A Brit's Guide to rlando and Walt Disney World

2001

★

Simon Veness

foulsham

The Publishing House, Bennetts Close, Cippenham, Berkshire, SL1 5AP, England

ISBN 0-572-02649-8

Text copyright © 2001 Simon Veness

Series, format, logo and layout design copyright © 2001 W. Foulsham & Co. Ltd

Other books in this series:
A Brit's Guide to Las Vegas and the West, Karen Marchbank, 0-572-02650-1
Choosing A Cruise, Simon Veness, 0-572-02562-9
A Brit's Guide to New York, Karen Marchbank, 0-572-02651-X

DEDICATION

To my wife, Karen, without whose non-stop support and assistance this book would never have become a reality.

SPECIAL THANKS

Special thanks for this edition go to: Airtours, Virgin Holidays, The Walt Disney Company, Alamo Rent A Car, Universal Orlando, the Holiday Inn All Suites Resort, Portofino Bay Hotel, Sheraton Safari Hotel, Walt Disney World Swan, Celebration Hotel and All In One Communications.

My sincere thanks also go to all the hard-working people at Foulsham who help to bring my work to life every year.

Contents

8. Off The Beaten Track

(or, When You're All Theme Parked Out). **A taste of the real Florida** – Winter Park, Aquatic Wonders Boat Tours, Boggy Creek Airboats, Orange Blossom Balloons, Everglades and the Bahamas, Flying Tigers Warbird Restoration Museum and Adventures, Green Meadows Petting Farm, Disney and Cruising, Seminole County, Forever Florida, *Disney's Wilderness Preserve*, Beach Escapes, Sports, including golf, fishing, water sports, horse riding, spectator sports and *Disney's Wide World of Sports*™.

9. Orlando by Night

(or, Burning the Candle at Both Ends). Church Street Station, *Downtown Disney*, Pointe*Orlando, Universal's CityWalk, Disney Shows, Arabian Nights, Pirate's Dinner Adventure, Mark II Dinner Theater, Medieval Times, Sleuth's, night-clubs, live music, discos, bars.

10. Eating Out

(or, Watching the Americans at Their National Sport). Full guide to local-style eating and drinking, rundown of the fast-food outlets, best family restaurants, American diners and speciality restaurants.

11. Shopping

(or, How to Send Your Credit Card into Meltdown). Your duty-free allowances, full guide to the main tourist shopping complexes, discount outlets, malls and speciality shops.

12. Safety First

(or, Don't Forget to Pack Your Common Sense!). General tourist hints, the Dos and Don'ts, how to look after your money and be safe behind the wheel.

13. Going Home

(or, Where Did the Last Two Weeks Go?). Avoiding last-minute snags, full guide to Orlando International and Orlando/Sanford Airports and their facilities for the journey home.

14. Your Holiday Planner

Examples of how to plan for a two-week holiday, with a Five-Day All-In-One Disney Hopper Pass and Seven-Day Pass, and blank forms for *your* holiday!

Foreword

Welcome to another new edition of the next best thing to actually being in Orlando! To first-time readers, a hearty Hello and a genuine warm reception for what's in store. To our repeat 'visitors' (and we know there are many of you – you know who you are!), welcome back for more of what you already realise is the most thrilling holiday experience you can take.

It now seems a long time since I sat down to draft the first edition of this book (it was 'only' 1993, but time flies when you're having fun in the Florida sun), and things have moved on at a breathless pace since then. This is the sixth edition of the UK's best-selling guidebook and it hasn't become any easier, thanks, largely, to the continued ferocious rate of development of this tourist wonderland.

The three principal counties that make up this vast holiday resort (Orange, Osceola and Seminole) remain vigorously engaged in making things newer, bigger and better almost by the day, and keeping up with them is a positively mind-boggling experience (not to mention exhausting. All together now – aaaahhh!).

Hot on the heels of an amazing Millennium year, 2001 is intent on upholding Orlando's best traditions of growth with style, including the promise of two dazzling new resort hotels – Animal Kingdom Lodge in Walt Disney World *Resort and* Loews Royal Pacific in Universal Orlando *– further enhancements to the International Drive and Highway 192 areas and even more attractions in the theme parks.*

However, despite all these attempts to keep us dazed and confused in the name of having fun, the Brit's Guide *remains dedicated to the simple principle of providing the most informed and user-friendly travel service you can find, especially if you use this book in conjunction with our friends at the website wdwinfo (see below), by far the best Internet resource on all things Disney-orientated out there.*

I like to think it is researched and written with a real tourist's eye for detail and value for money, and it includes all the information you really need to know, not just what the brochures want you to believe. It aims to give you a good idea of what to expect and (most importantly) how to plan and budget for it, as well as being a useful companion while you are there.

Most significantly, you will get the inside track on how to have the best holiday you can, at the best price and with the least fuss. Prepare to be amazed (and exhausted!) by what's in store, but don't say I didn't tell you so. Now, excuse me while I put my feet up for a while … have a nice day now.

Simon Veness
(e-mail me at simonveness.orlando1@virgin.net or join me at www.wdwinfo.co.uk)

Introduction
(or, Welcome to the Holiday of a Lifetime)

Welcome to the most exciting holiday experience in the world, bar none, guaranteed. This area of central Florida we call Orlando is a vast conglomeration of adventure rides, thrills, fun and fantasy the like of which exists nowhere else, and we are not talking just about the Walt Disney World Resort here.

First off, you need to be aware of the bewilderingly extensive and complex nature of most of what lies in wait in this tourist wonderland. Disney remains the leading attraction in town, but there is a strong supporting cast, of which Universal Orlando is an outstanding example.

There is something to suit all tastes and ages – young or old, familes, couples or singles – but it exacts a high physical toll. You'll walk a lot, queue a lot and probably eat a lot. You'll have a fabulous time, but you'll end up exhausted as well. It is not so much a holiday as an exercise in military-style organisation.

Eight theme parks

In simple terms, there are now eight major theme parks which are generally reckoned to be essential holiday fare, and at least one of those will require two days to make you feel it has been well and truly done. Add on a day at one of the water fun parks, a trip to see some of the wildlife or other more 'natural'

attractions, or the lure of the nearby Kennedy Space Center, and you're talking at least 11 days of pure adventure-mania. Then add in the night-time attractions of Church Street Station, *Downtown Disney* and Universal's new CityWalk and the various and numerous dinner shows, and you start to get an idea of the awesome scale of the entertainment on offer. Even given two weeks, something has to give – just make sure it isn't your patience/pocket/sanity!

So, how do we innocents abroad, many of us making our first visit to the good ol' US of A, make the most of what is still without doubt the most magical of holidays?

There is no set answer of course, but there are a number of pretty solid guidelines to steer you in the right direction and help you avoid some of the more obvious pitfalls. Central to most of them is **planning**. Towards the back of this guide there is a useful 'calendar' to fill in and use as a ready reference guide. Don't be inflexible, but be aware of the time requirements of each of the main parks, and (importantly) allow yourself a few quiet days either by the pool or at one of the smaller attractions to recover your strength.

Also, be aware of the vast scale and complexity of this wonderland, and try to take in as much of the clever detail and great breadth of imagination on offer, especially in *Walt Disney World* Resort.

Orlando

Orlando itself is a relatively small but bright young city which has been taken over to the immediate south-west by the *Walt Disney World* Resort Florida, to give it its full title, which opened with the Magic Kingdom® Park in 1971 and has encouraged a massive tourist expansion ever since. New attractions are being added all the time and the city of Orlando is in danger of being swamped by this vast out-pouring of rampant commercialism and aggressive tourist marketing. However, there is still a genuine concern for the environment and the dangers of over-commercialisation, and the development should not get out of hand, at least in the near future (although it is easy to imagine it already has in some parts).

The tourist area generally known as Orlando actually consists of three counties. Orange County is the home of the city of Orlando, but much of *Walt Disney World* Resort is in Osceola County, with Kissimmee its main town. Seminole County, home of Sanford Airport, is immediately to the north of Orange County.

The local population numbers slightly above 1.5 million, of which some 150,000 are actively employed in the tourist business, but in the year 2000 almost 40 million people were forecast to decide on Orlando as the place for their holiday, spending in excess of $16 billion in central Florida! Britain accounts for more than a third of all foreign visitors to Orlando, and in 1999 that was 1,137,000 of us. Those figures represent a near 100 per cent increase in the last 10 years, with the international airport seeing its traffic boom from eight million passengers in 1983 to a massive 29.2 million just 16 years later. In addition, the full Orlando area boasts more than 100,000 hotel rooms and almost 4,000 places to eat.

Walt Disney World Resort Florida

Walt Disney World Resort now consists of four distinct, separate theme parks, 20 speciality hotel resorts, a camping ground, three water fun parks, a state-of-the-art spectator sports complex, five 18-hole golf courses, four mini-golf courses and a huge *Downtown Disney* shopping and entertainment complex. It covers 47 square miles (almost 31,000 acres): Alton Towers and Thorpe Park would comfortably fit into one of its car parks. Indeed, Alton Towers, Britain's biggest theme park, is 60 times smaller than *Walt Disney World* Resort. Disney's most-frequented park, the *Magic Kingdom* Park, has a single-day record attendance in the region of 92,000 – Thorpe Park in Surrey (500 acres) peaks at around 20,000. The Disney organisation still does things with the most style, but the others have caught on fast and they are all creating new amenities almost as fast as they can think of them.

Intriguingly, only around half of Disney's massive site is currently developed, leaving plenty of room for new accommodation and attractions, while even the existing parks have potential for an extra ride or two, and there are several major projects on the drawing board. They think and plan on a massive scale (up to 20 years ahead) and completed

Life-size pinball at DisneyQuest

FLORIDA

How far from Orlando to . . .

Bradenton . . . . 130 miles	Miami . . . . 220 miles
Clearwater . . . . . . 110 miles	Naples . . . . .230 miles
Cocoa Beach . . . . . 40 miles	Sarasota . . . . 140 miles
Daytona . . . . 60 miles	Silver Springs . . . . .80 miles
Fort Lauderdale . . 205 miles	St Augustine . . . . .120 miles
Fort Myers . . . . . . 190 miles	St Petersburg . . . . 105 miles
Jacksonville . . . . . 155 miles	Tampa . . . . 75 miles
Key West . . . . .375 miles	Venice . . . . 160 miles

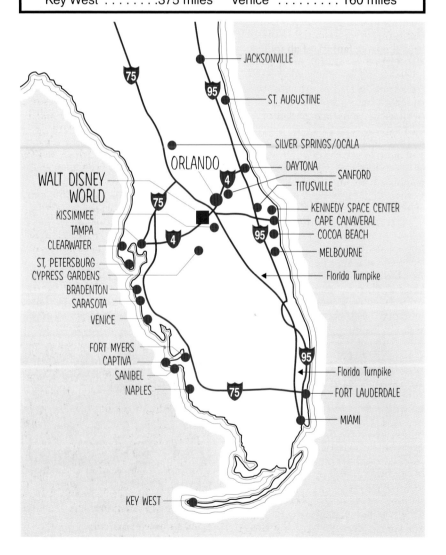

the biggest expansion programme in their history in 1999 with the opening of the final segment of *Disney's Animal Kingdom* Theme Park, the extensive redevelopment of the *Downtown Disney* area and the launch of their second cruise ship in two years. Their year-long Millennium celebration was truly dazzling, and there are likely to be more festivities from October 2001 as Walt Disney World's 30th anniversary gets under way.

Here's a quick rundown of what's on offer. **The Magic Kingdom Park**: this is the essential Disney, including the fantasy of all its wonderful animated films, the adventure of the Wild West and African Jungles, and the excitement of some classy thrill rides like Space Mountain, a huge indoor roller-coaster, and the ExtraTERRORestrial Alien Encounter. **Epcot:** this is Walt Disney World's look at the world of tomorrow through the gates of Future World, plus a potted journey around our planet in World Showcase. It's more educational than adventurous, but still possesses some memorable rides, including the new Test Track, and some great places to eat. **Disney-MGM Studios**: here you can ride the movies in style, meeting up with Star Wars, the Muppets and Indiana Jones, drop into the fearsome Tower of Terror or the thrilling new Rock 'n Roller Coaster and learn how films are *really* made. **Disney's Animal Kingdom Theme Park** is billed as 'a new species of theme park' and delivers another contrasting and hugely entertaining scenario. With cleverly realistic animal habitats, including a 100-acre safari savannah, captivating shows and two stunning thrill rides, it offers a chance to change pace from the other parks. **Disney's Typhoon Lagoon Water Park**: bring your swimming costume and spend a lazy day splashing down

water slides and learning to surf in the world's biggest man-made lagoon. **Disney's River Country Water Park**: more water fun 'n' games, with some great slides and the accent on nature. **Disney's Blizzard Beach Water Park**: this is the big brother of all the water parks, with a massive spread of rides and slides all in a 'snowy' environment. **Disney's Wide World of Sports Complex** offers the chance to watch world-class events like tennis, baseball, basketball, athletics, volleyball and many others. **Downtown Disney** incorporates **Pleasure Island**, **Marketplace** and the new **West Side** of themed restaurants, a cinema complex, the unique *DisneyQuest* arcade of interactive games, Virgin Megastore and world-famous Cirque du Soleil circus company. New Year's Eve is the Pleasure Island theme, with a choice of eight night-clubs. For *Walt Disney World* hotels, see Chapter 4, while Walt Disney World's **Wedding Pavilion** features in many brochures for the chance to get married in fairytale style.

Most people buy one of the multi-day passes which allow you to move between the various parks on the same day, while all grant unlimited access to *Walt Disney World* Resort's transport system of monorails, buses and ferries (always get your hand stamped if you leave one park but

Montu at Busch Gardens

intend to return). Make no mistake, you can't walk between the parks, and trying to do more than one in a day in any depth is a recipe for disaster. The choice of tickets for Disney in particular is becoming bewildering, and the addition of 7- and 9-day passes hasn't helped. Here are the main choices at the ticket booths: **1-day tickets**, giving access to one of the four main parks; **4-Day Park Hopper**, providing 4 days at the main parks, with multiple parks on the same day; **5-Day Park Hopper**, 5 main park days, with multiple same-day visits; **5-Day Park Hopper Plus**, 5 days at the four parks, with multiple same-day visits, plus TWO visits to any of Blizzard Beach, Typhoon Lagoon, River Country, Pleasure Island and Wide World of Sports™ (excluding special events at WWoS); **6-Day Park Hopper Plus**, 6 days at the main parks, plus THREE of the options above; and the **7-Day Park Hopper Plus**, a week at the main parks, plus FOUR of the options. All multi-day passes give savings on 1-day tickets, and unused days can be saved for the future. In the UK, you can buy the 5- and 7-Day Park Hopper Plus through tour operators, ticket brokers and **Disney Stores**, while the special **World Pass** is available ONLY over here, giving 10 days' entry to the four main parks, water parks, Pleasure Island and Wide World of Sports (excluding special events), plus FREE parking, which expires 13 days after its first use. Guests at Walt Disney World Resort hotels can also buy the **Unlimited Magic Pass**, giving entry to all the parks, Pleasure Island, Wide World of Sports AND DisneyQuest for the length of your stay, plus a choice of one extra item, such as a character breakfast or Epcot® guided tour. Price varies according to how long you stay.

When it comes to Universal Orlando (see page 12), SeaWorld and Busch Gardens, the choice is a little simpler. Again, you have **1-day tickets,** but it works out cheaper to buy a **2-, 3-** or even **5-Day Escape Pass,** giving access to Universal Studios Florida, the new Islands of Adventure park, Wet 'n Wild water park and the clubs of CityWalk for up to 5 consecutive days. There is also a clubs-only pass ($7.95 plus tax) or a clubs-plus-film ticket ($11.95 plus tax) as CityWalk also incorporates the new 20-screen Cineplex. Even better value are **Orlando FlexTickets**. The 4-Park, 7-Day Ticket gives unlimited admission for a week to USF, IoA, SeaWorld and Wet 'n Wild, while the 5-Park, 10-Day Ticket is also good for Busch Gardens. In summer 2000, Universal also offered early entry at 7am for all multi-day tickets, and it will be worth checking to see if this continues in 2001.

With price hikes every year, it is worth shopping around for tickets. **Tour operators** tend to be ABOVE gate price for the convenience of being able to pre-book and budget for all your main costs in one go. If you do want to pre-book, I recommend the **Keith Prowse** agency (01232 232425, or see your travel agent) as one of the best for competitive prices AND pre-booking convenience, while they do several one-off tickets, excursions and 2-day trips specially for the UK market. They also supply the actual tickets as opposed to a voucher

> BRIT TIP: Be wary of travel agent pressure to buy too many tickets. You may well find that you can't fit everything in, plus, for many attractions, you can often buy CHEAPER in Orlando, even from the tour operators' reps.

GETTING AROUND ORLANDO

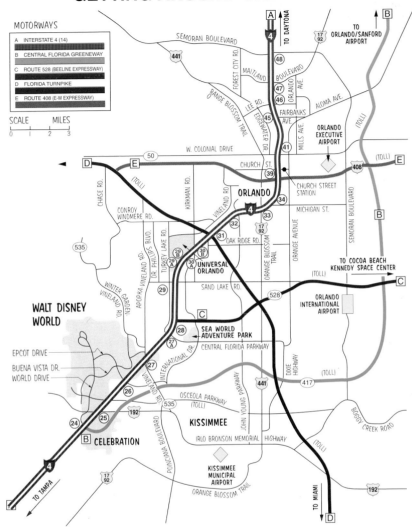

MOTORWAYS

A	INTERSTATE 4 (14)
B	CENTRAL FLORIDA GREENEWAY
C	ROUTE 528 (BEELINE EXPRESSWAY)
D	FLORIDA TURNPIKE
E	ROUTE 408 (E-W EXPRESSWAY)

SCALE   MILES
0   1   2   3

which you have to exchange at the main ticket booth.

You can also call one of the three big **ticket brokers** in Orlando (see page 67) for a price comparison, and to order tickets. All offer discounts BELOW gate prices, but these do vary seasonally. Prices for the dinner shows and smaller attractions in particular offer big savings.

A first word of warning: you don't want to try to do *Walt Disney World* Resort in one chunk. Apart from ending up with serious theme park indigestion, you'll probably also hit one of the parks on a busy day (check the Busy Day Guide on page 264). The *Magic Kingdom* Park and *Epcot* can be particularly exhausting (especially with children), and you'll need a quiet day afterwards.

Jungle Cruise at Silver Springs

The others

If *Walt Disney World* is what you think Orlando is all about, you'll be in for a pleasant surprise when you read this round-up of some of the other attractions on offer. **Universal Orlando** is the newest resort development that aims to rival Disney with its choice of two theme parks, water park, entertainment district and series of speciality hotels. **Universal Studios Florida**®: this features the state-of-the-art simulator ride Back to the Future, the mind-boggling Terminator 2 attraction, Jaws, Kongfrontation, the Twister experience, Earthquake, Woody Woodpecker's Kid Zone and the new Men in Black ride. **Islands of Adventure:** brand new in '99, Universal's second park is a superb blend of thrill rides, family attractions, shows and awesome, eye-catching design, with some of the most technologically advanced hardware in the world.

SeaWorld: don't be put off thinking it's just another dolphin show, this is *the* place for the creatures of the deep, with killer whales being the main attraction, a bright, refreshing atmosphere and a pleasingly serious ecological approach, plus their serious thrill rides Journey to Atlantis and

Kraken. SeaWorld also has an exclusive new sister park, **Discovery Cove,** that offers the chance to swim with dolphins, among other things. **Busch Gardens**: the sister park to SeaWorld, here it's creatures of the land, with the highlight being the Myombe Reserve, a close-up look at the endangered Central African highland gorillas, and the Edge of Africa safari experience. A real treat, plus a number of brain-numbing roller-coasters and other rides. **Cypress Gardens**: a chance to slow down and take in the more scenic attraction of beautiful gardens, water-skiing shows and circus acts. **Kennedy Space Center**: the dramatically upgraded home of space exploration. **Silver Springs**: a close look at Florida nature via jeep and boat safaris through real swampland, with several alligator displays. **Splendid China**: a magnificent alternative attraction, a 5,000-mile journey through China with miniaturised reproductions of features like the Great Wall and the Terracotta Warriors, plus films, live shows, acrobats, dancers, and great shopping and food. **Fantasy of Flight**: this aviation museum experience has the world's largest private collection of vintage aircraft plus fighter-plane simulators.

KEY TO ORLANDO – MAIN ATTRACTIONS

A1 = DISNEY'S ANIMAL KINGDOM THEME PARK
A = MAGIC KINGDOM PARK
B = EPCOT
C = DISNEY-MGM STUDIOS
D = UNIVERSAL ORLANDO
E = SEAWORLD ADVENTURE PARK
F = BUSCH GARDENS
G = KENNEDY SPACE CENTER
H = US ASTRONAUT HALL OF FAME
I = SPLENDID CHINA
J = CYPRESS GARDENS
K = SILVER SPRINGS
L = GATORLAND
M = DISNEY'S TYPHOON LAGOON WATER PARK

N = DISNEY'S BLIZZARD BEACH WATER PARK
O = DISNEY'S RIVER COUNTRY WATER PARK
P = WATER MANIA
Q = WET 'N WILD
R = DISCOVERY COVE BY SEAWORLD
S = MYSTERY FUN HOUSE
T = RIPLEY'S BELIEVE IT OR NOT
U = GUINNESS WORLD OF RECORDS/*TITANIC*
V = CHURCH STREET STATION
W = DOWNTOWN DISNEY
X = GREEN MEADOWS PETTING FARM
Y = FANTASY OF FLIGHT

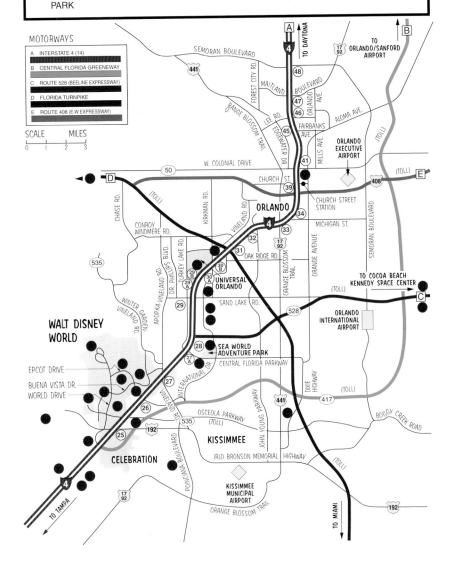

So that's a good taste of what's on offer, the next question is when to go? Florida's weather does vary a fair bit, from bright but cool winter days in November, December and January, with the odd drizzly spell, to furiously hot and humid summers punctuated by tropical downpours.

> BRIT TIP: The humidity levels – up to 100 per cent – and fierce daily rainstorms in summer take a lot of visitors by surprise, so take a lightweight, rainproof jacket or buy one of the cheap plastic ponchos available in local shops.

The most pleasant option is to go in between the two extremes, i.e., in spring or autumn. You will also avoid the worst of the crowds. However, as the majority of families are governed by school holidays, July to September remain the most popular months for Brit visitors, and so there will also be some pertinent advice on how to get one jump ahead of the high-season crush.

And now to business. Hopefully, we've whetted your appetite for the excitement in store. It's big, brash and fun, but above all it's American, and that means everything is exceedingly well organised, with a tendency towards the raucous rather than the reserved. It's clean, well-maintained and very anxious to please: Floridians generally are an affable bunch, but they take affability to new heights in the main theme parks, where staff are almost painfully keen to make sure you 'have a nice day'. Also close to every American's heart is the custom of TIPPING. With the exception of petrol pump attendants and fast-food restaurant servers, just about everyone who offers you any sort of service in hotels, bars, restaurants, buses, taxis, airports and other public amenities will expect a tip. In bars, restaurants and taxis, 15 per cent of the bill is the usual going rate while porters will expect $1 per bag. Brits are notoriously forgetful of this little habit but, as all service industry workers are automatically taxed on the assumption of receiving 15 per cent in tips, you will be doing a major service to the local economy if you remember those few extra dollars each time.

It is also useful to know that dollar

> BRIT TIP:
>
> | Bill | Suggested Tip |
> | --- | --- |
> | $15 | $2.25 |
> | $20 | $3.00 |
> | $25 | $3.75 |
> | $30 | $4.50 |
> | $40 | $6.00 |
> | $50 | $7.50 |

travellers' cheques can be used as cash, so it is not necessary (as well as not being advisable) to carry large amounts of cash around. **Take note that all Orlando prices, both where indicated in this book and on every price-tag you see, do not include the 6–7 per cent Florida Sales Tax. There is also a 4–5 per cent Resort Tax on hotel rooms.**

The use of credit cards is very nearly essential as they are accepted everywhere, are easy to carry and use and provide an extra degree of buying security. In some cases, notably car hire, you can't operate without your flexible friend, so don't leave your Visa or Mastercard at home!

Holiday visitors to America do not need a visa providing they hold a valid British passport showing they are a British Citizen (and which does not expire before the end of your holiday). Instead, all you do is fill in a green visa waiver form (usually you should apply at least a month in advance to the US Embassy.

In England, Scotland and Wales write to the Visa Office, US Embassy, 5 Upper Grosvenor Street, London, W1A 2JB (0891 200 290).

In Northern Ireland write to US Consulate General, 3 Queens House, Belfast, BT1 6EQ.

Alternatively, call 0991 500 590 (£1.50/minute) for more detailed visa advice, or log on to their Internet site at www.usembassy.org.uk.

Disney's Animal Kingdom Theme Park

handed out on your flight or when you check in) and hand it in with your passport to the US immigration official who checks you through first thing after landing. However, British Subjects do need a visa (£30), and

Plan your visit

The next few chapters will help you *plan* your days and tell you everything you need to know to make your holiday perfect. Draw up a rough itinerary, and then fine-tune it with www.wdwinfo.co.uk. Now read on and enjoy . . .

WHAT'S NEW IN 2001

Walt Disney World will celebrate its 30th Anniversary from October, and there could well be several additions to the parks, with a revamped **Star Tours** ride quite likely and an **Aladdin's Carpet** ride in store for the Magic Kingdom, similar to Dumbo. There are also distinct hints of a major thrill ride for Disney's Animal Kingdom, possibly a dramatic lay-down coaster called **Fire Mountain.** Disney's biggest opening, though, will be the 1,300-room **Animal Kingdom Lodge** in the spring, an African safari-type resort built on the edge of a new area of savannah featuring a host of wildlife. Having had a sneak preview, I can confirm it looks stunning.

Not to be outdone, Universal Orlando start work on the 1,000-room **Loews Royal Pacific Resort** to bring their high-quality hotels to three, with two more in the pipeline. And Busch Gardens will have **Rhino Rally**, their most ambitious ride project to date.

Away from the theme parks, there is a significant new resort development to the south of Walt Disney World called **Champions Gate**, a 1,200-acre complex of hotels, holiday homes, restaurants and sports, including some top-notch golf. The opening of **Festival Bay** at the north end of International Drive will add still more shopping, dining and entertainment choice to this area (plus a large amusement park), including the first Orlando outlet of the Ron Jon Surf Shop. The **Lake Buena Vista Factory Stores** are also adding more retail choice, almost doubling the size of their shopping plaza.

As ever, there will be other things and announcements that beat our deadline, so don't forget to check out www.wdwinfo.co.uk for the very latest information.

Planning and Practicalities

(or, How to Almost Do It All and Live to Tell the Tale)

There is one simple rule once you have decided Orlando is the place for you.

Sit down (preferably with this book) and PLAN what you want to do very carefully. This is NOT the type of holiday you can take in a freewheeling, carefree 'make it up as you go along' manner. Frustration and exhaustion lie in wait for all those who do not have at least a basic plan.

So this is what you do. First of all work out WHEN you want to go, then decide WHERE in the vast resort is the best place for you. Then consider WHAT sort of holiday you are looking for, WHO you want to entrust your holiday with and finally HOW much you want to try to do.

When to go

If you are looking to avoid the worst of the crowds, the best periods to choose are October to early February (but not the week of the Thanksgiving holiday in November or the Christmas to New Year

BRIT TIP: Thanksgiving is always the fourth Thursday in November; George Washington's birthday, or President's Day, is the third Monday in February. Try to avoid the weeks including those dates!

period), mid-February (after George Washington's birthday holiday) to the week before Easter, and April (after Easter) to the end of May. Orlando gets down to some serious tourist business from Memorial Day (the last Monday in May, the official start of the summer season) to Labor Day (the first Monday in September and the last holiday of summer), peaking on the Fourth of July, a huge national holiday. The Easter holidays are similarly uncomfortable (although the weather is better), but easily the busiest is the Christmas period, starting the week before 25 December and lasting until 2 January. It is not unknown for some of the theme parks to close their gates to new arrivals as their massive car parks become full by mid-morning.

The Touchdown Hotel at Disney's All-Star Sports Resort

The months offering the best combination of comfortable weather and smaller crowds are February and early March (pre-Easter) and October, but never let wet weather put you off. Few of the main theme park attractions are affected by rain (although the roller-coasters and water rides will close if lightning threatens), and you will be one jump ahead if you have remembered to bring a waterproof jacket as the crowds noticeably thin out when it gets wet. In any event, all the parks sell cheap, plastic ponchos (although they are even cheaper at Wal-Mart or other supermarkets). In the colder months, take a few lightweight but warm layers for early-morning queues, then, when it warms up later in the day, peel off and leave them in the lockers that are provided in all the parks. And, when it's too hot, take advantage of the air-conditioned facilities (of which there are many) during the warmest parts of the day, although you may also find the indoor facilities can be a bit chilly.

Where to stay

The choice of where to stay is equally important, especially if you have a family who will demand the

Isle of Bali Resort

extra amenities of swimming pools and games rooms. Having the use of a swimming pool is also a major plus for relaxing at the end of a busy day. Inevitably, there is a huge choice of accommodation areas and prices. As a guide, there are four main areas that make up the greater Orlando tourist conglomeration.

Walt Disney World Resort Florida: some of the most sophisticated, convenient and fun places to stay are to be found in *Walt Disney World's* 'resort' hotels sprinkled around its main attractions. The same imagination that has gone into the creation of the theme parks has been at work on the likes of *Disney's Wilderness Lodge* and *Disney's Contemporary Resort*. They all feature free, regular transport to all of the attractions and guests also get extra perks like special baby- and childcare services, early admission to theme parks on selected days, your own resort ID card (so you can charge meals and souvenirs to your room, and have your gifts delivered to the hotel), free parking and being able to book in advance for restaurants and shows in the parks, while Disney characters pop up for meals at some of them. The drawbacks here are that, with the exception of the new *Disney's All-Star Resort*, the *Walt Disney World*

© Disney Enterprises, Inc.

The Rock Hotel at Disney's All-Star Music Resort

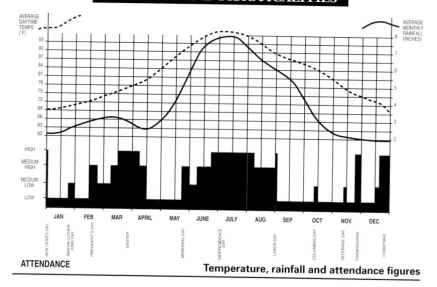

Temperature, rainfall and attendance figures

resorts are among the most expensive in Orlando, especially to eat in, and you still have a fair drive to get to the other attractions like Universal Orlando and the Kennedy Space Center. For a 1-week holiday it takes some beating, though.

Lake Buena Vista: is a loosely defined area around some pretty lakes to the eastern fringes of *Walt Disney World* Resort and along Interstate 4 that again features some of the more up-market hotels. It also has the convenience of being handy for all the *Walt Disney World* parks, with most hotels offering free transport, and excellent leisure and shopping facilities. It tends to be a bit pricey, but its proximity to Interstate 4 makes it convenient for the whole of Orlando.

International Drive: this ribbon development lies midway between Walt Disney World and downtown Orlando and is therefore an excellent central location. Running parallel to Interstate 4, it is about 15–20 minutes away from the main theme parks, while it is also a well-developed tourist area in its own right, with some great shopping, restaurants and minor attractions

like Wet 'n Wild, Ripley's Believe It Or Not, WonderWorks and Skull Kingdom. The downside is it does get congested and occasionally hazardous with tourist traffic in peak periods and you have to make a slightly earlier start in the morning for *Walt Disney World* Resort. But it does represent good value for money and it also possesses a rarity in Orlando in that you can go for a long stroll along real pavement. A sub-area off I-Drive is now the Universal maingate area of Kirkman Road and Major Boulevard, which is developing new hotels all the time.

Kissimmee: budget holiday-makers can be found in their greatest numbers along the tourist sprawl of Highway 192, an almost unbroken 12-mile strip of hotels, motels, restaurants and shops. It offers some of the best economy accommodation in the whole area and is handy for *Walt Disney World* Resort's attractions, although it gives you the longest journey to Universal Studios and downtown Orlando. A car is most advisable here, although there's a major project to enhance this tourist corridor, called Beauti-vacation. This will see a dramatic improvement in the heavily built-up stretch of 192 from Route 535 as far west as Splendid China, with road enhancements, pavements, landscaping, bus shelters, benches and water fountains all being added. The downside of all this is the choking **roadworks** on 192 all along here until the end of 2001. Try to use the toll road Osceola Parkway, which runs parallel to 192.

Split holidays

It is fair to say you can't really go far wrong no matter what you're seeking from your holiday, as long as you plan well. The Atlantic coast and some great beaches are only an hour's drive away to the east, the magnificent Florida Everglades are little more than 3–4 hours to the south, and there are more wonderful beaches and pleasant coast roads to the west. There are great shopping opportunities almost everywhere, while Orlando is also home to some of the best golf courses in the world, and there are plenty of opportunities either to play or to watch tennis, baseball and basketball as well. An increasingly popular choice is to split the holiday by having a week or two in Orlando as well as a week on the Florida coast or somewhere more exotic like the Caribbean. The main tour companies offer a huge variety of packages, with cruise-and-stay options increasingly popular.

If you can afford the time (and the expense), the best combination is to have two weeks in Orlando itself and then a week relaxing on one of Florida's many fabulous white-sand beaches. A 2-week half-and-half split is a popular choice, but can tend to make your week in Orlando especially hectic, unless you pick your additional week on the Atlantic coast at somewhere like Cocoa Beach. This resort, near to Cape Canaveral and the Kennedy Space Center, is only an hour from Orlando and offers the choice of being able to return to *Walt Disney World* Resort for the day. A few companies offer a good 10-day Orlando and 4-day coast split (and Jetlife also do a 9–5 option, see below). Fly-drives obviously offer the greatest flexibility of doing Orlando and seeing something else of Florida, but again there is a lot to tempt you in just two weeks and you may find it is better to book a one-centre package that includes a car as well as your accommodation so you can travel around and avoid too much packing and unpacking.

Travel companies

There is some serious competition for your hard-earned holiday money and in the last couple of years the travel companies have worked hard to keep the cost of an Orlando holiday down, making it excellent value for money, whether you fly-drive, book your own flights or take a straightforward package.

Shop around to get the best value for your holiday £, but I always recommend making sure your package is booked with an ABTA agent for holiday security should anything go wrong. At the last count, there were some 86 tour operators offering package holidays or fly-drives to Florida, and here is a rundown of the biggest and best.

Virgin holidays: the biggest operator to MCO (that's Orlando Airport in travel-agent-speak), Virgin also have the biggest and most exhausting brochure. They offer the largest variety of combinations, including Miami, the Keys, South Carolina, New Orleans, New York, the Bahamas, Mexico, nine Caribbean islands and some tempting cruises, as well as the Florida coasts. A strong selling point is Virgin's non-stop scheduled service to Orlando (now from Manchester as well as Gatwick) with

award-winning in-flight entertainment, free drinks and special kids' meals and games. They have a veritable army of well-briefed reps in Orlando and a good, all-round choice of accommodation in the different areas, and are popular for fly-drives, flying into Orlando and out from Miami. Flight upgrades to their Premium Economy (extra leg-room and bigger seats) or a full Upper Class service are available and the Virgin service throughout is impeccable. You can book Anny's Nannies baby-sitters through Virgin, too. Orlando is also an increasingly popular choice as a wedding venue, and Virgin have their own wedding co-ordinators, and even offer SeaWorld weddings! For golf, tennis and scuba-diving enthusiasts there are also activity packages. Other bonuses include single-parent discounts, Kids' Nite Out features, non-driver packages, 'kids eat free' deals at selected hotels and help and advice for disabled passengers. Virgin also have a unique return flight check-in service at *Downtown Disney*, open from 9am–1pm on your final day so you can get rid of your suitcases and make good use of the time. You can check out their Internet site on www.virginholidays.co.uk or call 01293 617181 for a brochure.
Airline: Virgin Atlantic.
Airport: Orlando International.

   Travel City: a relative newcomer, this direct-sell company has become one of the biggest Florida operators,

Azure waters and pure white sands at Castaway Cay with a Disney Cruise

cutting out travel agent overheads to offer a cheaper deal. They still have the full package of flights, car hire and accommodation, with their own reps and Welcome Centre in Orlando, while their tele-sales agents have good local knowledge, right down to choice of hotel. You can book fly-drives, fly-drives with hotels, two-centre options and a range of *Walt Disney World* resorts, which all come with Disney's resort guide as a useful bonus. Flights are with one of the more up-market charter airlines and there are up-grade scheduled flight choices. You can pre-book your seats at £10 per person. Travel City can be found on the Florida section of Teletext, page 222, or in the pages of the national press. You can call 01792 543481 (in the south) or 01253 757500 (in the north) to book.
Airline: American TransAir.
Airport: Orlando International.

   Thomson: another of the largest, mass-market operators, Thomson have an excellent reputation in Orlando, where they have a large team of reps and Service Centres on I-Drive and at Fort Liberty in Kissimmee, and offer six departure airports (including Birmingham, Newcastle and Glasgow). You can now pre-book your flight seats in advance for a small charge, and they

Orlando's downtown

also feature great in-flight entertainment. Thomson price their packages very competitively for the family market, with special children's fares and bonuses like 'kids eat free' and 'extra value' hotels, while they offer a decent selection of coastal resorts for two-centre holidays and an increasing number of private villas. They also organise wedding packages at either Leu Gardens, the Gulf Coast or Cypress Gardens. Flight up-grade options cost £60 and £120 extra for more leg-room and other services. Check out their website on www.thomson-holidays.com.

Airline: Britannia.
Airport: Orlando International.

Airtours: another of the leading group who take around 100,000 British tourists to Orlando every year, they fly mainly non-stop from nine UK airports, with good in-flight entertainment and fun-packs for kids. For £10/person (£20 from May 2001), seats can be pre-booked in the family areas. They offer a highly recommended comfort up-grade (extra leg-room, free bar, pre-selected menu, late UK check-in) for £99/person (£149 from May 2001). Airtours launches new 10- and 11-night packages in 2001 to offer a more flexible choice and are the only operator to offer a 15-seater mini-van. They work hard to be one of the most price-friendly outfits and also offer some imaginative two- and three-centre combinations, including the Florida Keys, and cruises with Carnival and Disney. Villa accommodations are now a prominent part of their programme, with good quality pool-homes on offer throughout Florida. Airtours make a feature of their fly-drive packages, with a range of 'Drive and Stay' holidays which offer a wide choice to the Florida sun-seeker, especially return visitors. For a brochure, call 01235 824428 or see www.airtours.co.uk.

Airline: Monarch, Airtours International.
Airport: Orlando/Sanford.

First Choice: a comprehensive flight programme uses eight UK airports (including Glasgow, Newcastle and Cardiff, but not always non-stop), plus a Classic

Great shopping at Pointe*Orlando

Premium up-grade (extra leg-room and in-flight services, plus special check-in facilities on the return flight) for £99 and pre-bookable seats on their smart in-house airline (£14/person). They offer an extended choice of twin-centre holidays, including an imaginative International Drive– Disney resort split (tip: do I-Drive first!), a range of Florida beach options (including coach transfers for non-drivers) and golf and diving facilities at selected hotels. First Choice have an admirable teenagers' programme, Teen Active, which offers basketball, baseball and evening events, and a family-friendly touch with price reductions, low-start prices and 'kids eat free' deals, plus villas and apartments (with their own reps) that can work out better value for large groups.

Airlines: Air 2000, Airtours International.
Airports: Orlando/Sanford.

Three other First Choice brands also sell Florida – **Sovereign**, for a more up-market choice (notably for villas), **Eclipse,** a direct-sell operator, and **Unijet** (see below). Their website is also worth checking out, www.first-choice.com, and you can request a brochure on 0208 880 8155.

Unijet: although bought out in 1998 by First Choice, Unijet continue to operate in their own right, flying from eight UK airports. Unijet pride themselves on their value-for-money family packages (including 'kids eat free' hotel deals) and offer an increasing number of holiday homes as well as hotels, which are great value for larger families or groups. They feature ten of *Walt Disney World's* big resort hotels, from the budget options to the top of the range, and an expanded range of two-centre holidays (including some popular Caribbean cruises). You can also ask questions of their Florida resort team or pre-book excursions on floridainfo@unijet.com. Unijet's well-run wedding service offers Cypress Gardens and Leu Gardens, as well as *Disney's Wedding Pavilion.* Call 0500 767767 for a brochure.
Airlines: Air 2000, Airtours International, Britannia.
Airports: Orlando/Sanford and Orlando International (Britannia).

British Airways Holidays: another company to benefit from their direct, scheduled air service (kids' activity packs, etc), BAH offer great flexibility, with almost any duration and combination possible. Beach add-ons, cruises, twin centres (including Miami, Boston, New York, Washington and the Caribbean) and an extensive selection of quality but great value private homes are all on offer. They also fly to Miami and Tampa to open up plenty of fly-drive possibilities, and children under two go free. Call 0870 2424243 for a brochure or dial up www.baholidays.co.uk
Airline: British Airways.
Airport: Orlando International.

Jetsave: Florida specialists Jetsave put the accent on flexibility, with a wide range of just about everything for your Orlando holiday. For accommodation, you have the full selection of motels, hotels (especially the kid-friendly variety), resorts, apartments and holiday homes (or villas, as we would call them), and simple, accurate star ratings for each property. The Jetsave High Flyers Club (01235 824324) is also worth joining for a few little extras. You can fly (with connecting flights in some cases) from any of 23 UK airports into one of eight Florida gateways, fly any day, stay for any duration and up-grade to extra leg-room seats, business or even first class (expensive, though). Twin-centre options (which can be split any way for a fortnight) feature a good range of Florida beaches, plus New Orleans, Caribbean and various cruises. Check their fine website on www.jetsave.co.uk
Airlines: Britannia, Virgin Atlantic, British Airways.
Airport: Orlando International.

Cosmos: although better known for European holidays, their Orlando operation is very well organised with one of the most readable brochures, catering mainly for the family market and offering a full range of accommodation. They feature hotels, villas and apartments, and promise even more options in 2001, including Universal's fabulous new hotels, new cruises, and an increased selection of villas with pools (including top-of-the-range executive homes). Their 'Dream Weddings' feature includes balloons, Cypress Gardens and even a sunset yacht cruise, as well as Disney's Wedding specialities. Kids' prices lead in at £149 with free entrance at a choice of six attractions for under 13s (including Water Mania, WonderWorks and Pirates Cove mini-golf) and under 12s eat free at many hotels. Call Cosmos on 0161 476 5678 or log on to their website

at www.cosmos-holidays.co.uk.
Airlines: Monarch (Premium Cabin up-grade £110), Airtours International, Air 2000, Britannia.
Airports: Orlando/Sanford and Orlando International (Britannia). Pre-bookable seats £10/person.

jmc: the recent rebranding of this Thomas Cook firm (formerly Sunworld) continues to build on a reputation for being one of the most quality-conscious mass-market operations. Free kids' passes to a few of the smaller attractions, free kids' meals (under 12s), some all-inclusive accommodation and a wide choice of quite select villas are all jmc features, while they also offer many Disney properties and a good range of twin-centre choices, including Cancun (Mexico) and the Bahamas. New features include pre-planned Fly Tours, cruise-and-stay holidays, and Vehicle Not Vital properties for those not wanting to drive, with the chosen accommodation within easy reach of shops, bars and restaurants and with good transport to the attractions. There are even some 'all-in' deals that include your attraction tickets and free transport. Their wedding packages (from £379) are another stand-out, with six locations, including Winter Park and Cypress Gardens. Flights are from nine UK airports and – praise be for a charter operator! – there are FREE pre-allocated seats.
Airlines: JMC Airline, Monarch, Air 2000, Airtours International.
Airport: Orlando/Sanford.

Jetlife: another company which specialises in a tailor-made service, Jetlife are especially popular with second-time visitors as they offer an increasing number of private villas and apartments (great value for larger groups), and three- and four-bedroom houses with a private or communal swimming pool – plus the range of *Walt Disney World* Resort accommodation. Jetlife use scheduled airlines, with a large number of non-stop flights, have an excellent variety of two-centre holidays (some with an imaginative 9/5-day split, giving you more than a week in Orlando), including Jamaica, Mexico, Hawaii and various American cities, and their packages are competitively priced with some clever extras. New in the year 2000 were Disney and Caribbean cruise options. For a brochure, call 01233 211888.
Airlines: Virgin, Delta, Continental.
Airport: Orlando International.

Kuoni: as in all their holidays, Kuoni offer the up-market version of Orlando, with some of the best hotels, a strong tie-up with *Walt Disney World* Resort, a comprehensive wedding and honeymoon service and a new Price Watch guarantee (money back if you find an identical holiday for less). They have an extensive range of twin-centre options, including the Florida Keys, Boca Raton and Marco Island, and some excellent executive holiday homes. The average price reflects the more exclusive nature of many of their packages (plus their flexible, tailor-made choice facility), but there are some big child reductions, 'kids eat free' hotels, and Kuoni use only scheduled airlines. Call 087007 458664 for a brochure, or check out www.kuoni.co.uk.
Airlines: Virgin Atlantic, United (via Washington).
Airport: Orlando International.

TransAtlantic Vacations: you won't find this firm in the big league of any operation world-wide other than Florida and, more particularly, Orlando. That means they offer a specialist American service with 10 years' experience of the Sunshine State and a good family-orientated product. TransAtlantic offer an increasing range of holiday homes and apartments, as well as hotels, which are more popular with return visitors and larger family groups.

Their two-centre options are the fairly routine Gulf and Gold Coasts, the Bahamas and Jamaica, plus 3-, 4- or 7-day cruises. Call 01293 774441 for a brochure.
Airline: Britannia.
Airport: Orlando International.

Funway Holidays: this is the sister company of America's largest tour operator and a leading specialist in holidays to the US, hence they offer a tailor-made service to match Orlando with *any* other option, making for total flexibility of choice from no less than 22 UK airports. Their private homes are a big feature of the Florida programme, but they also serve up some terrific-value deals, especially with low children's prices, if you book early, making them consistently among the best prices for a family of four. They also use only scheduled airlines. Two-centre options include cruises of 3 to 7 nights to the Bahamas and Caribbean from Miami, plus the Gulf Coast and Mexico, with the latter offering all-inclusive resorts. Other extras include 'kids eat free' hotels, free kids' clubs, free hotel nights at certain times and free shuttle bus services at selected hotels for non-drivers. Look them up at www.funwayholidays.co.uk or call 0208 466 0222 for a brochure.
Airlines: various scheduled, including Virgin and Continental.
Airport: Orlando International.

Style Travel: one of the UK's top self-catering specialists (and a Thomas Cook-owned company), they offer a huge selection of private-pool homes and hotel suites, with accommodation from two-, three- and four-bed homes up to luxurious five-, six- and seven-bed varieties, as well as the usual range of hotel and Disney resort options. All properties are in named, well-described situations so that the location, facilites and size can be matched to needs. Their comprehensive Florida brochure has

an excellent variety of Gulf Coast villas and hotels (all of which can be combined with Orlando), while they maintain a high standard of in-resort service. Transfers can be arranged for non-drivers (£15 per person) and they offer the full range of pre-bookable attraction tickets. Wedding packages are equally stylish, with 10 options, from Disney and SeaWorld to Church Street Station and Leu Gardens. For bookings and brochures, call 0208 568 1999, or check out www.style-holidays.co.uk.
Airlines: Monarch, Caledonian.
Airport: Orlando/Sanford and Orlando International.

Walt Disney Travel Company: brand new at the end of 2000, Disney's own travel operation to Florida offers the deluxe package that comes with the inimitable Mouse Ears style. A sharp, informative brochure is backed up with what should be the most knowledgeable reservations consultants in the business. Every *Walt Disney World* resort is featured, as well as a handful of well-chosen non-Disney hotels and holiday homes, plus a series of up-market twin-centre options in the likes of St Petersburg and Marco Island. The detail looks good, with character-branded ticket wallets and luggage tags, autograph books for the kids and an information book. *Walt Disney World* Resort guests get an Unlimited Magic Pass included while non-Disney guests get a Five-Day Hopper Plus. Car rental is, uniquely, with National, which adds to the all-round quality of service, while there is a free airport transfer for those not wishing to drive straight away. To up-grade to the true all-inclusive package, there are two additional plans that include meals and a host of extras like spa treatments, golf, free access to childrens' activity centres at the resorts and backstage tours. However, these come at a serious price: £289 per adult (7 nights) for the Discovery Magic Plan, and £575 per adult (7 nights) for the Deluxe Magic Plan. As with all things Disney, you pay top dollar but should get the best service.

Airlines: Britannia, British Airways (for a supplement).

Airport: Orlando International.

There are plenty of other options worth checking out, including **Trailfinders** (highly recommended by a number of readers; 0207 937 5400, or www.trailfinders.co.uk) **USAirtours** (0345 353353), **Travel 4** (0541 550066), **Travelbag** (01420 88380), **Transolar Holidays** (0151 630 3737), **Totally Florida** (by Mercury Travel, 0870 8870060), **Phileas Fogg Travel** (0870 0747400), **Premier Holidays** (01223 516688), **Key To America** (01784 248777) and **Destination USA** (0207 253 2000), while **Flightbookers** (0207 757 2000) and the **Flight Centre** (08708 999888) feature keen flight-only services. Scanning Teletext (page 222) will often reveal many special deals on full packages or flights alone.

Establish a plan of what you want to do and then get a selection of brochures and compare the various prices and attractions of each one.

Finally, for those looking to book an independent package, but wanting help with Disney accommodation, meal reservations, etc, the excellent **Dreams Unlimited** internet service is a must. Check out www.dreamsunlimitedtravel.com for the essential information on this excellent no-cost service which can save you time, money and hassle.

What to see when

Once you arrive, the temptation is to head immediately for the nearest theme park, then the next, and so on. Hold on! If there is such a thing as theme park indigestion, that's the best recipe for it. Some days at the parks are busier than others; it is simply not possible to cover more than one a day, and may be inadvisable to attempt two of the main parks on successive days. So here's what you do.

With the aid of the Holiday Planner on pages 258–64, make a note of all the attractions you want to try to see and pencil them in over the duration of your holiday.

The most sensible strategy is to plan around the eight 'must see' parks of The *Magic Kingdom* Park, *Epcot, Disney-MGM Studios, Disney's Animal Kingdom* Theme Park, Universal Studios Florida and the new Islands of Adventure theme park, SeaWorld and Busch Gardens. If you have only a week, consider dropping Busch Gardens (it's furthest away from Orlando and doesn't have quite the same magical appeal as the others) and concentrate on the Disney parks and Universal Studios, with SeaWorld as an 'extra' if it fits into your plan. Science fact and fiction addicts will be hard-pressed not to include the Kennedy Space Center, but it will probably bore small children.

As a basic rule, the *Magic Kingdom* Park is the biggest hit with children, and families often find it requires 2 days. The same can be said of *Epcot*, but there are fewer rides to keep small children happy, and as much of the emphasis is on education as on entertainment,

Islands of Adventure

although it all has *Walt Disney World* Resort's slick, easily digestible coating. Only the most fleet of foot, given the benefit of a relatively crowd-free period, will be able to negotiate *Epcot* successfully in a day. *Disney's Animal Kingdom* Theme Park is also a little short on attractions for the youngest kids, but it still requires nearly all of its 7am–8pm opening hours. *Disney-MGM Studios* is a 9–5 park (where you can fit in all the attractions in a day), while SeaWorld needs rather longer and Universal Studios Florida can be a 2-day park when Orlando is at its busiest. Islands of Adventure will almost certainly keep everyone, except possibly the under-5 age group, busy all day, too. Busch Gardens is another full-day affair, extremely popular with British families, especially as it is 75–90 minutes' drive away to Tampa in the south-west, but an early start to the Kennedy Space Center (an hour's drive to the east coast) will mean you can be back in your hotel swimming pool by tea-time, confident you have fully enjoyed One Small Step For Man. All the attractions are detailed in Chapters 5–8, so try to get an idea of the time requirements of them all before you pick up your pencil.

Smaller attractions

Of the other, smaller-scale attractions, the nature park of Silver Springs is a full day out as it also involves a near 2-hour drive to get there, but everything else can be fitted around your Big Eight Itinerary. The water parks are all a good way to spend a relaxing afternoon, while Cypress Gardens is another quieter place to while away 4–5 hours. There are also a number of smaller-scale attractions in Orlando which will probably keep the children amused for several hours. Gatorland is a unique look at some of Florida's oldest inhabitants. The Mystery Fun House is a good bet for

2–3 hours for the kids, while Ripley's Believe It Or Not museum and WonderWorks interactive house of fun are both good family centres for several hours. Add in the terrific haunted house attraction Skull Kingdom, the new Guinness World Records Experience and *Titanic* exhibitions at The Mercado, and the more old-fashioned lure of go-karts and other fairground-type rides at Fun Spot (all of them on the I-Drive corridor), and you have a full day of alternative fun and frolics. Aviation fans must not miss a trip to Fantasy of Flight (further down I4) or the Flying Tigers Warbird Air Museum and Adventures in Kissimmee for a fascinating experience.

DisneyQuest, another new venture in *Downtown Disney*, is a hugely imaginative interactive 'arcade' that guarantees up to half a day's fun. Each main tourist area is also well served with imaginative mini-golf and go-kart tracks that will happily absorb any excess energy for an hour or two from those who haven't, by now, been exhausted!

Evenings

Then, of course, there is the evening entertainment, with a similarly wide choice of extravagant fun-seeking. By far the best, and a must for at least one evening each, are *Downtown Disney Pleasure Island* at *Walt Disney World* Resort, Universal's new CityWalk and Church Street Station in downtown Orlando. All will keep you fully entertained from 5pm until the early hours. Another popular source of fun are the various dinner shows: a 2–3 hour cabaret based on themes like the Wild West, medieval Spain, Arabian Nights and murder mysteries that all include a hearty meal. Then there are the huge variety of night-clubs and bars, many offering live music. See Chapter 9 for the full details.

What to do when

There are a couple of handy general guidelines for avoiding the worst of the tourist hordes, even in high season. The vast majority of fun-seekers in town are American, and they tend to arrive at the weekends, get settled in their hotels, and then head for the main theme parks, i.e. *Walt Disney World* Resort, first. That means that Mondays and Tuesdays are generally bad times for the *Magic Kingdom* Park and *Epcot*. Additional busy times are created by Disney's *Early Entry days* at three of their parks. These allow *Walt Disney World* hotel guests in an hour before official opening time and mean the parks stay especially busy on those days. If you are NOT staying in a Disney property and can't take advantage of *Early Entry*, these are best avoided: Sunday, *Disney-MGM Studios*; Monday, *Magic Kingdom* Park; Tuesday, *Epcot*; Wednesday, *Disney-MGM Studios*; Thursday, *Magic Kingdom* Park; Friday, *Epcot*; Saturday, *Magic Kingdom* Park. *Disney's Animal Kingdom* tends to be busiest on Monday, Tuesday and Wednesday and is a tough park to get round when it's crowded. The popular water parks of *Blizzard Beach*, *Typhoon Lagoon* and *River Country* hit high tide at the weekend, and Thursday and Friday during the summer.

At Universal Orlando, the picture is a little harder to predict after the opening of their Islands of Adventure park, and experiments with Express early opening (for all multi-day ticket holders). The weekends definitely see above-average crowds, while Universal Studios Florida also tends to be busier on Thursdays and IoA on Mondays and Wednesdays.

If *Walt Disney World* Resort is humming in the early part of the week, that makes it a good time to visit SeaWorld, Busch Gardens, Cypress Gardens, Silver Springs or the Kennedy Space Center. Wet 'n Wild and Water Mania are best avoided at the weekends when the locals come out to play (see also page 264, Busy Day Guide).

Making sure you get the most out of your days at the main theme parks is another art form, and there are a number of practical policies to pursue. The official opening times are all well publicised and don't

> **BRIT TIP:** If your hotel is not far from the park take a couple of hours out to return for a siesta or a swim. Have your hand stamped for re-entry when you leave (your car park ticket will also be valid all day so), and then enjoy the evening entertainment back at the park, which is often the most spectacular part of the day.

vary much between 8.30 and 9am. However, apart from the obvious advantage of arriving early to try to get at the head of the queues (and you will encounter some SERIOUS queues, or lines, as the Americans call them), the parks may well open earlier than scheduled if the crowds build up quickly before the official hour. So, you can get a step ahead of the masses by arriving at least 30 minutes before the expected opening time, or an hour early during the main holiday periods. Apart from anything else, you will be better placed to park in the vast, wide open spaces of the public car parks and catch the tram to the main gates (anything up to half a mile away!).

Once you've put yourself in pole position, don't waste time on the shops, scenery and other frippery which will lure the unprepared first-timer. Instead, head straight for some of the main rides and get a few big-time thrills under your belt before the main hordes arrive. You will quickly work out where the most popular attractions are as the majority of the other early birds will be similarly prepared and will flock in the appropriate direction. Use Chapters 5 and 6 to help you plan your individual park strategies.

As another general rule, you can also benefit from doing the opposite of what the masses do after the initial rush has subsided.

Pace yourself

A word of warning: the *Walt Disney World* Resort parks, notably the *Magic Kingdom* Park, stay open late in the evening during the main holiday periods, occasionally until midnight, and that can make for a long day for young children. Therefore it is important to pace yourself, especially if you have been one of the first through the gates. There are plenty of opportunities to take time-outs and have a drink or bite to eat, and you can take advantage of the American propensity to take meal-times seriously by avoiding lunchtime (around 12.30pm) and dinnertime (around 6pm). So, after you've had a couple of hours of real adventure-mania, it pays to take an early lunch (i.e. before midday), plunge back into the hectic thrill of it all for another 3 hours or so, have another snack-sized meal in mid-afternoon and then return to the main rides, as the parks tend to quieten down a little in late afternoon.

Finally, a word about shopping in Orlando – it's world class. Your battle plan should also include at least an afternoon to visit one of the spectacular shopping malls in Orlando, as well as a chance to sample

some of the discount outlets and speciality centres like Old Town in Kissimmee, the Church Street Exchange in downtown Orlando, the Mercado and the stunning new Pointe*Orlando on I-Drive.

Clothing and comfort

The most important part of your whole holiday wardrobe is your footwear. You are going to spend a lot of time on your feet, even during the off-peak periods. The smallest of the parks covers 'only' 100 acres, but that is irrelevant to the amount of time you will spend queuing. Don't decide to break in those new sandals or trainers. Comfortable, well-worn shoes or trainers are ESSENTIAL. Otherwise, you need dress only as the climate dictates. T-shirts and shorts are quite acceptable in all of the parks (but swimwear is not acceptable away from pool areas) and most restaurants and other eating establishments will happily accept informal dress.

If, after a long day, you feel the need for a change of clothes or a sweater for the evening, use the handy lockers which all the theme parks provide. All the main parks are also well equipped with pushchairs (or strollers) for a small charge, and baby services are freely located at regular intervals.

It is absolutely vital to use high-factor sun creams at all times, even during the winter months when the sun may not feel that strong but can still burn. Nothing is guaranteed to make you feel uncomfortable for several weeks like severe sunburn.

BRIT TIP: Don't pack a lot of smart or semi-formal clothing – you really won't need it in hot, informal Florida.

Orlando has a sub-tropical climate and requires higher-factor sun creams than even a holiday in the Mediterranean. Use sun blocks on sensitive areas like your nose and ears, and splash on the after-sun cream liberally at the end of the day. Local skincare products are widely available and usually inexpensive (especially at Wal-Mart or K-Mart stores), while many tour operators now have a skincare specialist at their welcome meetings.

BRIT TIP: The summer is mosquito time. Buy a spray-on insect repellent. Alternatively, try Avon's Skin So Soft which works wonders at keeping the bugs at bay.

Don't forget a waterproof sun cream if you are swimming. Wear a hat if you are out theme park-ing in the hottest parts of the day, and try to avoid alcoholic drinks until the evening as there is nothing like alcohol for making you dehydrated (except, perhaps, strong coffee and caffeine-based soft drinks) and susceptible to heatstroke. You will need to increase your fluid intake *significantly* during the summer months in Orlando, but stick to still soft drinks (try Gatorade, a squash-like energy drink) or water.

Should you require medical treatment, whether it be for sunburn or other first aid, consult your tour company's information about local hospitals and surgeries. In the event of a medical, or other, emergency, dial 911 as you would 999 in Britain.

It cannot be over-stressed that you should have comprehensive travel and health insurance for any trip to America as there is NO National Health Service and ANY form of medical treatment will need to be paid for – and is usually expensive. Keep all the receipts and reclaim on your return home.

Emergency out-patients departments can be found with Centra Care at Florida Hospital Medical Center (in four locations: 12125 South Apopka-Vineland Road, near the Crossroads at Lake Buena Vista; 7848 West Irlo Bronson Memorial Highway, near Splendid China; 6001 Vineland Road, near Universal Studios; and 1462 West Oakridge Road, near Florida Mall) and Sand Lake Hospital on 9400 Turkey Lake Road, while the East Coast Medical Network (407 648 5252) and House Med Inc (407 239 1195) both make hotel 'house calls' 24 hours a day. House Med also operates MediClinic, a walk-in facility on 2901 Parkway Boulevard, Kissimmee, open daily from 9am to 9pm, and Orlando Regional Healthcare System (operators of Sand Lake Hospital) have Walk-In Medical Care centres on

The Grand Staircase on *Titanic*

International Drive (407 351 3035 and 239 6679) open 8am–8pm. The two largest chemists (drug stores) are Eckerd Drugs at 908 Lee Road and Walgreens at 6201 I-Drive (both open 24 hours).

Travel insurance

Having said you should not travel without good insurance, you should also not pay over the odds for it. Tour operators are notoriously expensive or may imply you need to buy their insurance policy when you don't. In all cases make sure your policy covers you in the USA for: **medical cover** of at least £2 million; **personal liability** up to £2 million (though this won't cover driving abroad; you would still need Supplementary Liability Insurance with your car-hire firm); **cancellation** or **curtailment** cover up to £3,000; **personal property** cover up to £1,500 (but check on expensive individual items, as most policies limit single articles to £250); **cash** and **document** cover, including your passport and tickets; and finally that the policy gives you a 24-hour **emergency helpline.** If you are going bungee jumping or even horse riding, check that your policy includes **dangerous sports cover**.

Shop around at reputable dealers like **American Express** (0800 700 737), **AA** (0191 235 6513), **Bradford & Bingley** (0800 435642), **Club Direct** (0800 0744 558), **Columbus** (0207 375 0011), **Direct Travel** (01903 812345), **GA Direct** (0800 121007), **Options** (0870 848 0870), **Premier Direct** (0990 133218), **Primary Direct** (0870 444 3434), **Thomas Cook** (0845 600 5454), **Travel Insurance Direct** (0990 168113), **Worldcover Direct** (0800 365121) and **Worldwide Travel Insurance** (01892 833338).

Travellers with disabilities

The main parks pay close attention to the needs of holiday-makers with disabilities. There are few rides and attractions that cannot cater for them, while wheelchair availability and access is almost always good. *Walt Disney World* Resort publish a *Guidebook for Disabled Guests,* as do Universal, available in all three main parks. Life-jackets are on hand at *Disney's River Country* and *Typhoon Lagoon,* while there are special tape cassettes for blind visitors, and guide dogs are not discouraged.

Disabled drivers should take their orange car badge with them as this is honoured in the US and there are designated parking areas at all theme parks. Disney resorts also have special services and rooms for guests with disabilities, call 407 939 7807 for details. For more local assistance, **Walker Medical & Mobility Products** specialise in three-wheeled electric scooters and wheelchair rentals, with free delivery and pick-up from your hotel or holiday home. Call 407 331 9500 for more information. Reader *Les Willans* confirms: 'Orlando is superb when it comes to accessibility for wheelchair users like myself, but Americans often use quite offensive language, such as the term "handicapped", when referring to the disabled.'

Measurements

American clothes sizes are smaller, hence a US size 12 dress is a UK size 14, or an American jacket sized 42 is really a 44. Shoes are the opposite: a US 10 should fit a British size 9 foot. Their measuring system is also still imperial and NOT metric.

American-speak

Another thing to watch out for are words or phrases that have a different meaning across the Atlantic. For instance, when Americans say the first floor, they mean the ground floor, the second floor is really the first, and so on. (PS: NEVER ask for a packet of fags. Fag is a crude, slang term for homosexual, hence you will get some VERY funny looks.)

American	English	American	English
Check or Tab	Bill	Lines	Queues, so 'Stand in line' not 'Queue up')
Restroom	Public toilet		
Bathroom	Private toilet		
Eggs 'over easy'	Eggs fried both sides but soft	Elevator	Lift
		Underpass	Subway
Eggs 'over hard'	Eggs fried both sides but hard!	Subway	Underground
		Mailbox	Postbox
Eggs 'sunny side up'	Eggs fried on just one side (soft)	Faucet	Tap
French fries	Chips	Collect call	Reverse charge phone call
Chips	Crisps	Gas	Petrol
Cookie	Biscuit	Trunk	Car boot
Grits	Porridge-like breakfast dish made out of ground, boiled corn	Hood	Car bonnet
		Fender	Car bumper
		Antenna	Aerial
		Windshield	Windscreen
		Stickshift	Manual transmission
Biscuit	Savoury scone		
Hash browns	Grated, fried potato (delicious!)	Trailer	Caravan
		Freeway	Motorway
Jelly	Jam	Divided highway	Dual carriageway
Silverware or place-setting	Cutlery	Denver boot	Wheel clamp
		Turn-out	Lay-by
Liquor	Spirits	No standing	No parking OR stopping
Seltzer	Soda water		
Shot	Measure	Parking lot	Car park
Liquor store	Off-licence	Semi	Articulated truck
Broiled	Grilled	Ramp	Slip-road
Grilled	Flame-grilled	Intersection	Junction
Sub	Torpedo roll	Construction	Roadworks
Shrimp	King prawn	Yield	Give way
Sherbet	Sorbet	Purse	Handbag
Eggplant	Aubergine	Fanny pack	Bumbag
Appetiser	Starter	Pants	Trousers
Entree	Main course	Undershirt	Vest
To go	Take-away (as in food)	Vest	Waistcoat
		Pantyhose	Tights
Candy	Sweets	Sneakers	Trainers
Drug store	Chemist	Shorts	Underpants
Movie theater	Cinema	Facecloth	Flannel
Sidewalk	Pavement	Quarter	25 cents
Pavement	Roadway	Dime	10 cents
Bill	Note (as in $5 note)	Nickel	5 cents
		Penny	1 cent
Crib	Cot	Downtown	The city or town centre (not the run-down part!)
Cot or rollaway	Fold-up bed		
Diaper	Nappy		
Stroller	Pushchair	A/C	Air-conditioning

Wedding bells

Florida is increasingly sought after by couples looking to tie the knot (some 20,000 couples a year at the last count), and Orlando offers a terrific range of wedding services, from ceremony co-ordinators, photography and flowers to a wonderfully scenic range of venues like Cypress Gardens, Winter Park and Leu Gardens, plus more unusual venues like the pit-lane of the Richard Petty Driving Experience at Walt Disney World or even at 145mph around the speedway itself! **Walt Disney World's Wedding Pavilion** offers true fairytale romance, with the backdrop of Cinderella Castle and Seven Seas Lagoon. You can opt for traditional elegance in this Victorian setting with up to 260 guests or the full Disney experience, arriving in Cinderella's glass coach and with Mickey and Minnie among the guests. Disney's wedding organisers can tailor-make the occasion for individual requirements (407 828 3400). Universal have a wedding service based on their beautiful Portofino Bay Hotel. Call 407 503 1120 for their wedding specialist. All the main **tour operators** feature wedding options and co-ordinated services, and offer ceremonies as varied as aboard a hot air balloon or helicopter (Virgin), Caledesi Island beach (Airtours and Jetsave), Church Street Station (Jetsave, Sunworld and Style Travel) or luxury yacht (Cosmos). Prices vary from £349 (Chapel of Love – Airtours) to £1,399 (Disney Pavilion – Unijet). You can also **do it yourself** by calling at the Osceola County Administrative Building, 17 South Vernon Street, Room 231-A, Kissimmee 8.30am–4.30pm Mon–Fri (407 847 1424). Both parties must be present to apply for the marriage licence, which costs $88.50 (in cash) and is valid for 60 days, while the ceremony (equivalent to a British registry office) can be performed at the same time for an extra $20. Passports and birth certificates are required and, after acquiring a marriage licence, a couple can get married anywhere in Florida. The County's Marriage Department can also supply names of public notaries to conduct the ceremony if you want to get married elsewhere, like one of the more picturesque resort hotels, which are usually amenable to providing the venue. For more information, you can call the Orlando/Orange County Convention & Visitors' Bureau for an information pack (407 363 5872).

© Disney Enterprises, Inc.

The Disney Wedding Pavilion

Know before you go

You can contact these organisations for advance information. Florida Tourism (FLA USA) have an info line on 09001 600555 (60p/minute) that lists all Florida destinations and gives other consumer lines in the

UK, while they are also on the Internet at www.flausa.com and have a free information pack if you call 01737 644882. The Orlando Tourism Bureau in London has a 24-hour information line on 0800 092 2352, on which you can request their free *Destination Imagination* information pack or check out www.orlandoflusa.co.uk. Their excellent official website is www.go2orlando.com. Kissimmee's UK office has a brochure request line on 01235 824334 and their website is www.floridakiss.com. You can also write to the Kissimmee-St Cloud Convention & Visitors' Bureau, Roebuck House, Palace Street, London, SW1E 5BA, fax 020 7630 0245.

When you arrive in the area, it is also worth checking out Orlando's ONLY official **Visitor Center** at 8723 International Drive (407 363 5872) for discounted attraction tickets, free brochures and accommodation advice and free information pamphlets and maps. The Kissimmee **Visitor Center** is at the eastern end of the Highway 192 tourist drag (407 847 5000 or 1-800 327 9159 in the States) and they have a toll-free accommodation line in the US of 1-800 333 KISS.

Of course, THE Internet site for all things Orlando and Disney is the information- and fun-packed www.wdwinfo.co.uk (and www.wdwinfo.com), to which I also contribute. The creation and maintenance of this independent site is a truly mind-boggling feat. It is a huge achievement, with its complete range of theme park info (right down to rides under refurbishment, park hours and ride height requirements), news, weather, facts, figures and tips, plus discount offers throughout Orlando, discussion boards and a chat forum. For up-to-the-minute advice and assistance, there is no better Internet resource. And don't overlook www.usfinfo.com and www.swoinfo.com for the full picture.

Of course, the official sites aren't bad either, with Disney's the pick of the bunch: http://disney.go.com/disneyworld (check opening hours, parade times and book tickets on-line). Then there is Universal's, www.uescape.com, plus www.seaworld.com and www.buschgardens.com. The local newspaper is also worth checking out (especially for their Calendar section of what's on), www.orlandosentinel.com.

There are then a plethora of unofficial and fan websites, like www.wdwig.com (especially good for their restaurant section), www.wdwmagic.com (great for Disney trivia and rumours), www.arkstar.com/dreamfinder (for more insider info; creator Arlen Miller also runs auctions of Disney collectibles and an e-mail Disney news service if you e-mail him at dsnyana@kua.net) and www.orlandorocks.com (for all theme park addicts). Right, that's enough planning for now, on to the real thing ...

Cypress Gardens

3 Driving and Car Hire
(or, The Secret of Getting Around on Interstate 4)

For the vast majority, introduction to Orlando proper comes immediately after clearing the airport via the potentially bewildering complexity of the local road systems in a newly acquired hire car. Yet driving here is a lot more simple and, on the whole, enjoyable than driving in the UK. In particular, anyone used to the M25 will certainly find Orlando's motorways less pressured.

Before you get to your hire car, however, a quick note about Orlando International Airport and the new Orlando/Sanford Airport, which is primarily a British charter flight gateway 30 miles to the north of Orlando. There is a full breakdown of how both airports work in Chapter 12, but you need to be aware of a couple of quirks on arrival.

Orlando International is one of the most modern and enjoyable airports you will encounter, but it does have a double baggage collection system that is a bit bewildering at first. You disembark at one of three satellite terminals (a fourth will have been completed in 2000, aiming to ease international arrivals) and have to collect your luggage immediately, then put it on another baggage carousel that takes it to the main terminal while you ride the passenger shuttle. Once in the main terminal you will be on Level Three and need to descend to Level Two for baggage reclaim. There are porters here to help you tote your luggage down to Level One for car pick-up, while the trolleys require $1 in change to operate. Taxis and limos are also on Level One.

The Big Four hire companies who all have check-in desks at the airport are Dollar, National, Budget and Avis and all offer the most comprehensive hire services, if rather lacking in the personal touch. However, there is also a telephone desk at Level One that connects you directly to one of another 10 hire companies who often work out better value if you haven't already booked your car (notably Alamo). A quick call brings their bus to pick you up and take you to their nearby depot, which also gives you a look at the surrounding roads before you have to drive on them. Hertz and Avis are the biggest companies in the US, but Dollar and Alamo are the tops for tourist business. Dollar include Thomson, Airtours, Virgin, Style Travel, Travel City, Cosmos, First Choice and Sunworld in their typical packages, while Alamo are the main clients for Unijet, Funway, Jetlife, Jetsave, Kuoni, British Airways Holidays and Thomas Cook

BRIT TIP: Make sure you follow the correct instructions to collect your hire car. There are several different desks for each of the main hire companies and if you do not check in at the right one you will waste a lot of time.

Holidays, among others. Alamo's new international tour centre, a 10-minute bus ride from the airport, features no less than 52 terminals, plus desks for the tour operator reps (handy for any paperwork wrangles), a changing area and a well-planned childcare area. Alamo are also a *Brit's Guide* partner company and can offer our readers a special rate in conjunction with the book. *See inside front cover for details.*

Orlando without a car

Although being mobile is advisable, it is possible to survive without a car. Be aware, though, that few of the attractions are within walking distance of anywhere and taxis can be expensive. If you decide not to drive, your best base is either *Walt Disney World* Resort (free transport throughout, but harder to get to the rest of Orlando) or International Drive for its location, good pavements (or 'sidewalks') and the I-Ride Trolley. Many hotels also have free shuttles to the main parks (notably in Kissimmee) or a regular mini-bus service for a small charge.

There are basically three different routes for your transport. The reliable, cheap, but slightly plodding **Lynx bus system** covers much of Metro Orlando. Their website is at www.golynx.com and their information line is on 407 841 8240. Ask for a copy of their excellent System Map, which shows all their routes (or 'Links') and the main attractions. Worth noting are Link 42 from the International Airport to I-Drive, Link 56 from Kissimmee to *Walt Disney World* Resort, and Link 4 from Kissimmee to downtown Orlando. They are only $1 a ride (plus 10c for any transfers) or $10 for a weekly pass (children 6 and under go free with a full-fare passenger). They average a bus every 30 minutes in the main areas, every 15 minutes from 6–9am and

3.30–6.30pm. Remember to have the right change (including any transfers). Buses are wheelchair accessible. Look for the pink paw-print signs that are the Lynx bus stops. International Drive also has the great value **I-Ride trolley** along an 8-mile stretch from Belz at the top, to SeaWorld via Westwood Boulevard and Sea Harbor Drive and to the new Orlando Premium Outlets (see www.iridetrolley.com or call 407 354 5656). Running every day, 7am to midnight, it costs 75c per trip (25c for seniors) – please have the right change – or you can buy passes for 1, 3, 5 or 7 days at $2, $3, $5 or $7. Kids 12 and under go free with an adult, and all trolleys have hydraulic lifts for wheelchairs. Passes are sold at most hotel service desks and visitor centres.

There is also a daily bus ($10/person) from SeaWorld to Busch Gardens in Tampa at 9am, called **The Busch Express**. You must have Busch tickets in advance (included in the 10-day, 5-Park Orlando FlexTicket). See page 142.

After public transport, there is a raft of well-organised firms who offer **shuttle services** to the attractions for a set fee and excursions to places like Kennedy Space Center and Busch Gardens that pick up at the hotels. The main firms are Mears (www.mears-net.com, tel 407 839 1570), Transtar (www.transtar1.com, tel 407 856 7777) and Coach USA (tel 407 826 9999). They also operate airport–hotel shuttles at about $26/person (plus tip) and even limousines. The excellent **Tiffany Town Car** services (www.tiffanytowncar. com) also come highly recommended for airport transfers and feature a 30-minute grocery stop if you are self-catering. Then there are the **excursion services** offered by the likes of Gray Line (www.grayline.com, 303 433 9800),

The colourful I-Ride Trolley

Real Florida Excursions (a British company), tel 407 345 4996, ext. 3012 (and on www.weruse.com), and Keith Prowse (see page 10). Finally, for groups of four or five, **taxis** can be a convenient occasional option. The journey from the International Airport to I-Drive would cost $35–$40 (about $8 each for five), $15 from I-Drive to Universal Orlando and $20–$25 from I-Drive to *Walt Disney World* Resort. Try Central Florida Taxi on 407 851 7523 (freephone 1-800 441 3276 in Florida) or Yellow Cab Co on 407 422 4561.

The car

Ultimately, having a car is the key to being in charge of your holiday, and on a weekly basis it tends to work out quite reasonable price-wise, too.

Weekly rates can be as low as $100 for the smallest size of car (an **Economy**, usually a Fiesta-sized hatchback; next up is the **Subcompact**, an Escort-sized car; the **Compact**, a small family saloon

> BRIT TIP: The boot size on American cars tends to be smaller than the British equivalent. And you will not get seven people PLUS their luggage in a seven-seater van!

like an Orion; the **Midsize** is a more spacious four-door, five-seater like a Vectra; and the **Fullsize** would be a large-style executive car like a Granada, and you can get larger still). But beware these low, low starting rates. There are a number of insurances, taxes and surcharges which are pretty much essential, and these can easily take the final weekly rate to $280 or more. However, all the big rental companies now offer all-inclusive rates which do away with the 'hidden extras', and which can work out significantly cheaper if booked in advance in the UK. Rates can be as low as £159 a week, and you also benefit from easier processing at the Orlando end, making the whole business quicker. To book, call **Alamo** (see inside front cover for our special readers' offer) or **Dollar** on 0800 252897. Or you could try **Avis** (0990 900 500); **Budget** (0880 181181); **Thrifty** (0990 168 238); **Hertz** (0990 906090); **National** (0345 222525); or **Suncars** (0990 005566).

> BRIT TIP: Be FIRM with the hire company check-in clerk as many are quite pushy and will try to get you to take extras, like car up-grades, you don't need.

Once again, the scale of the car-hire operation is huge, and, with upwards of 300 tourists arriving at a time, it can be a pretty formidable business getting everyone off and running. The currently widespread practice of British holiday companies offering free car hire with their packages does NOT mean it won't cost you anything. It is only the *rental* cost which is free and you will still be expected to pay the insurance, taxes and other extras BEFORE you can drive the car away (which makes the all-inclusive packages even more attractive). Having a credit card is *essential*, and there are two main kinds of insurance, the most important being the Loss or Collision Damage Waiver, LDW or CDW. This currently costs around $17 a day and covers you for any damage to your hire car. You can manage without it, but the hire company will then insist on a huge deposit in the order of $1,000 on your credit card, and that could wipe out your credit limit in one go (and you are also liable for ANY damage). You will also be offered Supplemental Liability Insurance or Extended Protection at around $11 a day. This covers you against being sued for astronomical amounts by any court-happy American you may happen to bump into (not strictly essential, but good for your peace of mind). Drivers under 25 have to pay an extra $10–20 per day, while all drivers must be at least 21. Other additional costs (which all mount up over a two-week holiday) include local and Florida state taxes which can add another $6 a day to your final bill, Airport Access Fee at $4 per day and then there's your petrol, although this is still appreciably cheaper than ours in the UK.

Drivers also please note: you may feel the effects of jet-lag for a day or two after arrival, but this can be reduced during the flight by avoiding alcohol and coffee and instead drinking plenty of water.

Most soon find that US driving is a pleasure rather than a pain, mainly

International Drive at night

because nearly all hire cars are automatics and rarely more than a year old. And, because speed limits are lower than we're used to at home (and rigidly enforced), you won't often be rushed into taking the wrong turn. Keep your foot on the brake when you are stationary as automatics tend to creep forward, and always put the automatic gear lever in 'P' (for Park) after turning off the engine.

Controls

All cars are also fitted with air-conditioning, which is absolutely essential during spring, summer and autumn. The button to turn it on will be marked A/C, Air, or will be indicated by a snowflake symbol. (Handy hint: to make it work, you also have to switch on the car's fan!) Don't be alarmed by a small pool of liquid forming under your car in summer – it's condensation off the A/C unit.

Power steering is also a common feature on many hire cars, so be gentle around corners until you get the feel of it. Some larger cars also have cruise control which lets you set the desired speed and take your foot off the accelerator (or gas pedal in American-speak). There will be two buttons on the steering wheel, one to switch the cruise control on, the other which you push to set the desired speed. To take the car off cruise control either press the first

BRIT TIP: You probably won't be able to take the keys out of the ignition unless you put the car in 'Park' first. This sometimes causes much consternation!

button again or simply touch the brake. Wait until you have a clear stretch of motorway before you try this! The handbrake may also be different. Some cars have an extra foot pedal to the left of the brake, and you need to push this to engage the handbrake. There will then be a tab just above it which you pull to release it, or a second push on the pedal if there is no tab. The car probably won't start unless the gear lever is in 'P', which can be confusing at first. To put the car in 'D' for Drive, you also have to depress the main brake pedal. D1 and D2 are extra gears for steep hills (none in Florida!). Few cars have central locking so make sure you lock ALL the doors.

Getting around

Your car-hire company should provide you with a basic map of Orlando plus directions for getting to your hotel. Insist that these are provided as all the hire companies make a big point of this in their literature. To begin with, familiarise yourself with the main roads of the area and learn to navigate by the road *numbers* (it's much easier than names, and the directional signs will feature the numbers primarily) and the exit numbers of the main roads.

When you drive out of the International Airport (or the hire company's off-airport depot) DON'T look for signs to 'Orlando' – the airport's new signage should be a big help here. The main tourist areas are all south and west of the city proper, so follow the appropriate signs for your hotel. For the International Drive area you want the Beeline Expressway (usually just listed as Route 528) all the way west until it crosses International Drive just north of SeaWorld. The main hotel area of I-Drive (as it is known locally) is to the north, so keep right at the exit. For western Kissimmee

and Walt Disney World, go south out of the airport and pick up the new Central Florida Greeneway (Route 417) all the way west until it intersects with State Route 536 at Exit 6. You can then follow 536 straight across into Walt Disney World or take the Interstate 4 west for one junction until it hits the main Kissimmee Routeway, Highway 192 (or the Irlo Bronson Memorial Highway). For eastern Kissimmee, come off Route 417 at Exit 11 with the Orange Blossom Trail (Highway 441), and going south brings you into Highway 192 at the other end of the main tourist drag.

Leaving **Orlando/Sanford Airport** is also a straightforward affair, boosted by the airport's simple design. Dollar and Alamo have made a big impression here with their British-dedicated operations. There is no off-airport shuttle to your car to slow you down, just a quick walk from the airport's baggage reclaim hall to the car-hire office. But please remember to have your paperwork and especially your driving licence with you or you WILL find yourself either delayed or refused a car altogether (in the case of forgetting your licence).

It may be much further to the north and involve more driving time, but you should save time overall. You leave the airport on East Lake Mary Boulevard and quickly hit the junction with the Central Florida Greeneway (Highway 417) on which

BRIT TIP: The Beeline Expressway (528) and Greeneway (417) are both toll roads, so it's handy to have some change. Toll booths are reluctant to change more than $20 notes.

BRIT TIP: Watch out for one small hiccup on the Greeneway heading south. Just after Junction 34 it appears to split into two where it meets Highway 408. Stay in the RIGHT lane to keep on the south-bound motorway.

you head south. The slip-road on to this toll motorway is just under the fly-over on your LEFT, and you will need about $4.50 in total to reach Kissimmee or Walt Disney World or $3.75 to reach International Drive (via the Beeline Expressway, Route 528).

You can avoid the tolls by staying on Lake Mary Boulevard for four miles until you hit Interstate 4, but you will encounter much more traffic this way and possibly hit the 4–6pm snarl-up through the city centre. The Greeneway is an excellent, easy-driving introduction to Orlando roads, even if it does cost an extra few dollars. PS: The car-hire firms do not receive a kick-back for recommending 417 either!

Signs and road names

It's best to be aware of a few other potential pitfalls. First, the system of signposting and road-naming can be confusing. For instance, you cannot fail to find the main attractions, but retracing your steps back to the hotel afterwards can prove tricky because they often take you out of the parks a different way. (Disney is notoriously poor at sign-posting to help find your way out. A good tip is to get a copy of their Transportation Guide/Map from Guest Services at any park and use it to help navigate.) Here, it is vital to learn the main road numbers (and directions, either

east–west or north–south) around the attractions so you know where you are heading, and if you want I4 east or west or 192 as you exit Epcot or Disney-MGM Studios. Also, exits off the Interstate and other main roads can be on EITHER side of the carriageway, not just on the right. This potential worry is offset by the fact you can overtake in ANY lane on multi-lane highways, not just the outside ones. Therefore, you can happily sit in the middle lane and let the rest of the world go by until you see your exit. However, you don't get much advance notice of turn-offs. You get the sign and then the exit in very quick succession. The local police also take a dim view of late and frequent lane-changing. But once again, the speeds at which you are travelling tend to minimise the dangers of missing your turn-off. It is handy if your front-seat passenger acts as navigator. Orlando has yet to come up with a comprehensive tourist map of its city streets and the maps supplied by the car-rental companies tend to be simplified. It helps that none of the main attractions is off the beaten track, but the support of your navigator can be useful.

Around town, and in the main tourist areas, you will come across another method of confusing the unwary in the way road names are displayed. At every junction you will see a road name hung underneath the traffic lights suspended ABOVE the road. This road name is NOT the road you are on, but the one you are CROSSING. Once again there is no advance notification of each junction and the road names can be difficult to read as you approach them, especially at night, so keep your speed down if you think you are close to your turn-off so you can get in the correct lane. If you do miss a turning, nearly all the roads are arranged in a simple grid system so it is usually easy to work your way

Panoramic view of Universal Orlando

back. Occasionally you will meet a crossroads where no right of way is obvious. This is a four-way stop, and the priority goes in order of arrival, so when it's your turn you just indicate and pull out slowly (America doesn't have roundabouts, so this is the closest you will get to one).

Several major highways, notably the Beeline Expressway and Florida Turnpike and Greeneway, are also toll roads, so have some change handy in varying amounts from 25 cents to $1. They all give change (in the GREEN lanes), but you will get through much quicker if you have the correct money (in the BLUE lanes). On some of the minor exits of the Greeneway and Osceola Parkway (another toll route in Kissimmee), there are auto-toll machines *only*, so try to keep some loose change in your car at all times.

As well as the obvious difference of driving on the 'wrong' side of the road (a particular hazard in car parks), there are also several differences in procedure. The most frequent British errors occur at traffic lights (which are hung above the road, not on posts – easy to miss occasionally). At a red light it is still possible to turn RIGHT, providing there is no traffic coming from the left and no pedestrians crossing,

unless otherwise specified (signs will occasionally indicate 'no turn on red'). Turning LEFT at the lights, you have the right of way with a green ARROW, but you have to give way to traffic from the other direction on a SOLID green light. The majority of accidents involving overseas visitors take place on left turns, so do take extra care here. There is also no amber light from red to green, but there IS an amber light from green to red.

Restrictions

Speed limits are always well marked with black numbering on white signs and, again, the police are pretty hot on speeding and on-the-spot fines are steep. Limits vary from 55 to 70mph on the Interstates (and can change frequently), where there is also a 40mph *minimum* speed, to just 15 or 20mph in some built-up areas.

Flashing orange lights suspended over the road indicate a school zone so proceed with caution, while school buses *cannot* be overtaken in either direction when they are unloading and have their hazard lights on. U-turns are forbidden in built-up areas and where a solid line runs down the middle of the road. It is illegal to park within 10ft of a fire hydrant or a lowered kerb, and *never*

BRIT TIP: The Osceola Parkway toll road which runs parallel to Highway 192 is a much handier route in to Walt Disney World from much of Kissimmee and costs only $1.

park in front of a yellow-painted kerb – they are stopping points for emergency vehicles and you will be towed away. Never park on a kerb, either. Seat belts are compulsory for all front-seat passengers, while child seats *must* be used for children under 4 and can be hired from the car companies at around $5 a day. Children of 4 or 5 must either use a seat belt, whether sitting in the front or back, or have a child seat fitted.

You *must* put your lights on in the rain, and you *must* park bonnet first. Reverse parking is frowned upon because number plates are often found only on the rear of cars and patrolling police cars like to be able to read them without the officers having to stop and walk round the car. If you park parallel to the kerb you must be facing in the direction of the traffic. Disabled drivers should note their orange disabled badge IS recognised in Florida for parking in the well-provided disabled parking spaces. *Don't drink and drive.* Florida has strict laws, with penalties of up to six months in prison for first-time offenders. The

legal limit for the blood-alcohol level is lower than in Britain, so it is safer not to drink at all if you are driving. It is also illegal to carry open containers of alcohol in the car itself.

Attention AA members – here comes a bonus for you. Not only is your membership recognised by the equivalent AAA in the States, but you also benefit from several special deals, including area maps and ticket and hotel discounts. The Florida AAA centre is situated in Heathrow, north of Orlando, just off junction 50 of I4 (turn left on Lake Mary Boulevard, then first right on to International Parkway and the AAA is half a mile down on the left). For details (and savings like $5.75 off SeaWorld tickets, $12 off Wild Bill's dinner show, and special hotel rates) call the info number on the back of your AA card and ask for their USA pack, which gives you a special AAA

BRIT TIP: The Kissimmee-St Cloud tourist information office on east Highway 192 has the best free map of the area, clearly indicating all the main routes and attractions.

card and their entitlements. It is even worth joining the AA (about £40) for the AAA discounts, which could add up to several hundred dollars if you take full advantage of them. Call 0870 544 4444.

Accidents

In the unlikely event of having an accident, no matter how minor, the police must be contacted before the cars can be moved (except on the busy I4). Car-hire firms will insist on a full police report for the insurance paperwork. In the case of a break-

Downtown Orlando

down, there should be an emergency number for the hire company among their essential literature, or, if you are on a major highway, raise the bonnet of your car to indicate a problem and wait for one of the frequent police patrol cars to stop for you (or, if you have a mobile phone, dial ✱FHP). Remember, also, always to carry your driving licence and your hire agreement forms with you in case you are stopped by the police. Should you be pulled over, remain in your car with your hands on the wheel and be polite to the officer who comes over. Once they learn you are British, you *may* just get away with a ticking-off for a minor offence!

Key routes

As already mentioned, the main route through Orlando is **Interstate 4** (or I4), a six- to eight-lane motorway linking the two Florida coasts. Interstates are always indicated on blue shield-shaped signs. For most of its length, I4 travels almost directly east–west, but, around Orlando, it swings north–south, although directions are still given east (for north) or west (for south). All main motorways are prefixed I, the even numbers generally going east–west and the odd numbers north–south. Federal Highways are the next grade down and are all numbered with black numerals on white shields, while state roads are known as Routeways (black numbers on white circular or oblong signs). All the attractions of Walt Disney World, plus those of SeaWorld and Universal Orlando are well signposted from I4. Cypress Gardens is a 45-minute drive from central Orlando (south) west on I4 and Highway 27, while Busch Gardens is 75 minutes down I4 to Tampa. The Kennedy Space Center is a good hour's drive along the Beeline Expressway (Route 528)

which intersects I4 at junction 28.

International Drive is the second key local roadway, linking as it does a 12-mile ribbon of hotels, shops, restaurants and some of the smaller attractions like Wet 'n Wild, the Mercado Shopping Center, The Pointe, Skull Kingdom, Guinness World Records Experience, WonderWorks and Belz Factory Outlet shopping malls. (Be aware that International Drive South, from Highway 192 north to Route 536, is NOT the main stretch, although they will, ultimately, link up.) From I4, take junctions 27A, 28, 29 or 30A travelling (north) east, or 30B, 29A or 28 travelling (south) west. To the north, International Drive runs into Oakridge Road and then the South Orange Blossom Trail, which leads into downtown Orlando (junctions 38–41 off I4). International Drive is also bisected by Sand Lake Road and runs away into Epcot Drive, via World Center Drive, to the south, which is another handy way to the attractions of *Walt Disney World* Resort. It is a major tourist centre in its own right and makes an excellent base from which to operate, especially to the south of Sand Lake Road, near the Mercado Shopping Center, where you can actually enjoy a walk around on real pavement. It's a 20-minute drive from *Walt Disney World* Resort's attractions and 10 minutes from Universal and SeaWorld. However, I-Drive can become congested at peak times, especially at the junction with Sand Lake Road, so it can be better to use I4 for north–south journeys. Universal Boulevard (formerly Republic Drive) is the new I-Drive link to Universal Orlando and is also a less congested alternative to I-Drive.

The other main tourist area is the town of **Kissimmee** to the south of Orlando and the south-east of *Walt Disney World* Resort. It's an attraction in its own right, being the home of Water Mania, the Old Town shopping complex, Gatorland, Green Meadows Petting Farm and the Medieval Times dinner show, plus more hotels and restaurants. It is all grouped in a rather untidy straggle along a 19-mile stretch of **Highway 192** (The Irlo Bronson Memorial Highway), which intersects I4 at junction 25B, and is not much more than 10 minutes from Walt Disney World, 20 from SeaWorld and 25 from Universal Studios (but look out for major roadworks on 192 during 2001). The downtown area of Kissimmee (off Main Street, Broadway and Emmett Street) is much prettier and accessible by foot.

A handy tourist addition to Highway 192 is a series of markers along its western stretch from Splendid China (Number 4) to just past Medieval Times (Number 15). These highly visible numbered signs make for accurate locators of many of the hotels, restaurants and attractions on local maps.

Fuel

Finally, a quick word about re-fuelling your car at an American gas station. You will often have a choice of attendant or self-serve. You do not tip the attendant but you do pay a slightly higher price to cover the service. Most gas stations will also require you to pay in advance at night, i.e. before filling the car, and will require the exact amount in cash or your credit card. Some pumps also allow you to pay by credit card without having to go in to the cashier's office. The American gallon is smaller (by about a fifth) than the British version. Always use unleaded fuel and, to make American petrol pumps work, you must first lift the lever underneath the pump nozzle. RaceTrac petrol stations are usually the cheapest locally (even for soft drinks and cigarettes), although they don't take credit cards.

Local maps

The best and most up-to-date free maps are the bright orange **Welcome Guide-Map** (also full of discount coupons), available in the main tourist areas, and the pull-out map inside the **Kissimmee-St Cloud Visitors' Guide** (from the official Visitor Center on east Highway 192, tel 407 847 5000). AA members are well catered for (see page 41), but the best paid-for maps are the **Trakker** series, with four products covering Orlando: the Pocket Map ($3.25) is almost as detailed as the AAA ones, while the City Slicker (a laminated fold-out of the main areas, $5.95) is useful in the car, and the Orlando/Walt Disney Popout Map is a handy theme park reference guide. They also do a full Orlando Atlas ($16.95), and Trakker Maps are found in all good bookshops in central Florida. You can contact them (and order maps) via www.trakkermaps.com or phone 305 255 4485 in Florida.

Mobile phones can be rented from $5 a day (plus $0.99/minute air time) and they will deliver to your hotel. Another of our *Brit's Guide* partners provides this service, so call **Airwave Communications** for details on 407 843 1166. They even rent pagers ($20/week) and small two-way radios ($75/week) which are a great idea for families who like to do their own thing but want to stay in touch around the parks.

Now, on to your holiday accommodation …

4 Accommodation
(or, Making Sense of American Hotels, Motels and Condos)

To list all the various hotels, motels, holiday homes, guesthouses, condominiums, campsites and other forms of accommodation available in the Orlando area would fill a book, so it is not the intention here to attempt a comprehensive guide. The metropolitan Orlando area can boast the second highest concentration of hotels anywhere in the United States and more are being built all the time, with the number of rooms now in excess of 100,000. Therefore, the following detail is intended only as a general guide to the bigger, better or budget types.

Hotels

The first thing to be aware of is that American hotels, particularly in the largest tourist areas like this, tend towards the motel type, even among some of the bigger and more expensive 'hotels'. This doesn't mean you will be short-changed as far as facilities and service are concerned, but you won't necessarily be located in one main building. The chances are that your room will be in one of several blocks arranged around the other facilities such as the swimming pool, restaurant, etc. This is a significant distinction because of the safety aspects – it is possible for non-hotel guests to gain access to parts of a motel-style hotel, so it is important to be security-conscious in matters like ensuring the room is locked and checking the ID of anyone who knocks at the door (although it is not something to be worried about. See also Chapter 12, Safety First). The size of rooms rarely alters, even between two-star and four-star accommodation. In general, it is the extra amenities of the hotel which give it extra star rating and not the size of the rooms themselves. A standard room usually features two double beds and will comfortably accommodate a family of four.

BRIT TIP: Few hotels have got round to providing hair-dryers as standard, although they can often be ordered from the front desk. If you bring your own, you will need a US plug adaptor (with two flat pins). Their voltage is also different, 110–120 AC, as opposed to our 220, so your hair-dryer/electric razor will work rather sluggishly.

The other feature of motel-type accommodation which frequently takes British visitors by surprise is the lack of a restaurant in many cases. This is because the American hotel scene operates purely on a room-only basis – meals are always extra, and hence dining facilities are not always provided. This means you may have to get out of your hotel/motel and drive to the nearest restaurant (of which there are a multitude – see Chapter 10) just for breakfast. Check the brochure carefully to see what dining facilities the various hotels provide if this would be a concern for you.

As a general rule, hotels in Orlando are big, clean, efficient and great value for money (one room usually suits a family of four quite comfortably). Another standard feature is the abundance of soft-drink and ice machines, with ice buckets in all the rooms (although you may find that you are paying well over the odds for a can of Coke, or whatever, from the machine at the end of your corridor).

All types of accommodation will also be fully air-conditioned and, when it is really hot, you will have to learn to live with the steady drone of the A/C unit in your room at nights. NEVER turn the air-conditioning off when you go out, even when it is cool in the morning because, by the time you return, the chances are your room will have turned into an oven.

Note also that the most expensive place to make a telephone call from is your hotel room! Nearly every hotel adds on a whacking 45–70 per cent surcharge (Disney resorts add a $15 'connection fee') on every call (you can also be charged for a call even if no one answers if it rings five or more times). A better way to make your calls is to buy a local phonecard, which even the holiday companies now sell, and use a normal payphone. To call Britain from the USA, dial 01144, then drop the first 0 from your area code.

Remember also that hotel prices (both in this book and in Orlando) are always per room and NOT per person. They will be cheaper out of the main holiday periods, but prices are still likely to vary from month to month, with special deals offered from time to time. Always ask for rates if you book independently and check if any special rates apply during your visit (don't be afraid to ask for their 'best rate' at off-peak times which can be lower than any published rate). There can also be an additional charge ($5–$15 per person) for more than two adults sharing the same room. It pays to book in advance in high season because Orlando's popularity as a convention centre means it can get very busy.

If you've just arrived and are looking for accommodation, head for one of the two official Visitor Centers in the area, one on International Drive just south of the Mercado Mediterranean Village (on the corner of Austrian Court and open every day 8am–7pm) and the other at the eastern stretch of Highway 192 in Kissimmee (open 8am–5pm), where they keep an updated list of all the hotels and their rates, with brochures on the latest special deals.

Alternatively, you can call the **Central Reservation Service** for a good choice of accommodations, often at discounted rates, on 407 740 6442 or toll-free in Orlando on 1-800 548 3311 (or www.reservation-services.com). They specialise in last-minute bookings in the price range and location you require, and there is no pre-charge or minimum stay requirement. Similarly, **Discount Hotels America** (407 294 9600 or 1-877 766 6787 or www.discounthotelsamerica.com) are worth checking as they occasionally offer free attraction tickets, while the full-service tourist centres of **Know Before You Go** (407 396 5400 or 1-800 749 1993) or **Vacation Works** (407 396 1844 or 1-800 396 1883) deal in discounted accommodation as well as attraction tickets. Of course, our friends at www.wdwinfo.co.uk can also help with accommodation at discounted rates, while www.hotelconxions.com is a another good Internet service.

We place hotels, motels and holiday homes in four price bands to give you a rough ready reckoner, although bear in mind no price is ever set in stone! These bands are:

$ = up to $45 per night
$$ = $46–$90
$$$ = $91–$150
$$$$ = $151-plus

Also, there is no widely accepted rating system for American hotels, so, bearing in mind that there is little difference in the size of rooms (usually quite generous, with two double beds, TV and full en-suite facilities) we have our own C grades, based on the number of facilities and extra creature comforts. Hence, a CCCCC grading will include the highest level of hotel facilities and service, while a CC or C will be the more basic motel-type.

> BRIT TIP: Buy your soft drinks at the supermarket, and a neat polystyrene cooler for about $4 that you can fill with ice from your hotel ice machine to keep your drinks cold.

Resort hotels for Walt Disney World

In keeping with the rest of this guide, a review of Orlando's hotels starts with *Walt Disney World* Resort. With the convenience of being almost on the doorstep of the resort's main attractions, and linked by an excellent free transport system of monorail, shuttle buses and boats, *Walt Disney World* Resort hotels, holiday homes and campsites are all magnificently appointed and maintained. They range from the futuristic appeal of *Disney's Contemporary Resort* (the monorail travels right through the main building) to the oversized fun of

Disney's All-Star Resort, and their landscaping, imagination and attention to detail are as good as the theme parks themselves. In all, there are more than 25,000 rooms throughout the 47 square miles of *Walt Disney World* Resort, while the 780-acre *Disney's Fort Wilderness Resort & Campground* has 1,192 sites. However, all this grandiose accommodation comes at a price. A standard room at *Disney's Grand Floridian Resort & Spa* can cost up to $390 a night in high season and even *Disney's Caribbean Beach Resort* can be more than $100 a night. Eating out in the hotels and resorts is not cheap, and you won't find as many fast-food outlets as you do along International Drive and Highway 192.

However, there is a budget choice for holiday-makers in *Walt Disney World* Resort itself – *Disney's All-Star Sports, Music and Movies Resorts*. This means the convenience of being so close to some of Orlando's biggest attractions has been opened to a lot more holiday budgets, and it is worth a lot, especially in high season when the surrounding roads are packed.

> BRIT TIP: It is usual in American hotels to tip the housemaid by leaving $1/adult each day before your room is made up.

Staying with The Mouse is one of the great thrills, for the style, service and the extras involved. The 20 resorts offer a superb array of facilities, and children especially love being a part of Disney full time. Here are the benefits: **Resort ID card**, every guest gets a 'charge' card with which to charge almost all your food, gifts and services in Walt Disney World to your room account, plus have any purchases shipped to your room. **Early entry**: every day, one of the parks is open to resort guests an hour early. These are known as EE days (see page 27). **Free parking**: with your ID card, there is no charge for your car at any of the parks. **Free transport**: forget the car and use the monorail-bus-boat network to get around. **Dining priority**: guests can make Priority Seating arrangements for all restaurants, shows and special events between 60 and 120 days in advance (two years in the case of dinner shows). Call 407 939 3463. NB: A Priority Seating (or PS, as it is known) is not strictly a reservation but a guarantee of the first available table when you turn up. **Priority golf**: the best tee times are reserved for *Walt Disney World* Resort guests and can be booked 90 days in advance on 407 939 4653.

Children's services: all resorts have in-room or group baby-sitting (subject to availability; you can book in advance on 407 827 5444) and the eight Deluxe resorts have supervised activity centers and dinner clubs (around $6 per child per hour), usually open until midnight.

E Nights: periodically, resort guests get the chance to buy a $10 ticket for an extra three hours doing the main rides at one of the parks after official closing time (great value). **Mickey on call**: okay it's a bit twee, but what better way to wake up than with an alarm call from the Mouse himself?

Around the **Magic Kingdom** Resort area you will find four of the grandest properties. The 15-storey **Disney's Contemporary Resort** boasts 1,050 rooms, a cavernous foyer, shops, restaurants, lounges, a real sandy beach, a marina, two swimming pools, six tennis courts, an electronic games centre and a health club – and magnificent views, especially from the highly acclaimed hotel-top California Grill restaurant. Don't miss Chef Mickey's for a breakfast or dinner buffet with all your favourite characters. There is

also the Mouseketeer Club for 4–12s. As with all **Walt Disney World** Resort accommodation, rooms are large, scrupulously clean and extremely well furnished. $$$$+, CCCCC.

Disney's Polynesian Resort is a South Seas tropical fantasy brought to life with ultra-modern sophistication and comfort. Beautiful sandy beaches, lush vegetation and architecture disguise the fact that 853 rooms can be found here, built in film-set wooden longhouse style and all with balconies and wonderful views. There are excellent eating opportunities, plus canoe rentals, two popular kids' pools, a games room, shops and children's playground. The Neverland Club caters for 4–12s from 5pm–midnight. $$$$+, CCCCC.

BRIT TIP: Dine in wonderful South Seas style at the 'Ohana restaurant, but don't ask for the salt – unless you want to spark an amazing reaction!

Disney's Wilderness Lodge Resort, opened in 1994, is one of the most picturesque places to stay. It is an imposing re-creation of a National Park lodge in amazing detail, down to the hot stream running through the massive wooden balcony-lined atrium lobby and out into the gardens, past the swimming pool (with hot and cold spas) and ending in the resort's own Old Faithful geyser, erupting every hour! It offers authentic backwoods charm with five-star luxury but is connected to the **Magic Kingdom Park** by boat and bus only. It also has two full-service restaurants: the outstanding Artist's Point and the Whispering Canyon Café (for a lively breakfast and huge all-you-can-eat buffets), a snack bar and a pool bar. The Cubs

4

Den is for 4–12s (4.30pm–midnight). $$$$, CCCCC.

The lobby of Disney's Wilderness Lodge

Disney's Grand Floridian Resort & Spa completes the quartet of **Magic Kingdom** Resort area hotels, a hugely elaborate mock Victorian mansion with 900 rooms, an impressive domed and towered foyer and staff in Edwardian dress. The rooms are luxurious, hence the mega price range, and it is worth a look even if you are staying somewhere else. It also has six restaurants, including *Walt Disney World* Resort's top-of-the-range establishment, Victoria and Albert's (where their set, six-course dinner with wine will set you back more than $100 per person) and the chic French style of Citricos, with its excellent view over Seven Seas Lagoon and the nightly Electrical Water Pageant, four bars and a comprehensive array of sporting and relaxation facilities. The Mouseketeer Club caters for 4–12s (7am–midnight), and the 1900 Park Fare restaurant is one of the most popular for character breakfasts and dinner. $$$$+, CCCCC.

Disney's Grand Floridian, Contemporary and *Polynesian* Resorts

are situated on the monorail, the best and fastest system for getting into the *Magic Kingdom* Park and *Epcot*.

Epcot Resort area

The Epcot resort area features six hotels, including arguably the best value properties of them all. The unmistakable **Walt Disney World Swan** and **Dolphin** hotels are perfectly-situated to be within walking distance of the *Epcot* and *Disney-MGM Studios* parks, the Boardwalk entertainment district and the Fantasia Gardens mini-golf courses. The 'entertainment architecture' style is fun and quite extensive, they have the full range of resort benefits, facilities and style, yet they are privately run and so come up a little cheaper than Disney's other deluxe hotels. The Swan features a 45ft statue atop the hotel, which boasts 758 large rooms (including 55 suites), while the Dolphin (1,509 rooms, with 136 suites) is crowned by two even bigger dolphin-fish statues. The duo effectively make up one mega-resort, with no less than 17 restaurants, four tennis courts, three pools (one, an amazing grotto pool with hidden alcoves and water slide), a kids' pool and a white-sand beach, two health clubs, bike and paddle boat rentals, a great range of shops, video arcade and the Camp Dolphin centre for kids 4–12 (1–4.30pm, 6–11pm, $12/hour). Even for non-guests, the Italian restaurant Palio's (the Swan) and Shula's Steak House (Dolphin) are worth seeking out. The Coral Café also features Disney character breakfasts, and some of their little touches for children are immensely thoughtful. And, at night, the whole resort looks just magnificent. Check out www.swandolphin.com for even more detail on these two gems. Transportation is by boat (to Epcot and Disney Studios) and bus. $$$$, CCCCC (tel 407 934 3000).

KEY TO WALT DISNEY WORLD AND LAKE BUENA VISTA ACCOMMODATIONS

1 = DISNEY'S CONTEMPORARY RESORT
2 = DISNEY'S POLYNESIAN RESORT
3 = DISNEY'S WILDERNESS LODGE
4 = DISNEY'S GRAND FLORIDIAN LODGE AND SPA
5 = WALT DISNEY WORLD SWAN
6 = WALT DISNEY WORLD DOLPHIN
7 = DISNEY'S CARIBBEAN BEACH RESORT
8 = DISNEY'S YACHT CLUB RESORT
9 = DISNEY'S BEACH CLUB RESORT
10 = DISNEY'S BOARDWALK
11 = DISNEY'S ALL-STAR RESORTS
12 = DISNEY'S DIXIE LANDINGS RESORT
13 = DISNEY'S PORT ORLEANS RESORT
14 = DISNEY'S CORONADO SPRINGS RESORT
15 = THE VILLAS AT THE DISNEY INSTITUTE
16 = DISNEY'S OLD KEY WEST RESORT
17 = DISNEY'S FORT WILDERNESS RESORT & CAMPGROUND
18 = DISNEY'S ANIMAL KINGDOM LODGE (Open Apr 2001)
19 = HILTON AT WALT DISNEY WORLD
20 = THE GROSVENOR
21 = WYNDHAM PALACE RESORT & SPA
22 = DOUBLETREE GUEST SUITES RESORT
23 = BEST WESTERN AT WALT DISNEY WORLD
24 = HOTEL ROYAL PLAZA
25 = COURTYARD BY MARRIOTT
26 = HYATT REGENCY ORLANDO GRAND CYPRESS
27 = MARRIOTT'S ORLANDO WORLD CENTER
28 = EMBASSY SUITES RESORT LAKE BUENA VISTA
29 = SIERRA SUITES HOTEL
30 = RADISSON INN LAKE BUENA VISTA
31 = BUENA VISTA SUITES
32 = SUMMERFIELD SUITES AT LAKE BUENA VISTA
33 = VISTANA RESORT
34 = SHERATON SAFARI RESORT
35 = HOLIDAY INN SUNSPREE RESORT
36 = CLUB HOTEL BY DOUBLETREE

4

The 45-acre **Disney's BoardWalk Inn and Villas** resort is the most extravagant property in **Walt Disney World**, featuring a 378-room Inn, 532 villas, four themed restaurants, a TV sports club and two night-clubs, plus an impressive array of unique shops, sports facilities and a huge, free-form swimming pool with a 200ft water slide, all situated on a re-created semi-circular boardwalk around Crescent Lake. The overall effect is stunningly pretty, and the attention to detail in the rooms is quite breathtaking. Outstanding features are the summer-cottage style villas, Mediterranean restaurant Spoodles (for arguably the best buffet breakfasts in Orlando) and the Big River Grille & Brewing Works for a magnificent array of beers. Top of the range is the expensive but magnificent seafood restaurant, the Flying Fish. Even if you are not staying here, it is a delightful resort to visit for a meal, the night-life (especially Jellyrolls piano bar) or just a wander along the boardwalk. The Harbor Club caters for 4–12s (4pm–midnight). $$$$+, CCCCC.

Disney's Caribbean Beach Resort is one of the largest resort-type hotels anywhere in America, with 2,112 rooms and the accent on moderate price and value for money. The rooms tend to be a little plainer (although they still comfortably house a family of four), but the facilities in the form of restaurants, bars and outdoor activities (including a lakeside recreation area with themed waterfalls and slides) are a big hit with children. The six counter-service outlets in the food court at Port Royale (the hub of this pretty resort) can get busy in the morning, and the Trinidad South and Barbados 'islands' are a fair walk from the centre, but it is an action-packed resort with some imaginative touches, like Parrot Cay Island with its tropical birds and kids' play area. Transportation from the five Caribbean 'islands' that make up the resort to the theme parks is by bus. $$$, CCCC. Going up-market again, the refined, almost intimate, **Disney's Yacht Club** has 635 rooms designed with nautical themes, all set around an ornamental lake. For a hearty breakfast, the Yacht Club Galley (one of three restaurants and two bars) offers some of the best fare in Walt

BRIT TIP: Although these two resorts are firmly in the Deluxe bracket, you can still visit to try out Beaches & Cream Soda Shop for arguably the best burgers in Walt Disney World.

Disney World. Sister hotel **Disney's Beach Club** completes the **Epcot** line-up. With 580 spacious rooms set along a man-made white-sand beach, it's like a tropical island paradise. You can go boating or catch a water-shuttle service to **Epcot,** while other theme park transportation is provided by bus. Water fun is provided for both Yacht and Beach Club resorts at the shared Stormalong Bay, a magnificent 2½-acre recreation area with water slides and a sandy-floored lagoon. The Sand Castle Club caters for 4–12s (4.30pm–midnight). Both $$$$+, CCCCC.

Disney's Animal Kingdom Resort area

The **Disney's All-Star Resorts** are Disney's first serious venture into capturing a big share of the budget accommodation market. Here, for just $74–$104 a night year-round, you can stay in one of the five sports-themed blocks (Surfing, Basketball, Tennis, Baseball and American Football) centred around a massive food court, two swimming pools, a games arcade and shops, the music-themed version (Jazz, Rock, Broadway, Calypso and Country), or the newest, the *Disney's All-Star Movies Resort* (Mighty Ducks, 101 Dalmatians, Fantasia, Love Bug and Toy Story). The latter is possibly the most imaginative, with its Fantasia pool and kids' play areas, and the most popular blocks are Toy Story and 101 Dalmatians (both of which are non-smoking only). All three centres, which have a total of 5,760 rooms, have pool bars, shops, laundry facilities, video games rooms and a pizza delivery service, and, while their bright, almost garish decor lacks the refined touches of other resorts, and rooms tend to be a lot smaller than their higher-priced counterparts, they are well designed for budget-conscious families who still want to enjoy all the *Walt Disney World* conveniences. Transport to other areas of *Walt Disney World* Resort is provided free by bus. $$-$$$, CCC½. There is also the bonus of a large McDonald's (one of only two in *Walt Disney World*) at the entrance to the All-Star complex.

Disney's Coronado Springs Resort is possibly the best value of the moderate resorts (Caribbean Beach, Port Orleans and Dixie Landings) and it's also the newest. With slightly more in the way of facilities for its 1,967 rooms spread throughout its 136 acres (four pools, including the beautiful – and massive – Lost City of Cibola feature pool, with water slide, jacuzzi and kids' pool/play area; pool bar and grill; two games arcades; a boating marina; bike rentals; restaurant, food court and convenience store; lounge bar; gift shop; beauty salon and health club; business centre; and two guest launderettes) and a wonderfully scenic Mexican/Spanish architecture theme in three 'villages' (Casitas, Ranchos and Cabanas), Coronado is an often overlooked treasure. Check out the Maya Grill

and its new Latino cuisine style for a memorable meal, the lovely one-mile walk around the 15-acre central lagoon, and the main pool's changing facilities, which mean you can have checked out of your room but still take advantage of the pool area before your flight home. Coronado is also only five minutes from *Disney's Animal Kingdom* and is well served by Disney's bus network. $$$, CCCC.

Disney's Animal Kingdom Lodge, due to open in April 2001, promises an African safari version of the Wilderness Lodge. It will be a private game reserve lodge on the edge of a 33-acre animal-filled savannah, which most rooms will overlook. The African theme covers the architecture, shopping, cuisine and restaurants, with the lobby featuring a stream that runs out to the 'watering-hole' main pool area (and kids' pool). This will be a deluxe resort (like Wilderness Lodge, Yacht and Beach Club, etc.), and its opening will be one of the highlights of the year. The attention to detail and the sheer quality of the facilities promise something quite stunning. The Cub's Den will be for 4–12s (4.40pm–midnight), and Disney transport will be by bus. $$$$, CCCCC.

Downtown Disney Resort area

The other main accommodation centre within *Walt Disney World* is the area surrounding Downtown Disney. Here you will find: **Disney's Dixie Landings Resort**, a 2,048-room resort which has a steamboat as a reception area, a wonderful cotton mill-style food court in addition to a Cajun-themed full-service restaurant and an old-fashioned general store (i.e. gift shop). Rooms are either *Gone With The Wind*-style mansionesque (surrounded by grand staircases and columns) or rural Bayou backwoods (decorated with wooden and brass fittings). It also has Ol' Man Island, a magnificent 3½-acre playground, incorporating swimming pool, kids' area and a fishing hole! **Disney's Port Orleans Resort** by comparison adopts the atmosphere of the French quarter of New Orleans for its 1,008 rooms. Turn-of-the-century-style fittings and a Mardi Gras feel make this one of the most pleasantly imaginative hotels, with full-service dining at Bonfamilles café plus the Sassagoula Floatworks and Food Factory court, two bars, a games room, shopping arcade and a fun pool, Doubloon Lagoon. Kids will especially enjoy the Mardi Gras dragon slide and alligator fountains, as well as their own play area and games arcade. Transportation for both resorts is provided mainly by bus, with a lovely boat service to *Downtown Disney*. $$$–$$$$, CCCC. **Disney's Old Key West Resort** is partly a holiday ownership scheme set-up of five-star proportions, but the one-, two- or three-bedroomed studios in a magnificent Key West setting can also be rented out on a nightly basis ($$$$, CCCC) when not in use by club members. Additional facilities include swimming pools, tennis courts, games room, shops and fitness centre. Finally, right next door to *Downtown Disney* are the **Villas At The Disney Institute**, a selection of extremely well-appointed bungalows (sleeping up to five) and townhouses (sleeping four or six), the latter with daily housekeeping. The excellent Seasons Dining Room is also here, along with six pools, four tennis courts, fitness facilities, beauty salon and spa, jogging trails, nature walks and bike paths. The peaceful setting among woodland and waterways is a long way from the hustle-bustle of the big resorts, but the Villas still

cater well for children, with a playground and Camp Disney fun and educational programmes (7–15 year olds). Transport by bus and also boat to *Downtown Disney*. $$$$, CCCC.

Camping Disney Style

Disney's Fort Wilderness Resort & Campground, on Bay Lake, opposite the Magic Kingdom, offers an impressive array of camping facilities and chalet-style homes that can house up to six people. Two 'trading posts' supply fresh groceries, while there are two bars and cafés and a range of on-site activities, including the thrice-nightly Hoop-Dee-Doo Musical Revue, campfire programme, films, sports, games and a prime position from which to view the nightly Electrical Water Pageant. Buses and boats link the campsites with other Walt Disney World areas. $–$$$$, CCCC.

> BRIT TIP: To make a reservation at any *Walt Disney World* Resort, call 407 934 7639. For information, don't forget www.disneyworld.co.uk and the best bookings service, www.dreamsunlimited.com.

Disney Hotel Plaza

In addition to the official *Walt Disney World* hotels, there are another seven 'guest' hotels inside *Walt Disney World* Resort itself at the Disney Hotel Plaza on the doorstep of *Downtown Disney*. These benefit from a free bus service to the attractions and guaranteed admission to the theme parks, and

KEY TO INTERNATIONAL DRIVE ACCOMMODATIONS

1 = PEABODY ORLANDO
2 = WYNDHAM ORLANDO RESORT
3 = RENAISSANCE ORLANDO RESORT
4 = SHERATON STUDIO CITY
5 = DELTA ORLANDO RESORT
6 = DAYS INN LAKESIDE
7 = HOLIDAY INN EXPRESS
8 = QUALITY INN INTERNATIONAL
9 = QUALITY INN PLAZA
10 = EMBASSY SUITES JAMAICA COURT
11 = HOWARD JOHNSON PLAZA
12 = HOWARD JOHNSON INN
13 = ROSEN PLAZA HOTEL
14 = LAS PALMAS HOTEL
15 = ENCLAVE SUITES
16 = QUALITY SUITES AT PARC CORNICHE

17 = WYNFIELD INN
18 = SUMMERFIELD SUITES HOTEL
19 = COMFORT SUITES
20 = THE DOUBLETREE CASTLE
21 = ROSEN CENTRE HOTEL
22 = HAWTHORN SUITES
23 = HOLIDAY INN & SUITES AT UNIVERSAL
24 = BEST WESTERN PLAZA
25 = EMBASSY SUITES INT. DRIVE/CONV. CENTER
26 = RADISSON HOTEL UNIVERSAL ORLANDO
27 = PORTOFINO BAY HOTEL
28 = HARD ROCK HOTEL
29 = AMERISUITES CONV. CENTER
30 = SHERATON WORLD RESORT
31 = SIERRA SUITES
32 = HOMEWOOD SUITES

4

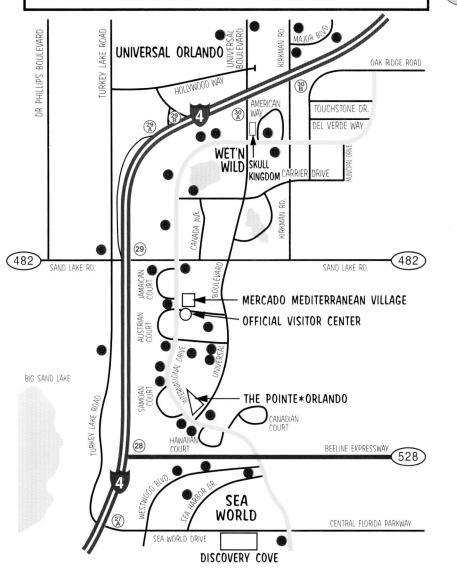

you can make reservations for shows and restaurants before the general public, but they are almost without exception more expensive than similar hotels outside *Walt Disney World*. Top of the list (for service, mod cons and price) is the 814-room **Hilton at Walt Disney World Resort** (407 827 4000, $$$$+, CCCC). Also fairly expensive are the **Grosvenor Resort** (626 sumptuously appointed rooms, exceptional service, colonial decor, $$$–$$$$, CCCC, 407 828 4444), **Wyndham Palace Resort & Spa** (a bustling, 27-storey cluster offering 1,014 rooms, many with a grandstand view of Epcot's Spaceship Earth, plus a European-style spa, three heated pools, tennis courts and a marina with boat rentals, tel 407 827 2727, $$$$, CCCC) and the **Doubletree Guest Suites Resort** (229 family-sized suites offering every conceivable in-room convenience and great kids' facilities, tel 407 934 1000, $$$$, CCCC). More modest ($$$, CCC) are the **Best Western Lake Buena Vista** (325 rooms, good views over the Marketplace, in-room coffee-makers, two restaurants, cocktail lounge and night-club, tel 407 828 2424), and the **Courtyard by Marriott** (323 rooms in a 14-storey tower and six-storey annex featuring glass-walled lifts, three pools, tel 407 828 8888, $$$, CCC). My current favourite for this area, though, is the **Hotel Royal Plaza**, with a lovely, welcoming aspect, 372 wonderfully spacious and well-equipped rooms and 22 suites, a neat, full-service diner-restaurant and relaxing lounge bar, a landscaped pool area, four tennis courts, a health club and a Disney gift shop. Like all the hotels in the Boulevard, it is well positioned for a stroll to Downtown Disney's attractions and features free bus transport and guaranteed access to the parks, plus preferred tee times at all five Disney golf courses ($$$,

CCCC, tel 407 828 2828).

As you move further away from *Walt Disney World* Resort the prices tend to moderate. This is a round-up of what's on offer.

Lake Buena Vista

You can still spend a small fortune at the **Hyatt Regency Grand Cypress** in Lake Buena Vista, for example, which is considered to be Orlando's top hotel. This 1,500-acre resort offers three nine-hole and one 18-hole golf course (all designed by Jack Nicklaus), a swimming pool with waterfalls and slide, 21-acre boating lake, tennis complex, health club and equestrian centre. Rates START at $200, but the 750 rooms and suites are magnificently appointed (it also has five restaurants, three lounges and a pool-side bar, tel 407 239 1234, $$$$+, CCCCC). Nearby is **Orlando World Center Marriott**, another personal favourite and an impressive landmark as you approach *Walt Disney World*, set as it is in 200 landscaped acres and surrounded by another golf course. An elaborate lobby, Chinese antiques and the sheer size of the hotel (1,503 rooms, 85 suites, seven restaurants, four pools and a health club) put it in the expensive range ($$$$, CCCCC, tel 407 239 4200), but it is very conveniently situated and it possesses one of the most stunningly picturesque pool areas, complete with waterfalls and palm trees, in Orlando, plus the whizziest glass-fronted lifts anywhere! It does, however, get very busy, especially with convention business. Extra facilities include a separate wading pool for kids, an indoor pool, a sports pool, four whirlpool spas, a golf school, tennis centre, five shops and a well-organised kids' programme. A 500-room expansion was due to be completed by late 2000, adding even more to this excellent resort. Similarly, but on more budget lines, the **Holiday Inn Sunspree Resort at Lake Buena Vista** (507 rooms, tel 407 239 4500, $$$, CCCC) is excellent for children's facilities, featuring a highly rated supervised childcare programme, a good range of pools, restaurants and other facilities. All rooms feature mini-kitchenettes. It also features the trademark 'Kidsuites' which offer an attractive novelty for families – a private playhouse/bedroom built into the hotel room, equipped with its own TV, cassette player, video game player, clock, fun phone, table and chairs. They offer a refreshing alternative to normal hotel family accommodation – right down to the separate check-in facilities for the youngsters. Sunspree, perfectly situated for Disney and with free transport, has recently added a 2,100-sq-ft Cyber Arcade, with access to the Internet and other high-tech elements, while it also has the extra option of 50 two-room suites for more family comfort. Outside of Disney, this has to be one of the best family-equipped hotels anywhere in Orlando. Kids 12 and under eat free.

A novel choice is the wonderful African-themed **Sheraton Safari Hotel** (www.sheratonsafari.com), which boasts the Python water slide, heated pool and kids' pool, with free transport to Disney's theme parks and kids eat free with parents at Casablanca's restaurant. Rooms are extremely well equipped, with hair-dryers, coffee-makers and ironing boards, all this within walking

---

BRIT TIP: When booking one of the chain hotels, make sure you have its full address – it is easy to end up at the wrong Holiday Inn or Howard Johnson!

---

distance of the Crossroads shopping centre and close to *Downtown Disney Marketplace* tel 407 239 0444, $$$, CCC½). There are 489 rooms, including 96 huge, superbly equipped suites, all with an exotic safari theme, and the breakfast buffet at Casablanca's (highly recommended) is worth checking out. With its great location and expansive style, the Sheraton Safari is an ideal mid-range family choice. Some of the big hotel chains also have one or two of their smartest properties in this area, notably the **Radisson Inn Lake Buena Vista** (200 rooms, tel 407 239 8400, $$$, CCC) and the recently refurbished **Club Hotel by Doubletree** (246 rooms, tel 407 239 4646, $$$, CCC½), while there are some excellent suites hotels (see also under Suites and Holiday Homes, page 63), such as the **Embassy Suites Resort Lake Buena Vista** ($$$$, CCCC), the **Sierra Suites Hotel Lake Buena Vista** ($$$, CCC) and the extensive **Buena Vista Suites** ($$$, CCC½), which all offer great value for larger families.

Kissimmee

Moving out along Highway 192 (the Irlo Bronson Memorial Highway) into Kissimmee, you will find the biggest choice of budget accommodation in the area. Facilities generally vary very little and what you see is what you get. All the big hotel chains can be found along this great tourist sprawl, and rates can be as low as $25 per room off-peak, or $35 for room with a kitchenette (what the Americans call an 'efficiency'). Be prepared to shop around for a good rate (discounts may be available at off-peak times), especially if you cruise along Highway 192 where so many hotels advertise their rates on large neon signs. As a general rule, prices drop the further you go from *Walt Disney*

KEY TO HIGHWAY 192 ACCOMMODATIONS

1 = KNIGHTS INN MAINGATE
2 = HOLIDAY INN MAINGATE WEST
3 = COMFORT INN MAINGATE
4 = HOLIDAY INN SUNSPREE RESORT
5 = HOLIDAY INN HOTEL & SUITES
6 = HAMPTON INN MAINGATE WEST
7 = RESIDENCE INN BY MARRIOTT
8 = CASA ROSA INN
9 = PARK INN INTERNATIONAL
10 = CELEBRATION HOTEL
11 = RAMADA RESORT MAINGATE
12 = FOUR POINTS BY SHERATON LAKESIDE
13 = HOMEWOOD SUITES
14 = HOLIDAY INN NIKI BIRD RESORT
15 = HYATT ORLANDO
16 = DAYS SUITES
17 = OPRYLAND HOTEL (FEB 2002)
18 = ADVANTAGE VACATION HOMES
19 = QUALITY SUITES
20 = PARKWAY INTERNATIONAL
21 = BRYAN'S SPANISH COVE
22 = ISLE OF BALI
23 = ORBIT ONE
24 = HAMPTON INN MAINGATE
25 = ORANGE LAKE RESORT
26 = PREMIER VACACTION HOMES (OFFICE)
27 = WELCOME HOMES (OFFICE)
28 = TROPICAL PALMS FUNSUITES
29 = ALEXANDER HOLIDAY HOMES (OFFICE)
30 = HOLIDAY INN FAMILY SUITES RESORT
31 = BUENAVENTURA LAKES
32 = MAGIC CASTLE INN & SUITES MAINGATE
33 = TRAVELODGE SUITES KISSIMMEE
        MAINTAGE
34 = WESTGATE RESORTS
35 = UNICORN INN
36 = CARIBE ROYALE RESORT & SUITES
37 = COMFORT SUITES HOTEL

BRIT TIP: Hotels designated Maingate East/West should be close to Disney's main entrance on 192, although it is wise to check.

World. Don't be afraid to ask to see inside rooms before you settle on your holiday base. Take into consideration how much time you'll have to use extra facilities.

Chains

Among the leading chains are **Best Western** (all with pools, family orientated but large, in the budget $–$$ range), **Days Inn** (rather characterless and some without restaurants, but always good value – $$ in most cases – and convenient, with some rooms available with kitchenettes), **EconoLodge** (see under Best Western, but slightly more expensive), **Howard Johnson** (also a bit dearer, but with more spacious rooms and some with free continental breakfast), **Quality Inn** (sound, popular chain, and in $–$$ range), **Ramada** (rates can vary more widely between hotels in the $$–$$$ range, some offer free continental breakfast) and **TraveLodge** (another identikit group, but also on the budget $–$$ side). The **Fairfield Inns** are the budget version of the impressive Marriott chain, while the **Budgetel** group also rate highly for hotel security as well as lower prices (both in the $$ range). **The Holiday Inn** chain varies so widely in both price ($$–$$$) and service, I have picked out only some worthy of note. **Doubletree** hotels and suites are another up-market chain with excellent facilities, as are the **Radisson** group (both in the $$$ range). The Marriott chain also has two other brands, which are

exceptionally family-friendly, in Orlando, the **Residence Inn by Marriott** and **Courtyard by Marriott** (both $$$).

In pure budget territory, the motel-type **Inns of America, Knights Inn, Motel 6, Comfort Inn** and **Super 8 Motel** brands all deliver a basic $ service, but the **Hampton Inn** and **Red Roof** groups seem to manage a more quality-conscious approach in the same price category. The chain that seems most anxious to please at the moment, though, are the **La Quinta Inn and Suites** series, in the $$–$$$ range, which has half a dozen well-equipped new properties in the area, notably two on International Drive.

Independent organisations

In addition, there are literally dozens of smaller, independent outfits who offer special rates from time to time in order to compete with the big boys. Look out in particular for offers of 'kids eat free' as this can save you quite a bit. Of the non-chain operators, the **Casa Rosa Hotel** offers simple, relatively peaceful Mediterranean-style hospitality (on west Highway 192, tel 407 396 1060, $–$$$, CC). The

Celebration Hotel

Park Inn International (same location, tel 407 396 1376) also has one of the better lake-front locations to go with its budget rates ($–$$, CCC); some rooms have kitchenettes.

For pure budget price, the **Magic Castle Inn and Suites Maingate** take some beating with their range of amenities – free continental breakfast, free Disney transport, fridges in all rooms, kids' playground, guest laundry and picnic area (107 rooms and 15 suites, tel 407 396 2212 or 1-800 446 5669, $–$$, CC½).

> BRIT TIP: For the smoothest entry to *Walt Disney World* Resort from Highway 192, take Seralago Boulevard opposite the Holiday Inn Hotel & Suites, turn left on to a non-toll stretch of Osceola Parkway and follow the signs to your chosen theme park.

A firm personal choice is the **Holiday Inn Hotel and Suites Maingate East**, which shares the Kidsuite and Camp Holiday children's programmes with the Holiday Inn Sunspree, making it an outstanding family resort. Good attention to detail (hair-dryers, coffee-makers, microwaves and fridges even in standard rooms), free Disney transport and its proximity next door to Old Town make for great holiday flexibility and add up to great value for money (614 rooms and 110 suites, tel 407 396 4488, $$–$$$, CCC½). Children get their own check-in area too, which is a neat touch. Kids 12 and under also eat free, as they do at the smart **Holiday Inn Maingate West**, with its tropical courtyard, free-form

heated pool and kiddie pool (287 rooms, tel 407 396 1100, $$, CCC).

The Holiday Inn Nikki Bird Resort, just west of Disney's Highway 192 entrance, is another good family location with its 23-acre tropical setting, three pools, basketball and volleyball courts and children's entertainment (529 rooms, tel 407 396 7300, $$, CCC).

The **Four Points Hotel by Sheraton Lakeside** on west Highway 192, is surprisingly good value for a big-name group, especially with three pools, tennis courts, kids' playgrounds, mini-golf, paddleboats and two restaurants. Kids 10 and under eat breakfast and dinner free with paying adults and there is free Disney transport (651 rooms, tel 407 396 2222, $$–$$$, CCC½).

Slightly off the beaten track but with extra charm is the new **Celebration Hotel** in the Disney-inspired town of Celebration. Just off Highway 192, the Central Florida Greeneway (417) and I4, this unique hotel is still handy for the parks, yet offers a small-town America style. With only 115 rooms in its three-storey, 1920s wood-frame design, the Celebration has a classy ambience a long way removed from the usual tourist hurly-burly. Rooms come in four choices – an attic-like Retreat, Traditional (with either one king- or two queen-size beds), a Studio with separate seating area or two-room Suite – and are all beautifully furnished. Lovely artwork, hardwood floors, unhurried, courteous staff and a good array of facilities – pool, jacuzzi and fitness centre, plus breakfast restaurant (dinner is not served) and bar – mark this out as a real gem. In the heart of Celebration (Disney's bid to recreate a traditional community town), it is within walking distance of the boutique shops, restaurants and peaceful walks that highlight the area. A shuttle service to the theme parks is also offered (for a small fee). For couples looking for a quieter or more initimate romantic holiday base, this member of the Grand Theme Hotels group (with the Sheraton Safari, Doubletree Castle, Sheraton Studio City and new Westin Grand Bohemian in downtown Orlando), is an ideal choice. Tel 407 566 6000 or see www.celebrationhotel.com. $$$$, CCC.

Still under construction but worthy of special note is the 1,400-room **Opryland Hotel**, due to open in February 2002 and arguably the most ambitious hotel project in Orlando. A cross between a convention centre and a vast turn-of-the-century Florida mansion, it will feature four acres of indoor gardens and landscaped waters under a glass dome. Themed restaurants, immaculate rooms, an extensive pool-beach spread, a full-service spa, and entertainment architecture on a huge scale should mark this out as one of the must-see properties. Ask for the Emerald Tower for the most lavish area of the hotel. For a preview, check out www.oprylandhotels.com/florida.

International Drive

Further away from *Walt Disney World* Resort, but handily situated for Universal Orlando, SeaWorld and closer to downtown Orlando is the final main tourist area of International Drive. For overall location and value for money I-Drive is hard to beat. It is more thoughtfully laid out, some attractions are within walking distance, and it is a good base for non-drivers. Top of the range for quality is the **Peabody Orlando**, a luxurious, 891-room tower block with every possible facility you could wish for, including an Olympic-size pool, health club, four tennis courts with professional coaching available

and some of the best restaurants in Orlando, notably the exclusive gourmet cuisine of Dux and the amazing B-Line Diner (see Eating Out, Chapter 10). Service is superb and the whole atmosphere is a cut above normal tourist fare. Check out the Royal Duck Palace on the tennis

BRIT TIP: For an attraction with a difference, don't miss the Peabody Hotel's twice-daily Duck March, which sees their trademark ducks take up residence 11am–4pm in the huge lobby fountain! It's a fascinating sight and a great place for afternoon tea. Just sit and watch them roll out the red carpet for the resident mallards!

deck if you don't believe me. However, rates are also suitably impressive ($$$$+, CCCCC) and, if there are any large conventions in town, don't expect a quiet stay (407 352 4000). The Peabody is also due to begin a massive expansion project in 2001, with the addition of 1,000 rooms in a 42-storey tower block (the tallest in central Florida), plus more restaurants and shops and a full-service spa. The recently refurbished **Wyndham Resort** (1,064 rooms, tel 407 351 2420, $$$, CCCC) is similarly extravagant, with three swimming pools in its beautifully landscaped grounds at the junction of I-Drive and Sand Lake Road (not to mention a café, pool-side food court, two bars, children's playground and arcade, plus a health club and four floodlit tennis courts), as is the magnificently appointed **Renaissance Orlando Resort** (on Sea Harbor Drive, 780 rooms, tel 407 351 5555, $$$,

The Peabody Orlando

CCCCC), claiming the world's largest atrium lobby and with some enormous rooms and suites, an Olympic-size swimming pool, tennis courts, fitness centre including sauna and steam room, five restaurants and special kids' activities. The Renaissance also boasts some magnificent restaurants, including the seafood-themed Atlantis and a stupendous Sunday buffet.

On slightly more budget lines but still in a grand style, the remodelled 21-storey **Sheraton Studio City Hotel** (formerly Universal Tower) is an I-Drive landmark at the entrance to Universal Orlando and features a full art deco film-theme design, from the shower curtains and mirrors to the large-scale architecture and landscaping. Facilities include a heated outdoor pool and a paddling pool, games room, fitness room, Starlight Grille restaurant and free shuttle service to Universal, Wet 'n Wild (within walking distance) and SeaWorld. The clever 1950s film styling is truly startling and even the staff add to the theme, which makes you feel like you are 'on set'. Check

out www.sheratonstudiocity.com for more details of this I-Drive icon. All rooms have hair-dryers, coffee-makers and Nintendo games (302 rooms, tel 497 321 2100, $$$, CCCC).

The **Quality Inn International** (728 rooms, in the heart of I-Drive, kids under 12 eat free, tel 407 996 1600, $$, CCC), and **Quality Inn Plaza** (a massive 1,020 rooms in multiple blocks with multiple pools and another 'kids eat free' restaurant, tel 407 345 8585, $–$$, CCC), are both firmly in budget territory but make for excellent bases in this popular area.

Another I-Drive landmark (next door to the Mercado) is the **Doubletree Castle Hotel**, a nine-storey fantasy palace modelled on Cinderella's castle at the Magic Kingdom. It features tower and turret rooms, a grand outdoor heated pool, hot tub, pool bar and grill, fitness centre, gift shop and a kids' play area. Rooms are immaculately furnished and there is a free shuttle to Walt Disney World, SeaWorld and Universal (216 rooms and seven suites, tel 407 345 1511, $$$–$$$$, CCCC).

The other eye-catching property on I-Drive is the monolithic **Rosen Centre Hotel**, the third largest hotel in Orlando, right next to the Beeline Expressway. It caters primarily for the convention trade (it is right next door to the massive

Sheraton Studio lobby

Convention Center), but also offers excellent tourist facilities with its 1,334 rooms and 80 suites featuring state-of-the-art security, a huge swimming grotto, an exercise centre, tennis courts, two top-quality restaurants (including the seafood-based Everglades) and two bars. Call 407 354 9840 for more details.

Two more Brit-popular properties are the **Howard Johnson Plaza** (just off I-Drive on Kirkman Road) with its family-friendly style that includes two pools, kids' pool and playground, free attractions transport, mini-golf, food court and the fun atmosphere of the Crazy Horse Saloon (354 rooms, tel 407 351 2000, $$, CCC) and the **Wynfield Inn** (just off I-Drive at Westwood Boulevard, near SeaWorld), which features free transport to all the theme parks, two pools (and two for kids), coffee-makers in all rooms and laundry facilities. Kids 12 and under also eat free with their parents (299 rooms, tel 407 345 8000, $$, CCC).

Universal Orlando

With the expansion of Universal as a major resort destination has come the development of the locale around it on Kirkman Road and Major Boulevard. It is highlighted by the first of Universal's own on-site resort hotels, and these are easily some of the best in the area. The **Portofino Bay Hotel** is the jewel in the crown, a splendid visual re-creation of the famous Italian port and a stunning resort in its own right, with every possible facility and a little bit more. The elaborate porticos and facades, the genuine trompe l'oeil (false 3-D) painting, the lovely harbourside piazza and the faithful ornamentation of the waterfront make it one of the most memorable settings of any hotel in Florida, and the 750 rooms are all impeccably appointed, with lashings

Italian village at Portofino Bay

of Italian style. The standard rooms are truly deluxe, with huge beds (and proper duvets, a first for an Orlando hotel), spacious bathrooms, mini-bar and coffee facilities, ironing board and hair-dryer, while the exclusive Villa rooms feature butler service, fax facility, CD and video players and separate showers, plus their own private pool area. There are also 18 elaborate Kids' Suites for extra family fun, with separate themed rooms that include TV, Sony Playstation, CD player and play area. The resort facilities are equally breathtaking – a Roman aquaduct-style pool with waterslide, a completely enclosed kids' play area and wading pool, a separate, smaller Hillside pool, jacuzzis, a full (if expensive) health spa, business centre, gift shops (check out Galleria Portofino for some magnificent artwork and jewellery), video arcade and jogging, walking and cycling paths. There is also the Campo Portofino supervised activity centre for kids 4–14, from 5–11.30pm every day ($45 for the first child and $35 for each additional child). For wining and dining, the Portofino boasts eight restaurants and lounges, including Mama Della's authentic Italian family dining experience and the Delfino Riviera featuring fine dining Tuscan style, plus a wonderful Deli, a pizzeria and gelateria serving home-made ice cream. Finally, all Universal resort guests benefit from free water taxi transport and early admission to their parks, express line privileges at the most popular attractions for the first hour, priority seating at restaurants, resort ID cards for all your spending around Universal Orlando and delivery of all purchases to guest rooms. All in all, a quite spectacular choice. $$$$+, CCCCC.

Due to open in late 2000 is the **Hard Rock Hotel**, 650 rooms and suites in the architectural style of a California mission, with public areas decorated with pieces from the Hard Rock group's extensive collection of rock 'n' roll memorabilia. The 14-acre site includes three bars, two restaurants, a fitness centre, plus oodles of casually elegant style, the hallmark of the Loews Hotel group, Universal's hotel partner. $$$$, CCCC. A third hotel, the **Royal Pacific Resort**, is scheduled for 2002, adding a tropical South Seas touch at a more moderate price level. For all Universal hotels, tel 407 503 1000.

The hotel choice around Universal is also growing apace. There are recent examples of the budget Days Inn, Hampton Inn, TraveLodge and Country Inn chains, plus the Extended Stay America group (good, clean efficiency studios, but few other amenities), but there are also three excellent mid-range properties. The **Radisson Hotel Orlando** is a twin-tower, 742-room complex, recently refurbished to provide a smart resort with spacious, tropical-themed rooms, a large pool, kids' playground and jacuzzi, pool bar, video games room, hair salon, gym and sauna, plus Scuba Joe's sport bar, the full-service Palm Court Restaurant and Food Court. It also offers a free shuttle service to Universal (right across the road), SeaWorld and Wet 'n Wild (tel 407 351 1000; $$, CCC). The **Holiday Inn Hotel & Suites** is a similar proposition, with 256 rooms and 134 one- and two-bedroom suites for great flexibility, a large heated outdoor pool and on-site TGI Friday's restaurant (tel 407 351 3333, $$–$$$, CCC.

Worthy of particular British note is the **Delta Orlando Resort** (800 rooms, tel 407 351 3340, $$$, CCCC), which also benefits from being slightly off the main drag (on Major Boulevard). The 25-acre Delta is a highly popular hotel with several tour operators, notably Thomson, and goes out of its way to provide home-from-home touches, like coffee-makers and bottled water in the rooms, English beer in the lively Studio 70 disco-bar and proper bacon and baked beans with the food court's breakfast buffets. Facilities are above average for this price range, including three pools, a hot tub grotto, saunas, mini-golf, floodlit tennis, free year-round kids' club and playground, a babysitting service and a refreshing full-service restaurant, Mango's, where kids 12 and under eat free with their parents.

As a final word on new hotels, the all-suite **Westin Grand Bohemian** is due to add a touch of class to the downtown area when it opens in May 2001. Part of the quality-conscious Grand Theme Hotel group, the Grand Bohemian will feature an early twentieth-century Austrian theme, with the accent on fine art, fine dining and fine service. Its 14 storeys will make it a distinct downtown landmark, and it will also boast a 150-seat signature restaurant, piano lounge, and 14th-floor concierge suite. Call 407 996 9999 for more details or check out www.grandthemehotels.com.

Suites and holiday homes

Finally, here is a quick look at a fast-growing area of accommodation in Orlando – suites hotels and holiday homes. These are popular with Americans and beginning to catch on with us Brits as a neat way of larger family groups or friends staying together and cutting the cost of their stay both by doing much of their own cooking and the extra value of sharing. The homes, whether individual houses, collections of houses, resorts or condominiums (holiday apartment blocks), all usually have access to excellent facilities in the form of swimming pools and recreation areas, and are fully equipped with all mod cons like microwaves, TVs and washer-dryers. For these, you MUST be prepared to use a hire car to get around, but the savings for, say, a group of eight staying together are obvious. Once again, the following can be only a representative selection.

Basically, the choice is between what the Americans call suites – apartments built in hotel-like blocks around communal facilities but lacking some hotel features like bars, room service and lounges – or out-and-out holiday homes, some in private residential areas and others in estate-type developments, most of which have their own pools and tend to work out slightly cheaper.

Suite things

Suites hotels seek to provide extra value for larger families or groups staying together. Typically, a suites room gives you a living room and mini-kitchen, including microwave, coffee-maker, fridge, cutlery and crockery, while many offer a complimentary continental breakfast (or better). All have swimming pools and grocery stores or snack bars. They vary only in the number of bedrooms and can usually sleep six to ten people.

They include the **Comfort Suites** (on west Highway 192 near Splendid China, tel 407 390 9888, on Turkey Lake Road, 407 351 5050, adjacent to I4 and International Drive, plus their smart new 198-room development behind Old Town in Kissimmee, which even offers a fitness centre, tel 407 397 7848, $$–$$$, CCC); the **Tropical Palms Funsuites** (on Holiday Trail, next to Old Town, 407 396 4595, $$–$$$, CCC½) with well-equipped studio and two-bedroom suites; the two-bedroom, two-bath studios of **Enclave Suites** (on Carrier Drive, just off Kirkman Road, $$–$$$, CCC½) where kids eat free with their parents; or the new **Ameri-Suites** (on I-Drive and by the International Airport, tel 1-800 833 1516), which include a fitness centre, laundry facility and a substantial free breakfast.

Family choice

The most striking new property, though, is the **Holiday Inn Family Suites Resort** at Lake Buena Vista (almost opposite Marriott's Orlando World Center, on International Drive South). From the main lobby, themed as a turn-of-the-century railway station, through the amazing range of facilities (food court, general store, Club Car casual dining, lounge-bar, toddlers' play area, interactive video games room, fitness centre, swimming pool and elaborate kiddie pool), to the choice of seven different one- and two-bedroom suites (classic suites, Kidsuites, Sweetheart suites, cinema suites, business suites, fitness suites – with their own mini-gyms – and residential suites), here is a dazzling family choice, especially with their Camp Holiday activity programme and separate check-in for kids, that really gives Disney resorts a run for

Delta Orlando Resort

choice of one-bedroom suites and two-bedroom villas, super pool area with water slide and one of the best free breakfast buffets in town. Similarly, the **Hawthorn Suites** (four properties in Orlando), **Homewood Suites** (two in Lake Buena Vista and one on I-Drive) and the new **Sierra Suites** (also in Lake Buena Vista and I-Drive) offer a more up-market feel with mid-range pricing ($$–$$$, facilities vary). The two **Summerfield Suites** (on I-Drive, tel 407 352 2400, and Lake Buena Vista, tel 407 238 0777, or www.summerfield-orlando.com) are another excellent example here, with suites sleeping up to eight, complimentary breakfast, convenience store and lovely fresh, inviting ambience ($$$, CCC).

Holiday resorts

Another accommodation type which combines the best of hotels, suites and private villas are the handful of genuine resort-style complexes (as opposed to timeshare resorts which are becoming increasingly common).

These purpose-built resorts are a kind of cross between condominiums and motels, with the advantage of a great range of in-resort facilities. The best of these include the **Orange Lake Resort** (4½ miles west of Maingate on

their money. The Kidsuites feature a semi-private bedroom with bunk beds (additional fold-out child's sleeper available), TV, video and CD/cassette player, video game system, activity table and chairs, plus, of course, the private adult king bedroom. The Club Car Restaurant has an excellent free buffet breakfast daily, and there is also complimentary regular transport to all the Disney parks. The walk-in kiddie pool with its array of different squirty fountains will ensure your young ones don't want to go anywhere else! For more info, check out www.hifamilysuites.com or tel 407 387 5437. $$$, CCCCC.

Other one-off suites properties worthy of note include the well-appointed **Buena Vista Suites** (tel 407 239 8588, $$$, CCC) and the massively eye-catching **Caribe Royale Resort Suites** (both at the lower end of I-Drive, tel 407 238 8000, $$$$, CCCC½), with their

Holiday Inn Family Suites

Highway 192, tel 407 239 0000, $$$–$$$$, CCCC), with a mixture of two-bedroom, two-bath villas and suites, golf, watersports and even a cinema, and the **Villages at Mango Key** (on Lindfields Boulevard, 4 miles west of Maingate, tel 407 239 7100, $$$, CCC), a collection of smart, new two- and three-bedroom townhouses, with pool, jacuzzi, tennis and volleyball.

Ron Jon's Resort (formerly the Isle of Bali resort) on the western fringe of 192 is a timeshare set-up that often has very good value apartments to rent on a weekly basis. Their newest blocks offer huge two-bedroom flats, with well-equipped kitchens (down to coffee-makers and ice-makers), while the complex itself has two pools plus the Liki Tiki Lagoon mini water park, tennis courts, paddle boats, bikes, pool-side bar and grill and a free continental breakfast Mon–Fri (when timeshare presentations are held). You don't have to attend any timeshare hard-sell, just enjoy the great facilities of this resort, now 'twinned' with the Ron Jon Surf Shop empire, (tel 407 239 5000). $$$, CCCC. Look up www.islandone.com for more details.

Top of the range in this category, though, is the **Vistana Resort** (just off the lower end of I-Drive in Lake Buena Vista, tel 407 239 3100, $$$–$$$$, CCCCC), where facilities include fitness centres with steam and sauna rooms, five pools and 13 tennis courts, to back up their luxurious two-bedroom villas that sleep up to eight.

Holiday homes

There are now dozens of companies offering private homes with pools throughout central Florida, some more reliable than others, so here are just a select few who all pass the *Brit's Guide* credibility test.
Welcome Homes USA are one of the foremost operators for condos,

villas and private homes in the Kissimmee area, with some of the smartest properties (especially their fully fitted designer-decorated kitchens) at a broad range of prices and an impeccable reputation for customer service. Their full-size houses (3–5 bedrooms) come with communal or private pools. Homes are only 10 or 15 minutes' drive from *Walt Disney World*, in residential areas, and feature everything from dishwashers to teaspoons (but not hair-dryers). For details, call 407 933 2233 ($$–$$$$, CC) for their holiday homes and 407 933 2889 for their well-equipped condo complex. Check out their website on www.welcome-homes.com. For similar great value and excellent properties, **Alexander Holiday Homes** (tel 407 932 3683), also in Kissimmee, have almost 250 properties, from standard condo villas to ultra-luxury large executive homes sleeping up to 10, all with pools and immaculately furnished, within 15 minutes of Walt Disney World. From fully fitted kitchens to walk-in wardrobes and private pools, these are a great way to enjoy a bit of Florida freedom. Alexander were the first company of their kind in Orlando, and still offer a friendly, efficient service in keeping with the Sunshine State ($$–$$$, CC).

A true B&B – the Unicorn Inn

They also boast one of the largest Internet sites in Florida on www.floridasunshine.com.

UK-based **Something Special Holidays**, one of the biggest operators in Florida for *named* accommodation, offer an all-inclusive service or accommodation only. They have 87 hand-picked villa properties in Kissimmee and their staff all have first-hand knowledge of the area and can tailor your booking to two or more centres. For a brochure or to book, call 01992 557700 ($$–$$$$, CC).

Finally, **Premier Vacation Homes** offer a terrific range of spacious properties with two to six bedrooms, sleeping up to 14, all in secure residential communities within a 15-minute drive of *Walt Disney World*. The homes are privately owned and have been purchased and furnished as a 'vacation' home, with screened pools, two TVs, fully equipped kitchens (including dishwasher, washer-dryer, microwave and coffee-maker), at least one king or queen bed, and free local phone calls. Maid service can be provided for an additional fee. The Luxury homes (two–four bedrooms) are their standard accommodation, while the Executive homes (three–six bedrooms) are bigger still, with an extra TV, a VCR and a gas barbecue grill. For privacy, convenience and value for money, they take some beating (tel 407 396 2401, or 0500 892634 in the UK, see www.premier-vacation-homes.com $$$, CC).

Bed and breakfast

The range of accommodation even includes a few places offering bed and breakfast. However, these are a long way removed from a traditional British B&B with one notable and laudable exception. The **Unicorn Inn**, on the corner of Orlando Avenue and Emmett Street in downtown Kissimmee, is run by a Yorkshire couple who turned a ramshackle building into a luxurious but homely bed and breakfast inn that really caters for the individual. Rates start at just $85 per night ($75 single rate), and there are discounts for stays of one week or longer in their eight individually styled rooms. They keep a few pushchairs and high-chairs for parents with young children and can arrange babysitting for you. They even provide their own personalised maps of the area with up-to-the-minute advice on local events and bargains. Their location is ideal for walking around the prettier parts of town (they are even included on the district's historic walking tour) and you can be sure of a decent cup of tea for a change! Call Don or Fran for more information on 407 846 1200 (or e-mail on unicorn@gate.net).

Babysitting

For folks who want an evening off from parenthood to take advantage of Orlando's night-life, babysitting is a ready option. The two most relied-upon, fully trained and licensed companies are **KinderCare** (who are also contracted to *Walt Disney World* Resort and Airtours, tel 407 846 2027) and **Anny's Nannies** (with Virgin Holidays, among others, tel 407 826 8949). Both will visit hotels, motels, condos and homes, while KinderCare also organise group events and activities. Some of the larger hotels offer babysitting (see the Accommodation guide on www.go2orlando.com).

Right, that's enough planning and preparation for now, it's time to HIT THE THEME PARKS … !

The Theme Parks – Disney's Fab Four

(or, Spending the Day with Mickey Mouse and Co.)

By now you should be prepared to deal with the main business of any visit to Orlando: Walt Disney World Resort and the other main theme parks of Universal Orlando, SeaWorld and Busch Gardens.

If you have only a week in the area this is where you should concentrate your attention but even then you may decide Busch Gardens is a bridge too far. If you have less than a week you should concentrate on seeing as much of *Walt Disney World* Resort as possible. There is SO much packed into every park and the main tourist areas, even two weeks will scarcely be enough to give first-timers more than an outline picture of central Florida.

BRIT TIP: Beware offers of cheap or free tickets for *Walt Disney World* theme parks as they are used as inducements to visit timeshare operations. And NEVER buy a Disney ticket from an unofficial source as it may be stolen or non-transferable.

First off, you can save money of many of the attractions if you shop around. Disney tickets are available at *The Disney Stores* in the UK, but try not to buy ALL your tickets in advance (many people *still* get too many for the time they have there – be sensible), as you will find

discount coupons in many of the tourist publications which are distributed in Orlando, while the **tour operators'** welcome meetings often have special deals or packages worth checking out. The main **local ticket agencies** also have great deals periodically: the official **Visitor Center** at 8723 International Drive (in the Gala Center on the corner of Austrian Row, tel 407 363 5871 or www.go2orlando.com); **Vacation Works** (at various locations in the main tourist areas, tel 407 396 1844 or www.vacationworks.com); and **Know Before You Go** (on International Drive and Highway 192, tel 407 396 5400 or www.1travel.com/knowbeforeyougo). It is also possible to pick up free park tickets for attending timeshare presentations but I don't recommend it as they can take up to half a day of your precious holiday time.

BRIT TIP: If you DO want to check out timeshare possibilities, look first at *Disney Vacation Club* for the guaranteed way to secure memorable holidays. Call 407 566 3300 for details or look it up on http://disney.go.com

Ratings

All the rides and shows are judged on a unique rating system that splits them into the Thrill Rides and the

Beauty and the Beast

Scenic ones. Thrill rides earn T ratings out of five (hence a TTTTT is as exciting as they get) and scenic rides get A ratings out of five (an AA ride is likely to be over-cute and missable). Obviously it is a matter of opinion to a certain extent, but you can be fairly sure that a T or A ride is not worth your time, a TT or AA is worth seeing only if there is no queue, a TTT or AAA should be seen if you have time, but you won't miss much if you don't, a TTTT or AAAA ride is a big-time attraction that should be high on your list of things to do, and finally a TTTTT or AAAAA attraction should not be missed! The latter will have the longest queues and so you should plan your visit around these rides. Some rides are restricted to children over a certain height and are not advisable for people with back, neck or heart problems, or for pregnant women. Where this is the case I have just noted 'Restrictions; 3ft 6in', and so on. Height restrictions (which are strictly enforced) are based on the average 5 year old being 3ft 6in tall, 6s being 3ft 9in and 9s being 4ft 4in.

Where families have small children, but mum and dad still want to try the ride, you DON'T have to queue twice. When you get to the front of the queue, tell the operator you want to do a 'baby swap'. This means mum can ride while dad looks after junior, and, on her return, dad can ride while mum does the babysitting, and there is often a special waiting area.

Disney's Animal Kingdom – the thrill of the Dinosaur ride

Magic Kingdom Park

The starting point for any visit has to be the **Magic Kingdom**, the park that best embodies the spirit of utter delight that *Walt Disney World* Resort bestows on all its visitors. It's the original development that sparked the tourist explosion of Orlando when it opened in 1971. In comparative terms, the *Magic Kingdom* Park is closest to *Disneyland* Paris® and *Disneyland* Park in Los Angeles. Outside those, it has no equal as an enchanting and exciting day out for all the family.

What I will now attempt to do is steer you through a typical day at the *Magic Kingdom* Park, with a guide to all the main rides, shows and places to eat, how to park, how to avoid the worst of the crowds and how much you should expect to pay.

This essential park takes up just 100 of *Walt Disney World* Resort's near 31,000 acres but attracts almost as many visitors as the rest put together! It has seven separate 'lands', like slices of a large cake centred on the most famous

The Magic Kingdom Park at-a-glance

Location	Off World Drive, Walt Disney World
Size	100 acres in 7 'lands'
Hours	9am–7pm off peak; 9am–10pm Washington's birthday, spring school holidays; 9am–11pm high season (Easter, summer holidays, Thanksgiving and Christmas)
Admission	Under 3, free; 3–9 $37 (one-day ticket), $142 (4-Day Park Hopper), $192 (5-Day Park Hopper Plus); adult (10+) $46, $176, $236.
Parking	$6
Lockers	Yes; under Main Street Railroad Station; $5 ($2 refund)
Pushchairs	$7 and $13 (Stroller Shop to right of main entrance, $1 deposit refunded)
Wheelchairs	$7 ($1 deposit refunded) or $40 ($10 deposit refunded) (Main Ticket Centre or Stroller Shop)
Top Attractions	Splash Mountain, Space Mountain, Alien Encounter
Don't Miss	Disney's Magical Moments Parade, Mainstreet Electrical Parade (high season and weekends) and Fantasy in the Sky fireworks
Hidden Costs	**Meals** Burger, chips and coke $6.65 Three-course dinner $31 (Cinderella's Table)
	Kids' meal $3.26
	T-shirts $19–$34
	Souvenirs $0.99–$375
	Sundries Mickey Mouse Hat (with ears!) $16

5

landmark of all Florida, Cinderella's Castle. There are more than 40 attractions packed in here, not to mention numerous shops and restaurants (although the eating opportunities are less impressive than *Epcot* and *Disney-MGM Studios*). It's easy to get lost or overwhelmed by it all, especially as it does get so busy (even the fast-food restaurants have serious queues in high season), so study the notes and plan your visit around what most takes your fancy.

> BRIT TIP: If you have pre-paid vouchers for park entrance rather than the actual tickets, you have to exchange them at a ticket window. Go to the Guest Relations window to redeem your vouchers and you will avoid the queues here.

Another essential note on queuing here is *Disney's FastPass* system. All the main attractions at the parks now have this wonderful service that allows you to roam while you wait for your allotted time to ride. How it works: just insert your main park entrance ticket into the FastPass turnstile (to the side of each attraction entrance) and you get another ticket out which gives you an hour's 'window' in which to return and do the ride with only a minimal wait. You can hold only one FastPass ticket at a time, but if you start by going to one of the FastPass rides, collecting your ticket and returning later, you can do so much more without standing in line for ages. Many people still miss this, but it is absolutely FREE (FastPass rides are indicated FP in my text for each attraction).

Location

The *Magic Kingdom* Park is located at the innermost end of the vacation kingdom, with its entrance toll plaza three-quarters of the way along World Drive, the main entrance road off of Highway 192. World Drive runs north–south through *Walt Disney World*, while the Interstate 4 entrance, Epcot Drive, runs basically east–west. Unless you are staying at one of the hotels at *Walt Disney World* Resort you will have to pay your $6 parking fee at the toll plaza and that brings you to the *Magic Kingdom* Park car park (or 'parking lot' in American-speak), an enormous stretch of tarmac that can accommodate more than 10,000 cars. The majority arrive between 9.30 and 11.30am, so the car parks can become pretty jammed then, which is another good reason to get here EARLY. If you are not here by 8am during peak periods you might want to wait until after 1pm, or even later when the park is open late into the evenings (as late as 11pm at the height of summer and at Christmas).

> BRIT TIP: Note on your parking ticket exactly what area you are parked in and the row number, e.g. Mickey, Row 30. You will struggle to remember otherwise, and all hire cars look exactly the same! (Try leaving a familiar, non-valuable item in the window for extra help.)

To give you another idea of the size of the operation, a system of motorised trams carries you from the car park to the Transportation and Ticket Center at the heart of the *Magic Kingdom*'s operation. Unless

BRIT TIP: Save paying up to three times more for your drinks by bring your own bottled water and sodas in a back-pack to all the parks and use the many drinking fountains for refills.

you already have your ticket (which will save you valuable time if you have), you will have to queue up at the ticket booths here to go any further. Once you have ticket in hand, you pass the booths to either the monorail or ferryboats that will bring you to the doorstep of the *Magic Kingdom* Park itself. Of course, if you are staying on a *Walt Disney World* property, you can also catch the monorail directly or one of the buses that make up the free transport system (both the bus and monorail deliver you to the park's front door). If you're at the head of the queue and can get straight on, the monorail (dead ahead of you) is slightly quicker. Otherwise, if you have to queue for the monorail, it is usually better to bear left and take the ferryboats which may be slightly slower but involve less queuing.

BRIT TIP: You can often get to ride up front on the monorail if you ask a Cast Member when you get onto the platform.

One final note, in all the main theme parks you may well find one or two attractions closed for refurbishment to mark the constant process of keeping everything as fresh and new as possible. However, you'll never be short of things to do!

Main Street, USA

Right, we've finally reached the park itself … but not quite. Hopefully you've paid heed to the need to arrive early and you're among the leading hordes aiming to swarm through the main entrance. The published opening times may say 9am, but the gates to the *Magic Kingdom* Park are quite likely to open anything up to 45 minutes before then. This will bring you into **Main Street, USA**, the first of the seven lands. Immediately on your right is **Exposition Hall**, a photographic centre featuring archive film material, a mini cinema showing Disney classics and a series of interactive games, plus some cartoon photo opportunities. On your left is **City Hall**, from where you can pick up a park map and schedule of the day's events, if you haven't been given them at the toll plaza, and make reservations for the main restaurants. Ahead of you is **Town Square**, where you can take a one-way ride down Main Street, USA on a horse-drawn bus or fire engine and visit the **Car Barn** mini museum and shop at the **Main Street Gallery** for exclusive Disney collectibles. The Street itself houses some of the best shopping in the *Magic Kingdom* Park, plus the **Walt Disney World Railroad**, the park's Western-themed steam train that runs the full circumference of the *Magic Kingdom* Park and is one of the better attractions when the queues are at their longest elsewhere. You can eat breakfast, lunch and dinner at Tony's Town Square Restaurant, a full-service diner specialising in Italian meals, The Plaza Restaurant (lunch and dinner, sandwiches, salads and sundaes), The Crystal Palace (breakfast, lunch and dinner, buffet-style food with Winnie the Pooh, Tigger and Co.), the Main Street Bake Shop (delicious pastries, tea

5

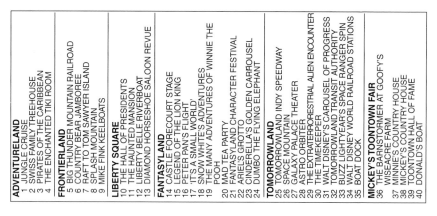

ADVENTURELAND
1 JUNGLE CRUISE
2 SWISS FAMILY TREEHOUSE
3 PIRATES OF THE CARIBBEAN
4 THE ENCHANTED TIKI ROOM

FRONTIERLAND
5 BIG THUNDER MOUNTAIN RAILROAD
6 COUNTRY BEAR JAMBOREE
7 RAFT TO TOM SAWYER ISLAND
8 SPLASH MOUNTAIN
9 MIKE FINK KEELBOATS

LIBERTY SQUARE
10 THE HALL OF PRESIDENTS
11 THE HAUNTED MANSION
12 LIBERTY BELLE RIVERBOAT
13 DIAMOND HORSESHOE SALOON REVUE

FANTASYLAND
14 CASTLE FORECOURT STAGE
15 LEGEND OF THE LION KING
16 PETER PAN'S FLIGHT
17 'IT'S A SMALL WORLD'
18 SNOW WHITE'S ADVENTURES
19 THE MANY ADVENTURES OF WINNIE THE POOH
20 MAD TEA PARTY
21 FANTASYLAND CHARACTER FESTIVAL
22 ARIELS GROTTO
23 CINDERELLA'S GOLDEN CARROUSEL
24 DUMBO THE FLYING ELEPHANT

TOMORROWLAND
25 TOMORROWLAND INDY SPEEDWAY
26 SPACE MOUNTAIN
27 GALAXY PALACE THEATER
28 ASTRO ORBITER
29 THE EXTRATERRESTRIAL ALIEN ENCOUNTER
30 THE TIMEKEEPER
31 WALT DISNEY'S CAROUSEL OF PROGRESS
32 TOMORROWLAND TRANSIT AUTHORITY
33 BUZZ LIGHTYEAR'S SPACE RANGER SPIN
34 WALT DISNEY WORLD RAILROAD STATIONS
35 BOAT DOCK

MICKEY'S TOONTOWN FAIR
36 THE BARNSTORMER AT GOOFY'S WISEACRE FARM
37 MINNIE'S COUNTRY HOUSE
38 MICKEY'S COUNTRY HOUSE
39 TOONTOWN HALL OF FAME
40 DONALD'S BOAT

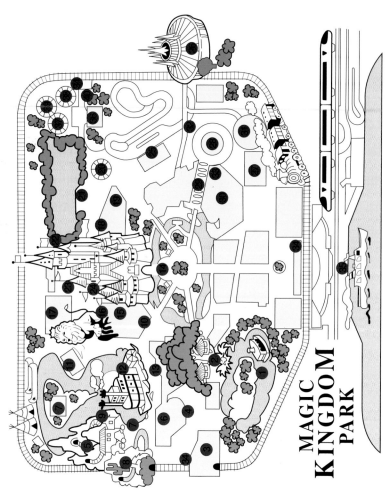

MAGIC KINGDOM PARK

and coffee), Casey's Corner (hot-dogs and soft drinks), or the Plaza Ice Cream Parlor.

Look out for the **Guest Information Board** at the top of Main Street USA (on the left) that gives waiting times for all the attractions through the day.

Unless you are a late arrival, give Main Street, USA no more than a passing glance for the moment and head for the end of the street where you will find the real entrance to the park. This is where you will have to wait for the final opening hour to arrive, the famous 'Rope drop', and you should adopt one of three tactics here, each aimed at doing one or two of the most popular rides before the queues become substantial (an hour for Splash Mountain is not unknown on the busiest days). **One:** if you fancy heading straight for the five-star log-flume ride Splash Mountain, keep left in front of the Crystal Palace and the majority of the crowd will head for the same place. **Two:** if you have young children who can't wait to ride on Cinderella's Golden Carrousel or the other Fantasyland rides, stay in the middle and head directly through the castle. **Three:** if the thrills of the ExtraTERRORestrial Alien Encounter and the indoor roller-coaster Space Mountain appeal to

you first, move to the right by the Plaza Restaurant and you'll get straight into Tomorrowland. Now you'll be in pole position for the opening rush to the main attractions (and it will be a rush – take care if you're here with small children).

Adventureland

If you head for the first option, to the left (effectively going clockwise around the park), you will first come to **Adventureland**. If you are heading for Splash Mountain, with the rest of the early-morning queue-beaters, you will pass the Swiss Family Treehouse on your left and bear right through an archway (with restrooms on your right) into Frontierland, where you bear left and Splash Mountain is dead ahead. Stopping to admire Adventureland, however, these are the attractions you will encounter.

> **BRIT TIP:** If you are determined to get the most from your day, have a good breakfast BEFORE you arrive to give you plenty of energy and save time once the park is open!

Swiss Family Treehouse: this imitation Banyan tree is a clever replica of the treehouse from Disney's 1960 film *Swiss Family Robinson*. It's a walk-through attraction where the queues (rarely long) move steadily if not quickly, providing a fascinating glimpse of the ultimate treehouse, complete with kitchen, rope bridges and running water! AAA.

Jungle Cruise: it's not so much the scenic, geographically suspect boat ride (where the Nile suddenly becomes the Amazon) that is so amusing here as the patter of your

© Disney Enterprises, Inc.

Main Street Electrical Parade

boat's captain, who spins a non-stop yarn about your jungle adventure that features wild animals, tropical plants, hidden temples and sudden waterfalls. Great detail but long queues, so visit either early morning or late afternoon (evening queues are shortest, but you'll miss some of the detail in the dark). AAAA (FP).

Pirates of the Caribbean: one of Disney's most impressive attractions that involves their pioneering work in audio-animatronics, life-size figures that move, talk and, in this instance, lay siege to a Caribbean island! Your underground boat ride takes you through a typical pirate adventure and the wizardry of the special effects is truly amazing. This is worth several rides, although it may be a bit spooky for very young children. Queues are rarely long and almost non-existent late in the day. AAAAA.

The Enchanted Tiki Room: one of the park's original audio-animatronics ventures has been given a lively update with the addition of Iago (from *Aladdin*) and Zazu (*The Lion King*) to lead a colourful, 16-minute revue that will appeal particularly to younger children. Queues are rare here, too. AAA.

Both the Pirates and Tiki Room are air-conditioned and offer a cooling break in the heat of the day.

Additional entertainment is provided by the Adventureland CongOasis, for the chance to meet *Lion King* and *Jungle Book* characters, and the best of the shopping is the House of Treasure as you come out of the Pirates ride. For food, you have Aloha Isle, for yoghurt and ice cream, El Pirata Y el Perico (Mexican snacks, hot-dogs and salads) and Sunshine Tree Terrace (fruit snacks, yoghurt, tea and coffee).

Frontierland

Passing through Adventureland brings you to **Frontierland**, the target of many of the park's early birds. This Western-themed area is one of the busiest parts of the Magic Kingdom and is best avoided from late morning to late afternoon.

Splash Mountain: based on the 1946 classic Disney cartoon *Song of the South*, this is a watery journey into the world of Brer Rabbit, Brer Fox and Brer Bear. The first part is all magnificent cartoon scenery and jolly fun with the main characters and a couple of minor downward swoops in your eight-passenger log-boat. The conclusion, a five-storey plummet at an angle of 45 degrees into a mist-shrouded pool, will seem like you are falling off the edge of the world! A huge adrenaline rush, but busy at nearly all times of day (try it first thing or during one of the main parades to avoid the worst of the queues). You will also get VERY wet! Restrictions; 3ft 6in. TTTTT (FP).

Big Thunder Mountain Railroad: when Disney do a roller-coaster they make it one of the classiest, and here it is, a runaway mine train that swoops, tilts and plunges through a mock abandoned mine filled with clever props and scenery. You'll need to ride it at least twice to appreciate all the detail, but again queues are heavy, so go first thing (after Splash Mountain) or late in the day. Restrictions; 3ft 4in. TTTT.

Country Bear Jamboree: now here's a novelty, a 16-minute musical revue presented by audio-animatronic bears! It's a great family fun show with plenty of novel touches (watch out for the talking moose-head). Again, you'll need to beat the crowds by going early morning or early evening. AAAA.

Frontierland Shootin' Arcade: apart from the Penny Arcade in

Main Street, USA, this is the only other attraction that costs extra, as you shoot at a series of animated targets. TT.

Tom Sawyer Island: take a raft over to this overgrown playground, complete with mysterious caves, grottos and mazes, rope bridges and Fort Sam Clemens, where you can fire air guns at passing boats. A good get-away in early afternoon when the crowds are at their highest, while Aunt Polly's Dockside Inn is a refuge within a refuge for snacks and soft drinks. TT.

Mike Fink Keelboats: a Davy Crockett journey along the same waters as the Riverboat, encountering the same dangers and escaping the same crowds! AA.

Shops here sell cowboy hats, guns and badges as well as Indian and Mexican handicrafts, while for food try Pecos Bill Café (salads, sandwiches and burgers), the Frontierland Kiosk (french fries and soft drinks) or the Turkey Leg Wagon (tempting, smoke-grilled turkey legs).

Liberty Square

Continuing the clockwise tour of the Magic Kingdom brings you next into **Liberty Square**, a homage to post-Independence America. A lot of the historical content here will go over the heads of British visitors, but it still has some great attractions.

The Diamond Horseshoe Saloon Revue: after all the audio-

BRIT TIP: When you are faced by more than one queue for an attraction, head for the left-hand one. Almost invariably this will move slightly quicker than that on the right.

animatronic gadgetry here's an honest-to-goodness Western saloon show performed by real people. If you fancy a slapstick song-and-dance routine featuring can-can girls, corny comedy and audience participation, this is for you. Snacks and drinks are available before the show. AAA.

Liberty Belle Riverboat: cruise America's 'rivers' on an authentic paddle steamer, be menaced by Indians and thrill to the tales of the Old West. This is also a good ride to take at the busiest times of the day, especially early afternoon. AAA.

The Haunted Mansion: a very clever delve into the world of ghost train rides that is neither too scary for kids nor too twee for adults. Not so much a thrill ride as a scenic adventure, hence AAAA. Watch out for the neat touch at the end when your car picks up an extra 'passenger'. Longish queues during the main part of the day, however.

The Hall of Presidents: this is the attraction that will mean least to us, a two-part show that is first a film about the history of the Constitution and then an audio-animatronic parade of all 42 American presidents. Technically, it's very impressive but dull for young children, although it is another air-conditioned haven when it's really hot. AAA.

Shopping here includes Ye Olde Christmas Shoppe and The Yankee Trader, while eating opportunities consist of the full-service Liberty Tree Tavern (serving hearty soups, steaks and traditional dishes like meatloaf and pot roast), Columbia Harbour House (for counter-service fried chicken or shrimp and chips) or Sleepy Hollow (a picnic area serving snacks, drinks and vegetarian meals).

Fantasyland

Exiting Liberty Square you walk past Cinderella Castle and come into **Fantasyland**, the spiritual heart of

5

© Disney Enterprises, Inc.

Frontierland – Splash Mountain

the *Magic Kingdom* Park and the area with which young children are most fascinated. The attractions here are all designed with kids in mind, but some of the shops are quite sophisticated in their wares, while Cinderella's Royal Table is a must for a fun family meal.

'it's a small world': this could almost be *Walt Disney World's* theme ride, a family boat trip through the different continents, each represented by hundreds of dancing, singing audio-animatronic dolls in delightful pageants of set-pieces. It sounds twee, but it actually creates a surprisingly striking effect, accompanied by Disney's annoyingly catchy theme song which younger children adore. Crowds are steady and peak in early afternoon. AAAA.

Dumbo the Flying Elephant: parents hate it but kids love it and all want to do this 2-minute ride on the back of a flying elephant that swoops in best Dumbo style, even if the ears do not flap. Do this one early or expect to queue. TT (TTTT under 5s).

Mad Tea Party: again the kids will insist you take them in these spinning, oversized tea-cups that have their own 'steering wheel' to add to the whirling effect. Actually, they're just a heavily disguised version of many similar fairground rides. Again, go early or expect serious crowds. TT (TTTT under 5s).

The Many Adventures of Winnie the Pooh: building on the timeless popularity of Tigger and Co. is this new family ride which offers a fairly predictable jaunt through Hundred Acre Wood with several notable special effects and another original soundtrack. AAA (AAAAA under 5s) (FP).

Snow White's Adventures: this lively, fast-paced ride tells the cartoon story of Snow White with a few ghost train effects that may scare small children. Good fun, though, for parents and kids. Again, you will need to go early or late (or during the main afternoon parade) to beat the queues. TTT (TTTTT under 5s).

Cinderella's Golden Carrousel: the centrepiece of Fantasyland shouldn't need any more explanation other than it is a vintage carousel ride the kids all adore. Long queues here during the main part of the day. TT (TTTT under 5s).

Legend of the Lion King: children will also love this cleverly staged version of the recent Disney cartoon, using puppets, actors and special effects to tell the story of the young lion cub born to be king. It is a bit of a test of endurance, though, as queues are long and then there is a pre-show you have to stand through before taking your seat in the air-conditioned theatre. AAAA.

Peter Pan's Flight: don't be fooled by the long queues at this one, it is a rather tame ride by Magic Kingdom standards, although it is still a big favourite with kids. Its novel effect of flying up, up and away with Peter Pan quickly wears off, but there is still a lot of clever detail as your 'sailing ship' journeys over the roofs of London and into Neverland. AA (AAAA under 5s).

In addition to the main rides, there are also different musical shows daily on the Castle Forecourt Stage in front of Cinderella Castle. **Fantasyland Character Festival**

Buzz Lightyear's Space Ranger Spin

behind Dumbo allows you to meet some more Disney characters, as does **Ariel's Grotto**, although this quickly draws quite a queue at peak periods. A recent addition is the **Fairytale Garden**, on the corner of the Castle facing Tomorrowland, where youngsters can enjoy *Storytime with Belle*. Eating opportunities are at The Pinocchio Village Haus (salads, burgers and hot-dogs), Hook's Tavern (beverages and shakes) and the Enchanted Grove, Scuttle's Landing and Mrs Potts' Cupboard (for ice creams and sundaes). Cinderella's Royal Table is a lovely setting for a meal, be it breakfast, lunch or dinner (book for all three on 407 939 3463). The majestic hall, waitresses in costume and well-presented food make for a memorable dining experience, with the food consisting of salads, seafood, roast beef, prime rib and chicken. It's a touch pricey for dinner, though. Shopping is provided by Tinkerbell's Treasures and Sir Mickey's.

Mickey's Toontown Fair

In the top corner of Fantasyland (just past the Mad Tea Party) is the shrub-lined entrance to **Mickey's Toontown Fair**. It is easy to miss, but it does have its own station on the railroad. Its primary appeal is to children, and they won't want to miss out on the chance to meet their favourite Disney characters. It is exceptionally kid-friendly and beautifully landscaped and features a huge merchandising area, the County Bounty, so wallets beware!

Mickey's Country House: here is a walk-through opportunity to see Mickey at home and have your picture taken with him in the Judge's Tent. AAAA (plus TTTTT for the Mickey photo opportunity. Just watch those awed young faces!).

Minnie's Country House: this is a chance to view Minnie's home and 'unique memorabilia', all designed in a country and western style. AAA.

Toontown Hall of Fame: here there are three opportunities to meet a host of other Disney favourites. The Villains Room features the likes of Captain Hook and Jafar, Mickey's Pals lets you meet Goofy, Pluto, Minnie and Co., and Famous Faces introduces characters such as Cinderella, Snow White and Pocahontas. TTTTT (for kids!).

The Barnstormer at Goofy's Wiseacre Farm: this is a mini roller-coaster just for the young 'uns (although possibly a bit too much for the under 5s) and is another masterpiece of design as it swoops through the barn, even if it is a pretty short ride for all the queuing. Watch out for the chance to meet Goofy. TTT (TTTT for 5–9s).

Donald's Boat: parents beware, your youngsters could get very wet here. If you have encountered the dancing fountains at *Epcot* between Future World and World

The Barnstormer at Goofy's Wiseacre Farm

Showcase, prepare for more watery delights as this boat-themed fountain spouts off in all sorts of ways. You might want to bring a change of clothes or swimsuit for your offspring. AAAA (under 10s).

Tomorrowland

Continuing down from Fantasyland finally brings you into the last of the seven Lands, **Tomorrowland**. It boasts a cartoon-like space-age appearance guaranteed to appeal to youngsters, and has some of the park's more original shops.

Space Mountain: this is one of the three most popular attractions, and its reputation is quite deserved. It is a fast, tight-turning roller-coaster completely in the dark save for occasional flashes as you whizz through 'the galaxy'. Don't do this one after you've just eaten! The only way to beat the almost non-stop crowds here is to go either first thing, late in the day or during one of the parades or the fireworks show. Restrictions; 3ft 8in. TTTTT (FP).

Tomorrowland Indy Speedway: despite the long queues, this is a rather tame ride on supposed race tracks that just putt-putts along on rails with little real steering required. Restrictions; children must be 4ft 4in to drive alone. TT (TTTT under 5s).

Astro Orbiter: this is a jazzed-up version of the flying Dumbos in Fantasyland, just a bit faster and higher and on rockets. Large, slow-moving queues are another reason to give this one a miss unless you are under 10. TT (TTTT under 9s).

Walt Disney's Carousel of Progress: this one will surprise, entertain and amuse. It is a 100-year journey through modern technology with audio-animatronics and a revolving theatre that reveals different stages in that development. Its 22 minutes are rarely threatened by crowds. AAA.

Tomorrowland Transit Authority: a neat 'future transport system', the TTA provides an elevated view of the area, including a glimpse inside Space Mountain, in electro-magnetically powered cars. If the queues are short, which they usually are, give it a go. AAA.

ExtraTERRORestrial Alien Encounter: this attraction draws some HUGE queues (go early) to its clever, high-tech preamble and awesomely scary show: a 'tele-portation' demonstration that goes wrong and brings an Alien to life in the middle of the audience. The fear factor adds a new dimension to the *Magic Kingdom* Park, but it will be too strong for most under 9s (and anyone scared of the dark!). Restrictions; 3ft 8in. TTTT.

The Timekeeper: this 360-degree film show features an amusing time-travel 'experiment', with comedian Robin Williams providing the voice of robot operator Timekeeper, who guides his assistant Nine Eye back and forth in time. AAAA.

Buzz Lightyear's Space Ranger Spin: kids will not want to miss this chance to join the great *Toy Story* character and his battle against the evil Emperor Zurg. Ride into action against Zurg's robot army – and shoot them with laser-cannons! A sure-fire family winner, especially as you get to keep score. AAAA.

The **Galaxy Palace Theater** hosts live musical productions featuring Disney characters and talent shows, at various times throughout the day. For food, Cosmic Ray's Starlight Café has burgers, chicken and salads, The Plaza Pavilion does pizza, subs and salads, Auntie Gravity's (ouch!) Galactic Goodies serves up frozen yoghurt and fruit juice and the Lunching Pad at Rockettower Plaza offers hot-dogs, snacks and drinks.

Other events

Having come full circle you are now back at Main Street, USA, and you should return here in early afternoon to avoid the crowds and look at the impressive array of shops. Watch out for the Dapper Dans, a strolling barbershop quartet.

In addition to the permanent attractions, the *Magic Kingdom* Park also has several other daily events which should not be missed. Watch out for **'character greetings'** around the park of various Disney cartoon characters, who will pose for photographs and give autographs. *The Sword In The Stone* is re-enacted daily in Fantasyland. The imaginative detail of the architecture and landscaping also mark this out as a great family entertainment achievement.

Watch out, too, for the show-stopping **Disney's Magical Moments Parade** every day at 3pm. It goes from Main Street, USA up to the Castle Forecourt, then left into Liberty Square and Frontierland (or vice versa). It features colourful floats and characters from Disney films in a terrific, interactive cavalcade that will captivate the children and use up several rolls of film! And, if you think the park looks good during the day, prepare to be amazed at how wonderful it looks at night when some of the lighting effects are truly astounding. When the park is open in the evenings (during the main holiday periods and weekends), there is also the twice-nightly **Main Street Electrical Parade** (wait for the second one to beat the crowds), a mind- and eye-boggling light and sound extravaganza full of glitter and razzamatazz, featuring more than half a million twinkling bulbs on 26 Disney-themed floats. It's difficult to do it justice in words, so make sure

you see it (the Main Street Electrical Parade is due to be replaced by the more high-tech **Spectromagic** Parade in Spring 2001, but the main theme is similar). Evening hours are also highlighted by **Fantasy in the Sky** firework show over the Castle which is sparked off every night in peak periods by Tinkerbell (seeing is believing!). People start staking out the best spots to see the parades up to an hour in advance along Main Street, USA. At Christmas and Easter there are special Santa Claus and Easter Bunny parades. You can also breakfast with Disney characters at Cinderella's Royal Table ($14.95 for adults, $7.95 for 3–11s), have dinner with them at the Liberty Tree Tavern ($19.95 and $9.95) or visit the Crystal Palace for breakfast ($13.95 and $7.95), lunch ($14.95 and $7.95) and dinner ($19.95 and $9.95) with Pooh, Tigger and Co. You can book a Disney character meal (from a choice of 19) up to 60 days in advance, on 407 939 3463.

If the crowds get too heavy, you CAN escape by leaving the park in early afternoon (get a hand-stamp for re-admission and keep your car park ticket which is valid all day) and returning to your hotel for a few hours' rest or a dive into *Disney's River Country* Water Park, just a short boat ride away.

Finally, one of the park's best-kept 'secrets' is the **Keys to the Kingdom**, a 4-hour guided tour of many backstage areas, including the service tunnel under the park, and entertainment production buildings. It costs an extra $45 (not available for under 16s), call 407 939 8687 for details of this or Disney's **Family Magic Tour**, a 2-hour guided adventure that takes you on a search for clues throughout the park, at $25 ($15 for children).

Epcot

Amaze and annoy your friends by revealing that *Epcot* stands for 'Experimental Prototype Community Of Tomorrow' (or the tourist's version: Every Person Comes Out Tired!), once you have marvelled at the double-barrelled entertainment value of this 260-acre Future World playground. Actually, it is not so much a vision of the future as a look at the world of today, with a strong educational and environmental message which children in particular are quick to pick up on.

At more than twice the size of the *Magic Kingdom* Park, it is more likely to require a 2-day visit (although under 5s might find it less entertaining) and your feet in particular will notice the difference!

Monorail at Epcot

Location

Epcot is located on Epcot Drive and the parking fee is again $6 as you drive into its main entrance (there is a separate entrance for guests of *Disney's Yacht and Beach Club* Resorts, *Disney's BoardWalk Inn and Villas* and the *Walt Disney World Swan* and *Dolphin* Hotels). It opened in October 1982 and its giant parking lot is big enough for 12,000 vehicles, so again a tram takes you from your car to the main entrance (although if you are staying at another of the

Walt Disney World hotels you can catch the monorail or bus service to the front gate). Once you have your ticket, you wait by the turnstiles for the opening moment (often accompanied by a Disney character or two) and are then admitted to the central plaza area, surrounded by the two Innoventions centres.

Epcot is divided into two distinct parts arranged in a figure of eight and there are two tactics to avoid the worst of the early morning crowds. The first or lower half of the '8' consists of **Future World**, seven different pavilions arranged around Spaceship Earth (the giant 'golfball' that dominates the Epcot skyline) and Innoventions. The second part, or the top of the '8', is **World Showcase**, a potted journey around the world via 11 internationally presented pavilions that feature a taste of their culture, history, shopping, entertainment and cuisine. Once you are through the gates, start by heading for the Future World pavilions to your left (Universe of Energy, Wonders of

'Honey, I Shrunk the Audience' is an outstanding Epcot attraction

Epcot at-a-glance

Location	Off Epcot Drive, Walt Disney World
Size	260 acres in Future World and World Showcase
Hours	9am–9pm (Future World), 11am–9pm (World Showcase).
Admission	Under 3, free; 3–9, $37 (one-day ticket), $142 (4-Day Park Hopper), $192 (5-Day Park Hopper Plus); adult (10+) $46, $176, $236.
Parking	$6
Lockers	Yes; to left underneath Spaceship Earth and International Gateway; $5 ($2 refund)
Pushchairs	$7 (to right underneath Spaceship Earth and International Gateway, $1 deposit refunded)
Wheelchairs	$7 ($1 deposit refunded) or $40 ($10 deposit refunded) (same location)
Top Attractions	Spaceship Earth, Body Wars, Honey I Shrunk the Audience, Test Track, Maelstrom, Universe of Energy, American Adventure
Don't Miss	IllumiNations, live entertainment (including Off Kilter in Canada) and dinner at any of the World Showcase pavilions.

Hidden Costs		
	Meals	Burger, chips and coke $7.59 Three-course dinner $31 (Le Cellier, Canada)
	Kids' meal	$3.25
	T-shirts	$19–$32
	Souvenirs	$0.80–$800
	Sundries	Test Track 'Cone' Hat $21

Life and Test Track) and then continue up into World Showcase. This way you will visit some of the best rides in *Epcot* ahead of the main crowds. Alternatively, if the rides don't appeal quite so much as a visit to such diverse cultures as Japan and Morocco, spend your first couple of hours in the Innoventions centres (which are very popular from mid-morning), then head into World Showcase as soon as it opens at 11am and you will be ahead of the crowds for several hours. If you time your journey around the Showcase (which is a full 1½-mile walk) to arrive back in Future World by late afternoon, you will find the worst of the milling throng will have passed through (except for Test Track).

The other thing you will want to do early on is book a table for lunch or dinner at one of the many fine restaurants around World Showcase (Mexico, Morocco, Canada and Japan all come highly recommended). The best reservations go fast, but check in at the Guest Relations office (immediately on the left as you enter the Innoventions Plaza) and they will be able to give you advice and make a Priority Seating booking (never just a reservation at Disney, remember).

Future World

Here is what you will find in Future World.

Universe of Energy

There is just the one attraction here but it is a stunner as you are taken on a 45-minute show-and-ride in the company of American comedienne Ellen DeGeneres that explores the creation of fuels from the age of dinosaurs to their modern day usages. The film elements convince you that you are in a conventional theatre, but then your seats suddenly rearrange themselves into 96-person solar-powered cars and you are off on a journey through the sights, sounds and even smells of the prehistoric era. The dinosaurs are very convincing! Queues are steady but not overwhelming throughout the day from mid-morning. AAAAA.

Wonders of Life

This is one of Future World's most popular pavilions, hence you need to be here either early or late in the day. **Body Wars** is a terrific simulator ride through the human body as in the films *Fantastic Voyage* or the more recent *Inner Space*. It is quite a violent adventure, too, hence it is not recommended for people who suffer from motion sickness, anyone with neck or back injuries, or pregnant women. Restrictions; 3ft 4in. TTTT. **Cranium Command** is a hilarious theatre show set in the brain of a 12-year-old boy, showing how he negotiates a typical day. It is both audio-animatronic and film-based. See how many famous TV and film stars you can name in the 'cast'. AAAA. **The Making of Me** is a sensitive film on

the creation of human life and will therefore require parental discretion for children as it has its explicit moments, although not without humour. AAA. The **Fitness Fairground**, with hands-on exhibits like exercise bikes, gives you the chance to see just how far all the holiday fun has taken its toll on your body! The Pure and Simple restaurant offers delicious – and nutritious – alternatives to the usual burgers and chips. Hot tip: this is a good pavilion to spend time in if you need to cool down!

Mission: Space

The old Horizons pavilion has been pulled down and, in its place, is the construction for **Mission: Space**, a dramatic new high-tech attraction which will feature a simulated shuttle launch and space travel, among other things. It sounds quite dazzling, but sadly it is not due to open until 2003.

Test Track

The newest ride at *Epcot* is a big production, a 5½-minute whirl along the Walt Disney World's longest and fastest track to date. **Test Track** starts with a pre-show into the world of General Motors' quality and safety techniques, preparing riders for first-hand experience of vehicle testing. The way the cars whizz around the *outside* of the building (at up to 60mph) gives you just a glimpse of what's in store. The reality is far more thrilling as you are taken on a thorough tour of a GM proving ground, including a hill climb test, suspension test (hold on to those fillings!), brake test, environment chamber, barrier test (remember those crash test dummies?) and the steeply banked high-speed finale. For those who manage to regain their breath, there is a post-show area with a multimedia film and the chance to view the latest GM models. There are some interactive driving tests, plus a smart gift store, and it all adds up to an extremely involved exhibit (although a bit technical for youngsters). The downside is the HUGE queues it attracts, up to three hours at peak times. Head straight for here after opening or come back in the evening to keep your standing to bearable levels. If you are on your own, you can save some time by using the Singles Queue here. Restrictions; 3ft 4in. TTTT (TTT for teenagers) (FP).

The next door **Odyssey Center** offers baby-care and first aid facilities, telephones and restrooms.

Imagination!

The two-part attraction here starts with **Journey Into Your Imagination**, a fairly zany ride through the experiments and illusions of the Imagination Institute designed to measure your IQ (Imagination Quotient). Narrated by Eric Idle and featuring a gravity-defying section (seeing is not believing in this case!), it is gentle fun but not worth the queues that build up here during the main part of the day. AAA. (It is also unpopular with fans of the Dreamfinder ride it replaced, but the baby dragon Figment does pop up in the new version – keep your eyes peeled!). You exit into Image Works, an interactive playground of unusual sights and sounds, which will probably amuse children more than adults (although you are also tempted here to part with more money, on various cartoon images and select-your-own CDs). Come out of the building and turn right for the fabulous 3-D experience of **Honey, I Shrunk The Audience**, as Rick Moranis reprises his hapless inventor character Wayne Szalinski. A neat 8-minute pre-show is the

perfect prelude to the fun and games in store. If you have already seen *Muppet*Vision 3-D* at *Disney-MGM Studios* you might have an idea what to expect. Special effects and moving seats add to the entertainment that makes you feel you have been miniaturised. And beware the sneezing dog! AAAAA (Extremely popular right through the day, hence another FastPass attraction). Outside, kids are always fascinated by the Jellyfish and Serpentine Fountains that send water squirting from pond to pond, and there is always one who tries to stand in the way and 'catch' one of the streams of water. Have your cameras and camcorders ready! Once again, if you have young children, bringing a change of clothing is advisable.

The Land

This pavilion features four elements that combine to make a highly entertaining but educational experience on food production and nutrition. **Living with the Land** is an informative 14-minute boat ride that is worth the usually long queue. This journey through various types of food production sounds a pretty dull idea, and it may not appeal much to younger children, but adults and school-age kids will sit up and take notice of the three different ecological communities, especially the greenhouse finale. AAAA. Having ridden the ride you can also walk the walk on a guided tour through the greenhouse complex and learn even more about *Walt Disney World* Resort's horticultural projects. It takes an hour ($6 for adults, $4 for children), but you have to book up in person at the desk near the Green Thumb Emporium. **Food Rocks**, just to the right as you exit the ride, is easy to overlook, but don't! This musical tribute to nutrition, presented by Food Rappa (what a great name!) and featuring

FUTURE WORLD

1 SPACESHIP EARTH
2 INNOVENTIONS EAST
3 UNIVERSE OF ENERGY
4 WONDERS OF LIFE
5 MISSION: SPACE (Opening 2003)
6 TEST TRACK
7 ODYSSEY CENTER
8 IMAGINATION!
9 THE LAND
10 INNOVENTIONS WEST
11 THE LIVING SEAS

WORLD SHOWCASE

12 MEXICO
13 NORWAY
14 CHINA
15 GERMANY
16 ITALY
17 THE AMERICAN ADVENTURE
18 JAPAN
19 MOROCCO
20 FRANCE
21 INTERNATIONAL GATEWAY (TO EPCOT RESORT HOTELS)
22 UNITED KINGDOM
23 CANADA

EPCOT

Pita Gabriel (ouch!) is a hilarious 12-minute skit that will amuse kids and adults alike. AAAA. **The Circle of Life** is a 15-minute live-action/animated story that explains environmental concerns, easily digestible for kids. Queues not a problem here, either. AAA.

The Sunshine Season food court offers the chance to eat some of Disney's home-grown produce, and again there are healthy alternatives to the usual fast food fare, while the Garden Grill Restaurant is a slowly revolving platform that offers more traditional food, including pasta, seafood and delicious rotisserie chicken. Mickey and friends also turn up here for character breakfasts ($8.25 for kids 3–11 and $14.95 for adults), lunch ($9.95 and $16.95) and dinner ($9.95 and $18.95), but book early.

Test Track in Future World at Epcot

The Living Seas

This pavilion does for the sea what The Land Pavilion does for the land. A 7-minute film pre-show leads on to the ride, a 3-minute trip around the man-made 5.7-million-gallon aquarium that takes you to Sea Base Alpha, the main attraction. This two-level development takes visitors through six modules that present stories of undersea exploration and marine life, including a research centre that provides a close-up encounter with the endangered manatee. Crowds build up substantially through the day, so go either early or late. AAA.

The pavilion also includes the highly recommended Coral Reef restaurant that serves magnificent seafood, as well as providing diners with a grandstand view of the massive aquarium. Dinner for two will cost around $60, which isn't cheap, but the food is first class.

Spaceship Earth

This ride spirals up the 18 storeys into the 'golfball', telling the story of communication from early cave drawings to modern satellite technology. This is one of the most popular rides in the park, largely because of its visibility and location, hence you need to do it either first thing or early evening when the crowds have moved on from Future World into World Showcase. The highlight is the depiction of Michelangelo's painting of the Sistine Chapel, which will be lost on small kids, but it's an entertaining 15-minute journey all along. AAAA. As you exit the ride you come into the Global Activity Center, presented by AT&T, with a host of interactive educational exhibits.

Innoventions East and West

These two centres of hands-on exhibits and computer games – subtitled **The Road to Tomorrow**

– were revamped as part of the Millennium celebrations, and include a glimpse of *Walt Disney World* Resort's latest investigations into virtual reality entertainment, and other demonstrations of current and future technologies, especially the Internet, by companies like IBM, Xerox, Motorola and General Motors. The kids will automatically gravitate to the free **Video Games of Tomorrow** selection presented by Sega and they may take a bit of moving along! Both sides are routed like a journey into the future and will reward the enquiring mind. Worth waiting for are the **Ultimate Home Theater Experience** (West) and the opportunity to send a video e-mail to friends in the **Internet Zone** (East). Musical entertainment is provided periodically in the Innoventions Plaza, along with other innovative live acts. Food outlets include the counter service Electric Umbrella Restaurant for lunch and dinner (sandwiches, burgers and salads), the Pasta Piazza Ristorante, which offers tempting pizzas and pasta, and the Fountain View Espresso and Bakery for tea, coffee and pastries. Visit **Ice Station Cool**, presented by Coca-Cola™, for some free product samples and the chance to encounter some real snow! You'll also find the huge shopping plaza **Mouse Gear** in Innoventions East, featuring stacks of quality Epcot and Disney souvenirs.

World Showcase

If you found Future World a huge experience, prepare to be amazed also by the more down-to-earth but equally imaginative pavilions around the World Showcase Lagoon. Each features a glimpse of the host country in dramatic settings. Several have either amusing rides or films that show off the tourist features of the countries, while in nearly every case the restaurants offering national fare are some of the best in Orlando.

Mexico

Starting at the bottom left of the circular tour of the lagoon and moving clockwise, your first encounter is the spectacular pyramid that houses **Mexico**. Here you will find the amusing boat ride along **El Rio del Tiempo**, the River of Time, which gives you a potted 9-minute journey through the people and history of the country. Queues here tend to be surprisingly long from mid-morning to late afternoon. AAA. The rest of the pavilion is given over to a range of shops in the **Plaza de los Amigos** that vary from pretty tacky to sophisticated, and the **San Angel Inn**, a dimly-lit and romantic full-service diner offering traditional and tempting Mexican

> BRIT TIP: The Cantina is a great spot from which to watch the nightly IllumiNations fireworks and laser show, but you need to arrive at least an hour early.

fare. Outside, on the lagoon, is the **Cantina de San Angel**, a fast-food counter for tacos, chili and burgers, while, as with all World Showcase pavilions, there is live entertainment and music.

Norway

Next up is **Norway**, which features probably the best of the rides in World Showcase, the Viking-themed **Maelstrom**. This 10-minute longboat journey through the history and scenery of the Scandinavian country features a short waterfall drop and a North Sea storm, and attracts longish queues during the day, so again the best tactic is to go soon after World Showcase's 11am opening. TTT. There are periodical Norwegian-themed exhibits in the reconstruction **Stave Church** and twice-daily guided tours (sign up at the Tourism desk). The pavilion also contains a clever reproduction of Oslo's Akershus fortress. **Restaurant Akershus** offers lunch and dinner buffets and the **Kringla Bakeri Og Kafé** serves open sandwiches, pastries and drinks.

China

The spectacular architecture of **China** is well served by the pavilion's main attraction, the stunning **Wonders of China**, a 20-minute, 360-degree film in the circular Temple of Heaven. Here you are surrounded by the sights and sounds of one of the world's most mysterious countries in a special cinematic production, the technology of which alone will leave you breathless. If you were ever tempted to pay a visit to the country itself, this film will convince you. Queues build up to half an hour during the main part of the day. AAAA. **Land of Many Faces** is a new exhibit introducing China's ethnic peoples. Two restaurants, the **Nine Dragons** (table service, decent if unremarkable food) and the **Lotus Blossom Café** (counter service, fairly predictable spring rolls and stir-fries) offer tastes of the Orient, while the **Yong Feng Shangdian Department Store** is a virtual warehouse of Chinese gifts and artefacts. Don't miss the periodic shows of Oriental music and acrobatic acts on the plaza in front of the Temple.

The **Outpost** between China and Germany features hut-style shops and snacks, with entertainment from Africa and the Caribbean.

Germany

Germany offers more in the way of shopping and eating than it does entertainment, although you will still find strolling players, courtyard musicians and a lively **Biergarten**, with its brass band. It also offers hearty portions of German sausage, sauerkraut and rotisserie chicken. The **Sommerfest** is fast food German-style (bratwurst and strudel), while this pavilion boasts the highest number of shops of any *Epcot* pavilion, including chocolates, wines, china, crystal, toys and cuckoo clocks.

Italy

Similarly, **Italy** has pretty, authentic architecture (including a superb reproduction of St Mark's Square in Venice), lively music and amusing Italian folk stories, three tempting gift shops (including Perugina chocolates and Armani collectibles), and its restaurant, **L'Originale Alfredo di Roma Ristorante**. It's a touch expensive, but the atmosphere, decor and singing waiters (!) add extra zest to the meals, which include world famous fettucine, chicken, veal and seafood. Expect a three-course meal to cost you about $35.

America

At the top of the lagoon and dominating World Showcase is the **American Adventure**, not so much a pavilion as a celebration of the country's history and constitution. A colonial fife and drum band add authentic sounds to the eighteenth-century setting, overlooked by a faithful reproduction of Philadelphia's Liberty Hall. Inside the Hall you will find the spectacular **American Adventure** show, a magnificent film and audio-animatronic production lasting half an hour which details the country's struggles and triumphs, its presidents, statesmen and heroes. It's a glossy, patriotic performance, featuring outstanding audio-

5

animatronic special effects, and, while some of it will leave foreign tourists fairly cold, it is difficult not to be impressed by the overall sense of pride and achievement inherent in so much American history. It doesn't pull any punches on the subject of Native American issues, either. Avoid at midday for the queues. AAAA. Outside, handcarts offer touches of American nostalgia and antiques, while the **Liberty Inn** offers fast-food fare for lunch and dinner. The **America Gardens Theater** facing the lagoon presents regular musical performances from worldwide artists and Disney characters which vary seasonally.

Japan

Next up on the clockwise tour is **Japan**, where you will be introduced to typical Japanese gardens and architecture, including the breathtaking Chi Nien Tien, a round building one-half scale reproduction of a temple, some magnificent art exhibits (notably the Bijutsu-kan Gallery), musical performances and live entertainment like kite-making. For one of the best and most entertaining meals in *Epcot*, the **Teppanyaki Dining** rooms and **Tempura Kiku-Sushi** both offer a full, table-service introduction to Japanese cuisine while **Yakitori House** is the fast-food equivalent and the **Matsu No Ma Lounge** features sushi and speciality drinks. The restaurants are hosted by Mitsukoshi, as is the superb department store.

Morocco

Morocco, as you would expect, is a real shopping experience, with artfully crafted bazaars, alleyways and stalls selling a well-priced array of carpets, leather goods, clothing, brass ornaments, pottery and antiques (seek out that Magic Lamp!). All of the building materials were faithfully imported and hand-built to give Morocco an outstanding degree of authenticity, even by the World Showcase's high standards, and will keep you gazing at its clever detail around the winding alleyways to the **Nejjarine Fountain** and gardens, which can be enjoyed on a guided walking tour. **Restaurant Marrakesh** offers a full Moroccan dining experience, complete with traditional musicians and a belly dancer. It's slightly pricey ($55 for the Moroccan feast for two) but the atmosphere is always lively.

France

France is predictably overlooked by a replica Eiffel Tower, but the smart streets, buildings and the sheer cleanliness of it all is a long way removed from modern-day Paris! This is pre-World War One France, with official buskers, comedy street theatre and mime acts adding to the rather dreamy atmosphere. Don't miss **Impressions de France**, another stunning big-film production that serves up all the grandest sights of France to the accompaniment of the music of Offenbach, Debussy, Saint-Saëns and Satie. Crowds get quite heavy from mid-morning to early evening but it is a stunning performance (although kids might feel left out). AAAA. If you are looking for a gastronomic experience this is also the pavilion for you as there is the choice of three restaurants, of which **Chefs de France** and **Bistro de Paris** are major discoveries. The former is an award-winning, full-service and therefore expensive establishment featuring top quality French cuisine created by French chefs on a daily basis, while the latter offers more intimate bistro dining, still with an individual touch and plenty of style. Alternatively, the **Boulangerie Patisserie** is a sidewalk café offering more modest fare at a more modest price. Shopping here is also suitably chic.

United Kingdom

Coming next to the **United Kingdom** will be something of a disappointment to British visitors. Sad to say, but this is the dullest of all the 11 international pavilions, certainly with little to entertain those of us who have been inside a traditional pub before or shopped for Royal Doulton or Pringle goods. Add in some street entertainers, a good Beatles tribute band and that really is the sum total on offer here. The **Rose and Crown Pub** is a fairly authentic pub, but you can certainly get better food and drink (steak and kidney pie $13, cottage pie $12 and a pint of Bass, Harp Lager or Guinness for a whopping $5) at these prices. Many people rave about the fish and chips served at Harry Ramsdens here, but I'm not over-eager. Other shops are the Tea Caddy, the Magic of Wales, the Queen's Table, the Lords and Ladies (perfumes, tobacco, family trees) and the Toy Soldier (traditional games and toys).

Canada

Canada completes the World Showcase circle, with its main features being **Victoria Gardens**, based on the rightly world-famous Butchart Gardens on Vancouver Island, some spectacular Rocky Mountain scenery, a replica French gothic mansion, the Hôtel du Canada, and another stunning 360-degree film, **O Canada!** As with China and France, this beautifully showcases the country's sights and scenery, and serves as a terrific, 17-minute advertisement for the Canadian Tourist Board. Their resident band, **Off Kilter**, are also one of the most entertaining I've seen anywhere. Want to hear rock 'n' roll bagpipes? This is the group

for you! It gets busiest from late morning to late afternoon. AAA. **Le Cellier Steakhouse** is a modestly priced cafeteria offering steaks, prime rib, seafood, chicken, soup and salads for lunch and dinner.

If you plan a 2-day visit, it makes sense to spend the first day in World Showcase, arriving early and heading there while most of the rest of the morning crowds linger in Future World, booking your evening meal around 5.30pm, and then lingering around the lagoon for the evening entertainment. For your second visit, try arriving in late afternoon and then doing Future World in more leisurely fashion than is the case in mid-morning to mid-afternoon. Queues at most of the pavilions are almost non-existent for rides like Universe of Energy, Body Wars and The Land, although Spaceship Earth and especially Test Track stay busy nearly all day (except for the evening, when everyone is out around the lagoon for the firework finale). Take best advantage of the FastPass system here by grabbing a FastPass for Test Track early on and then riding Universe of Energy or Body Wars. You CAN do *Epcot* in a day – if you arrive early, put in some speedy legwork and give some of the peripheral detail a miss. But, of all the parks, it is a shame to hurry this one. In the shops (almost

5

World Millennium Celebration

70 in all), try to save your browsing for the busiest times when most people are on the rides. The Innoventions Centers are also busiest from mid-morning to late afternoon, and less crowded in the evening.

Finally, there is the day's finale at *Epcot*. This received a dramatic revamp for the magnificent Millennium celebrations in 2000. A new parade, **Tapestry of Nations**, was introduced twice a day around World Showcase Lagoon (the second in early evening) featuring a stunning array of dancers and musicians in a carnival setting. More than 100 performers were involved, many dressed in elaborate costumes designed like giant puppet-figures that danced, swayed and interacted with guests (especially children). Fifteen rolling percussion units, like huge time-pieces, beat out the rhythm, backed by inspirational music by British composer Gavin Greenaway and the award-winning Hans 'Lion King' Zimmer. It was a combination of Rio's Carnival, Mardi Gras in New Orleans and typical Disney style, and the good news is that it will continue beyond the end of the Millennium celebrations on January 31, 2001. Tapestry of Nations also builds superbly into the nightly finale of **IllumiNations: Reflections of Earth**, a firework and special-effect extravaganza that is awesome even by Disney standards. Again, Greenaway provides original music for a 15-minute performance of vivid brilliance. Some 2,800 firework shells are launched as a celestial backdrop to a series of fire-and-water effects on the World Showcase lagoon. The central icon is a 28ft video globe of Earth that opens in a spectacular climax of choreographed pyrotechnics. Don't miss it! However, be aware that people start staking out the best Lagoon-side spots, including the terrace of the Rose and Crown pub, 2 hours in advance. The ultimate way to view IllumiNations is by private boat on one of five **cruises** from Disney's BoardWalk or Yacht/Beach Club resorts (for non-residents, too). They vary from $120–$230 per boat (holding 4–12 guests) and can be used for special celebrations. Call 407 939 7529 well in advance to book.

Epcot also has some special **behind-the-scenes tours** which are worth knowing about (but not for under-16s). **Dolphins In Depth** ($140, including souvenir video, T-shirt and refreshments) is a 3½-hour delve into the backstage and research areas of the Living Seas pavilion, including a chance to meet the resident dolphins. **Gardens of the World** ($49) is a 3-hour botanical tour of the gardens in Epcot, and includes tips for your own garden. **Hidden Treasures** is a 3- ($49) or 5-hour ($85, including lunch and gift) tour of the 11 countries of World Showcase. Brand new is **Undiscovered Future World**, a 4½-hour journey into the creation of *Epcot*, Walt's vision for the whole Resort and backstage areas like IllumiNations ($45). **Backstage Magic** ($199) takes you behind the scenes of *Epcot*, *Magic Kingdom* Park and *Disney-MGM Studios* on a 7-hour tour into little-seen aspects of the parks, including animators at work in *Disney-MGM Studios* and tunnels below the *Magic Kingdom* Park. Tours must be booked on 407 939 8687.

Finally, you can enjoy *Epcot's* wonderful **International Flower and Garden Festival** from mid-April until early June. You can really slow down and smell the roses – and it's free!

Disney-MGM Studios

Welcome to Hollywood! Well, the Walt Disney version of it. When it opened in May 1989, Michael Eisner, Chairman of the Walt Disney Company, insisted it was 'the Hollywood that never was and always will be'. Sounds double Dutch? Don't worry, all will be revealed in your day-long tour of this real-life combination of theme park and working TV and film studio. It's the most common question about *Disney-MGM Studios*, and yes, there really are genuine film and TV productions going on even while you're riding around the park peering into the backstage areas.

Rather bigger than the *Magic Kingdom* Park at 135 acres but substantially smaller than *Epcot*, *Disney-MGM Studios* is a different experience yet again with its combination of rides, spectacular shows (including the unmissable

5

Disney-MGM Studios at-a-glance

Location	Off Buena Vista Drive or World Drive, Walt Disney World	
Size	135 acres	
Hours	9am–7pm off peak; 9am–10pm high season (Easter, summer holidays, Thanksgiving and Christmas)	
Admission	Under 3, free; 3–9, $37 (one-day ticket), $142 (4-Day Park Hopper), $192 (5-Day Park Hopper Plus); adult (10+) $46, $176, $236.	
Parking	$6	
Lockers	Yes; next to Oscar's Super Service, to right of main entrance; $5 ($2 refundable)	
Pushchairs Wheelchairs	$7 (from Oscar's Super Service, $1 deposit refunded) $7 ($1 deposit refunded) or $40 ($10 deposit refunded) (same location)	
Top Attractions	Twilight Zone™ Tower of Terror, Rock 'n Roller Coaster, Star Tours, Great Movie Ride, Muppet*Vision 3-D	
Don't Miss	Daily Parade, evening fireworks (high season only), Indiana Jones™ Stunt Spectacular, Fantasmic!	
Hidden Costs	**Meals**	Burger, chips and coke $6.65 Three-course dinner $20.95 (Sci-Fi Dine-In Theater)
	Kids' meal	$4.75
	T-shirts	$18–$28
	Souvenirs	$2.50–$385
	Sundries	Full colour caricature $20

Fantasmic!), street entertainment, film sets and smart gift shops. Like the *Magic Kingdom* Park, the food on offer won't win awards, but some of the restaurants (notably the Sci-Fi Dine-in Theater and 50s Prime Time Café) have superbly imaginative settings to keep everyone amused. *Disney-MGM Studios* also has rather more to keep the attention of smaller children than *Epcot*, but you can still easily see all it has to offer in a day, and, if you make an early start, you can safely say you have 'done' it by 5pm unless the crowds are really heavy.

Location

The entrance arrangements will be fairly familiar if you have already visited either the *Magic Kingdom* Park or *Epcot*. *Disney-MGM Studios* are located on Buena Vista Drive (which runs between World Drive and Epcot Drive) and the parking fee is $6. Look out for the landmark 130ft water tower adorned with Mickey Mouse ears and dubbed – wait for it – the **Earffel Tower**!

Again, make a note of where you park before you catch your tram to the main gates, where you must wait for the official opening hour. If the queues build up quickly, the gates will again open early, so be ready to jump the gun and get a running start!

Once through the gates you are into Hollywood Boulevard, which is a street of mainly gift shops, and you have to decide which of the three main ride attractions to head for first as these are the ones where the queues will be heavy nearly all day. Try to ignore the lure of the shops as it is better to browse in the early afternoon when the queues build up at the rides. Incidentally, if you thought *Walt Disney World* Resort had elevated queuing to an art form in their other two parks, wait until you see the clever ways they are arranged here! Just when you think you have got to the ride itself there is another twist to the queue you hadn't seen or an extra element to the ride which holds you up. The latter are called 'holding pens' and are an ingenious way of making it

© Disney Enterprises, Inc.

The unmissable Fantasmic! special effects show at Disney-MGM Studios

DISNEY-MGM STUDIOS

1 MULAN PARADE ROUTE
2 DISNEY'S DOUG LIVE!
3 INDIANA JONES™ EPIC STUNT SPECTACULAR!
4 ABC SOUND STUDIO 'SOUNDS DANGEROUS'
5 STAR TOURS
6 DISNEY'S HUNCHBACK OF NOTRE DAME – A MUSICAL ADVENTURE
7 JIM HENSON'S MUPPET*VISION 3-D
8 HONEY, I SHRUNK THE KIDS MOVIE SET ADVENTURE
9 CATASTROPHE CANYON ON DISNEY-MGM STUDIOS BACKLOT TOUR
10 AMERICAN FILM INSTITUTE SHOWCASE COSTUMES & PROPS
11 DISNEY-MGM STUDIOS BACKLOT TOUR
12 THE GREAT MOVIE RIDE
13 VOYAGE OF THE LITTLE MERMAID
14 THE BACKSTAGE PASS TOUR
15 THE MAGIC OF DISNEY ANIMATION
16 THE TWILIGHT ZONE™ TOWER OF TERROR
17 'BEAUTY & THE BEAST' – LIVE ON STAGE
18 GUEST INFORMATION BOARD
20 TOY STORY PIZZA PLANET
21 FANTASMIC!
22 ROCK 'N ROLLER COASTER: starring Aerosmith
23 BEAR IN THE BIG BLUE HOUSE

seem like you are being entertained instead of queuing. Look out for them in particular at the Great Movie Ride, Twilight Zone™ Tower of Terror and Jim Henson's Muppet*Vision 3-D. An up-to-the-minute check on queue times at all the main attractions is kept on a Guest Information Board on Hollywood Boulevard, just past its junction with Sunset Boulevard, where you can also book for one of the feature restaurants.

Disney-MGM Studios is laid out in rather more confusing fashion than its two main counterparts, which both have neatly packaged 'lands' or pavilions, so you need to consult your map frequently to make sure you are going in the right direction.

The main attractions

Having said that, the opening-gate crowds will all surge in one of four directions which will give you a pretty good idea of where you want to go. By far the 'biggest' attraction in *Disney-MGM Studios* is **The Twilight Zone™ Tower of Terror**, a magnificent haunted hotel ride that culminates in a 13-storey drop in a lift. The queues here build up to two hours at peak periods. Consequently, if the Tower appeals to you, do it FIRST! Head up Hollywood Boulevard then turn right into Sunset Boulevard and it is at the end of the street, looming ominously over the rest of the park. The new **Rock 'n Roller Coaster: starring Aerosmith**, at the end of Sunset Boulevard on the left, is another huge draw, but it is also a FastPass ride like the Tower of Terror, so you can get a FP for one and then ride the other if you head here first.

Star Tours, the great Star Wars™ simulator ride, and **Voyage of the Little Mermaid** are the other serious queue-builders and are also FP attractions. If you are not up for the really big thrills, grab an FP for Mermaid (straight up Hollywood Boulevard, past Sunset, turn right into Animation Courtyard) then head for Star Tours (back across the main square, past Doug Live).

Here's a full rundown of all the current attractions in more detail, working around the park in a clockwise direction.

The Great Movie Ride

The Great Movie Ride: this faces you as you walk in along Hollywood Boulevard and is a good place to start if the crowds are not too serious. An all-star audio-animatronics cast recreate a number of box office smashes, including Jimmy Cagney's *Public Enemy*, Julie Andrews in *Mary Poppins*, Gene Kelly in *Singing in the Rain* and many more masterful set pieces as you ride through on your conducted tour. Small children may find the menace of the Alien a bit too strong, but otherwise it has fairly universal appeal and features some live twists it would be a shame to spoil by revealing. AAAA.

Disney's Doug Live!: this 30-minute show based on the American cartoon series will mean little to anyone not familiar with the character of 11-year-old Doug and his Bluffington friends. Well sung and presented, but with minimal staging, it is hard to see its appeal stretching to anyone other than fans of the cartoon. AA.

ABC Sound Studio 'Sounds Dangerous': another recent presentation is this sound FX special featuring American comedian Drew Carey in an instalment of a spoof undercover police show *Sounds Dangerous*. The majority of the show is in the pitch dark – which upsets some young children – and is centred on your special headphones as Carey's stakeout goes wrong. Clever and amusing – if a little tame for older children – you exit into the SoundWorks Studio to try your hand at a number of well-known sound effects. AAA.

Indiana Jones™ Epic Stunt Spectacular!: consult your park map for the various times during the day when this rip-roaring stunt cavalcade hits the stage. A specially made movie set creates three different backdrops for Indiana Jones'™ stunt men and women to put on a dazzling array of clever stunts, scenes and special effects from the Harrison Ford film epics. Again there is an audience participation element and some amusing sub-plots I won't reveal. Queues for the near-45-minute show begin to form up to half an hour before showtime so be prepared for a wait here, but the auditorium holds more than 2,000 so everyone usually gets in. TTTT (FP).

Star Tours

Star Tours: anyone remotely amused by the *Star Wars*™ films will enjoy just queuing up for this ride, one of my personal favourites, a breathtaking 7-minute spin in a Star Speeder. The elaborate walk-in area is full of Star Wars™ gadgets and gizmos that will completely take your attention away from the fact you often have to wait in line here for up to an hour. From arguing robots C-3PO and R-2D2 to your robotic 'pilot', everything has a brilliant sense of space travel, and the ride won't disappoint you! Restrictions; 3ft 4in, no children under 3. TTTT (plus AAAAA).

Jim Henson's Muppet*Vision 3-D: the 3-D is crossed out here and 4-D substituted in its place, so be warned some strange things are about to happen! A wonderful 10-minute holding-pen pre-show takes you in to the specially built Muppet Theater for a 20-minute experience with all of the Muppets, 3-D special effects and much more.

When Fozzie Bear points his squirty flower at you, prepare to get wet! It's a gem, and children in particular will love it. Queues are substantial through the main parts of the day, but Disney's queuing expertise always makes them seem shorter than they actually are. AAAAA.

Honey, I Shrunk the Kids Movie Set Adventure: this adventure playground for kids gives youngsters the chance to tackle gigantic blades of grass that turn out to be slides, crawl through caves, investigate giant mushrooms and more. However, some may turn round and say 'Yeah. A giant ant. So what?' and head back for the rides. There can be long queues here, too, so arrive early if the kids demand it (and bring plenty of film). TT (TTTT under 8s).

Backstage Pass: the first element of a three-part sequence takes you behind the scenes of Disney film-making. This 25-minute section showcases the recent remake of *101 Dalmatians* starring Glenn Close, with a look inside the clever animal animation, a glimpse of *Disney-MGM Studios* soundstages and their current productions and finally a full-scale set-up of the world of Cruella De Vil. It is a fascinating tour, but it won't hold the attention of small children and you will find it hard going with pushchairs. AAA.

The Disney-MGM Studios Backlot Tour: part two, which takes 35 minutes, starts with some more special effects (involving a lot of water) before you board the special trams for a look at the off-limits part of the Studios. You are introduced to the production backlot, famous 'houses' and props before visiting **Catastrophe Canyon** for a demonstration of special effects that try both to drown you and blow you up! AAA (plus TTTT!).

You exit into the **American Film Institute Showcase** of costumes and props from recent films.

Hollywood Boulevard

Voyage of the Little Mermaid: this 17-minute live performance is primarily for children who have seen and enjoyed the Disney cartoon. Like Legend of the Lion King in the *Magic Kingdom* Park it brings together live actors, animation and puppetry to recreate the highlights of the film. Parents will still enjoy the special effects, but queues tend to be surprisingly long so go either early or late. Those in the first few rows may get a little wet. AAA (AAAAA under 9s) (FP).

The Magic of Disney Animation: an amusing and entertaining 40-minute tour through the making of cartoons. It's up to you how you pace the walk-through tour, but don't miss Robin Williams in a special cartoon, *Back to Neverland*, with Walter Cronkite, and the fascinating view of some of Disney's animators at work. It concludes with a film of some of the highlights of Disney's many animated classics, and you will be amazed at how much you have learned in the course of your tour (although small children might be a bit lost by it all). Queues are rarely serious here, so it's a good one for the afternoon. AAAA.

Bear In The Big Blue House: straight out of the popular kids' TV series is this 15-minute live show featuring Bear and his friends who invite you to sing along in this rather makeshift arena (formerly the Soundstage Restaurant) up to seven times a day. Older kids won't be impressed, but the young 'uns (and their parents) love it. AAA (AAAAA under 6s).

Fantasmic!: this epic special-effects spectacular is simply not to be missed. Staged every night in a 6,900-seat amphitheatre behind the Tower of Terror™, it features the 'dreams' of Mr M Mouse, portrayed as the Sorcerer's Apprentice, through films such as *Pocahontas*, *The Lion King* and *Snow White*, but hijacked by various Disney villains, leading to a tumultuous battle, with Our Hero emerging triumphant. Dancing waters, shooting comets, animated fountains, swirling stars, balls of fire and more combine in a truly breathtaking presentation – just watch out for the giant, fire-breathing dragon! The 25-minute show begins seating up to 90 minutes in advance and it is advisable to head there at least half

The Wicked Witch in Fantasmic!

an hour beforehand to be sure of a seat (watch out for the splash zones!). AAAAA.

BRIT TIP: Beat the crowds by booking a Fantasmic dinner package when you enter the park (or in advance on 407 939 3463). Just make an early-evening Priority Seating for the Brown Derby or Mama Melrose's restaurant, and you get no-wait VIP seating later for the show

Tower of Terror

The Twilight Zone™ Tower of Terror: the tallest landmark in *Walt Disney World* Resort (at 199ft) invites you to experience another dimension in this mysterious Hollywood hotel that time forgot. The exterior is intriguing, the interior is fascinating, the ride is scintillating and the queues are mind-blowing! The only unfortunate aspect of this really thrilling attraction, which is so much more than just the advertised 13-storey free-fall, is the fact that the majority of queuing time is outside in the sun, and, when it is hot, you are almost melting by the time you reach the air-conditioned inner sanctum of the spooky hotel. Typically, just when you think you have got through to the ride itself, there is another queue, but the inner detail is so clever you can spend the time inspecting how realistic it all is – before you enter the Twilight Zone itself. You have been warned! Restrictions; 3ft 6in. TTTTT (FP).

Rock 'n Roller Coaster: starring Aerosmith: Disney's first big-thrill inverted coaster is a sure-fire draw for the high-energy ride addicts, with a magnificent indoor setting and nerve-jangling ride. It features a clever 3-D film show starring rock band Aerosmith in their recording studio. That preamble leads to the real fun, set to specially recorded tracks from the band themselves and with outrageous speaker systems, as riders climb aboard Cadillac cars for this memorable whizz through a mock Los Angeles setting (watch out for a close encounter with the 'Hollywood' sign!) The high-speed launch and multiple inversions ensure an up-to-the-minute coaster experience. Go first thing or expect serious queues. Restrictions; 4ft 4in TTTTT (FP).

'Beauty and the Beast' – Live on Stage: a live performance of the highlights of this recent Disney classic will entertain the whole family for 20 minutes in the nearby Theater of the Stars. Check the daily schedule for showtimes. AAA.

More characters

Another popular show is **Disney's The Hunchback of Notre Dame – A Musical Adventure**, a clever 32-minute musical and animated/

© Disney Enterprises, Inc.

The Twilight Zone™ Tower of Terror

puppetry show that highlights the key elements of the Disney film. It is staged five times a day in the Backlot Theater and features a wonderfully elaborate stage setting. AAA. Have your cameras handy in this area for the **Backlot**, a collection of clever façades that look like city scenery, which you can wander around on foot. In the best Disney tradition, there is also a daily parade. At the time of writing this was based on the animated hit **Mulan**, but whatever it turns out to be, you can be sure of a guaranteed family success. AAAA. During peak periods, the **Sorcery in the Sky** Fireworks Show presents a dazzling end to the evening. Best viewing point is in front of the Great Movie Ride as a certain mouse appears at the grand finale. You can also meet Disney characters in Animation Courtyard, along Mickey Avenue, at the Backlot Theater and on the streets of New York.

> BRIT TIP: I always recommend the Sci-Fi Diner or 50s Prime Time Café to make your main meal a bit different.

Food and shops

While the choice of food may not be wide, there is plenty of it and at a reasonable price. **The Hollywood Brown Derby** offers a full-service restaurant in fine Hollywood style (reservations necessary – special Early Evening Value meals 4–6pm), while **Mama Melrose's Ristorante Italiano** is a similar table-service Italian option. The **Sci-Fi Dine-In Theater Restaurant** is a big hit with kids as you dine in a mock drive-in cinema, with cars as your 'table', waitresses on roller-skates and a big film screen showing corny old black-and-white science fiction

clips. The **50s Prime Time Café** is another hilarious dining experience as you sit in mock stage sets from American 50s TV sitcoms and eat meals 'just like Mom used to make'. (The waiters all claim to be your brother and warn you to take your elbows off the table, etc. Hilarious!). Reservations are also necessary. The fast-food eateries consist of the **ABC Commissary**, **Studio Catering Co.**, **Backlot Express**, **Rosie's All-American Café** or the **Toy Story Pizza Planet & Arcade** for various counter-service options, from sandwiches and salads to pizza, pasta and fajitas. Disney character meals are available at **Hollywood & Vine** for breakfast and lunch ($14.95 and $15.95 for adults, $8.95 for 3–11s) but you need to book first thing for these (or call 407 939 3463).

There are also 18 gift and speciality shops, six of them along Hollywood Boulevard, which are worth checking out in early afternoon. **Sid Caheunga's One-of-a-Kind** (just to the right of the main entrance gates as you look out) stocks rare movie and TV items, including many celebrity autographs. Try the **Legends of Hollywood** (on Sunset Boulevard) for a rather different range of souvenirs and **It's a Wonderful Shop** (in the Backlot) for Christmas gifts and collectibles. **Keystone Clothiers** (at the top of Hollywood Boulevard) offer some of the best Disney apparel in any of the parks. All the main rides and film attractions also have their own shops.

For a detailed look behind the scenes at Disney animation, the **Inside Animation** tour provides 3 hours of in-depth fascination of this art (not for under 16s) at $49/person. Call 407 939 8687 to book.

At Christmas, don't miss the incredible **Osborne Family Lights**, switched on in the evening in the Backlot Tour area. Amazing!

Disney's Animal Kingdom Theme Park

Disney's newest, smartest and most radical theme park opened its gates for the first time in April 1998, and represents an outstanding and completely different Disney park experience. With its emphasis on nature and conservation, it largely avoids the non-stop thrills and attractions which mark out the other three parks and instead offers a change of pace, a more peaceful and relaxing motif, as well as Disney's usual seamless entertainment style – plus two decent thrill rides (and more to come!).

The attractions are relatively few, just three out-and-out rides, plus two scenic journeys, two elaborate nature trails, five shows, including the hilarious 3-D film It's Tough to Be a Bug! and the full-blown theatre of Festival of the Lion King, an elaborate adventure playground, petting zoo and Disney character greeting area. It's a far cry from the hustle-bustle of the *Magic Kingdom* Park, and it carries a strong environmental message that aims to create a greater understanding of the world's ecological problems. School-age children should find it quite educational, though under 5s may be a little left out. It is outrageously scenic, notably with the 145ft Tree

Disney's Animal Kingdom Theme Park at-a-glance

Location	Directly off Osceola Parkway, also via World Drive and Buena Vista Drive
Size	500 acres divided into 6 'lands'
Hours	8am to 6, 7 or 8pm
Admission	Under 3, free; 3–9, $37 (one-day ticket), $142 (4-Day Park Hopper), $192 (5-Day Park Hopper Plus); adult (10+) $46, $176, $236.
Parking	$6
Lockers	Yes; either side of Entrance Plaza; $5 ($2 refundable)
Pushchairs	$7 and $13 ($1 refundable) at Garden Gate Gifts, through entrance on right
Wheelchairs	$7 ($1 refund) and $40 ($10 refund), same location
Top Attractions	Dinosaur, Kilimanjaro Safaris, It's Tough to Be a Bug, Kali River Rapids, Festival of the Lion King
Don't Miss	Pangani Forest Exploration Trail, Maharajah Jungle Trek, Conservation Station, dining at Rainforest Café
Hidden Costs	Meals	Burger, chips and coke $7.40
	Kids' meal	$3.25
	T-shirts	$14–$29
	Souvenirs	$2–$250
	Sundries	Disney character-imposed photo $12.95

© Disney Enterprises, Inc.

Some of the cast at Disney's Animal Kingdom Theme Park

of Life and the Kilimanjaro Safaris, but it won't overwhelm you with Disney's usual sense of grand style. Rather, it is a chance to experience a part of the world that is both threatened and threatening in a safe, secure manner. It is obviously not the Real Thing, but it does open up a vital taste of some of the world's most majestic areas to people who would otherwise never have the chance to see them. Here, ecology and Disney's commercial touch meet and find a peaceful co-existence.

The most conclusive word on Disney's first full-blown animal adventure goes to Professor David Bellamy, who told me: 'This park has been designed and looked after by the best animal welfare people you can think of. Bad zoos are bad news and should be closed down, but good zoos are good news and the only hope for keeping about 500 species of animals alive in the future'. The park does get horribly crowded and the walkways can be very congested. Take advantage of the 8am opening and use the FastPass rides to minimise queueing.

Getting there

If you are staying in the Kissimmee area, *Disney's Animal Kingdom* Theme Park is the easiest to find. Just get on the (toll) Osceola Parkway and follow it all the way to the toll booths, where the parking fee is $6. Alternatively, coming down I4, take Exit 26 for Epcot and follow Epcot Drive as far as Buena Vista Drive, which leads on to Osceola Parkway. From the western end of Highway 192, come in on World Drive and then Osceola Parkway.

If you arrive early (which is advisable), you will be able to walk up to the Entrance Plaza. Otherwise, the usual tram system will take you in, so make a note of the area in which you park (e.g. Unicorn, row 67). The Plaza is overlooked by the mountainous Rainforest Café with its 65ft waterfall, which is a must for an (early) lunch or late dinner (rarely busy). The park's scheduled opening time is 8am to allow the animals the earliest opportunity to roam their habitats (they return to secure pens at night). With Orlando getting so hot through the summer months, this early start also gives visitors the best chance to view the animals before they seek shade.

For the early birds, here is your best plan of campaign. Once through the gates, animal lovers should head first for Kilimanjaro Safaris, through the Oasis, Safari Village and into Africa. From there, head straight into Pangani Forest Exploration Trail and you will have experienced two of the most satisfying animal encounters in the park. Alternatively, thrill-seekers should turn right in Safari Village and head for DinoLand USA, where the DINOSAUR ride (formerly Countdown to Extinction) is the big attraction. With that one safely under your belt before the serious crowds arrive, head back through the Village to Asia and Kali River

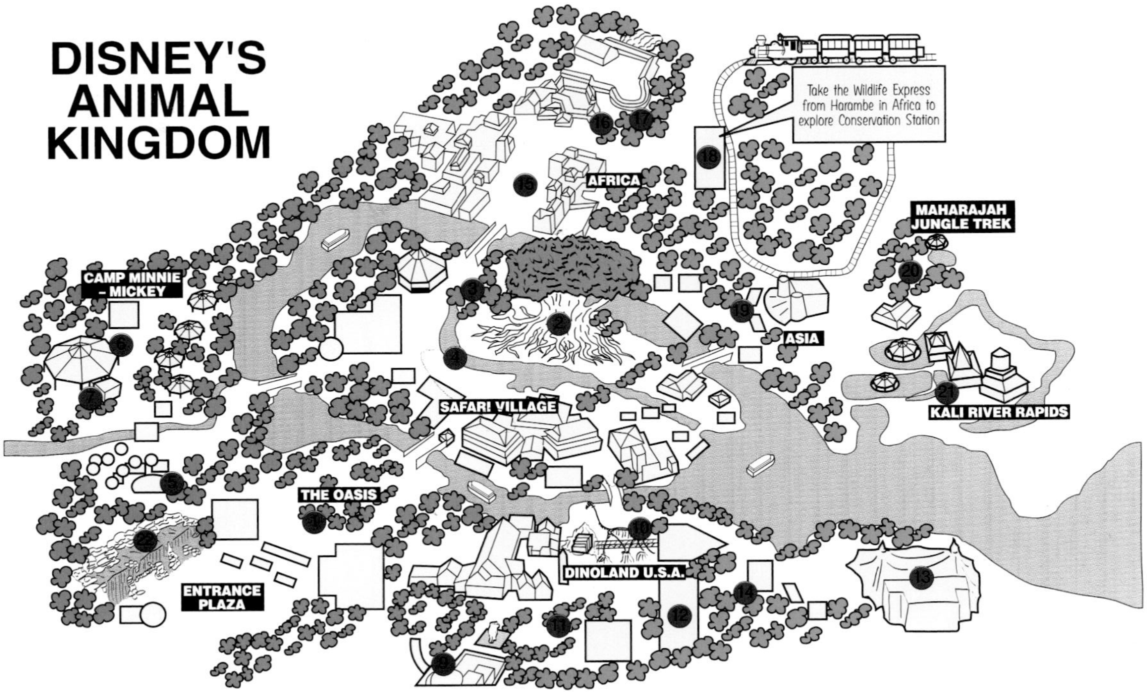

THE OASIS
1 THE OASIS TROPICAL GARDEN

SAFARI VILLAGE
2 THE TREE OF LIFE
3 SAFARI VILLAGE TRAILS
4 IT'S TOUGH TO BE A BUG!

CAMP MINNIE-MICKEY
5 POCAHONTAS AND HER FOREST FRIENDS
6 CHARACTER GREETING AREA
7 FESTIVAL OF THE LION KING

DINOLAND USA
9 DINOSAUR
10 THE BONEYARD
11 CRETACEOUS TRAIL
12 DINOSAUR JUBILEE
13 TARZAN ROCKS!
14 FOSSIL PREPARATION LAB

AFRICA
15 HARAMBE
16 KILIMANJARO SAFARIS
17 PANGANI FOREST EXPLORATION TRAIL
18 WILDLIFE EXPRESS TO CONSERVATION STATION

ASIA
19 FLIGHTS OF WONDER
20 MAHARAJAH JUNGLE TREK
21 KALI RIVER RAPIDS

22 RAINFOREST CAFE

DISNEY'S ANIMAL KINGDOM

Take the Wildlife Express from Harambe in Africa to explore Conservation Station

MAHARAJAH JUNGLE TREK

KALI RIVER RAPIDS

ASIA

AFRICA

SAFARI VILLAGE

DINOLAND U.S.A.

CAMP MINNIE-MICKEY

THE OASIS

ENTRANCE PLAZA

5

Rapids raft ride followed by the scenic Maharajah Jungle Trek. The best combination for the first arrivals is to get a FastPass for DINOSAUR then head straight for the Safaris, and once you have done that (and depending on your FP time) either do your DINOSAUR ride (followed by a Kali River Rapids FP) or go straight to the Rapids. Check your show schedule times for the Legend of the Lion King and try to catch one of the first two performances as the later ones draw sizeable queues. The 'wait time' board at the entrance to Safari Village is also helpful.

> BRIT TIP: The early start is especially advised for the Kilimanjaro Safaris. You will see far more in the first few hours of the day than during the afternoon.

Right, those are your main tactics, here is the full rundown.

The Oasis

This is a gentle, walk-through introduction to the park, a rocky, tree-covered area featuring several animal habitats and studded with streams, waterfalls and lush plant life. Here you will meet miniature deer, macaws, parrots, iguanas, sloths and tree kangaroos in a wonderfully understated environment that leads you across a stone bridge and brings you out into the main open park area. AAA.

Safari Village

This hugely colourful 'village' is the hub of *Disney's Animal Kingdom* Theme Park, from which the other four lands radiate. Its theme is a tropical artists' colony, with animal-inspired artwork everywhere, four main shops and two eateries.

The Tree of Life: this 145ft-high arboreal edifice is the centrepiece of the park, an awesome creation that seems to give off a different perspective from wherever you view it. The 'trunk' and 'roots' are covered in 325 animal carvings representing the Circle of Life, from the dolphin to the lion. Trails lead round the Tree, interspersed with more natural animal habitats that showcase flamingos, otters, ring-tailed lemurs, macaws, axis deer, tamarin monkeys, cranes, storks, ducks and tortoises. For stats lovers, the Tree canopy spreads 160ft wide, the trunk is 50ft wide and the roots spread out 170ft in diameter. There are 103,000 leaves (all attached by hand) on more than 8,000 branches! AAAA.

It's Tough to Be a Bug!: winding down among the Tree's roots brings you 'underground' to a 430-seat theatre and another example of Disney's artistry in 3-D films and special effects. This hysterically funny 8-minute show, a homage to 80 per cent of the animal world, features grasshoppers, beetles, spiders, stink bugs and termites (beware the 'acid' spray!) as well as a number of tricks I couldn't possibly reveal. Sit towards the back in the middle of the row (allow a good number of people in first as you fill up the rows from the far side) to get the best of the 3-D effects. Parents please note: some of the creepy-crawlies can scare young ones. Queues build up from midday onwards, but they do move quite steadily. Don't miss the 'forthcoming attractions' posters in the foyer for some excruciating bug puns on well-known films. AAAAA.

Watch out, too, for Disney musicians and storytellers, here and in Africa and Asia in native dress, who combine mime, puppetry and acting.

Shopping is at its best here, with a huge range of merchandise, souvenirs and gifts (notably in **Disney Outfitters** and **Island Mercantile**), while the two counter-service restaurants, **Pizzafari** and **Flame Tree Barbecue**, are possibly the best of the park's rather average eating options (with the exception of the Rainforest Café). Indeed, provided it is not too hot, the Flame Tree Barbecue offers quite a relaxing and picturesque experience, set among some pretty gardens, pools and fountains on the edge of Discovery River.

Camp Minnie-Mickey

This woodland retreat features gently winding paths and some more of Disney's typically clever scenery, like the benches, lighting and the gurgling stream, with Donald Duck and his nephews hiking down the side, that develops into a series of kid-friendly squirt fountains.

Character Greeting Areas: here, four trails lead to a series of jungle encounters with Disney characters like Mickey and Minnie (naturally), Winnie the Pooh and Tigger, Chip 'n' Dale, Baloo and King Louie, Timon and Rafiki. AAAAA (for kids).

Pocahontas and Her Forest Friends: based on characters from the Disney Film *Pocahontas*, this 15-minute show sees various animals – racoons, rabbits, cranes, a skunk, armadillo and porcupine – interacting with the central actress and Mother Willow in the question of who can save the forest. It doesn't seem to do much for small children, there is not much shade in summer and it is standing room only once the 350 seats have been filled. AAA.

Festival of the Lion King at Lion King Theater: not to be missed, this high-powered 40-minute production brings the hit film to life in quite spectacular fashion with giant, moving stages, huge animated figures, singers, dancers, acrobats and stilt-walkers. All the well-known *Lion King* songs are given an airing in a coruscation of colour and sound, and it serves to underline the quality Disney bring to their live production shows. Its quality is matched only by its popularity – people begin queuing a good 30 minutes in advance for the 1,000-seater amphitheatre. Try to take in one of the first two shows of the day. AAAAA.

DinoLand USA

5

Rather at odds with the natural theming of the rest of the park, DinoLand USA is a full-scale palaeontology exercise, with this mock 'town' taken over by a university fossil dig. Energetically tongue-in-cheek (the 'students' who work in the area have the motto 'Been there, dug that' and you enter under a mock brachiosaurus skeleton, the Oldengate Bridge – ouch!), it still features some genuine and fascinating glimpses into dinosaur research at the **Fossil Preparation Lab** and the **Dinosaur Jubilee** mini-museum of artefacts.

DINOSAUR: this has been re-named after Disney's blockbuster animated film and its original fast, jerky ride has been toned down a little for a more family-friendly ride (although the dinosaur menace is still pretty scary for many children). It is a mind-blowingly realistic journey back to the end of the Cretaceous Period and the giant meteor that put paid to dinosaur life. You enter the high-tech Dino Institute, 'a discovery center and on-going research lab dedicated to uncovering the mysteries of the past', to be presented with a multimedia show of dinosaur history that leads you in to a briefing room. Here you learn your 'mission', to go back 65 million years for a glimpse

© Disney Enterprises, Inc.

The Festival of the Lion King

of Cretaceous life. However, one of the Institute's scientists hijacks your journey for his own project, to capture a dinosaur just before the fateful meteor's arrival, and you are sent careering back to a prehistoric jungle in your 12-passenger Time Rover. The threat of a carnivorous carnotaurus and the impending doom of the meteor add up to a breathtaking whizz through a stunning environment. You will need to ride at least twice to appreciate all the clever details, but queues build up quickly, so go either first thing or late in the day. Restrictions; 3 ft 4 in. TTTT plus ÁÁÁÁÁ (FP).

BRIT TIP: Ride at the front left of your Time Rover car for maximum effect of the twists and turns and the dinosaur menace.

The Boneyard: a hugely imaginative adventure playground, it offers kids the chance to slip, slide and climb through the 'fossilised'

remains of triceratops and brontosaurs, explore caves, dig for bones and splash through a mini-waterfall. The amusing signage will go over the heads of most kids, but it is ideal for parents to let their young 'uns loose for up to an hour (although not just after the neighbouring Tarzan show has finished). TTTT (kids only).

Tarzan™ Rocks!: and he really does. This amazing show is basically a 30-minute rock concert show-casing the songs from the animated film, with special effects provided by dancers, acrobats and roller-bladers, all in wonderful costumes and superbly choreographed. Tarzan and Jane make only a brief appearance, and then mainly as acrobats (ladies – no staring at that loincloth!), while its loud, high-energy style is not everyone's cup of tea (especially for sensitive young ears), but it is visually stunning and the quality of the performers – singers, musicians and acrobats – leaves you gasping. AAAA.

© Disney Enterprises, Inc.

The Boneyard adventure playground

Cretaceous Trail: landscaped, walk-through animal encounter featuring lush, tropical forest and 'living' dinosaurs like soft-shelled turtles and Chinese crocodiles. AA.

Dining options include the **Restaurantosaurus**, counter-service burgers and hot-dogs (presented by McDonald's, so you get McDonald's fries, Chicken McNuggets and Happy Meals but no Big Macs) and two snack bars, while shopping is centred on **Chester and Hester's Dinosaur Treasures**, the 'Fossiliferous Gift Store' with groan-inducing slogans like Merchandise of Extinction, Prehistoric Prices and Last Stop for 65 Million Years!

> BRIT TIP: Restauranto-saurus also features Donald's Prehistoric Breakfastosaurus 7–10.30am with Mickey, Donald Duck and other character favourites. It costs $13.95 for adults and $7.95 for 3–11s.

Africa

The largest land in *Disney's Animal Kingdom* Theme Park, it recreates the forests, grasslands and rocky homelands of equatorial Africa's most fascinating residents in a richly landscaped setting that is part run-down port town setting and part endless savannah. The outside world seems thousands of miles away and there is hardly a glimpse of *Walt Disney World* Resort (there is one, but I'm not telling!).

Harambe, a reconstruction Kenyan port village, complete with white-coral walls and thatched roofs, is the starting point for your African adventure. The Arab-influenced Swahili culture is depicted in the native tribal costumes and architecture. Here you will find two

5

Kilimanjaro Safaris

more shops, including the **Mombasa Marketplace Ziwani Traders**, where you can suit up safari-style, and the counter-service **Tusker House Restaurant** for spit-roasted prime rib, rotisserie and fried chicken and salads, as well as four snack and drink outlets. Themed entertainment, with the African Contemporary Band, adds spice to the location and whets the appetite for the attractions in store.

Kali River Rapids

Kilimanjaro Safaris: the queuing area alone earns high marks for authenticity, preparing you for the sights and sounds of the 110-acre savannah beyond. You board a 32-passenger truck, with your driver/guide relaying information about the flora and fauna on view and a bush pilot overhead relaying stats on the wildlife, including the dangers threatening them in the real world. Hundreds of animals are carefully spread out in various habitats, with no fences in sight – the ditches and barriers are all well concealed – as you splash through fords and cross rickety bridges (will one of them collapse?), and you are likely to get a close-up view of rhinos, elephants, giraffes, zebras, lions, baboons, antelope, ostriches and hippos. Halfway round, your journey becomes a grim race to stop elephant poachers, although the outcome is fairly obvious. Once

> BRIT TIP: The best (and most jolting) ride is at the back of the truck, while the Safari is best avoided from midday to late afternoon when many animals take a siesta.

again, the authentic nature of everything you see (okay, so some of the tyre 'ruts' and termite mounds are concrete and the baobab trees are fake) is quite awesome with the spread of the vegetation and the landscaping, and the only drawbacks are the lack of photo stops along the route (and the ride can be pretty bumpy). Also you are not guaranteed to see some of the animals as they are free to roam over quite a large area and can disappear from view. The ride is not recommended for expectant mothers or anyone with back or neck problems. AAAAA (FP).

Pangani Forest Exploration Trail: as you leave the Safari you turn into an overgrown nature trail that showcases gorillas, hippos, meerkats, rare tropical birds and naked mole rats(!). You wander the trail at your own pace and visit several research stations where you can learn more about the animals on display, including the swarming, ant-like colony of naked mole rats (see, I wasn't making it up), the underwater view of the hippos (check out the size of a hippo skull and those teeth!) and the savannah overlook, where giraffe and antelope graze and the amusing meerkats frolic. The walk-through aviary gives you the chance to meet the carmine bee-eater, pygmy goose, African green pigeon, ibis and brimstone canary, among others, but the real centrepiece of the Trail is the silverback gorilla habitat, in fact, two of them. The family group can often be seen just inches away from the giant plate-glass window, while the bachelor group further along can prove more elusive. Again, the sheer natural aspect of the Trail is breathtaking and it provides a host of good photo opportunities. It is best to visit early in the day to see the animals at their most active. AAAAA.

Wildlife Express to Conservation Station: the clever little train journey here, with its peek into some of the backstage areas, is just the preamble to the park's interactive and educational exhibits, including the **Affection Section**, the petting zoo of lambs, goats, donkeys, sheep and guinea hogs. The main part of Conservation Station is quite educational, though, and aimed at children with enquiring minds. The first exhibits are interactive information stations about the environment and ecological dangers in **Song of the Rain Forest**, and the story progresses through endangered species like the manatee at the **Mermaid Tales Theater** to a self-guided tour of the park's backstage areas on interactive screens and the work of the world's eco-heroes, who can also be quizzed on screen. Finally, you can look into the wildlife tracking centre, the animal hospital, bird hatchery and neonatal care centre. You could easily spend an hour here as the environmental message sinks home, along with that of Disney's Wildlife Conservation Fund.

Asia

The final land of the park is elaborately themed as the gateway to the imaginary south-east Asian city of Anandapur, with its temples, ruined forts, landscape and wildlife.

Flights of Wonder at Caravan Stage: another wildlife show, this one showcases the talents and traits of a host of birds, built into a production of mythical proportions as a treasure-seeking student encounters Phoenix, the birds' guardian, in a crumbling, fortified town. Vultures, eagles, toucans, macaws and many other feathered friends take a bow as Phoenix reveals the treasure of the avian world. Unfortunately, the Caravan Stage where all this takes place is not air-conditioned and is fiendishly hot in summer. AAA.

Kali River Rapids: part thrill-ride, part scenic journey is this bouncy, watery, raft-ride journey that will get you pretty wet (not great for early morning in winter unless you bring a change of clothes). It starts out in tropical forest territory before launching into a scene of logging devastation, warning of the dangers of clear-cut burning. Your raft then plunges down a significant waterfall (and one unlucky soul – usually the rider with his back to the drop – gets seriously damp) before you complete your journey in more sedate style, albeit with a few more unanticipated watery encounters. Queues build up here quickly through the main part of the day and you will probably want to ride at least twice to appreciate all the clever detail involved. Restrictions: 3ft 6in. TTT (plus AAAA) (FP).

Maharajah Jungle Trek: Asia's version of the Pangani Forest Trail, this is another picturesque walk-through journey past decaying temple ruins and various animal encounters. Playful gibbons, tapirs, Komodo dragons and a bat enclosure (including the world's largest variety, the flying fox-bat) lead up to the main viewing area, the five-acre Tiger Range, which includes a pool and fountains, a popular playground early in the day for these magnificent big cats. An antelope enclosure and walk-through aviary complete this breathtaking Trek in fine style. AAAAA.

Finally, returning to the front entrance gives you the chance to sample or just visit (and shop at) the **Rainforest Café**, the second in *Walt Disney World* Resort. If you haven't seen the one at *Downtown Disney* Marketplace, you should definitely call in here to sample the amazing jungle interior with its audio-animatronic animals, waterfalls, thunderstorms and unique bar area. A three-course meal would set you back about $25 (kids' meals at $5.99), but the setting alone is worth it and the food is way above average.

For a behind-the-scenes look at *Disney's Animal Kingdom* Theme Park, the **Backstage Safari** is a wonderful 3-hour-long journey into the handling and care of the animals ($65, not for under 16s. Call 407 393 8687 to book).

5

IllumiNations at Epcot

Walt Disney World Resort at Christmas

If you can visit prior to the seriously busy days from just before Christmas Day to New Year's Day, you get the benefit of all the added decorations and atmosphere and none of the overwhelming crowds. Each of the three parks takes on a suitably festive character, with the addition of artistic artificial snow, Christmas lights and a huge, magnificently decorated fir tree.

Disney-MGM Studios also features an eye-popping extravaganza of exterior house decorations on the Backlot Tour with over 2 million lights! Donated by the Osborne family, they open up as a walk-through attraction every evening.

The Magic Kingdom Park turns Main Street into its Christmas extravaganza, with the 60-foot tree dominating the scene. There is also the unmissable Mickey's Very Merry Xmas Parade, which replaces the 3pm Disney's Magical Moments Parade in December, a positive delight for its lively music and eye-catching costumes. Another seasonal extra is the lively *Twas the Night before Xmas* show at the Galaxy Palace Theater.

Epcot is the jewel in the Christmas crown, with two outstanding extra features. At 6pm, the elaborate daily Christmas tree lighting ceremony is quite breathtaking as the rest of the park lights go out and then the World Showcase bridge and the tree itself are illuminated in dramatic stages to some grand musical accompaniment. It is tasteful, dramatic and eye-catching, but you should arrive EARLY as people start queuing two hours in advance! **Disney's Yuletide Fantasy** is an extra 3-hour tour ($55, not for under 16s) into how all the elaborate decorations are done.

Five More of the Best
(or, Expanding Orlando's Universe)

It is time to leave wonderful Walt Disney World and venture out into the rest of central Florida's great choice of attractions. And, believe me, there is still a terrific amount in store.

For a start, they don't come much more ambitious than Universal Orlando. The area that used to consist of just the one theme park, Universal Studios Florida, is fast developing into a fully fledged resort of similar scope to Disney's. A second dynamic theme park, Universal's Islands of Adventure, opened in 1999, hot on the heels of the 30-acre CityWalk entertainment district. The first resort hotel, the Portofino Bay, also made its debut in 1999, followed by the Hard Rock Hotel in 2000, and the Royal Pacific Hotel is due in 2002.

There is also a waterway network connecting the hotels to the CityWalk hub of Universal Orlando, while their multi-storey car parks, handling more than 20,000 vehicles, have done away with the need for any other transport system, and it is quite convenient to move from park to park.

The marketing tie-up with SeaWorld, Busch Gardens and Wet 'n Wild has proved another success, with the 7- and 10-day Flex Tickets both excellent value. The opening of Islands of Adventure has added a 2- and 3-day Escape Pass allowing movement between the two parks, and an experimental early-entry policy for multi-day ticket holders (extremely popular in 2000; check with your ticket supplier for the latest situation) that allowed entry at 7am, with most of the main attractions open. They were also looking into a FastTrack system for the most popular rides.

Back to the Future ... The Ride at Universal Studios

Universal Studios Florida

Universal opened its Florida park in June 1990 (it has had its original Los Angeles site open to the public since before World War II) and quickly became a serious competitor to Disney. The two are currently going head-to-head with all their new attractions and, for the visitor, it means a consistently high standard and good value in everything on offer (although the choice is beginning to be utterly bewildering!). Also, if you have already been to the LA Universal Studios, this one is better.

The obvious question to ask here is whether you need to go to Disney-MGM Studios as well as Universal, and the answer is an emphatic YES! Universal is a very different kettle of fish to Disney-MGM Studios, with a more in-your-face style of entertainment that goes down well with older kids and younger adults. Younger children are also well catered for in Woody Woodpecker's KidZone. Universal can require more than a full day in high season. As with Disney's parks, the strategies for a successful visit

Universal Studios Florida at-a-glance

Location	Off Exits 30A and 29B from I4; Universal Boulevard and Kirkman Road
Size	110 acres in seven themed areas
Hours	9am–7pm off peak; 9am–10pm high season (Washington's birthday, Easter, summer holidays, Thanksgiving, Christmas)
Admission	Under 3, free; 3–9, $37 (one-day ticket), $70 (2-Day Escape Pass), $80 (3-Day Escape Pass), $128 (7-Day, 4-Park Flex Ticket), $158 (10-Day, 5-Park Flex Ticket); adult (10+) $46, $85, $100, $160, $197.
Parking	$7
Lockers	Yes; immediately to left in Front Lot; $5 ($2 refundable)
Pushchairs **Wheelchairs**	$7 and $13 (next to Locker hire) $7 and $30 (same location)
Top Attractions	Men In Black, Jaws, Back to the Future, ET, Earthquake, Kongfrontation, Terminator 2 3-D
Don't Miss	Curious George Playground (for kids), The Blues Brothers

Hidden Costs		
	Meals	Burger, chips and coke $6.78 Three-course dinner $34 (Lombard's Landing)
	Kids' meal	$6.75 (Finnigan's and Lombard's Landing only)
	T-shirts	$16–$28
	Souvenirs	$0.95–$145
	Sundries	Universal Studios PAL video $19.95

are the same. Arrive EARLY (i.e. up to 30 minutes before the official opening time), do the main rides first, avoid main meal times if you want to eat, and step out for a few hours in the afternoon (try shopping or dining at CityWalk) if the crowds get too much.

Highlights are the new Men In Black ride, Terminator 2 3-D show, five-star simulator ride Back To The Future (state-of-the-art technology here), the Jaws ride, the Funtastic World of Hanna-Barbera (another simulator, slightly toned down for young children) and the other two blockbuster rides of Kongfrontation and Earthquake. Queues at all of these top an hour at peak periods, and even the smaller attractions get seriously busy.

Location

Universal Studios Florida® is sub-divided into six main areas, set around a huge, man-made lagoon, but there are no great distinguishing features between many of them so keep your map handy to steer yourself around. The main entrance is found just off the new exit to I4 or by the Universal Boulevard link from International Drive by Wet 'n Wild. Parking costs $7 in their massive new multi-storey car park (one of the largest in the world) and there is quite a walk (with some moving walkways) to the front gates. Once through with the madding crowd, your best bet is to turn right on to Rodeo Drive, along Hollywood Boulevard and Sunset Boulevard and into World Expo for Back to the Future … The Ride and Men In Black. From there, head straight across the bridge to Jaws, then go back along the Embarcadero for Earthquake and into New York for Twister and Kongfrontation. This will get most of the main rides under your belt early on before the crowds really build up, and you can

then take it a bit easier by putting your feet up for a while at one of the several shows. Alternatively, try to be among the early birds flocking to the blockbuster Terminator show at the entrance to Hollywood Boulevard to avoid the queues that build up very quickly for this much-publicised attraction, then head for Back to the Future and Men In Black.

Here's a full blow-by-blow guide to the Studios. For the rundown on CityWalk, see Chapter 9.

The Front Lot

Coming straight through the gates brings you into **The Front Lot**, which is basically the administrative centre, with a couple of large gift stores (have a look at these in mid-afternoon) plus The Fudge Shoppe and the Beverly Hills Boulangerie (sandwiches, pastries and tea and coffee). Call at Guest Services here for written guides for disabled visitors, TDD and assisted listening devices, as well as to make restaurant bookings. If you are here early, you can sign up to be in the audience for one of Universal's TV shows at the **Studio Audience Center**. First aid is available here and on Canal Street between New York and San Francisco, while there are facilities for nursing mothers at Family Services by the bank through the gates on the right.

Production Central

Ahead and to the left is **Production Central**, and this brings you into the main business of the park.

Hitchcock's 3-D Theater: this tribute to the film-making genius of the late Alfred Hitchcock is a touch over-long for most children at 40 minutes, although it has two separate elements to keep you guessing at what happens next. The effects from his horror film *The Birds* come to the rescue of the first

1 KONGFRONTATION
2 TWISTER
3 GUEST SERVICES
4 STUDIO AUDIENCE CENTER
5 PRODUCTION CENTRAL
6 HITCHCOCK'S 3-D THEATER
7 NICKELODEON STUDIO TOUR
8 TERMINATOR 2 3-D
9 THE FUNTASTIC WORLD OF
  HANNA-BARBERA
10 LUCY: A TRIBUTE
11 THE BONEYARD
12 EARTHQUAKE – THE BIG ONE
13 JAWS
14 BEETLEJUICE'S GRAVEYARD REVUE
15 THE WILD, WILD, WILD WEST STUNT SHOW
16 MEN IN BLACK: ALIEN ATTACK
17 BACK TO THE FUTURE . . . THE RIDE
18 ANIMAL ACTORS SHOW
19 FIEVEL'S PLAYLAND
20 ET ADVENTURE
21 THE GORY, GRUESOME & GROTESQUE
   HORROR MAKE-UP SHOW
22 AT&T AT THE MOVIES
23 A DAY IN THE PARK WITH BARNEY
24 THE BLUES BROTHERS
25 WOODY WOODPECKER'S NUTHOUSE
   COASTER
26 CURIOUS GEORGE PLAYGROUND

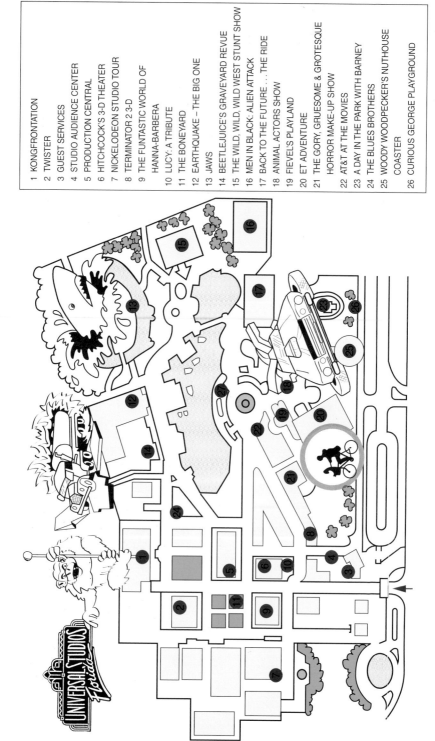

The five-storey tornado at Twister

section, which is basically just a series of clips from his 53 films for Universal Studios. Part two goes 'inside the movies' as some special effects from *The 39 Steps* are explained with film techniques. Queues build up quickly here after opening time, so save it for late in the day. It also advises parental discretion for children under 13, but few seem put off by the horror elements, which are fairly tame by modern standards. TTT.

Nickelodeon Studios: a lot of this American kids' TV series will be lost on us Brits (although it's now on satellite TV in Britain) as visitors are taken behind the scenes into the production set. All kids will be able to identify, however, with the chance to get gunged in green slime by the Gakmeister! And they'll love the restrooms which feature green slime 'soap' and sirens when you flush the loo. Long queues build up quickly, though. AAA.

The Funtastic World of Hanna-Barbera: this is one of Universal's simulator rides that is always a big hit with kids. It involves a cartoon chase of the funniest order, with your seats becoming jet-propelled in the bid to save an all-star cartoon cast. Humongous queues, so go

either first thing or late. Expectant mothers, those with heart, back or neck problems and children under 3ft 4in must use the stationary seats. TTTT.

The **Bone Yard** is now a rather

> BRIT TIP: The interactive do-it-yourself cartoon world as you exit the ride (in the Hanna-Barbera Store) is also a great place for parents to unleash the kids for half an hour (or when it rains).

depleted area reserved for famous old props after they were discarded by the films in which they starred. AA.

Almost next door to the Bone Yard, **Production Central** is a seasonal exhibit offering a close-up look at props and scenery from recent Universal film blockbusters. In 2000 it was the *Flintstones in Viva Rock Vegas*. AAA.

The main eating outlet here is the magnificently themed **Monsters Café**, specialising in salads, pasta, pizza and chicken. The counter-service area is done up like

Men in Black Alien Attack

Frankenstein's lab, with the dining areas sub-divided into Swamp, Space, Crypt and Mansion Dining, all to the accompaniment of old black and white horror film clips on the many video screens. There is also monster face painting for kids ($6–$15). Shopping includes the Hanna-Barbera Store, Jurassic Park Visitors' Center and Bates Motel Gift Shop.

New York

From Production Central you head on to **New York** and some great scene-setting in the architecture and detail of the buildings and streets. It's far too clean to be authentic, but the façades are first class and worth a closer look.

Twister: newly opened in 1998, this experience, based on the hit film, breaks new ground in live special effects as audiences are brought 'up close and personal' with the awesome destructive forces of a tornado. The five-storey terror will shatter everything in its path (okay, so it's pretty tame compared with the real thing), building to a shattering crescendo of destruction (watch out for the flying cow!). The noise is quite stunning, but it's a bit much for young children (parental discretion advised for under 12s). The pre-show area is almost a work of art but, unless you can get here early, save this for late in the day. TTTT.

Kongfrontation: Universal's engineers have really gone to town on this attraction, a full-scale encounter with the giant ape on a replica of the Roosevelt Island tram. The startlingly real special effects (King Kong even has banana breath!) and clever spiel of your tram driver all add up to a breathtaking experience that will convince you that you have met King Kong and lived to tell the tale. It's only a 5-minute ride and queues regularly

top an hour, so going early is the best plan of campaign. Restrictions; 4ft (but smaller children can ride with an adult). TTTT.

The Blues Brothers: fans of the film will not want to miss this live show as Jake and Elwood Blues (well, pretty good doubles, anyway) put on a stormin' performance on New York's Delancey Street four or five times a day. They cruise up in their Bluesmobile and go through a selection of the film's hits before heading off into the sunset, stopping only to sign a few autographs. Terrific entertainment, not to be missed. AAAA.

For dining, you have the choice of two contrasting restaurants. **Finnegan's Bar and Grill** offers the likes of shepherd's pie, fish and chips, corned beef and cabbage along with more traditional New York fare like prime rib, burgers, fries and a good range of beers as well as live Irish-tinged entertainment and Happy Hour from 5–7pm (half-price beer and wine). **Louie's Italian Restaurant** has counter-service pizza and pasta, Italian ice cream and the delicious tiramisu (the Italian version of trifle only jazzier). For shops you have the choice of Safari Outfitters Ltd (and the chance to have your picture taken in the grip of King Kong!), The Aftermath for Twister souvenirs, and Bull's Gym and Second Hand Rose for discontinued Universal merchandise bargains. New York also boasts a particularly noisy, and therefore kid-friendly, amusement arcade presented by Sega.

San Francisco/Amity

Crossing Canal Street brings you all the way across America to **San Francisco/Amity** and two of the biggest queues in the park.

Earthquake – The Big One: this three-part adventure has them lining up from first thing in the morning until almost last thing at night. Go behind the scenes first of all to two special stage sets where, with audience help, some of the special effects of the blockbuster film, starring Charlton Heston, are explained in detail. Then you enter the Bay Area Rapid Transit underground and arrive in the middle of a full-scale earthquake that will shake you to your boots. Tremble as the walls and ceilings collapse, trains collide, cars fall in on you and fire erupts all around, followed by a seeming tidal wave of water. It's not for the faint-hearted (or small children), while those who have bad backs or necks, or are pregnant, are advised not to ride. Restrictions; 4ft (but children under 4ft CAN ride if accompanied by an adult, with parental discretion). TTTT.

Jaws: the technological wizardry alone will leave you gasping on this attraction, where queues of more than an hour are commonplace. The man-made lagoon holds five million gallons of water; nearly 2,000 miles of wire run throughout the seven-acre site, which required 10,000 cubic yards of concrete and 7,500 tons of steel; and the 32-foot monster shark attacks with a thrust equal to a Boeing 727 jet engine! Yes, this is no ordinary ride (at more than $45m to build, it couldn't be) and its 6-minute duration will seem a lot longer as your hapless tour boat guide tries to steer you through an ever more spectacular series of stunts, explosions and watery menace from the Great White. Yes, of course it's only a model, but I defy you not to be impressed – and just a little terrified – by this fabulous ride. TTTTT.

Beetlejuice's Graveyard Revue: Disney-MGM Studios has Beauty and the Beast and the Little Mermaid, Universal goes for Dracula, Frankenstein, the Wolfman, the Phantom of the

Opera and Frankenstein's Bride in this 18-minute musical extravaganza. It eschews completely the twee prettiness of Disney's attractions yet still comes up with a fun family show, with versions of hits like 'Wild Thing' and 'Great Balls Of Fire' all in a spectacular stage setting, especially in the evening. AAAA.

The Wild, Wild, Wild West Stunt Show: corny gags, fistfights, explosions, high-level falls and dramatic shootouts all add up to 15 minutes of rootin', tootin' Wild West adventure, Universal Studios style. A hilarious finale and some very loud bangs (not good for small children) are accompanied by large crowds, but the auditorium seats almost 2,000 so there is usually no serious queuing here (provided you arrive 15 minutes early). AAAA.

San Francisco also has the best choice of eating establishments in the park, with **Lombard's Landing** the pick of the bunch (reservations accepted). Great seafood, pasta and sandwiches are accompanied by a good view out over the main lagoon, and there is a separate pastry shop for desserts and coffee. **Richter's Burger Co.** offers a few interesting burger variations, while the **Midway Grill** serves smoked sausages and Italian sausage hoagies. For a quick snack, **Chez Alcatraz** has shrimp cocktails, clam chowder and speciality hot sandwiches, while **Boardwalk Snacks** does corn dogs, chicken fingers, candy floss and frozen yoghurt.

For shopping, try Quint's Nautical Treasures for seaside souvenirs and Shaiken's Souvenirs for more up-market mementoes. The added attraction of this area is a boardwalk of fairground games (which will cost you an extra few dollars to take part), including a Guess Your Weight stall which usually attracts a good crowd for the fun patter of the person in charge.

6

Six tons of howling fury awaits visitors in Kongfrontation

Expo Center

Crossing the footbridge from Amity brings you into **Expo Center** and Universal's other five-star thrill attraction.

Back To The Future ... The Ride: simulators just do not come more realistic than this journey through space and time in Dr Emmit Brown's time-travelling De Lorean. The queues are immense, but a lot of the queuing time is taken up by some attention-grabbing pre-ride information on the many TV screens above your head. Once you reach the front of the queue, there is still more information to digest and clever surroundings to convince you of the scientific nature of it all. Then it's into your time-travelling car and off in hot pursuit of baddie Biff, who has stolen another time-car. The huge, wraparound screen and violent movements of your vehicle bring

the realism of the ride to a peak, and it all adds up to a huge experience, well worth the wait. Restrictions; 3ft 4in. TTTTT.

Men In Black – Alien Attack: new in 2000 and huge fun (especially for kids) is this combination thrill/ scenic ride which takes up where the hit film starring Will Smith and Tommy Lee Jones left off. Visitors are secretly introduced to the MIB Institute in a wonderfully inventive mock-futuristic setting and enrolled as trainees for a battle around the streets of New York with a horde of escaped aliens. Your six-person car is equipped with laser zappers for an interactive shoot-out that is like a real-life arcade game as the aliens can also shoot back and send your car spinning out of control. The finale features a close encounter with a 30ft bug that is all mouth – will you survive? Only your collective shooting skill can save the day, and

Excitement at the Terminator 2 experience

> BRIT TIP: Along the lagoon in the World Expo/KidZone area is Central Park, a quiet area where you can escape the theme park whirl for a while.

there are numerous ride variations according to your accuracy as each rider's score is totted up. Will Smith and Rip Torn are your on-screen hosts, and Will returns at the end to reveal if your score makes you Galaxy Defenders, Cosmically Average or Bug Bait! Fast, frantic and a bit confusing, this will have you coming back for more until you can score over 250,000 (Defender status). Restrictions; 4ft 6in. TTTT. (Beat my best score – 256,410!)

For food here there is the **International Food Bazaar** (a food court-style indoor diner) offering Greek, Italian, Chinese, German and American dishes in air-conditioned comfort.

Woody Woodpecker's Nuthouse Coaster

Woody Woodpecker's KidZone

Animal Actors Stage: prepare to be amazed now by the feats of acting giants like Lassie, Mr Ed, Beethoven and Babe as they put on their own show to upstage all those pesky humans. It's a big theatre, too, and there is never much of a wait, so roll up and see those dogs put their trainers through the hoops! This is also a good one to avoid the afternooon crowds. AAAA.

Fievel's Playland: strictly for kids but also a big hit with parents for taking them off their hands for a good half-hour or so, this playground based on the enlarged world of the cartoon mouse offers youngsters the chance to bounce under a 1,000-gallon hat, crawl through a giant cowboy boot, climb a 30-foot spider's web and shoot the rapids (a 200ft water slide) in Fievel's sardine can. TTTT (young 'uns only!).

A Day in the Park with Barney: again, this is strictly for the younger set (ages 2–5). The purple dinosaur from the hugely popular kids' TV show is brought to Super-Dee-Duper life on stage in a 65,000-sq-ft arena that features a pre-show before the main event, which lasts about 15 minutes, plus an interactive post-show area. The show and its jokes are guaranteed to make mum and dad cringe, but the youngsters seem to love it and they are the best judges in this instance. PS: Check out the state-of-the-art restrooms! AAA (AAAAA under 5s).

ET Adventure: this is as glorious as scenic rides come, with a picturesque queuing area made up like the pine woods from the film and then a spectacular leap on the trademark flying bicycles to save ET's home planet. Steven Spielberg (Universal's creative consultant) has added some extra special effects and characters, and the whole experience is a huge hit with young to teenage kids and their parents. Queues here occasionally touch two hours at peak periods, so be aware that you need to do this one either early or late. There is a 4ft height restriction, but smaller children can ride with parents. AAAAA.

Woody Woodpecker's Nuthouse Coaster: anchoring this excellent under 10s' adventure land is this child-sized but still quite racy roller-coaster. The brilliant red 800ft track reaches only 28ft high and 22mph, but it will seem like the real deal to the youngsters. Minimum ride age is 3 years old and children under 4ft must be accompanied by an adult. TTTT (juniors only).

Curious George Goes to Town: this American children's book character means little to me, but kids of all ages will just love this amazing adventure playground with its huge range of activities – and plenty of opportunities to get wet (it is definitely advisable to bring swimsuits or a change of clothing for them here). It combines toddler play, water-based play stations and a hands-on interactive ball area, and adds up to a real boon to harassed parents. The town theme, upon which Curious George has wreaked havoc, includes buildings to climb, pumps, hoses and sprays to get wet with, a ball factory in which to shoot, dump and blast thousands of foam balls and – the tour de force – two 500-gallon buckets of water on the clock tower balconies which regularly dump their contents in spectacular fashion on the street below. TTTTT (under 12s only).

For snacks, **Animal Crackers**, offers hot-dogs, chicken fingers, smoked sausage hoagies and frozen yoghurt. Shop at Back to the Future Gifts, Universal's Cartoon Store, the Barney Store or ET's Toy Closet and Photo Spot.

Hollywood

Finally, your circular tour of Universal brings you back towards the main entrance via **Hollywood** (where else?). Visit **AT&T at the Movies** for a number of hands-on exhibits taking you through the history and future of film-making. Another unusual attraction is the **Gory, Gruesome and Grotesque Horror Make-Up Show** (not recommended for under 13s) which demonstrates some of the often highly amusing ways in which films have attempted to terrorise us. It's a 20-minute show, queues are rarely long and the secrets of the special effects are well worth learning. AAA.

Terminator 2: 3-D Battle Across Time: another first-of-its-kind attraction, this is quite hard to describe accurately. Part film, part show, part experience but all action, it cost a staggering $60 million to produce and is guaranteed to leave its audience stunned and awed. The 'Wow!' factor really works overtime here as you go through a 10-minute pre-show to represent a trip into the workshops of the Cyberdyne Systems, from the *Terminator* films, and then into a 700-seater auditorium for a 'presentation' on the company's latest robot creations. Needless to say, nothing runs according to plan and the audience is subjected to a mind-boggling array of (loud) special effects, including indoor pyrotechnics, real actors interacting with the screen and the audience, and a climactic 3-D film finale that takes the original film sequence a step further. The original cast, including Arnold Schwarzenegger and director James Cameron, all collaborated on the new 12-minute film footage (which, at $24 million, is the most expensive frame-for-frame film ever made) and the overall effect of this technological marvel is simply dazzling. Needless to say, you need to arrive early or expect queues well in excess of an hour all day. Not recommended for under 11s. TTTTT.

The last attraction (or first, depending on which way you go round the park) is **Lucy: A Tribute**, which will mean little to all but devoted fans of the late Lucille Ball and her 60s TV comedy *The Lucy Show*. Classic shows, home movies, costumes and scripts are all paraded for close viewing, but youngsters will find it rather tedious. AA.

If you haven't eaten by now there is a choice of four contrasting but highly enjoyable eateries. **Mel's Drive-In**, a re-creation from the film *American Graffiti*, serves all manner of burgers, hot-dogs and milkshakes, while **Café La Bamba**, a counter-service Mexican diner, offers tacos, burgers, barbecue chicken and steak, with margaritas and beer (Happy Hour 3–6pm). There is also **Schwab's Pharmacy** for old-fashioned milkshakes, sundaes and ice cream cones and the **Beverly Hills Boulangerie** for baked breakfast treats, pastries, juices and coffee. Shop for hats in the Brown Derby, for *Terminator* gifts and clothing in Cyber Image, for movie memorabilia (especially Lucille Ball) at Silver Screen Collectibles and for some of the smartest but most expensive clothing, hats and sunglasses at Studio Styles.

Photo opportunities

In addition to all the set-piece action, watch out for photo and autograph opportunities with cartoon characters like Scooby Doo, Fred Flintstone, Woody Woodpecker and Yogi Bear, and filmstar lookalikes of Charlie Chaplin, WC Fields, Marilyn Monroe and Groucho Marx.

The Studios also feature some brilliant extra entertainment for

Terminator 2 3-D

Mardi Gras (in March) and Hallowe'en, when their **Horror Nights** (throughout much of October) add a wonderfully bloodthirsty touch, as well as New Year's Eve and the Fourth of July, when the park gets into full party mode. There is an extra charge, however, for the attractions of Hallowe'en, when the Universal designers turn the park into recreations and set-pieces from various horror movies, with a parade and shows that include live character interaction. It is definitely not for kids (but goes down a treat with adults with the right sense of humour). The grisly fun of Hallowe'en Horror Night begins each evening at 7.30pm and costs $46, or an extra $19–$25 if you up-grade your Universal Studios ticket on the day.

Sadly, as part of their on-going updating process, Universal have closed down their Dynamite Nights water stunt show which used to be the evening finale and there is no news of a replacement for the central lagoon area. The Hercules and Xena show (which replaced the original Murder She Wrote Mystery Theater) has also bitten the theatrical dust and we await developments of the space there with interest. As ever, for up-to-the-minute Universal hints, gossip and advice, you can check out www.usfinfo.com. The park's change of ownership in summer 2000 from Rank and Seagram to Blackstone and giant French conglomerate Vivendi (which cost the latter some $30 billion!) promised to provide a further boost to Universal's growth curve, so stay tuned!

Islands of Adventure

In May 1999, Universal's creative consultant Steven Spielberg officially opened £1billion IoA, as it is known, with the words: 'These are not just theme park rides, these are entertainment achievements beyond anything I have ever seen anywhere else in the world.'

And that's only the beginning. Here is the most complete and thrilling theme park on offer. Complete, because the park is a genuinely rounded and consistent concept that has been carried through to the full extent of its designers' aims. And thrilling because it contains more T-rides (and the first TTTTT+ ratings) per square inch than almost all the other parks put together.

It has a full range of attractions from the real adrenalin overloads to pure family entertainment, the shopping and eating opportunities are way above average, and it even *sounds* good (with some 40 pieces of original music, you can even buy the CD of the theme park!). Okay, so they are not really *islands* (the six themed 'lands' form a chain around the central lagoon), but otherwise you get a lot more than you bargained for, unless you have extremely timid children under 5, in which case The Magic Kingdom is still your best bet. Seuss Landing has enough to keep them amused for several hours, and Camp Jurassic is a clever adventure playground for the 5–12 age range, but the rest of the park, with its seven five-star thrill rides and other heavyweight attractions is primarily geared to kids of 8-plus, their parents, and especially teenagers (although two new rides in summer 2000 are geared towards under 12s). There are five elements that look truly alarming (two of which produce moments of supreme terror), but

don't be put off – they all deliver a magnificent experience. In fact, there is as much spectator value as ride fun in some of the attractions!

If there is one ride that sums up the achievements of IoA, it is the Amazing Adventures of Spider-Man, the world's first moving 3-D simulator ride. It is guaranteed to leave you in awe of its technical wizardry and imagination, and it is the only ride I have seen where the people applaud at the end!

Port of Entry

You arrive for IoA as you do for Universal Studios Florida in the big multi-storey car parks ($7) off Universal Boulevard and either walk or ride the moving walkways into CityWalk, where you continue through to the entrance plaza (head for the 130ft-high Pharos Lighthouse).

Once through the gates, the lockers, pushchair and wheelchair hire are all immediately to your left as the **Port of Entry** opens up before you. This elaborate 'village' consists primarily of shops and eateries, so push straight on until you hit the main lagoon. Later in the day, return to Port of Entry to check out the fully themed retail

One Fish Two Fish …

experience at places like **Silk Roads Toy Shoppe**, the **IoA Trading Company** and **Ocean Trader Market,** enjoy a snack from **Spice Island Wings & Fries** or the **Croissant Moon Bakery** or chill out with a soft drink or Belgian waffle from the **Arctic Express.** Alternatively, sit down for lunch or dinner at **Confisco Grille** (and meet a range of IoA characters from noon to 2pm every day) or grab a beverage at the **Backwater Bar**. Above all, take a closer look at the wonderful

architecture, which borrows from Middle East, Far East and African themes and includes odd bits of bric-a-brac from all over the world dotted around the balconies.

When you come to the end of the Port thoroughfare, you are faced with three choices, and this is where you need a plan of campaign. There are five attractions where the queues build up quickly and remain that way. If you are here for the big thrill rides, turn left into Marvel Super-Hero Island and head straight to

Islands of Adventure at-a-glance

Location	Off Exits 30A and 29B from I4; Universal Boulevard and Kirkman Road
Size	110 acres in six 'islands'
Hours	9am–7pm off peak; 9am–10pm high season (Washington's Birthday, Easter, summer holidays, Thanksgiving, Christmas)
Admission	Under 3, free; 3–9, $37 (one-day ticket), $70 (2-Day Escape Pass), $95 (3-Day Escape Pass), $128 (7-Day, 4-Park Flex Ticket), $158 (10-Day, 5-Park Flex Ticket); adult (10+) $46, $85, $100, $160, $197.
Parking	$7
Lockers	Yes; immediately to left through main gates; $5 ($2 refundable)
Pushchairs **Wheelchairs**	$7 and $13 (next to Locker hire) $7 and $30 (same location)
Top Attractions	Amazing Adventures of Spider-Man, Dueling Dragons, Incredible Hulk Coaster, Jurassic Park River Adventure, Dudley Do-Right's Ripsaw Falls
Don't Miss	Eighth Voyage of Sindbad, Poseidon's Fury, Jurassic Park Discovery Centre, If I Ran the Zoo playground (for kids)

Hidden Costs	**Meals**	Burger, chips and coke $7.28 Three-course dinner $30 (Mythos Restaurant)
	Kids' meal	$5–$5.99
	T-shirts	$18–$25
	Souvenirs	$2.95–$250
	Sundries	Dr Seuss character photos $12.95 and $17.95

Spider-Man, then do Dr Doom's Fearfall and the Incredible Hulk Coaster. Alternatively, dinosaur fans should jump in one of the Island Skipper boats for the trip across the lagoon to Jurassic Park, where you should be able to do the Triceratops Encounter and River Adventure before the majority arrive. Once you are nice and wet, you might as well go straight to Toon Lagoon and get Ripsaw Falls and the Bilge-Rat Barges under your belt.

If you have younger children, turn right into the amazing multi-coloured world that is Seuss Landing and take advantage of the Cat in the Hat and other family-friendly rides prior to the crowd build-up.

Marvel Super-Hero Island

Taking the journey in a clockwise direction, you arrive first in the elaborate comic-book pages of the super-heroes. As with all the Islands, the experience is an immersive one. The amazing façades of this two-dimensional world swallow you up and surround you with a totally believable alternative reality that is one of the park's great triumphs – and that is before you have ridden the rides.

The Incredible Hulk Coaster: roller-coasters don't come any more dramatic than this giant green edifice that soars out over the lagoon, blasting 0–40mph in 2 seconds and reaching a top speed of around 65mph. It looks awesome, it sounds stunning, and it rides like a demon as you enter the gamma-ray world of Dr Bruce Banner, aka the Incredible Hulk. You zoom straight

BRIT TIP: Keep left where the queue splits up and you will be in line for the front car for an even more extreme experience.

into a weightless inversion 100ft up, and it keeps getting better!

Just watching is quite mind-boggling, and the after-effects are distinctly brain-scrambling. You will need to deposit ANY loose articles (sunglasses, cameras, coins, etc.) in the lockers provided at the front of the building as the ride is guaranteed to shake just about anything free. Crowds build up rapidly here, but the queues move quite quickly. Restrictions; 4ft 6in. TTTTT+.

The Amazing Adventures of Spider-Man: just queuing is a novel experience as your visit to the *Daily Bugle*, home of ace reporter Peter Parker (or Spider-Man to his enemies), unravels into a reporting secondment in one of the 'Scoop' vehicles. Prepare yourself for an audio-visual extravaganza as the combination of 3-D and motion simulator takes you into a battle between Spidey and arch-villains like Dr Octopus with his anti-gravity gun, culminating in a 400ft sensory drop off a skyscraper as the contest literally hots up. There are numerous jaw-dropping special effects and you will probably need to ride at least twice to appreciate all there is to see. In fact, you'll see it and you still won't believe it, and I defy anyone to be unimpressed. Do this ride early on or expect to queue for an hour or more. Restrictions; 3ft 4in. TTTTT+.

Dr Doom's Fearfall: stand by for one of those two moments of supreme terror I mentioned earlier. This is where, O hapless visitor, you have wandered into the lair of the evil Dr Doom – arch-enemy of the Fantastic Four – and his sinister cohorts. His latest creation is the Fearfall, a device for sucking every last ounce of fear out of its victims, and YOU are about to test it. Four riders at a time are strapped into chairs at the bottom of one of the two 200ft towers, the dry ice rolls, and whoooosh! Up you go at

6

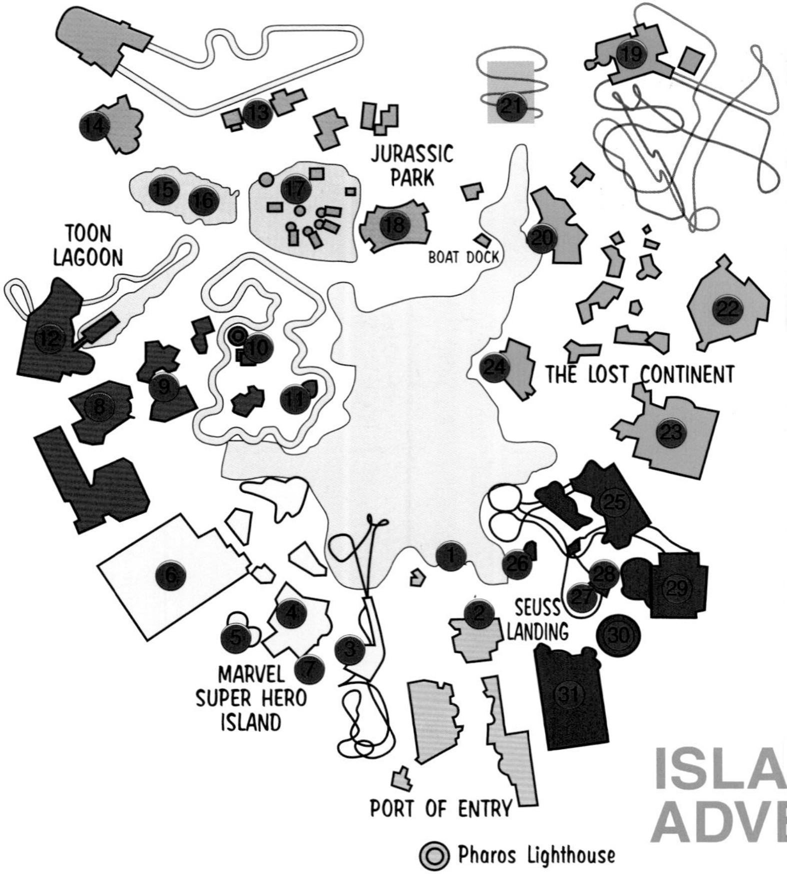

PORT OF ENTRY
1 Island Skipper Tours
2 Confisco Grille

MARVEL SUPER-HERO ISLAND
3 Incredible Hulk Coaster
4 Café 4
5 Doctor Doom's Fearfall
6 The Amazing Adventures of Spider-Man
7 Storm Force

TOON LAGOON
8 Comic Strip Café
9 Comic Strip Lane
10 Popeye & Bluto's Bilge-Rat Barges
11 Me Ship, The Olive
12 Dudley Do-Right's Ripsaw Falls

JURASSIC PARK
13 Jurassic Park River Adventure
14 Thunder Falls Terrace
15 Camp Jurassic
16 Pteranodon Flyers
17 Triceratops Encounter
18 Jurassic Park Discovery Center

THE LOST CONTINENT
19 Dueling Dragons
20 The Enchanted Oak Tavern (and Alchemy Bar)
21 The Flying Unicorn
22 The Eighth Voyage of Sindbad
23 Poseidon's Fury: Escape from the Lost City
24 Mythos Restaurant

SEUSS LANDING
25 Sylvester McMonkey McBean's Very Unusual Driving Machines (2001)
26 Green Eggs & Ham Café
27 If I Ran The Zoo
28 Caro-Seuss-el
29 Circus McGurkus Café Stoo-pendous
30 One Fish Two Fish Red Fish Blue Fish
31 The Cat in the Hat

ISLANDS OF ADVENTURE

© Pharos Lighthouse

THE LOST CONTINENT

BOAT DOCK

JURASSIC PARK

TOON LAGOON

SEUSS LANDING

PORT OF ENTRY

MARVEL SUPER HERO ISLAND

breakneck speed, only to plummet back seemingly even faster, with an amazing split-second in between when you feel suspended, weightless in mid-air. Summon up the courage to do this one and I promise a truly astonishing experience. Queues are also substantial during the main part of the day. Restrictions; 4ft 4in, and I reckon this is way too scary for under 10s. TTTTT+.

You exit Fearfall into the inevitable high-energy video arcade, or you may prefer to calm your nerves with a meal at the Italian buffeteria **Café 4** (pizza, spaghetti, sandwiches and salads) or a burger at the **Captain America Diner**. For shopping, each of the rides has its own character merchandise, while the **Comics Shop** and **Marvel Alterniverse** sell other souvenirs.

Storm Force: this new ride, aimed primarily at youngsters, was due to open in late summer 2000. It puts you in the middle of a battle between X-Men super-heroine Storm and arch-nemesis Magneto, with a full range of visual and sound effects. It is a fast, spinning, 360-degree whirl through an up-dated version of typical fairground attractions. Expected rating: TTT (TTTTT under 12s).

You can also meet the Marvel Super-Heroes for character autographs several times a day on the main street.

Toon Lagoon

The thrills continue here, albeit with a watery theme and with another comic-book element brought to life, that of the newspaper cartoon characters. Children will love the chance to play with the fountains, squirt pools and overflowing fire hydrants, plus their purpose-built playland **Me Ship, The Olive**, a three-storey boat full of interactive fun and games, including slides, bells and water cannons (with which to

squirt passers-by on the Bilge-Rat Barges below) in best Popeye style. TTTT (youngsters only). Have plenty of film here.

Popeye & Bluto's Bilge-Rat Barges: every park seems to have a variation on the white-water raft ride, but none is so outrageously themed and downright wet as this one. It's fast, bouncy and unpredictable, with water coming at you from every direction, a couple of sizeable drops and a whirl through the Octoplus Grotto that adds to the huge amount of fun. If you don't want to get wet, don't ride, because there is just no escaping the deluge here. This is also one of the top five rides for queues, but it's worth the wait. Restrictions; 3ft 6in. TTTTT.

6

BRIT TIP: A change of clothes is often advisable after riding the Barges, unless it's so hot you need to cool down in a hurry. Bring a waterproof bag for your valuables, too.

Dudley Do-Right's Ripsaw Falls: Universal's designers have again taken an existing ride concept and given it a new spin as this becomes the first flume ride to send its passengers *through* the water surface and out the other side at high speed. You join guileless mountie Dudley Do-Right, from the *Rocky and Bullwinkle* cartoon series, in a series of adventures to save girlfriend Nell from the evil Snidely Whiplash. The action builds (as does the height of the ride) to an explosive showdown at the top of a 60ft precipice that drops you down, in almost sheer fashion, through the rooftop of a ramshackle dynamite shack and into the 400,000-galloon lagoon below. Just awesome – as are the queues from mid-morning to late afternoon. Wet? You bet! Restrictions; 3ft 8in. TTTTT.

After you have dried off, take a walk along **Comic Strip Lane** to meet up with characters like Beetle Bailey, Hagar the Horrible, Krazy Kat and Blondie (some of whom will mean little to a British audience), brought to life for the first time. There is the usual array of character shopping outlets, like **Gasoline Alley** and **Toon Extra**, while you can grab a truly humongous sandwich at **Blondie's: Home of the Dagwood**, a trademark hamburger or hot-dog at **Wimpy's**, sample the food court in the **Comic Strip Café** or tuck into something colder at **Cathy's Ice Cream**.

Watch out for appearances of the **Toon Trolley** for a meet-and-greet with the Lagoon's various characters.

Jurassic Park

Leaving the comic-book lands behind, you travel back in time to the Cretaceous period and the utterly credible make-believe of the dinosaur film world. Again, the immersive experience is first class and the lavish scenery is enough to have you looking over your shoulder for stray dinos.

Jurassic Park River Adventure: the mood change from scenic splendour to hidden menace is startling as your journey into this magnificent waterborne realm brings you up close and personal with the most realistic dinosaurs created to date. Inevitably, your passage is diverted from the safe to the hazardous, and the danger increases as the 16-person raft climbs into the heights of the main building – with raptors loose everywhere. You are aware of something large lurking in the shadows – will you fall prey to the T-Rex, or will your boat take the 85ft plunge to safety (with a good soaking for all concerned)? I'll leave you to decide. Queues usually move

quite briskly here. Restrictions; 3ft 6in. TTTTT.

Triceratops Encounter: this is your face-to-face meeting with the park's resident 4-ton, 24ft-long 'living' dinosaur, which reacts to both its handler and visitors. The spiel is amusing and educational and the 'Trike' pretty convincing, especially for children. It also draws a crowd and there is little shade (one of the few minus points), but the queues do move steadily. AAAA.

Pteranodon Flyers: the slow-moving queues are a major turn-off, especially for a fairly average ride, which glides gently over much of Jurassic Park. It is designed mainly for kids, though, and the height range of 3ft–4ft 8in requires anyone over the upper limit (usually that is the over 11s) to be accompanied by a child of the right height! TTT.

Camp Jurassic: more excellent kids' fare here with the mountainous jungle giving way to an 'active' ancient volcano for youngsters to explore, climb over and slide down. Squirt guns and 'Spitter' dinosaurs add to the fun. TTTT (children first, but parents may explore too!).

Discovery Center: the designers' imagination has gone into overdrive here with terrific results. Interactive opportunities include creating a dinosaur through DNA sequencing, mixing your own DNA with a dino via a computer touchscreen, seeing through the eyes of various large reptiles and even watching a baby raptor hatch, plus a host of other hands-on exhibits that are fun and educational. This is also a good visit in the hotter part of the day. AAAA.

Best of the shopping is in the Discovery Center itself, while you can chow down at the **Burger Digs** there, visit the **Pizza Predatoria** or the **Watering Hole**, or go for the rotisserie chicken at the rustic **ThunderFalls Terrace** (counter service), which boasts a great view of the River Adventure splash-down.

The Lost Continent

This is one of my favourite lands for its original theming, gentle contrast after Jurassic Park, superb attractions, great eating options and a few amusing 'extras'.

Dueling Dragons: there is no disguising the intense nature of this magnificent double coaster, with its 100ft drop, multiple loops, twists and three near-miss encounters. There is a lot more, too, as the queuing area is a real mind-boggler – 1,060 yards, most of it along a dark tortuous path through the ancient castle that is the domain of the dragons, Fire and Ice. You get their story while you stand in line, and Merlin arrives in time to cast a spell and ensure you survive. You choose which dragon to ride (the tracks differ slightly), and you can then join an additional queue for the front seats. Unlike the Hulk, this is a suspended coaster, so your legs dangle free, and the initial drop is like going into free-fall (Supreme Terror moment Number Two!). Coaster afficionados reckon the best ride is in the back of the Ice (Blue) dragon, but it's all pretty amazing. Restrictions; 4ft 6in, and you will need to take advantage of the lockers provided to the left of the entrance in which to leave your loose articles. TTTTT+.

The Flying Unicorn: another new ride in late 2000, this junior-sized roller-coaster is also aimed primarily at youngsters. It is due to feature an elaborate wizard's workshop, hidden in an enchanted wood, that is the gateway to a magical journey inspired by the Unicorn. Expected rating: TTTT (for 6–12s).

The Eighth Voyage of Sindbad: this stunt and special effects show is another marvel, as much for its elaborate staging as for its performance. Mythical adventurer Sindbad and his side-kick Kabob (a name that's the cue for a truly awful pun) tackle the evil witch Miseria in a bid to rescue Princess Amoura, and the action springs up in surprising places. There are several loud bangs which could scare young children, but otherwise it is good, family fun. At peak times, arrive 15 minutes before showtime, but everyone usually gets in. TTT/AAAA.

Poseidon's Fury: Escape from the Lost City: this is a walk-through show that puts its audience at the heart of the action as you journey beneath the sea to the lost city of Atlantis. Again, there is a terrific element of suspense, so I won't reveal any surprises, but the showdown between Poseidon and Zeus is amazing as the arena seems to explode in water and fire around you. Queuing is a bit slow, but that's a bonus in summer as you are inside. TTTT.

Check out **Metal Smiths** for unusual trinkets, **Treasures of Poseidon** and **Shop of Wonders** for more up-market gifts and the **Psychic Readings** tent in Sindbad's Village for something new. The **Fire-Eater's Grill** (sausages, fries and drinks), **Frozen Desert** and **Oasis Coolers** provide the snacks, while there are the magnificent **Enchanted Oak Tavern** (in the dark, cool interior of a vast, sculpted oak tree, and with its Alchemy Bar) for counter-service meals (hickory-smoked chicken, ribs and salads) and the ultra-elaborate **Mythos Restaurant** for the best dining experience in IoA. Not only is the food great (seafood, grills, pizza and pasta), but the setting, inside a dormant volcano with streams, fountains and clever lighting, is an attraction in its own right.

Finally, watch out for **The Mystic Fountain** in Sindbad's Village – it has the ability to get you very wet when you least expect it!

6

Dr Doom's Fearfall

Seuss Landing

There is not a straight line to be seen in this vivid 3-D working of the books of Dr Seuss. The characters may not mean much to those unfamiliar with the children's stories, but everyone can relate to the fun here (although queues build up quickly for all rides). There is so much clever detail packed in, from squirt ponds to beach scenes, it is easy to miss something, so take your time.

Caro-Seuss-el: this intricate carousel ride on some of the Seuss characters – like cowfish, elephant-birds and dog-a-lopes – has rider-activated features sure to go down well with the young ones. AAA (AAAA under 5s).

One Fish Two Fish Red Fish Blue Fish: another fairground ride is given a twist here as you get to pilot these Seussian fish up and down according to the special rhyme that plays while you ride. Get it wrong and you get squirted! A big hit with the kids. TTT (TTTTT under 5s).

The Cat in the Hat: prepare for a ride with a difference as you board these crazy six-passenger 'couches' and meet the world's most adventurous Cat and his friends, Thing One and Thing Two. You literally go for a spin through this storybook world, and it may be a bit too much for very young children. The slow-moving queues are a bit of a drag, so try to get here early or leave it until much later in the day. AAAA (plus TTT).

If I Ran the Zoo: interactive playgrounds don't get much more fun for the pre-school brigade as they get 19 different Seuss character scenarios, most of which can get them quite wet. Hugely imaginative and great fun just to watch. TTTTT (young 'uns only).

Sylvester McMonkey McBean's Very Unusual Driving Machines (due to open in 2001): here's another novelty, an elevated ride around Seuss Landing on interactive cars that bump and honk their way round a track that runs in and out of many buildings, including the Circus McGurkus. AAAA (expected).

Jurassic Park River Adventure

Dr Seuss Presents: A Something for Everyone: specially for the youngsters is this 15-minute musical performance featuring travelling salesman Slinky Fuddnuddler and characters like Horton the Elephant, the Grinch and Thing One and Thing Two. AA (AAAA under 5s).

If you have been captivated by the land, you can buy the book at **Dr Seuss' All the Books You Can Read** store, or visit the **Mulberry Street Store** for all the characters. **Snookers & Snookers Sweet Candy Cookers** is a super sweet shop, while snacks and drinks can be had at **Hop on Pop Ice Cream Shop** and **Moose Juice Goose Juice**. **Circus McGurkus Café Stoo-pendous** is the mind-boggling cafeteria eatery for fried chicken, lasagne, pizzas and spaghetti, complete with clowns and pipe organs, while **Green Eggs and Ham Café** is a must for all Seuss fans to try the meal of the same name (and the eggs *are* green!).

To make sure they are extra family-friendly, there are private nursing facilities, an open area for feeding and resting (with high-chairs) and nappy-changing stations at the **Family Service Facility** at guest services (to the right inside the main gates), while ALL restrooms throughout the park are equipped with **nappy-changing** facilities. **First aid** is provided in Sindbad's Village in the Lost Continent, across from Oasis Coolers.

At peak periods, there is even a nightly **firework show** to provide a fitting finale to the day.

And that, my friends, is the full low-down on very possibly the best theme park in the world to date. Miss it at your peril.

6

The Dueling Dragons roller coaster

SeaWorld Adventure Park

Just a few years ago, SeaWorld was the ideal place in which to become gently acquainted with the idea of running yourself ragged in the cause of enjoyment in Florida. It was quiet, low-key and happy to live in the Second Division of the entertainment world. Not any more.

A dramatic and highly successful development programme by corporate owners the Anheuser-Busch Company has given SeaWorld the big-park treatment with an impressive new 12-acre entrance plaza and rebranding as an Adventure Park, and it is now one of the most refreshing and vibrant of them all, demanding a full day's attention.

The opening, in summer 2000, of an exclusive sister park to SeaWorld – Discovery Cove, an exotic tropical island with dolphin, stingray and snorkelling adventures – has added even more to this process.

Happily, the queues and crowds here have yet to reach the monster proportions of elsewhere, so this is a park where you can still proceed at a relatively leisurely pace, see what you want to see without too much shoulder-jostling and yet feel you have been superbly entertained (even if meal-times do get crowded in the various restaurants around the park).

SeaWorld is still a good starting point if this is your first visit to Orlando as it will give you the hang of negotiating the vast areas, navigating by the various maps and learning to plan your visit around the different showtimes which all the parks offer. There is also a strong educational and environmental message to much of what you see. To underline the educational points, there are three hour-long behind-the-scenes tours (book up as soon as you enter) which provide a greater insight into SeaWorld's marine conservation, rescue and research programme, as well as their entertainment resources. You can take the 1-hour **Polar Expedition,** which provides a close-up of the penguin and polar bear environments, **To the Rescue**, which showcases the park's animal rescue and rehabilitation programme, or the **Sharks!** tour for a backstage view of Terrors of the Deep. You have to pay an extra $6.95 ($5.95 for children) for these tours, but they are worth it and, if you take one of them early on, they will increase your appreciation of the rest of the park.

Two recent additions are the 5½-hour **Adventure Express Tour**, which offers guests their own guide to tour the park, with back-door access to the rides, reserved seating at shows and animal feeding opportunities (an extra $55 for adults, $50 for 3–9s; book up first thing at the Guided Tours counter), and the **Trainer For A Day**, an 8-hour programme open to just three people (at least 13 years old and in good physical condition), a day which shows how SeaWorld trainers care for and train their animals (cost is $349, including T-shirt, waterproof disposable camera and lunch with trainers; for reservations, call 407 370 1382).

Location

SeaWorld is located off Central Florida parkway, between I4 (exit 27A going [north] east or 28 heading [south] west) and International Drive, and the parking fee is $6. It is still a good idea to arrive a bit before the officially scheduled opening time so you're in good position to book one of the backstage tours at a time convenient to you or scamper off to one of the few attractions that does draw crowds, like **Wild Arctic**, **Journey to Atlantis** and, new in 2000, the **Kraken** roller-coaster.

The park covers in excess of 200 acres, with nine shows (ten with the nightly Aloha Polynesian Dinner Show which costs an extra $35, $24 for 8–12s and $12 for 3–7s, and for which you don't necessarily have to visit the rest of the park, tel 407 351 3600 to book), ten large-scale continuous viewing attractions and nine smaller ones, plus relaxing gardens, a kids' play area and a particularly smart range of shops (which is a noticeable feature of the Anheuser-Busch parks). Their hire pushchairs (strollers) are also the most amusing – shaped like baby dolphins so you push them along by the tail. Be warned, though, the size of the park will take you by surprise and requires a lot of to-ing and fro-ing to catch the various shows, which can be wearing. Keep a close grip on your map and entertainment schedule and try to establish your own programme that gives you regular time-outs to sit and enjoy some of the quieter spots. For something different, you can also sign up for the free 35-minute Anheuser-Busch Beer School at the Hospitality Center for a glimpse into beer-making (and tasting!). Here's how the attractions line up.

Wild Arctic: this interactive ride-and-view experience provides a

SeaWorld Adventure Park at-a-glance

Location	7007 SeaWorld Drive, off Central Florida Parkway (Junctions 27A and 28 off I4)
Size	More than 200 acres, incorporating 25 attractions
Hours	9am–7pm off peak; 9am–10pm high season (Easter, summer holidays, Thanksgiving, Christmas)
Admission	Under 3, free; 3–9, $37 (one-day ticket), $127.95 (7-Day Flex Ticket), $157.95 (10-Day Flex Ticket); adult (10+) $46, $159.95, $196.95
Parking	$6
Lockers	Yes, by main entrance; $1.50
Pushchairs	$8 and $814 (from Information Centre, to left of main entrance)
Wheelchairs	$6 and $30 (same location)
Top Attractions	Shamu Stadium, Terrors of the Deep, Journey to Atlantis, Kraken, Wild Arctic
Don't Miss	Red, Bright & Blue Fireworks, Manatees: The Last Generation?, Behind-the-Scenes Tours, Cirque de la Mer

Hidden Costs		
	Meals	Burger, chips and coke $7.08
	Kids' meal	$3.25 and $6.29 (Bimini Bay Café)
	T-shirts	$16.99–$26.95
	Souvenirs	$1.99–$426
	Sundries	Caricature Drawings $10–$20

1 MANATEES: THE LAST GENERATION?
2 JOURNEY TO ATLANTIS
3 PENGUIN ENCOUNTER
4 PACIFIC POINT PRESERVE
5 SEA LION & OTTER STADIUM
6 TERRORS OF THE DEEP
7 NAUTILUS THEATER
8 CLYDESDALE HAMLET
9 ANHEUSER-BUSCH HOSPITALITY CENTER
10 SHAMU'S HAPPY HARBOR
11 WILD ARCTIC
12 ATLANTIS BAYSIDE STADIUM
13 HAWAIIAN RHYTHMS
14 SEAWORLD THEATER
15 TROPICAL REEF
16 KEY WEST DOLPHIN STADIUM
17 SHAMU STADIUM
18 INFORMATION
19 KEY WEST AT SEAWORLD
20 TURTLE POINT
21 STINGRAY LAGOON
22 TIDE POOL
23 DOLPHIN NURSERY
24 DOLPHIN COVE
25 KRAKEN

SEA WORLD

SeaWorld Adventure Park

realistic environment that is both educational and thrilling. It consists of two elements, an exciting (simulator) jet helicopter journey into the Arctic wilderness which arrives at a cleverly recreated research base, Base Station Wild Arctic, where the 'passengers' are disgorged into a frozen wonderland to meet some denizens of the North, like real polar bears, Beluga whales and walruses. The imaginative detail includes a replica sunken galleon and other nautical touches, as well as some scientific research. Not to be missed (but not just after a Shamu show when the hordes descend en masse). TTTT plus AAAAA.

Shamu Stadium: SeaWorld has long since outgrown its tag as just the place to see killer whales, but the Shamu show is still one of its most amazing experiences. See the killer whales and their trainers pull off some spectacular stunts, as well as explaining all about these majestic creatures. There are two distinct

> BRIT TIP: Reader David Snelling from Cheshire, warns, 'Gentlemen, do not volunteer to participate in the Shamu display – it will be chauvinistically humiliating.'

shows, the more humorous Shamu Adventure during the day (25 minutes) and the louder Shamu Rocks America at night (20 minutes). Both are worth seeing, and are easily the park's most popular events, so do make an effort to arrive early. Also, be warned: the first 14 rows of the stadium will get VERY wet (watch out for your cameras). When a killer whale leaps into the air in front of you, it displaces a LOT of water on landing! AAAAA.

Sea Lion & Otter Stadium: this is home to the new show, Clyde and Seamore Take Treasure Island, featuring the resident sea lions who,

> BRIT TIP: The weather may occasionally mean the outdoor entertainment is cancelled, but don't let it stop you enjoying yourself. Cheap, plastic ponchos will appear in the shops at the first sign of rain!

with their pals the otter and walrus (plus a couple of humans to be the fall-guys!), put on a hilarious 25-minute performance of watery stunts and gags. Arrive early for some first-class audience mickey-taking from the resident pirate mimic. AAAA.

Shamu the killer whale

Marine research

Key West Dolphin Fest: more breathtaking marine mammal stunts and tricks in a funky beach theme, with the accent once again on informing and educating the audience in a gentle manner on the current state of research into dolphins and false killer whales and the dangers they face. The show is 25 minutes long and is rarely over-subscribed, but once again the first few rows face a soaking. AAAA.

Bayside Stadium: this arena showcases the half-hour Intensity Water Ski Show, with an explosion of high-energy action in water stunts and gymnastics featuring water-skiing, wakeboarders, jet skis and more. AAAA.

SeaWorld Theater: this air-conditioned venue is a little haven when it's hot during the main part of the day. Pets on Stage is the show here, a 25-minute giggle featuring the talents of a menagerie of dogs, cats, birds, rats, pot-bellied pigs and others, the majority of which were rescued from animal shelters. AAA.

Nautilus Theater: this is home to the quite spectacular *Cirque de la Mer* show, a unique 40-minute adventure of athleticism, acrobatics, modern dance, music and special effects. The South American cast exhibit a terrific élan as they illustrate the story of the Flight of the Condor. It's all air-conditioned, too. AAAAA.

> BRIT TIP: For all the main shows, make sure you arrive 20 minutes early during peak periods to grab one of the better seats and avoid the last-minute rush.

Hawaiian Rhythms: an amusing song-and-dance pastiche of Polynesian culture on SeaWorld's Beach Stage, lasting 25 minutes and with a welcome beverage service. Beware if you are chosen to go on stage – it's an embarrassing experience! AAA.

Clydesdale Hamlet: these massive stables are home to the Anheuser-Busch trademark Clydesdale dray horses. They make great photo opportunities when fully harnessed for one of their regular tours of the park, and there is a life-size statue outside on which to sit the kids to take their picture. AA.

Anheuser-Busch Hospitality Center: adjoining Clydesdale Hamlet, this offers the chance to sample the company's most famous product, beer (in fact, the world's Number One bottled beer, Budweiser, and its cousins). Sadly, it's only three small samples per over-21 visitor, but it still makes a nice gesture, and you can take your free drink and sit on a pleasant outdoor terrace which makes for a relaxing break from all the usual theme park hustle and bustle. AAA. It is also home to the **Beer School**, while the **Deli** restaurant here is an attractive proposition, serving fresh-carved turkey and beef, German sausage, sauerkraut, fresh-baked breads and delicious desserts.

> BRIT TIP: Touching the rays and dolphins is an experience at SeaWorld you won't easily forget.

Endangered

Manatees: The Last Generation?: here is an exhibit that will really tug at your heart-strings as the tragic plight of this endangered species of Florida's waterways is illustrated. Watch these lazy-looking creatures (half walrus, half hippo?) lounge around their man-made lagoon from above, then walk down the ramp to the special circular theatre where a 5-minute film with amazing 3-D effects will reveal the full dangers facing the harmless manatee. Then pass into the underwater viewing section, with hands-on TV screens offering more information about them. It's a magnificently staged exhibit and a few tears at the animals' uncertain future are not unknown. It is also right behind the Key West Dolphin Fest, so DON'T go just after one of the shows there. AAAAA.

Pacific Point Preserve: another SeaWorld first, this carefully recreated rocky coast habitat shows the park's seals and sea lions at their most natural. A hidden wave-making machine adds the perfect touch of reality, while park attendants are on hand at regular intervals to provide informative talks on the animals. You can also buy small packs of smelt from two stalls to throw to the ever-hungry sea beasts. AAAA.

Shamu's Happy Harbor: three acres of brilliantly designed adventure playground await youngsters of all ages here, with all things climbable or crawlable. Activities include a four-storey net climb, two tented 'ball rooms' to wade through, and a giant 'trampoline' tent. It does get busy in mid-afternoon, but the kids seem to love it at any time. Next door is the clever Shamu Splash Attack (water-balloon catapults), the inevitable video arcade and some funfair games for a few extra dollars. TTTTT.

Sharks and morays

Terrors of the Deep: the world's largest collection of dangerous sea creatures can be found here, brought vividly and dramatically to life by the walk-through tubes that surround you with prowling sharks, barracudas and moray eels. It's an eerie

experience (and perhaps too intense for small children), but brilliantly presented and, again, highly informative. Queues do build up here at peak times, though. AAAAA or TTTTT. Take your pick!

Tropical Reef: after the dramas and amusements elsewhere, this may seem a little tame, but stick with it. Literally thousands of colourful fish inhabit the centrepiece 160,000-gallon tropical reef, while 17 smaller tanks show off other intriguing species. AAA.

Penguin Encounter: always a hit with all the family (and hence one of the more crowded exhibits at peak periods) are the eternally comical penguins in this brilliantly presented (if decidedly chilly) showpiece. You have the choice of going close and using the moving walkway along the whole of the display or standing back and watching from a non-moving position, while both positions afford views of how the 17 different species are so breathtaking under water. Feeding time is the most popular time for visitors, so arrive early if you want a prime position, while there is also a special question-and-answer session at 1pm every day – the winner gets to pet a penguin. AAAA.

Key West at SeaWorld is a whole collection of exhibits grouped under the clever Key West theme. **Stingray Lagoon**, where you can feed and touch fully grown rays, has been enlarged to 40,000 gallons to include a nursery for newborn rays, while the park's rescued and rehabilitated sea turtles have been brought out from behind the scenes into a new exhibit, **Turtle Point**, which helps to explain the dangers to these saltwater reptiles. The centrepiece exhibit, the 2.1-acre **Dolphin Cove**, is a more spectacular, naturalistic development and offers visitors the chance to get right up close and feed this friendly community of Atlantic bottlenose

6

The Key West Dolphin Fest

Journey to Atlantis: unique in Orlando, this terrific 'water-coaster' gave SeaWorld its first five-star thrill attraction in 1998. The combination of extra elements here ultimately makes it unique, with a series of illusionary special effects giving way to a high-speed water ride that becomes a runaway roller-coaster. An amusing TV show preamble about the 'discovery' of Atlantis opens the way to your eight-passenger Greek fishing boat, which sets off gently through the lost city. The evil spirit Allura takes over and riders plunge into a dash through Atlantis, dodging gushing fountains and water cannons, with hundreds of dazzling holographic and laser-generated illusions, before the heart-stopping 60ft drop, which is merely the entry to the roller-coaster finale back in the candle-filled catacombs. An amazing creation. Once again, be prepared to get *seriously* wet (like, soaked) in the course of the ride, which is great in the heat of the

dolphins. There is an underwater viewing area to the 700,000-gallon lagoon, which also features waves, a sandy beach and a recreated coral reef. The whole area is designed in the tropical, seaside flavour of America's southernmost city, Key West, with beach huts, lifeguard chairs, dune buggies, themed shops and other eclectic lookalike elements, but it also underlines the environmental message of conservation through a series of interactive graphics and video displays adjacent to the animal habitats, and children of all ages will find it a fun, educational experience. The shops are above average, too. AAAA.

Shamu: Close-up: this backstage exhibit can be found at the opposite side of Shamu Stadium, affording a much closer and more natural look at the killer whales while at their leisure. Attendants are on hand to answer all your questions. AAA.

The touch pool at Stingray Lagoon

Journey to Atlantis

summer but not so clever first thing in the morning in winter. TTTTT. Riders exit into the **Sea Aquarium Gallery**, a combination gift shop

The Kraken rollercoaster

and 25,000-gallon aquarium full of sharks, stingrays and tropical fish (don't forget to look up!).

Kraken: brand new in 2000 was this outrageous addition to the coaster family, the longest, fastest and highest in central Florida. Based on the mythical sea monster, Kraken is an innovative pedestal ride (you are effectively sitting in a chair without a floor – pretty exposed!) that plunges an initial 150ft, tops speeds of 65mph, dives underground three times, adds seven inversions (including a 119ft vertical loop, a 101ft diving loop, a zero-gravity roll and a cobra roll) and a flat spin before riders escape the beast's lair. The ride from the front row, especially down that opening drop at an angle that can best be described as ludicrous, is positively blood-curdling, and the rear seats are pretty neat, too. Thrill seekers can do no better. Restrictions; 4ft 6in. TTTTT+.

SeaWorld Specials

In addition to the **Shamu Rocks America** show, night-time at SeaWorld is marked by an end-of-evening fireworks extravaganza in front of the Atlantis Bayside Stadium called **Red, Bright & Blue**. This 15-minute curtain-call features lasers, fountains and pyrotechnics and is well worth staying for. AAAAA.

There is also live entertainment daily around the Key West attractions, including the trademark **Sunset Celebration** street party.

As well as all the main set-pieces, there are several smaller ones which can be equally rewarding for their more personal touch. The **Flamingo, Pelican** and **Spoonbill Exhibits** offer, amongst other things, the answer to the eternal question 'Dad, why has that pink duck got only one leg?'. The **Tide Pool** is another hands-on experience with starfish and sea anemones, and, for an extra $3, you can ascend the **Sky Tower** for a lofty overview of the park (and the lower portion of International Drive). A recent addition are the flamingo pedal-boats, which rent for $6 per half-hour (for two people) in one corner of the lagoon. Watch out, too, for the best photo opportunity of the day as a big, cuddly Shamu greets kids just inside the main entrance.

There are also nine different places to eat, with the **Dockside Smokehouse** (barbecued, mesquite-grilled chicken, ribs and beef), **The Deli** (mentioned, above, in the Anheuser-Busch Hospitality Center), **Bimini Bay Café** (for a relaxing, full-service lunch or dinner) and **Mango Joe's Café** (delicious grilled fajitas, speciality salads and sandwiches) the best of the bunch. As in the other main parks, try to eat before midday or after 2.30pm for a crowd-free lunch, and before 5.30pm if you want a leisurely dinner.

Your wallet will also be in severe peril in any of the 23 shops and photo-opportunity kiosks. Make sure you visit at least **Shamu's Emporium** (for a full range of cuddly Shamu toys and souvenirs), **Manatee Cove** (more cuddlies), **Friends of the Wild** (dedicated to animal lovers everywhere) and **The Label Stable** for Anheuser-Busch gifts and merchandise (some of it very smart). Your purchases can be forwarded to Package Pick-up in Shamu's Emporium for you to collect on your way out, provided you leave at least an hour for this service to work.

Finally, non-drivers will want to make a note of the special daily bus service from SeaWorld (and other points on International Drive) direct to sister park Busch Gardens (see page 142).

Discovery Cove

Fancy a day on your own tropical island paradise, with the chance to swim with dolphins, encounter sharks, snorkel in a coral reef and dive through a waterfall into a tropical aviary? Well, this is the place for you. The unique Discovery Cove by SeaWorld is all that and more. The only drawback is the price. This mini theme park comes at a premium because it is restricted to just 1,000 guests a day, making for an exclusive experience, and the admission fee reflects that – a whopping $179, plus tax, per person, and no reduction for children (except to $89 for 3–5s; see full pricing below).

So, just what do you get for your money? Well, as you would expect, it is a supremely personal park. You check in as you would for a hotel rather than a theme park (the entrance lobby is wonderfully impressive), and you have your own guide to take you in and get you set for the day. All your basic requirements – towel, mask, snorkel, wet-jacket, lockers, lunch and soft drinks – are included in the price, and the level of service is excellent. The lunch provided at the buffet-style Laguna Grill is good without being outstanding, but you have to pay for any further snacks and any alcoholic drinks, while the gift shop and photographic prices reflect the entrance fee, i.e. expensive. Discovery Cove admission also includes a seven-day pass for SeaWorld.

The whole of the 30-acre park is magnificently landscaped, with lovely thatched buildings, palm trees, lush vegetation, brilliant white-sand beaches, gurgling streams and even hammocks, and the overall effect is as if you have been transported to some Caribbean or South Seas oasis.

The usual tourist hurly-burly is left far behind. The five-star resort feel is enhanced by waiter service to your beach lounger and the high staff-to-guest ratio (the lifeguards can outnumber the guests at times, it seems). There should be no queues for anything (okay, the buffet-service restaurant may get a little busy at lunchtime) and the highlight dolphin encounter is unquestionably world class.

The essence of a day at Discovery Cove involves up close and personal encounters with all the animals – although not too close in the case of the sharks – with a strong underlying message of conservation, as you get with SeaWorld. Here are the main attractions:

Coral Reef: a huge rocky pool, filled with several thousand tropical fish, offers the most amazing man-made snorkelling experience you'll find. The water teems with the likes of silverjacks, angelfish and yellowtail snapper and, even if the 'coral' is hand-painted concrete, it is a clever environment. Swimmers will also come within inches of sharks and barracuda – all safely behind a substantial Plexiglass partition – which adds another novel element. AAAAA/TTTT.

Ray Lagoon: another carefully sculpted pool provides the opportunity to snorkel and paddle with more than a hundred southern and cownose rays, quite harmless, but with just a hint of menace to the fascination. AAAA.

6

The author at Discovery Cove

Tropical River: this 800-metre circuit of gently flowing bath-warm water is a variation on the lazy river feature of many of the water parks, although with a far more naturalistic aspect and none of the inner-tubes. It is primarily designed for snorkellers and features rocky lagoons, caves, a beach section, a tropical forest segment and an underwater viewing window into the Coral Reef. However, the lack of fish means it seems a bit bland after the Reef and Ray Lagoon, and you start to yearn for one of those innertubes. There was a suggestion some freshwater fish might be added, which would give it the missing ingredient. AAA (without fish).

Aviary: this is both an area in its own right and a 30-metre section of the Tropical River. You can walk in off the beach or swim in through one of the two impressive waterfalls which guard each end, a beautifully scenic touch and fun for snorkellers. Some 300 tropical birds fill the 10m-high enclosure and, if you stand still for a while, they are likely to use you for a perch. There are guides to introduce you to specific birds, which you can also hand-feed, and tell you about their habits, habitats and conservation issues. AAAAA.

Animal encounters: a minor additional touch, but sure to be a hit with children in particular, is the chance to meet some of the Cove's lesser lights, like macaws, tree-sloths and anteaters on an individual basis at various points around the park. AAA.

The Aviary

Snorkelling in the Coral Reef

Dolphin Swim: the headline attraction at Discovery Cove is the 90-minute encounter with the park's Atlantic bottlenose dolphin community. A 30-minute orientation programme in one of the four thatched beach cabanas, with a film and instruction from two of the animal trainers, sets you up for this deeply thrilling experience. Groups of 12–20 guests go into the huge lagoon with careful supervision from the trainers and, starting off by standing in the waist-deep (and slightly chilly) water as one of the dolphins comes to you, you gradually become more adventurous until you are swimming next to them. Timid swimmers are catered for and there are life-jackets for those who feel they need them, but the lagoon is up to 12ft deep so there is a feeling of really being in the dolphins' environment. You will stroke, scratch, feed and even kiss (!) your dolphin – all the time with a trainer close at hand – and the encounter comes to a dramatic conclusion as you are towed back to shore by one of these awesome 600lb animals. TTTTT+.

Truly, this is an attraction with huge style and appeal – not to mention the stuff of which cherished memories are made – but it will take a big bite out of your holiday

budget. The entrance fee plus tax adds up to $190 per person, and the only reduction is to $89 (plus tax) for those not wishing to do the Dolphin Swim and for 3–5s (under 6s are not allowed into the dolphin lagoon; under 3s are free). That means a family of four, with children of 6 or

Ray Lagoon

older, would pay $760 for the day and, even with the 7-day SeaWorld pass included, it is a massive outlay. The park is located on Central Florida Parkway, almost opposite the SeaWorld entrance, and is open year-round from 9am– 5.30pm. For more details, look up www.discoverycove.com. You can book on-line or call 407 370 1280.

Discovery Cove

6

Busch Gardens

Question: when is a zoo not a zoo? Answer: when it is also a theme park like 335-acre Busch Gardens in nearby Tampa.

Busch Gardens, the second big Anheuser-Busch park in the area, started life as a mini-menagerie for the wildlife collection of the brewery-owning Busch family. In 1959, they opened a small hospitality centre next to the brewery and things have mushroomed ever since. Now, it is a major, multi-faceted family attraction, the biggest on Florida's west coast and little more than an hour from Orlando.

It is rated among the top four zoos in America, with more than 2,700 animals representing 340 species of mammals, birds, reptiles, amphibians and spiders. But that's just the start. It boasts a safari-like section of Africa spread over 65 acres of grassy veldt, with special tours to hand-feed some of the animals. Interspersed among the animals are 29 bona fide theme park rides, including the mind-numbing roller-coasters Kumba, Montu and Gwazi, which guarantee a new experience for coaster addicts, and yet another in the series of simulator rides, the amusing and novel Akbar's Adventure Tours. There are shows, comedians, musicians, strolling players and a family show extravaganza in the impressive Moroccan Palace Theater, *World Rhythms on Ice*.

The overall theme is Africa, hence the park is subdivided into areas like Nairobi and the Congo, and the dining and shopping opportunities are the equal of any of the other big theme parks. It doesn't quite have the pizazz of an Epcot or Universal, and the staff are a bit more laid back. In a way, it is like the big brother of the Chessington World of Adventures in Surrey, although admittedly on a much grander scale (and in a better climate). But it has guaranteed, five-star family appeal, especially with its selection of rides just for kids, and it is a big hit with the British market in particular.

Location

Busch Gardens is the hardest place to locate on the sketchy local maps and the signposting is not as sharp as it could be, but, from Orlando, the directions are pretty simple. Head (south) west on I4 for almost an hour (it is 55 miles from I4's junction with Highway 192) until you hit the intersecting motorway I75. Take I75 north for 3½ miles until you see the exit for Fowler Avenue (Highway 582). Continue west on Fowler Avenue for another 3½ miles, and, just past the University of South Florida on your right, turn LEFT into McKinley Drive. A mile down McKinley Drive and Busch Gardens' car park entrance will be on your left, where it is $6 to park.

Those without a car can use the daily bus service to Busch Gardens, with five round-trips a day from Orlando at $10 a time (free if you have a five-park, 10-day FlexTicket). You board the Shuttle Express at SeaWorld, the Mercado Center, Lake Buena Vista Factory Outlet shops, Universal Studios or Old Town in Kissimmee and pick-up times range from 8–10.15am for the one-hour journey, returning at 5, 6 and 8pm. You book at the Guest Services window at SeaWorld or call 1-800 511 2450.

You may think you have left the crowds behind in Orlando, but, unfortunately, in high season you'd be wrong. It is still advisable to be here in time for opening, if only to

Busch Gardens at-a-glance

Location	Busch Boulevard, Tampa; 75–90 minutes drive from Orlando
Size	335 acres in 11 themed areas
Hours	9.30 or 10am–6pm off peak; 9am–9pm high season (Easter, summer holidays, Thanksgiving, Christmas)
Admission	Under 3, free; 3–9, $36.74 (one-day ticket), $158 (10-Day Flex Ticket, inc. Universal Studios, SeaWorld and Wet 'n Wild); adults (10+) $45.68, $197
Parking	$6
Lockers	Yes; in Morocco, Congo, Egypt and Stanleyville; $1
Pushchairs **Wheelchairs**	$7 and $11 (in Morocco) $7 and $30 (same location)
Top Attractions	Kumba, Congo River Rapids, Edge of Africa, Gwazi, Tanganyika Tidal Wave, Myombe Reserve, Montu
Don't Miss	*World Rhythms on Ice*, Elephant Wash, Mystic Sheikhs band

Hidden Costs	**Meals**	Burger, chips and coke $6.38 Three-course meal $19 (Crown Colony House)
	Kids' meal	$2.99 and $3.49
	T-shirts	$15.99–$22.99
	Souvenirs	$0.79–$600
	Sundries	Cartoon caricatures $9.95–$19.95

be first in line to ride the dazzling roller-coasters Gwazi, Kumba and Montu, which draw queues of up to an hour during the main holiday periods. The Congo River Rapids, Stanley Falls log flume ride and Tanganyika Tidal Wave (all opportunities to get very wet!) are also prime rides, as is Akbar's Adventure Tours and the other two roller-coasters, Python and Scorpion. The queues take longer to build up here, so for the first few hours you can enjoy a relatively crowd-free experience, even in high season.

Busch Gardens is divided into 11 main sections, with the major rides all a bit of a hike from the main entrance. Gwazi, the wooden double-coaster which opened in summer 1999, attracts the majority of the early birds, so head here first for one of the best rides in Florida. Bear left through Morocco and you will soon arrive in its own purpose-built area, with Gwazi on your right. Then go through Stanleyville to Congo for Kumba, and retrace your steps to do Congo River Rapids, the Python and the other two water rides. Alternatively, turn right through the main entrance and visit Egypt for Montu and Akbar's. Here is the full 335-acre layout.

1 **CONGO**
2 CONGO RIVER RAPIDS
3 KUMBA
4 THE PYTHON
5 **TIMBUKTU**
6 DOLPHIN THEATER
7 THE SCORPION
8 FESTHAUS
9 **STANLEYVILLE**
10 TANGANYIKA TIDAL WAVE
11 STANLEY FALLS
12 STANLEYVILLE THEATER
13 **LAND OF THE DRAGONS**
14 **BIRD GARDENS**
15 KOALA DISPLAY
16 HOSPITALITY HOUSE/BEER SCHOOL
17 LORY LANDING
18 **MOROCCO**
19 MOROCCAN PALACE THEATER
20 **MYOMBE RESERVE**
21 **CROWN COLONY**
22 SKYRIDE STATION
23 CROWN COLONY RESTAURANT &
    HOSPITALITY CENTER
24 CLYDESDALE HAMLET
25 **EGYPT**
26 AKBAR'S ADVENTURE TOURS
27 TUT'S TOMB
28 MONTU
29 **SERENGETI PLAIN**
30 EDGE OF AFRICA
31 **GWAZI**
32 RHINO RALLY (SPRING 2001)
33 TRAIN STATIONS

BUSCH
GARDENS

ENTRANCE
GATES

Morocco

Coming through the main gates brings you first into **Morocco**, home of all the main guest services and a lot of the best shops. Epcot's Moroccan pavilion sets the scene rather better, but the architecture is still impressive and this version won't overtax your wallet quite as much as Disney does! For a quick meal try the **Zagora Café**, especially at breakfast when the marching, dancing, eight-piece brass band called the **Mystic Sheikhs** swing into action to entertain the early morning crowds. Alternatively, the wonderfully enticing **Sultan's Sweets** will serve you coffee and pastries. Watch out, too, for the strolling **Men of Note**, a four-piece *a cappella* group, and the costumed characters like TJ the Tiger and Hilda Hippo. The **Sultan's Tent** gives you your first animal encounter in the form of a resident snake charmer, while turning the corner brings you face to face with the alligator pen. Morocco is also home to two of the biggest shows in Busch Gardens. The **Marrakesh Theater** offers various variety shows that change from time to time (American Jukebox was featured in 2000; check the daily Entertainment Guide for full details), while the **Moroccan Palace Theater** houses the award-winning show *World Rhythms on Ice*. Even if the thought of an ice show doesn't immediately appeal to you, think again, because this is a surprising and highly entertaining 30-minute spectacular that celebrates different cultures around the world. The costumes are absolutely terrific, the music is vibrant and enhanced by video screens to either side of the stage, and there are a number of breathtaking special effects which sum up a brilliant design element here. It is also air-conditioned, a welcome relief in summer. AAAAA.

Crown Colony

Crown Colony sits in the bottom right-hand corner of Busch Gardens and has five distinct components.

6

The breathtaking Montu roller-coaster

Here, you can take the **Skyride** cablecar (AAA) on a one-way trip to The Congo. The station features various lemurs, monkeys and birds staring out of their cages at these strange humans all in long lines. Who's watching who, you wonder. The **Clydesdale Hamlet** is also here, but if you've seen the massive dray horses and their stables at SeaWorld, the set-up is identical.

Akbar's Adventure Tours (actually part of Egypt's attractions but located in Crown Colony because it replaced the Questor ride in 1998) is another in the array of simulator rides, though this relies as much on fun as thrills. The TV pre-show leads its audience into the world of down-at-heel Akbar (brilliantly played by comedian Martin Short) and his home-made (and untried) excursion machine. It explores, in unconventional fashion, the secrets and treasures of ancient Egypt, but don't expect a smooth ride – a mysterious force assumes control in the forbidden tomb and the journey takes a high-speed turn for the unexpected! It is not recommended for anyone who suffers back or neck problems or for expectant mothers, while the height restriction is 3ft 6in. TTTT.

The **Crown Colony Restaurant and Hospitality Center** is a large Victorian-styled building overlooking the Serengeti Plain and affording either counter-service salads, sandwiches or pizzas (downstairs) or a full-service restaurant upstairs with magnificent views of the animals roaming the Plain. For a memorable lunch, book here early in the day or, better still, come back for dinner in the early evening and see the animals come down to the water hole.

Serengeti

The **Serengeti Plain** itself is a recently enhanced 29-acre spread of African savannah that is home to buffalo, antelope, zebra, giraffe, wildebeest, ostriches, hippos, rhinos and many exotic birds, and can be viewed for part of the journey on the **Trans-Veldt Railroad**, a full-size, open-car steam train that chugs slowly from its main station in Nairobi to Egypt and all the way round to Congo, Stanleyville and back (AAA). The Railroad is a good ride during the main part of the day when queues build up at the thrill rides. Part of the Skyride also provides a view over the Serengeti.

Edge of Africa

This 15-acre safari experience guarantees a close-up encounter that is almost as good as the real thing. The walk-through attraction puts you in an authentic setting of natural wilds and native villages (right down to the imported plants and even the

> BRIT TIP: Edge of Africa offers some wonderful photo opportunities, but, in the hot months, come here early in the day as many animals seek refuge from the heat later in the day.

smells), from which you can view giraffes, lions, baboons, meerkats, crocodiles, hyenas, vultures and even get an underwater view of a specially designed hippopotamus habitat. Look out for the abandoned jeep – you can sit in the front cab while lions lounge in the back! Wandering 'safari guides' and naturalists offer informal talks, and the attention to detail is wonderful. AAAAA. You can also sign up here for the **Serengeti Safari** by truck (see below).

Nairobi

Nairobi is home to the awesome **Myombe Reserve**, one of the largest and most realistic habitats for the threatened highland gorillas and chimpanzees of central Africa. This 3-acre walk-through has a superb tropical setting where the temperature is kept artificially high and convincing with the aid of lush forest landscaping and hidden water mist sprays. Take your time, especially as there are good, seated vantage points, and be patient to catch these magnificent creatures going about their daily routine. It is also highly informative, with attendants usually on hand to answer any questions. AAAAA.

At **JR's Gorilla Hut** you can buy your own cuddly baby gorilla, while you can get a snack or soft drink at the **Myombe Outpost**. This is also the place to see the Gardens' Asian elephants (check the advertised times for the **Elephant Wash**, which is always worth watching) and the **Nairobi Animal Nursery**, which houses all manner of rehabilitating and hand-reared creatures that can be seen close up. Continuing round the Nursery brings you to the oddly out of place **Showjumping Hall of Fame**, the **Reptile House** and the inevitable **Petting Zoo**, for kids to stroke goats, sheep and baby deer. The **Curiosity Caverns**, just to the left of the Nursery, are easy to miss but don't if you want to catch a glimpse of various nocturnal and rarely seen creatures in a clever, cave-like setting.

Timbuktu

Passing through Nairobi brings you into the more ride-dominated area of the park, starting with **Timbuktu**. Here in a North African desert setting you will find many of the elements of a traditional fun fair, with a couple of brain-scrambling rides and two top-class shows. **Scorpion**, a 50mph roller-coaster,

features a 62ft drop and a full 360-degree loop that is guaranteed to dial D for dizzy for a while afterwards. The ride lasts just 120 seconds, but it seems longer! The queues build up here from late morning to mid-afternoon, and you have to be at least 3ft 6in tall to board. TTTT. The **Phoenix** is a positively evil invention, sitting its passengers in a gigantic, boat-shaped swing that eventually performs a full 360-degree rotation in dramatic, slow-motion style. Don't eat just before this one! TTTT. **Sandstorm** is a fairly routine whirligig contraption that spins and levitates at fairly high speed (hold on to your stomach). TTT. The **Crazy Camel** is an odd sort of ride resembling a giant sombrero that spins and tilts its riders into a state of dizziness. TT. Then there are a series of scaled-down **Kiddie Rides** that always seem popular with the under 10s (and give mum and dad a break for a few minutes as well). The **Carousel Caravan** offers the chance to ride a genuine Mary Poppins-type carousel, while there is also the inevitable **Electronic Arcade** and a **Games Area** of side shows and stalls that require a few extra dollars to play. The **Festhaus** is a combined German Bierfest and entertainment hall, offering a mixture of German and Italian food. It's a jolly, rather raucous establishment, with the International Celebration show featuring singers, dancers and musicians four or five times a day. The final element of Timbuktu is the **Dolphin Theater**, complete with its aluminium sculpture outside that is a homage to the value of recycling. The 25-minute Dolphins of the Deep show borrows heavily from SeaWorld's education-orientated dolphin offering, but still comes up with some terrific leaps, stunts and tricks. AAAA.

6

The Serengeti Safari

Rhino Rally: new in spring 2001 is scheduled to be this dramatic ride which starts out as an off-road jeep safari and changes into an innovative raft adventure as your 16-passenger vehicle gets caught up in a flash flood. The 8-minute whirl through the wilds of Africa includes encounters with elephants, rhinos, antelope and more, plus a thrilling raging river section that is unlike any attraction to date. Check this out! Expected rating: TTTT.

Myombe Reserve

Congo

You're really into serious ride territory as you come into the **Congo**, with the unmistakable giant turquoise structure of **Kumba**. First of all it's one of the largest and fastest roller-coaster in the south-east United States and, at 60mph, it features three unique elements: a diving loop which plunges the riders a full 110ft; a camelback, with a full 360-degree spiral that induces a feeling of weightlessness for three seconds; and a 108ft vertical loop. For good measure, it dives underground at one point! It looks

Congo River Rapids

terrifying close up, but it is absolutely exhilarating, even for non-coaster fans. The height restriction here is 4ft 6in. TTTTT. The **Congo River Rapids** look pretty tame after that, but don't be fooled. These giant rubber tyres will bounce you down some of the most convincing rapids outside of the Rockies, and you will end up with a fair soaking for good measure. TTTT. The **Ubanga-Banga Bumper Cars** are just that, typical fairground dodgems (TT), and you won't miss anything by passing them by for the more daring **Python**, the fourth of Busch Gardens' roller-coasters, with this one featuring a double spiral corkscrew at 50mph from a drop of some 70ft. Height restriction here is 4ft, and the whole ride lasts just 70 seconds, but it's

Hippos at the Edge of Africa animal attraction

Bengal tigers, to get to **Stanleyville**, which all rather merges into one area from the Congo. Here there are more watery rides, with the popular **Stanley Falls** log flume ride (almost identical to the ones at Chessington, Thorpe Park and Alton Towers), which guarantees a good soaking at the final drop (TTT) and the

Rhino Rally

distinctly cleverer **Tanganyika Tidal Wave**, which takes you on a scenic ride along 'uncharted' African waters before tipping you down a two-stage drop which really does set you down with tidal-wave force. TTTT.

a blast. TTTT. Nearby, the **Monstrous Mamba** is almost a carbon copy of Timbuktu's Sandstorm, but just with a different name and paint job, while there are more **Kiddie Rides** to stop the smaller visitors feeling left out. The **Vivi Storehouse Restaurant** offers chicken fajitas, club sandwiches, salads and desserts, while there are three gift shops, including the **Tiger's Den**.

Stanleyville

You pass over **Claw Island**, home of the park's spectacular rare white

> **BRIT TIP:** Don't stand on the bridge into the neighbouring **Orchid Canyon** unless you want to catch the full weight of the Tidal Wave!

Lory Landing

Stanleyville Theater is a good place to relax and put your feet up for a while as you are entertained by a number of circus-style acts. For a hearty, if somewhat messy, meal, visit the **Stanleyville Smokehouse** – their wood-smoked ribs platter is a real lip-smacking delight. As you leave Stanleyville behind, say hello to the warthogs and orang-utans (who are rarely active during the heat of the day) in the large pens either side of the Train Station.

Land of the Dragons

Parents will want to know about this large, wonderfully clever area of activities, entertainment, rides and attractions purely for the young 'uns. It features a three-storey treehouse complete with towers and maze-like stairways, a rope climb, ball crawl and outdoor **Dragon's Tale Theater**, which features the 15-minute show with Captain Kangaroo's Roo Crew – fun, friendship and ping-pong balls! It is all good, knockabout, well-supervised stuff, and some of the kiddie rides are superbly inventive, as well as offering plenty of opportunity to get wet. TTTTT (youngsters only – but mums and dads can watch!).

Bird Gardens

Your anti-clockwise route now brings you to the most peaceful area, the **Bird Gardens**. Here it is possible to unwind from the usual theme park hurly-burly. The exhibits and shows are all family-orientated, too, with the 30-minute For The Birds presented in the **Bird Show Theater** and the **Hospitality Patio** offering ragtime jazz at regular intervals. A recent addition is **Lory Landing**, a desert island-themed walk-through bird encounter featuring lorikeets, hornbills, parrots

and more, with the chance to become a human perch and feed the friendly lorikeets (and have your ear nibbled!). A cup of nectar costs $1, but is a great investment for a memorable photo. Take a slow walk round to appreciate the lush, tropical foliage, and special displays such as the walk-through **Aviary**, **Flamingo Island**, **Eagle Canyon** and the emus. The highlight of the Bird Gardens, confusingly enough, is the **Koala Display**, in the south-west corner, where these natives of Australia happily sit and seemingly do nothing all day while drawing large crowds for doing so. A free taste of Anheuser-Busch products is on offer in **Hospitality House**, and you can go a step further here by enrolling for **Beer School**, a 40-minute session into the age-old process of beer-making. It offers a fascinating glimpse into the brewery world, and is excellently explained, with the bonus of some tasting included! You also get a Brewery Master certificate. AAA.

Gwazi

Not so much a 'land' as the purpose-built area for Busch's newest and most elaborate roller-coaster, **Gwazi**, a massive 'duelling' wooden creation in the classic mould (i.e. no inversions). The two sets of cars, the Gwazi Lion and Gwazi Tiger, each top 50mph and generate a G-force of up to 3.5 as they career around nearly 7,000ft of track with six distinct fly-by encounters. You get to choose your ride in the intricately themed 8-acre village plaza and then you are off up the 90ft lift for a truly breathtaking 2½ minutes. The shake, rattle 'n' roll effect of a classic coaster is cleverly re-created and Lion and Tiger rides are slightly different so you need to do both. Even if you don't like coasters, try this one. Restrictions; 4ft. TTTTT.

Egypt

The final area of Busch Gardens is tucked away through the Crown Colony, so it is best visited either first thing or late in the day. **Egypt** is 8 acres of carefully recreated pharaoh country, dominated by the trademark roller-coaster **Montu**, named after an ancient Egyptian warrior-god. It is a truly breathtaking creation, one of the world's tallest and longest inverted coasters, covering nearly 4,000ft of track at speeds topping 60mph and peaking with a G-force of 3.85! Like Kumba, it looks terrifying, but in reality it is an absolute five-star thrill as it leaves your legs dangling and swoops and plunges (underground at two points) for almost 3 minutes of brain-scrambling fun. Restrictions; 4ft 6in. TTTTT.

You can travel back in time on a tour of **Tut's Tomb**, as it was discovered by archaeologist Howard Carter, with clever lighting, audio and even aroma effects. AAA. There is also a neat **Sand Pit** that invites youngsters to undertake their own excavations (and there are even some little 'treasures' to be found!), while the shopping here takes on a high-quality air with its hand-blown glass items, elaborate sculptures and authentic cartouche paintings.

You should finally return to Morocco for a spot of shopping there in the area's tempting bazaars. Middle Eastern brass, pottery and carpets will all try to tempt you into opening your wallet yet again, while there is also a full range of Anheuser-Busch products and gift ideas if you haven't already succumbed to the array of gift shops and cuddly-toy emporiums around the rest of the park.

And ...

In addition to all the aforementioned activities, you can enhance your visit to Busch Gardens by taking the **Serengeti Safari** tour, an excursion aboard flat-bed trucks to meet the Plain's giraffes, zebras, ostriches and rhinos close up and learn more about the park's environmental efforts. You book up at the entrance to Edge of Africa for an extra $20, and places soon fill up.

For a full family day out, you can combine Busch Gardens with next-door water park **Adventure Island** (on McKinley Drive) which is particularly welcome when it hots up (provided you plaster on the sun tan cream). The 25 acres of watery fun, in a Key West theme, offer a full range of slides and rides, like the new Wahoo Run adventure ride, the 76ft free-fall plunge of the Tampa Typhoon and the spiralling Calypso Coaster, kids' playground, cafés, gift shops, arcades and volleyball, plus the wonderful Splash Attack adventure, a water activity maze culminating in a 1,000-gallon bucket dump on the unwary! Adventure Island is open from mid-February to late October (weekends only Feb–Mar and Sept–Oct) 10am–5pm (later in high season) and a combined ticket with Busch Gardens costs $60.45 for adults and $50.74 for 3–9s. A combination Busch/ SeaWorld ticket is $79 for adults and $64 for children.

6

The Other Attractions
(or, One Giant Leap for Tourist Kind)

If you think you have seen everything Orlando has to offer by simply sticking to the theme parks, in the words of the song, 'You ain't seen nothin' yet'. It would be relatively easy to add the Kennedy Space Center to the parks in Chapter 6 because, although it's not strictly a theme park, it is adding new attractions all the time and is fast becoming a full day's excursion from Orlando to the east or 'space' coast.

Then there are Cypress Gardens and Silver Springs to give you a taste of the more natural things Florida has to offer, the Kissimmee attraction Splendid China for a completely different park experience, the mind-boggling Gatorland, with its multitude of alligators, crocs and gator shows (and great value, too), and the one-off family centres like Mystery Fun House, Guinness World Records Experience, WonderWorks, the Orlando Science Center and Ripley's Believe It Or Not.

For more individual attractions, you have the unique aviation experience of Fantasy of Flight, and the Warbirds Air Museum, the hair-raising haunted house walk-through of Skull Kingdom plus the area's magnificent array of water fun parks.

Chapter 8 then introduces a range of alternatives that help you Get Off the Beaten Track and discover some of the real Sunshine State, while Chapter 9 unveils all the options for an evening out in Orlando by Night. The choice is yours, but it is an immense selection. Let's start here with One Giant Leap for Mankind.

Kennedy Space Center

The recent change to a fully ticketed entrance fee is a reflection of the massive amount of new development that has taken place at the home of NASA's space programme. More than $120 million has been spent on revamping the Kennedy Space Center's Visitor Complex in the last couple of years and, while it was always a great visit in the past, now it is simply unmissable, in my opinion, for its hugely imaginative depiction of the past, present and future of space exploration.

There are five continuous-running shows or exhibitions, four static showcases, a kids' play area, an art gallery, the all-new Astronaut Encounter, three splendid IMAX films and a full bus tour of the Space Center, which adds up to great value for the Maximum Access Pass ticket.

You enter through the futuristic new ticket plaza and can spend several hours wandering around the exhibits and presentations of the 70-acre complex.

The new **Robot Scouts** is a walk-through display-cum-show in the company of Starquester 2000, your robot host who will explain the history of NASA's unmanned space probes in surprising and often amusing style. Next door, the **Quest for Life** film – narrated by Deep Space Nine star Avery Brooks – provides another illuminating view of our universe. Head on out and see some of the hardware of space flight in the **Rocket Garden**, and don't forget to stop by the **Astronaut Memorial**, a stark, sombre but very moving tribute to the men and women who have died in advancing the space programme.

Shuttle Plaza gives you the chance to inspect a full-size replica space shuttle, while the **Launch Status Center** displays actual flight hardware, plus live mission briefings. Free walking tours are available several times a day. **Early Space Exploration** is a clever and coherent walk-through trip into the recent past of the space programme, including the *Hall of Discovery*, the *Mercury Mission Control Room* – the original consoles from America's first manned space flights – and the *Hall of History*. The futuristic **Exploration in the New Millennium** exhibit provides more appeal for youngsters, with a fun educational element from the spaceship-like *Exploring Gallery*, the *Mars Rock exhibit* and a series of interactive panels. Perhaps the most innovative feature, though, is the **Astronaut Encounter**, with personal briefings, Q&A sessions, video footage and anecdotes from various veterans of the Mercury,

Kennedy Space Center

Gemini and Apollo programmes, plus several Space Shuttle astronauts. It is an amazingly insightful, inspirational and engrossing feature, and takes place up to three times a day at the Center Plaza. Kids have their own playground, too, inside the **Children's Play Dome**, complete with a one-fifth scale space shuttle.

Owners Delaware North Parks Services have lavished a fortune on upgrading the Center and, for my money, it's an essential experience for all but pre-school children. In many ways, it knocks the artificiality of Disney and Co. into a cocked hat.

The air-conditioned **coach tour,** fully narrated throughout, makes three important stops in addition to driving around much of the working areas of the Space Center, including the truly massive Vehicle Assembly Building. The first stop is the new $7m **LC39 Observation Gantry**, just one mile from shuttle launch pad 39A, a combination four-storey observation deck and exhibition centre. The exhibits consist of a 10-minute film on the preparation of a shuttle for launch, models and videos of a launch countdown and touch-screen information on the shuttle programme. Next is the awesome **Apollo/Saturn V Center**, one of the area's truly great exhibits, where you can easily spend 90 minutes. It highlights the Apollo programme and first moon landing with two deeply impressive theatrical presentations on the risks and triumphs, with an actual 363ft Saturn V rocket and a hands-on gallery that brings the past, present and future of space exploration into sharp focus. It is also quite a humbling experience. Third stop is the new $4-million **International Space Station Center**, another interactive attraction featuring the construction of this current project, with incredibly detailed mock-ups of the modules and a fascinating viewing gallery showing the workings of the Center. You should allow 3–4 hours to do the tour justice.

An additional tour – at an extra $20 per person – is **Cape Canaveral: Then and Now**, a 2-hour-plus in-depth journey into the early days of space exploration around the older part of the facility. Highlights include the Air Force Space Museum, Mercury launch sites and Memorial, original astronaut training facility and several active launch pads, all of which are otherwise off-limits.

Equally impressive are the IMAX cinemas – 55ft screens which give the impression of sitting on top of the action. The 37-minute film **The Dream Is Alive** puts you inside a space shuttle mission, the new 40-minute **Mission to Mir** depicts American–Russian co-operation, and the 3-D **L5: First City in Space** is a breathtaking slice of science fiction based on science fact. All the films are now included in the admission price.

The Visitor Complex boasts an excellent Space Shop, three restaurants, including the full-service Mila's, and three snack counters. Even the Apollo/Saturn V Center has its own café where you can sit and marvel at it all.

To get to the Kennedy Space Center, take the Beeline Expressway out of Orlando (Highway 528, and it's a toll road, remember) for about 45 minutes, then bear left on the SR 407 (DON'T follow the signs to Cape Canaveral or Cocoa Beach at this point) and turn right at the T-junction on to SR 405. The Space Center's Visitor Center is located 6 miles along SR 405 on the right-hand side. Opening hours are 9am to dusk every day except Christmas Day, and the Center gets busiest around lunchtime. The first tours and IMAX presentations start at 9.30am, and the final tour of the day

is 2 hours before dark. Adult admission is $24 and $15 for children 3–11. Parking is free. For more details, log on to www.kennedyspacecenter.com. **Total attraction rating: AAAAA.**

The greatest attraction of all, however, is an actual shuttle launch, of which there are six or seven a year. You can call 407 867 4636 for dates and information, while free car passes to a Launch Viewing area some 6 miles from the launch pad are available by writing 3 months in advance to NASA Visitor Services, Mail Code: PA-Pass, Kennedy Space Center, Florida 32899. There are also 1,500 $10 Launch Viewing Opportunity tickets for a bus trip to a site just a mile from the launch pad (or $15 for an LVO ticket, IMAX film and mission briefing). These go on sale on a first-come basis 5 days before launch and must be purchased in person from the Ticket Pavilion. However, in the event of a launch cancellation, there are NO refunds. Alternatively, prime viewing sites are along Highway 1 in Titusville and Highway A1A through Cape Canaveral and Cocoa Beach. To be on hand for a shuttle launch is an awe-inspiring experience.

Astronaut Hall of Fame

While the Kennedy Space Center tells you primarily about the machinery of putting men in space, the neighbouring Astronaut Hall of Fame (on SR 405, just before the main entrance to the Space Center)

BRIT TIP: Every Friday is Space Camp graduation day, so avoid the Hall of Fame then unless you want to be surrounded by dozens of highly enthusiastic 'space cadets' and their parents.

gives you the full low-down on the people involved. This museum to the space programmes houses some fascinating memorabilia, interactive exhibits and engaging explanations of the people behind the spacesuits. Prepare to be amazed at how incredibly small the cockpits of the early manned spaceflights were and amused by personal touches like Buzz Aldrin's High School report!

A recent reorganisation and expansion has created a more chronologically coherent approach divided into six main sections. The **Entry Experience** introduces the visions of space flight, with an 8-minute video of the astronauts as modern explorers, and leads into **Race to the Moon**, the stories of the Mercury, Gemini and Apollo missions and their people. The **New Frontier** opens the way for Skylab and Shuttle missions, adjacent to the **Astronaut Hall of Fame**, the museum's heart and soul. **Space Explorers Today and Tomorrow** includes the audio-visual experience aboard the replica Shuttle to Tomorrow and a glimpse of the Space Camp for kids, before introducing the hands-on **Astronaut Adventure** with its working models, G-force and flight simulators (a cabin that does six 360-degree rolls!), space-walk 'chairs', moon exploration, interactive computers and Mars Mission experience. Active minds will be more than rewarded. New in 1999 was the **First on the Moon** exhibit, focusing on the selection of the Apollo 11 crew.

Admission is $13.95 for adults and $9.95 for kids (6–12), with opening hours 9am–6pm (9am–7pm in summer), 7 days a week. **Total attraction rating: AAAA**. If you enjoyed the Kennedy Space Center, try to spend a couple of hours here. There is also the usual gift shop, with refreshments provided by the Cosmic Café. The residential **Space Camp** may be of interest to you if you have children of 9–12 who would like to train to be junior astronauts for 5 days. It's not a cheap programme – $699 – but it is a magnificent educational recreation for kids, and the Camp is happy to take visitors from the UK. You have to book up about 2 months in advance, but then just bring your youngsters along on Sunday afternoon and they are taken off your hands until Friday morning. They are arranged into groups and go through activities like flight and space-walk simulators, simulated space missions, studying rocket propulsion, space technology and other scientific experiments. If your youngster is mad keen on being an astronaut, sign him or her up for Space Camp! For details, phone 407 269 6100 or, look up their website at www.astronauts.org and www.spacecamp.com.

Cypress Gardens

Turning from the futuristic to the more natural, Cypress Gardens offers more than 200 acres of immaculate botanical gardens, spectacular flower festivals, world-famous water-ski shows and plenty of good ol' southern hospitality. It was, in fact, the first 'theme park' in Florida, pre-dating Walt Disney World by some 35 years, and it has gradually expanded in recent years to remain a pleasant alternative to the usual park experience.

It is about a 45-minute drive from Kissimmee, down I4, turning off at Exit 23 and south on to Highway 27 and then right on SR 540 6 miles past Haines City. Cypress Gardens is about 5 miles along SR 540, on the left-hand side.

After the major tourist hustle of Orlando, the Gardens are an island of peace and tranquillity. Plan on spending the best part of a day here, too, as there is plenty to keep everyone amused. Start with a boat

KEY TO ORLANDO – MINOR ATTRACTIONS

A = WINTER PARK
B = AQUATIC WONDERS TOURS
C = BOGGY CREEK AIRBOAT RIDES
D = PORT CANAVERAL
E = LEU GARDENS
F = WARBIRD AIR MUSEUM
G = GREEN MEADOWS PETTING FARM
H = SANFORD/RIVERSHIP ROMANCE
I = WONDERWORKS
J = POINCIANA GOLF AND RACQUET RESORT
K = DISNEY'S WILDERNESS PRESERVE
L = MARRIOTT'S ORLANDO WORLD CENTER
M = WEST ORANGE TRAIL BIKES
N = KISSIMMEE RODEO
O = RICHARD PETTY DRIVING EXPERIENCE
P = BLACK HAMMOCK FISH CAMP
Q = DAVE'S SKI SCHOOL
R = KATIE'S WEKIVA RIVER LANDING

S = GRAND CYPRESS EQUESTRIAN CENTER
T = HORSE WORLD RIDING STABLES
U = PIRATES DINNERSHOW
V = ORLANDO ARENA
W = CITRUS BOWL STADIUM
X = OSCEOLA COUNTY STADIUM
Y = CENTRAL FLORIDA ZOO
Z = SAK COMEDY LAB
A1 = SLEUTH'S MYSTERY DINNER SHOW
B1 = ARABIAN NIGHTS
C1 = FOREVER FLORIDA
D1 = ORLANDO SCIENCE CENTER
E1 = ORANGE COUNTY HISTORY CENTER
F1 = MARK II DINNER THEATER
G1 = MEDIEVAL TIMES
H1 = GUINNESS WORLD RECORDS EXPERIENCE
     TITANIC, SHIP OF DREAMS
J1 = SKULL KINGDOM

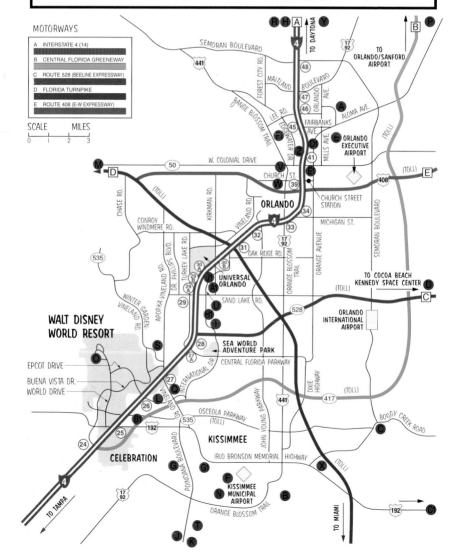

The beautiful Gazebo

tour round the canals of the **Botanical Gardens**, then stroll round the gardens themselves, taking note of the immense **Banyan Tree** (unlike the Magic Kingdom's Swiss Family Treehouse, this one is real!), the photogenic **Southern Belles** in their colourful period outfits and the beautiful **Gazebo**, which hosts more than 300 weddings a year. Visit the Oriental and French gardens, then retrace your steps and take in the spectacular **Ski Xtreme Show**, which features world-class skiers and world-famous routines (odd fact: Cypress Gardens' ski show is the world's longest-running single attraction, operating every day since 1942). There is also a new behind-the-scenes tour and skiing adventure programme for $25 per person. Have your picture taken in front of the scenic **Mediterranean Waterfall**, then marvel at the delights of the centrepiece garden attraction: the **Spring Flower Festival** runs from March to May, the **Victorian Garden Party** all year long, the **Mum Festival**

(featuring more than 2.5 million chrysanthemum blooms) in November and the **Poinsettia Festival** from the end of November to early January. For my money, the elaborate Victorian Garden Party, featuring clever topiary 'statues', is the highlight of four hugely imaginative programmes.

Continuing through the park brings you to the **Plantation Gardens**, which offers the practical side of gardening with tips on 'how to grow' herbs, vegetables, roses and other flowers. Also here is the **Wings of Wonder** exhibit, a huge butterfly house where more than 1,000 butterflies hatch from glass cabinets and flutter around in tropical splendour. Stop off for a *Gone with the Wind* experience at the beautifully restored **Magnolia Mansion**. The **Island in the Sky** will then lift you up 15 storeys on its circular revolving platform for a grandstand view of the park. Model railway fans are also well catered for with the **Historical Florida Garden Railway**, 5,000ft of lovingly recreated landscape, and the indoor 20-train **Cypress Junction**, while next door is **Carousel Cove**, a selection of games, rides and other activities to keep the youngsters amused for a while. There are four show arenas, offering contrasting live entertainment all day. The **Crossroads Arena** stages the new *European Circus Magic* up to three times a day. The **Palace** houses the

The Spring Flower Festival

spectacular *Fairy Tales on Ice* show (in great air-conditioned comfort), the **Gardens Theater** features botanical seminars, and **Nature's Arena** offers another recent show, *Calling All Animals*, three times daily. Recent additions are a mini zoo (including the inevitable gators) called **Nature's Way, Nature's Boardwalk**, which provides a superb natural setting down to the edge of the lake to discover animal habitats like wallaby and fallow deer, and the **Birdwalk Aviary**, a walk-through encounter with lorikeets that eat out of your hand. Another recent feature is an hour-long eco-tour cruise of the local lakes for an extra $6 (5 and under free). The pretty Southern Breeze paddle wheel riverboat provides historical excursions on Lake Eloise during the day for a small extra fee and themed dinner cruises in the evening and for Sunday brunch (separate ticket required – call 941 324 2111 to book, or call in at the ticket booth during your Gardens visit).

There are 14 shops and gift stores to tempt you into buying yet more souvenirs, from the children-friendly **Butterfly Shop**, to **Sweet Creations** (home-made fudge and real citrus juice, marmalades and jellies). The **Village Fare** food court offers a good choice of eating, from freshly carved roast beef to pizza and salads, while the **Cypress BBQ** serves up barbecue-smoked chicken and ribs, and the **Crossroads Restaurant** is full-service dining in air-conditioned comfort. Again, there's no shortage of choice, quality is consistently high and value for money is good.

Cypress Gardens is open from 9.30am to 5pm, with extended hours during the festivals, including until 9pm for the spectacular **Spring Lights** (Feb–April) and **Glitter, Glisten and Glow** (late Nov–Feb), which both feature laser shows, millions of lights and the 110ft Tree

of Life. Admission is $31.95 for adults, $27.15 for Seniors (55+) and $14.95 for children 6–17. One child 6–12 went free with an adult in 2000; check out www.cypressgardens.com for the latest info. Parking is $3. **Total attraction rating: AAAA.**

Silver Springs

Continuing the theme of more natural attractions, we have Silver Springs, just under 2 hours' drive to the north of Orlando. This 350-acre nature park (don't worry, you won't have to walk round all of it) surrounds the headwaters of the crystal-clear Silver River. Glass-bottomed boats take you for a close-up view of the artesian springs (the largest in the world) that bubble up here, along with plenty of wildlife. Expect close encounters with alligators, turtles, racoons and plenty of waterfowl, while the park also contains a collection of more exotic animals, like bears, panthers, giraffes, camels and zebras that can be viewed from either land or water. Four animal shows, an alligator and crocodile encounter, the world's largest bear exhibit, a petting zoo, a new kids' playground and a white alligator exhibit complete the rest of the attractions. Once again, you will feel you have left the crowds far behind. To ruin a few more illusions of the film industry, this was the setting for the famous 1930s and 40s films of the Tarzan series starring Johnny Weissmuller. This was where they staged all the spectacular scenes of Tarzan's great swimming exploits, including his regular wrestling battles with alligators, and once you have absorbed the amazing tropical nature of the undergrowth, you will understand why they decided to save on the cost of shipping the film crew all the way to Africa.

Silver Springs is located on SR 40 just through the town of Ocala, 72 miles to the north of Orlando. Take the Florida Turnpike north (it's a toll road, remember) until it turns into I75 and 28 miles further north you turn off and head east on SR 40. Another 10 miles brings you to Silver Springs, just past the Wild Waters water park on your right.

Silver Springs' main attraction is its **Glass-bottomed Boats**, 20-minute rides which go down well with all the family and give a first-class view of the seven different springs and a host of water life. Similarly, the **Lost River Voyage** is another 20-minute boat trip down one of the unspoilt stretches of the Silver River including a visit to the park's animal hospital where the local park ranger introduces you to all his current charges. The third boat trip on offer, the **Jungle Cruise**, is effectively a water safari along the Fort King Waterway, where animals from six continents are arranged in natural settings along the riverbanks. As an alternative to messing about on the river, the **Jeep Safari** is a 15-minute ride in the back of an open trailer through a natural forest habitat, home to more animals from other corners of the world, such as tapirs, marmosets, antelope and vultures. Then there are the three **Cypress Island Animal Shows**, each one lasting 15 minutes and featuring an entertaining – and occasionally hair-raising – look at the worlds of reptiles, household pets (with the addition of parrots, macaws and toucans) and creepy crawlies. The hair-raising occurs only if you are the unlucky victim chosen to display a large tarantula, giant cockroach or scorpion. As you exit the animal shows take 15 minutes to wander the **Board Walk** and see the largest American crocodile in captivity, the 16ft, 2,000lb Sobek, as well as a collection of alligators, turtles and Galapagos tortoises. The **Botanical Gardens** provide a peaceful haven to

sit and watch the world go by for a while, and the only odd note is struck by the somewhat out-of-place **A Touch of Garlits Museum**, which houses vintage American cars and racing cars. More recent additions are the **World of Bears**, an educational presentation including conservation information, all set in a 2-acre spread devoted to bears of all kinds (the largest of its type in the world), from grizzly to spectacled and black bears, the **Kids Ahoy!** playland, with its centrepiece riverboat featuring slides, rides, an air bounce, ball crawl, 3-D net maze, carousel, bumper boats and games and **Wings of the Springs,** a 30-minute show in the Silver River Showcase arena that highlights the strengths, beauty and conservation issues of the park's new collection of hawks, eagles, owls, falcons and vultures in a dramatic free-flight demonstration. **Doolittle's Petting Zoo**, with its deer and goats, is another draw for the young 'uns. The brand new **Big Gator Lagoon** showcases more than two dozen alligators in a natural cypress swamp, while the **Panther Prowl** offers a unique look at the endangered Florida panther and the Western cougar, with an educational presentation on their welfare several times daily. The **Florida Natives**

BRIT TIP: Silver Springs and Wild Waters both get busy at the weekend. Otherwise, you shouldn't encounter many queues here.

Exhibit provides a look into the state's 'native' species of snakes, turtles, spiders and mammals in a series of naturalistic enclosures. The usual collection of shops and eateries are fairly ordinary here, in contrast to the slick appeal of Orlando's

7

Ski Xtreme at Cypress Gardens

parks, although the **Deli** offers some pleasant sandwich alternatives for lunch. In all, you would probably want to spend a good half day here, with the possibility of a few hours in the neighbouring 9-acre water park of **Wild Waters** which offers slides like the new Twin Twister, a pair of 60ft-high flumes, the free-fall Thunderbolt, the twin-tunnelled Tornado, the 220ft-long Silver Bullet and the helter-skelter Osceola's Revenge, as well as a 400ft tube ride on the turbo-charged Hurricane, a huge wave pool, an area of junior slides 'n' fun called Cool Kids Cove and a nine-hole mini-golf course.

Parking is $4 and admission fees are $30.95 for adults and $21.95 for children (3–10 years). A joint ticket (Silver Springs and Wild Waters) is $35.95 and $24.95. Open 9am–5.30pm all year round. (Wild Waters open 10am–5 or 7pm March–September only.) **Attraction**

Silver Springs glass-bottomed boat

rating: **AAAA.** Check out www.silversprings.com for more info or call 352 236 2121.

Splendid China

New in 1994 and still expanding and modifying its various displays and exhibits, Splendid China is unique to central Florida and a completely different type of attraction. Here, you won't find rides and other flights of fancy, but you will be taken on a fascinating journey through one of the biggest and most mysterious and breathtaking countries of the world.

This elaborate 76-acre park offers a range of intricate, miniaturised features like the Great Wall of China, the Forbidden City and the Stone Forest, some fascinating full-size exhibits, thrilling acrobats and martial arts experts, and, naturally enough, some great food. Recent additions include five-person golf-cart tours around the park and an enlarged playground for young children. Realistically, it will not hold the attention of small kids for long, and in high summer there is little escape from the relentless heat, but where it scores impressively as an attraction is in its amazing eye for detail, its total air of authenticity (genuine Chinese craftsmen were brought in to hand-build every miniature) and its peaceful atmosphere – quite an achievement in the tourist bustle of Orlando!

Splendid China is located at the western end of the main tourist drag of Highway 192, three miles west of its junction with I4 and opposite the big Key W Kool Restaurant. The minimum time requirement here is 3–4 hours, and you can easily spend half a day taking in all the different shows and one of the excellent restaurants. Here's how its 10,000-mile journey through 5,000 years of history works. The four elements of the park are essentially:

Splendid China

1) The Exhibits. More than 60 painstakingly recreated scale models of China's greatest buildings, statues and landmarks. **The Great Wall** is one of the most striking, at half a mile long and up to 5½ft high. It is constructed of more than six million tiny bricks, all faithfully put into place by hand. Other highlights include Beijing's **Imperial Palace** and **Forbidden City**, the 26-storey **Grand Buddha of Leshan** (reduced to a 'mere' 36ft tall), and the **Mausoleum of Genghis Khan**. The stairs by the side of the **Mausoleum of Dr Sun Yat Sen** afford a wonderful high-rise overview of the park, while the famous **Terracotta Warriors** exhibit

offers a chance to get in the air-conditioned cool for a minute or two. Splendid China is fully three-quarters the size of The Magic Kingdom, so it demands a fair amount of leg work to appreciate fully all the exhibits (noting how the specially imported Chinese grass is manicured around the smallest figures!), and it is not the time to discard your walking shoes (although you can get a five-person guided tour by electric cart for $48. A guided walking tour is $5.35 extra per person).

2) The Shows. There are seven centres for the performing arts which showcase the talents of some of China's top musicians, artists, acrobats and martial arts exponents. The **Temple of Light Theater** is the main centre, featuring national song and dance exhibitions of around 30 minutes a time. **Harmony Hall** features films about China and the creation of Splendid China and its sister park near Hong Kong, which is a good starting point for any visit. Outside, the **Chinatown Show Arena** is home to various musical and martial arts specialities, while the **Pagoda Gardens** also stage acrobatic shows. The **Panda Playground**, where the kids can get rid of some excess energy, doubles

7

The spectacular Mysterious Kingdom of the Orient show at Splendid China

up as the venue for some more daring acrobats, and the **Imperial Bells Theater** holds other traditional acts, like the daring knife-climbing ceremony. The **Golden Peacock Theater** presents a special 1½-hour evening spectacular (not on Mondays), the *Mysterious Kingdom of the Orient*, which showcases the talents of some 70 dancers, acrobats and jugglers in magnificent costumes. You will need to get your entry ticket validated if you leave the park early and want to return for this show, or you can pay the $14.95 (children 5–12 $9.95) for the show on its own.

3) The Restaurants. The park sets great store by the quality of its food, whether it be in its sumptuous five-star restaurant or its cafeteria-style buffet. The jewel in the crown is the elegant **Suzhou Pearl Restaurant** for full-service, gourmet cuisine, while more budget-priced is the **Seven Flavors**, a cafeteria-style diner offering American food as well as Chinese dishes. The **Pagoda Garden**, in the furthest corner of the park, is a straightforward American deli-style establishment offering burgers and sandwiches while the **Wind and Rain Court Restaurant** has the greatest range of Chinese dishes outside the Suzhou Pearl. The **Great Wall Terrace** serves a mixture of authentic Chinese and traditional Western meals.

4) The Shops. Unlike all the other theme parks, Splendid China's shopping opportunities are all located in the Chinatown front area of the park which is open to the general public without park admission. The ten gift shops are also one up on their counterparts by stocking a more up-market and distinctive range of goods, from Bonsai trees to furniture, jewellery to T-shirts, silk and satin clothing to children's toys, and antique curios to contemporary artefacts. In many instances you can also watch the local craftsmen and women at work producing the various wares.

The mixture of Chinese and Floridian staff adds to the friendly atmosphere that the park generates, but ultimately it is a difficult concept to describe so the best advice is to see it for yourself. Adult admission is $26.99 ($25.15 for seniors), children (5–12) are $16.99 while children 4 and under are free. Opening hours are 9.30am–6pm 7 days a week and parking is free. **Attraction rating: AAAA.**

Gatorland

For another taste of the 'real' Florida, this is as authentic as it gets when it comes to the wildlife, and consequently it is hugely popular with children of all ages. When the wildlife consists of several thousand menacing alligators and crocodiles in various natural habitats and three fascinating shows, you know you're in for a different experience. 'The Alligator Capital of the World' was founded in 1949 and is one of the few family-owned attractions left in Florida, hence it possesses a home-spun charm which few of its big-money competitors can match.

Start by taking the **Gatorland Express Railroad** (under renovation in 2000) around the park to get an idea of its 50-acre expanse. Wander around the natural Florida countryside beauty of the 2,000ft **Swamp Walk**, as well as the **Alligator Breeding Marsh**

BRIT TIP: If you have an evening flight home, Gatorland is a handy place to visit on your final day. Conveniently located, it is the ideal place to soak up a couple of 'spare' hours.

Walkway, with its three-storey-high observation tower, and get a close-up view of these great reptiles who seem to hang around the 2,000ft walkway in the hope someone might 'drop in' for lunch. Breeding pens, baby alligator nurseries and rearing ponds are also situated throughout the park to give you an idea of the full growth cycle of the Florida alligator and enhance the overall feeling that it is the visitor who is behind bars and not the animals themselves. Many of the small-scale attractions have been designed with kids in mind and there is plenty to keep even the youngest amused, notably at **Lilly's Pad**, an imaginative water playground, guaranteed to get them good and wet (swimming costumes definitely advisable). **Allie's Barnyard** is the petting zoo, while you can feed some friendly lorikeets at the **Very Merry Aviary**. Other animals on view include bats, iguanas, turtles, turkey vultures, tortoises, snakes, flamingos, emus, a Florida bear and deer. However, the alligators are the main attraction and it is the two gator shows which really draw the crowds (although you will never find yourself on the end of a queue here). The 800-seat **Wrestling Stadium** sets the scene for some real Cracker-style alligator feats (a Cracker is the local term for a Florida cowboy) as Gatorland's resident 'wranglers' catch themselves a 7–8ft gator and proceed to point out the animal's various survival features, with the aid of some stunts that will have you seriously questioning your cowboy's sanity. The **Gator Jumparoo** is another eye-opening spectacle as some of the park's biggest creatures use their tails to 'jump' out of the water and be hand-fed tasty morsels such as whole chickens! You can also take in the **Snakes of Florida** show which demonstrates that these reptiles, although dangerous, are not slimy and nasty after all, but are, in fact, dry-skinned and shy (and that Florida is home to more venomous varieties than you would imagine).

A fascinating recent addition is the fearsome **Jungle Crocs of the World** exhibit and show, with some of the deadliest animals from places like Egypt, Australia and Cuba. Authentic lairs and brilliant presentation by the well-versed guides all add up to a superb extension to the park. Obviously, face-to-face encounters with these living dinosaurs is not everyone's cup of tea, but it's an experience you're unlikely to repeat anywhere else. In addition, you can dine on smoked alligator ribs and deep-fried gator nuggets at **Pearl's Smokehouse,** with excellent kids' meals at $3.99. The park is also home to hundreds of nesting herons and egrets, providing a fascinating close-up view of the nests from March–August.

Gatorland scores in its great value for money for 3–4 hours' entertainment, with adult tickets at $16.93, children 3–12 $7.48, while there is also an extremely worthwhile combination ticket with nearby **Boggy Creek Airboats** at $28 for adults and $14.75 for 3–12s. Gatorland is located on the South Orange Blossom Trail, 2 miles south of its junction with the Central Florida Greeneway and three miles north of Highway 192. Opening hours are 9am to dusk daily and parking is free. **Attraction rating: AAAA.** Look up www.gatorland.com for more info.

Mystery Fun House

This three-part adventure playground is primarily for kids and will happily occupy Junior for up to three hours. The three elements are the Mystery Fun House itself, the Jurassic Putt Golf Park, and Starbase Omega, an elaborate laser battle game that mum and dad get as much of a kick out of as the kids.

A Gatorland denizen

Start with the **Mystery Fun House** and work your way through the mirror maze into the Egyptian Tomb. Another 14 chambers of surprises await you, including a fire-breathing dragon in the Topsy-Turvy Tilt Room, the mysteries of the Forbidden Temple, the dangers of the Chamber of Horrors (why do kids seem to revel in the gruesome delights of death and torture?), and concluding in the Grand Ballroom with its circus theme.

BRIT TIP: The Mystery Fun House is ideal for kids of all ages – unless they are really afraid of the dark.

Next, take in the high-tech **Starbase Omega**. You'll be fully kitted out with electronic power-vest and laser blaster, briefed for your 'mission' (usually a battle with all the visitors divided into two teams) and then unleashed on the combat zone via the Millennium 333 transporter. The unique 'alien environment', space mist and rousing music add to the fun and this twenty-first-century version of cops and robbers is guaranteed to bring out the kid in everyone.

The **Mini-golf** set-up offers a few variations on the standard crazy golf courses with which Orlando is overstocked. The Jurassic Putt theme means you have to test your skill against a number of dinosaur

obstacles, including an 18ft brachiosaurus and a dangerous velociraptor.

If all that is not enough to keep your youngsters entertained, the Mystery Fun House has one of Orlando's largest video games arcades, an ice cream parlour, several gift shops, a shooting gallery, an 'old-tyme' photo booth, and a restaurant that features the periodic Wiz-Bang Revue. The Mystery Fun House also offers a number of birthday party packages from $10.50 per person ($11.75 with pizza or hot-dogs); for details call 407 351 3356.

BRIT TIP: On a (rare) wet day, the Mystery Fun House can be a boon to parents with active kids to keep amused for a few hours. There is no entry fee to play the video games.

The Mystery Fun House is located on Major Boulevard, just off Kirkman Road as you approach Universal Studios. It is open 365 days a year 10am–10pm (Mon–Thur), 2pm–9pm (Fri), 10am–11pm (Sat) and 10am–9pm (Sun), and a combination ticket for all three features costs $19.95. Individually, it is $10.95 for the Mystery Fun House, $9.95 for Starbase Omega, and $4.95 for the Jurassic Putt Mini-golf. **Attraction rating: TTT.**

Ripley's Believe It Or Not

You can't miss this particular attraction, next door to the Mercado Shopping Center on International Drive, as its extraordinary tilted appearance makes it seem as though it was designed by an architect with an aversion to the horizontal.

BRIT TIP: Like the Mystery Fun House, Ripley's is a handy retreat to know about on the occasional rainy days.

However, once inside you will soon find yourself back on the level and for an hour or two you can wander through this museum dedicated to the weird and wonderful.

Robert L Ripley was an eccentric and energetic explorer and collector who, for 40 years, travelled the world in his bid to assemble a collection of the greatest oddities known to man. The Orlando branch of this now world-wide museum chain features 8,900 sq ft of displays that include authentic artefacts, video presentations, illusions, interactive exhibits and music. The elaborate re-creation of an Egyptian tomb showcases an Egyptian mummy and three rare mummified animals, while the collection of miniatures includes the world's smallest violin and a single grain of rice handpainted with a tropical sunset. Larger-scale exhibits include a portion of the Berlin Wall, a two-thirds scale 1907 Rolls Royce built

entirely out of matchsticks and a version of the Mona Lisa textured completely from toast!

Admission is $12.95 for adults and $8.95 for 4–12s and it is open 9am–1am daily (last ticket sold at midnight). **Attraction rating: AAA.**

Ripley's is also the starting point for an excellent package of four I-Drive attractions called **A Day On The Drive**. The price undercuts the cost of all four individually and has the benefit of flexibility, so you can do them in a single day or over a series of days (after the main parks shut, for instance). The cost of Ripley's, Titanic – Ship Of Dreams, Fun Spot and Race Rock restaurant would normally be around $59.40 for adults and $44.40 for children (4–12) but is available through some tour operators and ticket outlets for $46 and $35. Ripley's serves as the starting point, and a full day would work out something like: 9.30am Ripley's, 11am Titanic, 1pm lunch at Race Rock, 3pm shopping at Pointe*Orlando, 6pm Fun Spot action park. For more details, call Ripley's on 407 345 0501 (Race Rock includes a special menu, Fun Spot provides a Track Sampler and four tokens; see below for other attraction details).

7

Skull Kingdom

Skull Kingdom

The walk-through haunted house idea takes on a new dimension in Orlando. Take **Skull Kingdom**, which was new in 1997, for example. Not content with a house, here is a full-blown *castle* on International Drive (opposite Wet 'n Wild) dedicated to frights, horrors and grisly goings-on at every turn. The setting and lavishness of the Kingdom of the Skull Lord marks it out as way above average, and the combination of elaborate light and sound effects, robotics and the scream-inducingly brilliant live actors (who are kept suitably creepy by two full-time make-up artists) makes for a hair-raising experience. Needless to say, the shock tactics are state of the art, with the best elements of horror films and haunted houses well maintained over the two-storey spread of mazes, caverns and other demonic challenges (watch out for the

> BRIT TIP: Friday and Saturday evenings are peak periods for Skull Kingdom, with queues of up to 30 minutes.

monster spit!). There is also the inevitable Haunted Gift Shop and Ghoulish Arcade Games at the end of your 20–30-minute (depending on how much you 'enjoy' the experience!) Skull Kingdom immersion. It is open 6pm–11.30pm (Sun–Wed), noon–midnight (Thur–Sat), with extended hours in peak season, with admission $11.79, and it gets a glowing recommendation from *Fright Times*, the official publication for the industry of haunted attractions – yes there *is* such a publication. Go with a few friends, or have a drink or three first! **TTTTT** (not recommended for under 10s).

Terror on Church Street is a downtown attraction that closed briefly in 1999 before being bought up and moved, lock, stock and haunted barrel, inside Church Street Station. Visitors move in groups of about eight at a time through 16 theatrical sets and scenes with an unforgettable array of costumed characters. The special effects, sound and climate control, plus the live contribution of the actors, add up to another terrifying half-hour or so. Admission is $12.95 for adults, $9.95 for under 13s (but again, way too scary for most kids), and Terror is open 6pm–midnight (Tue–Thur), 6pm–1am (Fri), 1pm–1am (Sat) and 1pm–11pm (Sun).

Fun Spot

While Orlando is also well served with small-scale attractions of the go-kart and funfair variety, the only one to deliver full-scale, family-sized fun is the aptly named **Fun Spot**, just off I-Drive on Del Verde Way (look for the 102ft-high Big Wheel just past the junction with Kirkman Road). With four different and highly challenging go-kart tracks, bumper cars and boats, four quite daring fairground-type rides (check out the Spider and Paratrooper), an impressive two-storey video arcade and food court, plus five Kid Spot rides for the little ones, the 4.7-acre park promises several hours of fun. Parking and admission are free, but you must buy tickets for the rides, which are $3 each ($22 for eight). Go-karts require two tickets, while the other rides are a ticket apiece. There is also a 3-hour 'unlimited everything' ticket for $30, a $20 go-kart ticket or $15 unlimited one-ticket ride package, and a freeplay video arcade ticket for $6. It is also included in the Day on the Drive package. **TTTT**. It opens 10am–midnight (high season), or 2pm–11pm (Mon–Thur), 2pm–

midnight (Fri) and 10am–midnight (Sat–Sun) in low season. Call 407 363 3867 or log on to www.fun-spot.com for details.

Guiness World Records Experience

Right in front of the Mercado Center on I-Drive is one of the most refreshing and enjoyable smaller attractions. New in 2000, it is an interactive showcase for all the myriad of fun and bizarre facts which the famous book highlights, all presented in a unique and highly entertaining way. You start in the Guinness World Theater for a look at how the book came to be and then move to the Computer Gateway/ Micro-Technology Playground where you play Guinness trivia on the 'Monster monitors' and are 'miniaturised' to enter the book's computer database. A variety of games, some quite energetic, await you before you pass on to the Molecular Expander/Transporter & Space Shuttle, which has more surprises in store (some rather gross, some quite breathtaking). The clever Space Shuttle segment brings you to Guinness Town and a multimedia streetscape of World Records brought to life in a host of amusing ways. Finally, you enter the Simulator Theater for a ride with a difference and exit into the inevitable gift shop. All in all, it is a novel way to spend a couple of hours and a great way to amuse the kids while mum and dad enjoy shopping or, perhaps, a drink in the Mercado itself. The Experience is open daily 10am–11pm and costs $12.95 for adults and $7.95 for 5–12s. **AAAA.**

Titanic

A new attraction in 1999 inside the Mercado was *Titanic* **– Ship of Dreams**, the first permanent exhibit

to the great maritime disaster of 1912. With a mixture of genuine artifacts, full-scale re-creations of the ship's interior, several clever scene-setting presentations (including a visit to the Harland and Wolff shipyard in Belfast during building of the 'unsinkable' liner), film memorabilia from *Titanic* and *A Night to Remember*, plus live interpretations by storytellers in period costume, you will see, hear and feel just about everything there is to know about the *Titanic* and her tragic fate. The live actor and actress participation, which is now carried right through the exhibit, makes for an enthralling and quite moving depiction of the tragedy. The full experience takes at least an hour, with the inevitable gift store at the end, and, while the basic premise is a touch macabre, there is no disguising the on-going fascination with the ship. Even the ticket hall is suitably atmospheric, and entry is $16.95 for adults and $11.95 for 6–12s (5 and under free). It is open 10am–9pm daily. **AAA½** (also in the Day on the Drive package).

If you enjoyed the Ship of Dreams, you will also want to know about the *Titanic* dining experience at the excellent Atlantis restaurant in the Renaissance Resort Hotel near SeaWorld. It features a sumptuous seven-course dinner with authentic period dishes and is a truly memorable meal (for more details see the Atlantis entry in Chapter 10, Eating Out).

WonderWorks

International Drive's most unmistakable landmark is the 'interactive entertainment centre' of **WonderWorks**, a three-storey chamber of real family fun with a host of novel elements. Unmistakable? You bet – how many buildings do you know that are *upside down?* That's right, all of the

The upside-down world of WonderWorks

82ft-tall edifice is constructed from the roof up! The basic premise (working on the theory that every attraction has to have a story behind it) is that WonderWorks is a secret research facility into unexplained phenomena that got uprooted by a tornado experiment and dumped in topsy-turvy fashion in the heart of this busy tourist district (yeah, right!). Well you've got to give them full marks for imagination, and the interior attractions are almost as entertaining as the exterior façade. You enter through an 'inversion tunnel' that orientates you the same way round as the building (look out of the window if you don't believe me) and there are then chambers of entertaining and mildly educational hands-on experiences that demand several hours to explore fully. Without ever actually using the words 'science' or 'museum', WonderWorks steers you through five different 'labs' of interactive activities, including the **Bermuda Triangle Corridor**, the **Mystery Lab** (experience earthquakes and hurricanes and see famous disasters on a bank of computer monitors), **Physical Challenge Lab** (virtual basketball, table tennis, hang-gliding and even horse racing, baseball test, health and lifestyle quizzes and the wonderfully creepy Shocker Chair, a high-voltage simulation that gives you the feeling of 2,000 jolts rather than volts – it's *weird*!), **Illusions Lab** (with the Bridge of Fire static electricity generator, a computer ageing process and 'elastic surgery', hall of mirrors and bubble table), plus the **WonderWorks Emporium** gift shop, souvenirs and pizza

BRIT TIP: WonderWorks is perfectly situated, next door to Pointe*Orlando. Mum and dad can happily dump the kids for a couple of hours' fun in WonderWorks while they enjoy a drink at Lulu's Bait Shack or Adobe Gilas, the Pointe's outstanding bars.

parlour. A new **Lazer Tag** game centre on the top floor adds even more appeal for youngsters. On no account miss the two virtual roller-coasters, a pair of amazing enclosed 'pods' which let you first design and then ride your own coaster. Truly, a topsy-turvy experience! The experience costs $14.95 for adults, $10.95 for seniors (55+) and $10.95 for kids 4–11; a WonderWorks/ Lazer Tag combo ticket is $18.95 and $13.95. Check out www.wonderworksonline.com for more info. Open 9am–midnight daily. **AAA** and **TTT**½.

Fantasy of Flight

Another recent addition to central Florida is this $30-million aviation museum attraction which is an absolute must even for anyone not usually interested in the history of flight or the glamour of the Golden Age of flying. Just 25 minutes down I4 towards Tampa (take Junction 21, Polk City, go north on SR 559 for half a mile, then turn left into the main entrance), Fantasy of Flight is a four-part adventure featuring the world's largest private collection of vintage aircraft, a series of expertly recreated 'immersion experiences' into memorable moments in aviation

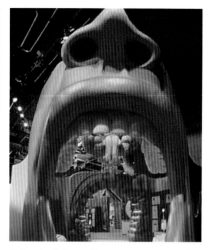

Orlando Science Center

history (like a World War Two bomber mission with a real Flying Fortress!) and eight incredibly realistic fighter simulators that take you through a WWII aerial battle. You get a pre-flight 'briefing' on how to handle your simulator (a Vought Corsair), and then climb in to the totally enclosed cockpit to do battle with the Japanese Air Force over the Pacific. It's difficult, absorbing, fun and totally addictive.

The whole experience is crafted in 1930s Art Deco style, including a full-service diner and original gift shop. There is strong British appeal with the war depictions and the exhibits, like a Mark IX Spitfire and the last airworthy Sunderland Flying Boat. Admission is $24.95 for adults, $21.95 for seniors (60+) and $13.95 for kids (5–12, under 5s free). It is open 9am–8pm in peak holiday periods, 9am–5pm at other times, and parking is free.

Other recent additions include the world's last flying B-26 Marauder in the collection of 30-plus historic aircraft. You can also take an **Ultralight flight** lesson over Fantasy of Flight for 15 minutes for $30 (weather permitting; not on

Immerse yourself in Fantasy of Flight

Mondays). Fantasy of Flight is the brainchild of American entrepreneur and aviation whizz Kermit Weeks and I have yet to encounter an attraction put together with more genuine love and care. In fact, it is as much a work of art as a tourist attraction, and the masses have yet to discover it, too. For more information call 863 984 3500 or look up www.fantasyofflight.com. **Attraction rating: AAAA.**

Orlando Science Center

Because this is Orlando, there is no such thing as a simple museum or science centre. Everything has to be all-singing, all-dancing just to compete. Hence, the new **Orlando Science Center** is more than a mere museum and far more fun than the average science centre. Here, you get a series of hands-on experiences and habitats that entertain as well as inform, and school-age children will get a lot from it (not to mention mum and dad). The Science Center has seven main components, plus an inviting café and a night sky observatory. **Natureworks** creates a number of typical Florida habitats, **Science City** introduces fun ways to understand and use physical science and maths (including some mind-bending puzzles) and the **Cosmic Tourist** offers a trip round our solar system with an amusing travel theme. The **Darden Adventure Theater** takes up more 'science is fun' topics with the Einstein Players, and **Bodyzone** offers some fascinating medical insights into the human body. For those a bit too young for the educational element, **Kids' Town** has plenty of junior-sized fun and games for under 8s while **TechWorks** completes the main tour, a three-part adventure into light, imaginary landscapes and showbiz science. You'll be amazed at how much you learn in the course of having fun.

In addition, the Center has two separate programmes based in the **Dr Phillips CineDome**, a 310-seat cinema that practically surrounds its audience with large-format films, digital planetarium shows (a virtual tour of the universe, anyone?) and

> **BRIT TIP:** The CineDome film and laser show can operate until midnight on Friday and Saturday for a show independent of the Science Center.

3-D laser shows. The underwater presentation *The Living Sea* is so lifelike you end up holding your breath! The CineDome also boasts a 28,000-watt digital sound system that helps make the experience unforgettable. The Science Center is located on East Princeton Street in downtown Orlando, just off exit 43 of I4, is open 9am–5pm Tuesday–Thursday, 9am–9pm Friday and Saturday and noon to 5pm Sunday, and costs $12.50 for adults, $11.50 for seniors (55+) and $9.25 for 3–11s with one CineDome show (film or planetarium); $14.25, $13.25 and $11.00 with two CineDome shows; $9.50, $8.50 and $6.75 for the Science Center only; or $6, $5 and $4.50 for one CineDome film. It is closed on Thanksgiving Day in November, Christmas Eve and Christmas Day. **Attraction rating: AAA½.**

   Orange County History Center: due to open downtown in autumn 2000 was a new journey into central Florida history, from the wildlife and Native Americans to today's tourist issues and the space programme. Again, the accent is on the interactive, with hands-on exhibits and live characters, and all in the ex-County Courthouse on renovated Heritage Square, complete with its huge fountains and open-air stage. Walking tours of historic downtown sites will also be available here. The History Center itself is a four-storey adventure starting with the Orientation Theater for a 14-minute multimedia presentation. Then you visit the Natural Environment (12,000 years ago), the First Peoples and European Contact exhibits. Re-creations of Settler Life, Cattle Industry and Citrus Industry complete the Fourth Floor level, and you move on to Courtroom B and Grand Jury Room for more re-enactments. Transportation, Tourism, the Land Boom and Aviation show how central Florida developed, and The Day We Changed marks the arrival of Walt Disney World. Second Floor highlights include The Place We Live (modern-day central Florida) and National Travelling Exhibits, while back on the First Floor (ground level to us) is the gift shop and the Dome, a huge 3-D metal arch rising up through the next level and depicting 200 scenes of Florida life. It sounds a remarkable effort to make history 'live' and should entertain all the family. Admission is $7 for adults, $4 for 3–12s and $5 for seniors (55+), and it is open 9am–5pm (Mon–Sat) and 11am–5pm (Sun). The History Center can be found off Washington Street and Magnolia Avenue downtown (Exit 40 off I4). Expected rating: **AAA½**. PS: combine a visit here with lunch at the wonderfully eclectic Globe restaurant on the corner of the Square.

BRIT TIP: Ladies, please remember that down some of the whizziest slides it is advisable to wear a one-piece swimsuit rather than a bikini. Your modesty could be at stake here!

The Water Parks

If anyone has been down the slides and flumes at the local leisure centre, they will have an inkling of what Orlando's five big water parks are all about. Predictably, *Walt Disney World* Resort weighs in with three of the most elaborate ones, but the independent Universal-owned Wet 'n Wild and Water Mania are equally adept at providing hours of watery fun with slides and wave pools in an amazing variety of styles that owe a lot to the imagination of the theme park ride creators.

All five parks require at least half a day of splashing, sliding and riding to get full value from their rather high admission charges, but, if you prefer to get your kicks in watery rather than land-borne fashion, these are definitely for you and you will want to try at least a couple of them. Lockers are provided for valuables and you can hire towels.

BRIT TIP: While these parks are a great way of cooling down, it is easy to forget this is also the best way to pick up a five-star case of sunburn. So don't forget high-factor (at least 15), waterproof suntan lotion.

7

172 ──── THE OTHER ATTRACTIONS

© Disney Enterprises, Inc.

Disney's Typhoon Lagoon Water Park

Disney's Typhoon Lagoon Water Park

Until *Disney's Blizzard Beach* Water Park opened in 1995, *Disney's Typhoon Lagoon* was the biggest and finest example of Florida's water parks. In high season, it is also the busiest, so be prepared to run into more queues and congestion in all the main areas. The 56 acres of *Disney's Typhoon Lagoon* Water Park are spread out around the 2½-acre lagoon that is fringed with palm trees and white-sand beaches. If it wasn't for the high-season crowds, you could easily convince yourself you had been washed up on some tropical island paradise. With the exception of *Disney's Blizzard Beach* Water Park, *Typhoon Lagoon* goes in for the most extravagant landscaping and introduces some unique and clever details. The walk up Mount Mayday, for instance, provides a terrific overview of the park as well as adding scenic touches like rope bridges and tropical flowers. Sun loungers, chairs, picnic tables and even a few hammocks are provided to add to the comfort and convenience of restful areas like Getaway Glen (although you need to arrive early to bag a decent spot with some shade).

The park is overlooked by the 90ft **Mount Mayday**, atop which is perched the luckless *Miss Tilly*, a shrimp boat that legend has it landed here during the typhoon that gave the park its name. Watch for the water fountains that shoot from *Miss Tilly's* funnel at regular intervals, accompanied by the ship's hooter, which signal the outbreak of another round of 6ft-high waves in the **Surf Pool** (where you can hire innertubes to bob around on or just try body-surfing). Circling the lagoon is **Castaway Creek**, a 3ft-deep lazy flowing river that offers the chance to float happily along on the rubber tyres that are provided for just this purpose (although around midday you may find yourself shoulder-to-shoulder with hundreds of people who all have the same idea).

The series of slides and rides are all clustered around Mount Mayday and vary from the breathtaking three slides of **Humunga Kowabunga**, which drop you 214ft at up to 30mph down some of the steepest inclines in waterdom (make sure your swimming costume is SECURELY fastened for this one!), to the children's area **Ketchakiddee Creek**, which offers a selection of slides and fun pools for all youngsters under 4ft tall. In between, you have the three **Storm Slides**, another body slide which twists and turns through caves, tunnels and waterfalls, **Mayday Falls**, a 460ft innertube ride down a series of twisting, turning drops, **Keelhaul Falls**, an alternative tube ride that takes slightly longer, and

> BRIT TIP: As the busiest of the water parks, *Disney's Typhoon Lagoon* can hit capacity quite early in the day in the summer. Call 407 824 4321 in advance to avoid being shut out.

Fun at Disney's Blizzard Beach Water Park

Gang Plank Falls, a group or family ride whose tubes take up to four people down the 300ft of mock rapids. The hugely imaginative **Shark Reef** offers the chance to snorkel around this upturned wreck and coral reef among 4,000 tropical fish and a number of real, but quite harmless, nurse sharks. Like all the areas, this one is carefully supervised, and those who aren't quite brave enough to dive in amongst the marine wildlife can still get a close-up through the underwater port holes of the sunken ship (Shark Reef is closed to swimmers during the coldest of the winter months). There are height and health restrictions on Humunga Kowabunga (it's not suitable for anyone with a bad back or neck, or for pregnant women), while the queues for this slide, plus the Storm Slides and Shark Reef, can touch an

arduous hour at times which can take a lot of the fun out of the experience (an hour's wait for a 20-second slide? Not for me, thanks). Getting out of the sun can also be slightly problematic as the provision of shaded areas is not overwhelming, but a quick plunge into Castaway Creek usually solves any overheating problems.

For snacks and meals, **Lowtide Lou's** and **Let's Go Slurpin'** both offer snacks and drinks while **Typhoon Tilly's** and **Leaning Palms** both serve a mixture of burgers, sandwiches, salads and ice cream. It is essential to avoid main meal-times here if you want to eat in relative comfort. You do, however, have the option of bringing your own picnic along here (unlike all the other theme parks) as there are several scenic areas laid out for you (but no alcohol or glass containers are allowed). You CAN'T bring your own snorkels, innertubes or rafts into the park, but snorkles are provided at Shark Reef and you need to hire innertubes only for the Lagoon. If you have forgotten any vital item like a sunhat or bucket and spade for the kids, or even your swimsuit, they are all available (along with the usual range of gifts and souvenirs) at **Singapore Sal's**.

To avoid the worst of the summer crowds (when the park's 7,200 capacity is frequently reached), Monday morning is about the best time to visit (steer clear of the weekends at all costs), while on other weekdays arrive either 30 minutes before opening time or in mid-afternoon when some people decide to call it a day to dodge the daily rainstorm. Early evening is pleasant as the park lights up.

Opening hours are 9am to dusk every day, with admission $27.95 for adults and $22.50 for kids 3–9 (under 3s free). It is free as one of the options with the Park Hopper Plus Passes. **Attraction rating: TTTT**.

Disney's River Country Water Park

At just a quarter of the size of *Disney's Typhoon Lagoon*, you might think this is a good, out-of-the-way spot that most people overlook. But you'd be wrong. It may be smaller, but the same number of folk seem to try to cram in here. As it is not unknown for the gates to close by late morning because capacity has been reached, it is a good idea to arrive early or after 4pm (when admission prices are also reduced).

BRIT TIP: Disney's River Country Water Park is not the best of the water parks in the winter. Despite the heated pool, Bay Lake can be pretty cold and the park often closes for refurbishment. Call 407 824 4321 to check opening times.

However, just because it is the country cousin to *Disney's Typhoon Lagoon* and *Blizzard Beach* in terms of size doesn't mean *Disney's River Country* is any less well organised or lacking in charm (although I believe it is looking a little ragged at the edges these days, especially the changing facilities). The overall theme is of an old-fashioned swimming hole, which gives it a rustic, backwoods America flavour straight out of *Huckleberry Finn*.

The heart of the park is **Bay Cove**, a roped-off section of Bay Lake which offers the chance to climb on ropes, tyre swings, a barrel bridge and boom swing, and ride the cable, all finishing with an emphatic splash into the lake. **Whoop-N-Holler Hollow** contains the two

main thrill opportunities, a pair of similar body-slide flumes that end with a drop into Bay Cove. **White Water Rapids** is a more sedate trip via innertube down a series of chutes and pools that gives you a chance to admire the scenery, while young children are also very well catered for with their own area, **Kiddie Cove**, with several small slides, pools and a separate stretch of beach, and **Indian Springs**, a neat fountain-cum-squirt pool. **Upstream Plunge** is a large, free-form pool, and the **Slippery Slide Falls** drop you 7ft into it! Each of the main activities will take you about half the time of those in *Disney's Typhoon Lagoon*, but there is a more relaxing feel to *Disney's River Country* that encourages you to stick around for a while longer. You can also take a boat ride or walk around on the **Nature Trail**, a 1,000yd boardwalk through a pretty, well-shaded cypress grove. The animals, pony rides and petting zoo of the neighbouring Fort Wilderness are another handy diversion for young 'uns.

Pop's Place serves the usual array of fast food (and a Kid's Picnic Basket at $3.59) while the **Waterin' Hole** offers snacks and drinks. There is no gift shop, however, and 3–4 hours will be probably the maximum you'll need here.

To find *Disney's River Country* Water Park, aim for *Disney's Fort Wilderness Resort & Campground* and you will find the (free) parking area at Gateway Depot. From there, you must leave your car and use the bus service to the *Disney's Fort Wilderness Campground*, where you walk the last 100 yards and bear left just before the boat jetty. Admission is $15.95 for adults and $12.50 for 3–9s, while it is free with a Park Hopper Plus Pass, and is open 10am to dusk. **Attraction rating: TTT/AAA.**

Disney's Blizzard Beach Water Park

Ever imagined a skiing resort in the middle of Florida? You haven't? Well, Disney have, and this is the result. *Disney's Blizzard Beach* Water Park aims to put the rest of the parks in the shade for size as well as extravagant settings, with the whole park arranged as if it were in the Rocky Mountains rather than the sub-tropics. That means snow-effect scenery, Christmas trees and water slides cunningly converted to look like skiing pistes and toboggan runs. It delivers a real feast for water lovers and Disney admirers in general, and the basic premise of snow-surfin' USA is an unarguable five-star knockout. Feature items are **Mount Gushmore**, a 90ft mountain down which all the main slides run (including the world's tallest free-fall speed slide, the terrifying 120ft-long **Summit Plummet**, which rockets you down a simulated ski jump at up to 60mph!), **Tike's Peak**, a kiddie-sized version of the park with scaled-down slides and a mock snow-beach and **Ski-Patrol Training Camp**, a series of slides and challenges for pre-teens. **Melt-Away Bay** is a one-acre pool fed by 'melting snow' waterfalls (actually blissfully warm), and **Cross Country Creek** is a lazy-flowing half-mile river around the whole park which also carries floating guests through a bone-chilling 'ice cave' (watch out for the mini-waterfalls of ice-cold water!). A clever ski chair-lift operates to the top of Mount Gushmore, providing a magnificent view of the whole park and the surrounding areas of *Walt Disney World* Resort. Don't miss the outstanding rides – **Teamboat Springs**, a wild, family innertube adventure, **Runoff Rapids**, a one-, two- or three-person tube plunge, and the **Snow Stormers**, a daring head-first 'toboggan' run.

Toboggan Racers give you the chance to speed down the 'slopes' against seven other head-first daredevils. All four go to new heights of water park imagination and provide good-sized thrills without overdoing the scare factor (yes, I know, I'm a total coward). A recent addition is the **Double Dipper**, two side-by-side slides which send you down 215ft-long tubes in a race that is timed on a big clock which you can see at the bottom, and which gives you a real jolt halfway down! For those not quite up to Summit Plummet lunacy, the wonderfully named **Slush Gusher** is a slightly less terrifying speed slide. There is also a 'village' area including the **Beach Haus** shop and **Lottawatta Lodge** fast-food restaurant, offering diners a grandstand view of Mount Gushmore and Melt-Away Bay beach. Snacks are also available at **Avalunch** (ouch!), the **Warming Hut** and **Polar Pub & Frostbite Freddie's**. Predictably, the crowds are suitably massive, so avoid the weekends and from mid-morning onwards on Wednesdays to Fridays.

Disney's Blizzard Beach Water Park is located just north of *Disney's All-Star Resorts* off Buena Vista Drive, and charges are $27.95 per adult and $22.50 per child (3–9); again it is one of the free optional extras with Hopper Plus Passes, with opening times from 9am to early evening. **Attraction rating: TTTTT**. Adjacent to Blizzard Beach is the wonderful **Winter Summerland** mini-golf challenge, with two elaborately themed courses, that makes for a great diversion with children.

Wet 'n Wild

If *Walt Disney World* Resort scores highest marks for its scenic content, the world's first water park back in 1977, Wet 'n Wild, goes full-tilt for thrills and spills of the highest quality. If you really want to test the material of your swimsuit to the limit, this is the place to do it!

Wet 'n Wild is repeatedly one of the best-attended water parks in the country, and its location in the heart of International Drive makes it a major tourist draw. It was also given a $1.5million facelift in 2000 to give it a fresh, new look. Consequently, you will once again encounter some serious crowds here, although the 12 slides and rides, **Lazy River** attraction, an elaborate kids' park (with mini versions of many of the slides), **Surf Lagoon** and restaurant and picnic areas all manage to absorb a lot of punters before the queues start to develop. Waits of more than half an hour at peak times are rare. Its popularity with locals means it is busiest at weekends, with July the month that attracts most crowds.

The Hydra Fighter at Wet 'n Wild

BRIT TIP: For all the water parks, it can be advisable to bring a pair of shoes or sandals that can be worn in water.

You are almost spoilt for choice of main rides, from the highly popular group innertube rides of the **Surge** and **Bubba Tub**, through the more demanding rides of **Raging Rapids** to the high-thrill factor of the two-person **Black Hole** (like the Magic Kingdom's Space Mountain, but in water!), **Blue Niagara** (also enclosed, but this one's a body slide) and **Mach 5**, to the ultimate terror of **Der Stuka** and the **Bomb Bay**. These latter are definitely not for the faint-hearted. Basically they are two 76ft-high body slides with a drop as near vertical as makes no difference. Der Stuka is the straightforward slide version, while

the Bomb Bay adds the extra terror of being hoisted into place and then allowed to free-fall on to the top of the slide. And they call it fun?! Suffice it to say, your author has not put himself at risk on these particular contraptions, and has absolutely no intention of doing so! For some reason only 15–25 per cent of the park's visitors pluck up the courage to try it. Can't think why. There are height restrictions (minimum 4ft required) on the Bomb Bay and Der Stuka and Blue Niagara, while older kids get their own chance for thrills on the huge, inflatable **Bubble Up**, which bounces them into 3ft of water.

Recent additions are the thrilling toboggan-like **Fuji Flyer**, which takes four passengers in 8ft-long, in-line tubes which whoosh down more than 450ft of banked curves and speed-enhancing straights, and the bungee-like **Hydra Fighter**, a two-person swing equipped with a fire-type hose that sends the contraption into mad gyrations as you increase the water pressure!

Wet 'n Wild

The neighbouring lake is also part of the fun (although not in winter when its temperature drops below that of merely chilly), adding the opportunities to try the cable-operated **Knee Ski** and (for a nominal fee) ride the **Wild One** (large innertubes tied behind a speedboat). Alternatively, take a breather in the slow-flowing **Lazy River** or abandon the water

Cruisin' Creek at Water Mania

altogether for one of several shaded picnic areas. Staying cool out of the water is rather harder, however, especially at peak times when the best spots are quickly snapped up.

For the energetic, there is also beach volleyball and the chance to ride the **Robo Surfer** at selected times, a watery version of the mechanical bucking bronco. All-day lockers, shower facilities, tube and towel rentals are all well provided,

Water Mania

but if you bring your own floating equipment is has to be checked by one of the many lifeguards on duty.

For food, **Bubba's Bar-B-Q** serves chicken, ribs, fries and drinks, the **Beach Club Snack Bar** features burgers, hot-dogs, chicken and sandwiches and there are another seven snack bars offering similar fast-food fare, including a pizza bar and a kiddies' counter (for the likes of peanut butter sandwiches, hot-dogs and chips).

BRIT TIP: The Children's Playground was built especially for those under 4ft – right down to the only junior wave pool in the world.

Picnics can also be brought in, provided you don't include alcohol or glass containers.

Wet 'n Wild is located half a mile north of International Drive's junction with Sand Lake Road at the intersection with Universal Boulevard and is open year-round from 9am in peak periods (10am at other times) until variously 5, 6, 7, 8 or 11pm. The extended hours from late June to late August, known as the Summer Nights programme, offer particularly good value as admission is $10 off after 5pm and you still have 6 hours of watery fun ahead of you. There is also live music, dancing, karaoke and competitions, including the interactive challenges of the rock-climbing walls and the catapult-orientated Water Wars, plus the bungee trampoline and dunk tank, in a real fun, party atmosphere. Admission is $28.95 for adults, $22.95 for 3–9s and free for under 3s, while Wet 'n Wild is included in both the 7- and 10-Day Flex Tickets with Universal Studios, SeaWorld and Busch Gardens and the 5-Day Universal Express ticket. Tube rentals are $4 ($2 deposit), towels $2 and lockers $5 ($2 deposit), or $9 for all three ($4 deposit). Parking is $4. **Rating: TTTTT.** Check out www.wetnwild.com.

Water Mania

If Wet 'n Wild attracts the serious water-thrill seekers, Kissimmee's version, Water Mania, is more family-orientated and laid back, with the crowds highest at weekends when the locals flock in and lowest early in the week. That's not to say Water Mania doesn't have its share of scary slides (or Wet 'n Wild doesn't cater for families), it's just their emphasis is slightly different and those looking to avoid the crowds often end up here. Where this 36-acre park scores a minor victory over its rivals is in the provision of 3 acres of wooded picnic area that makes a welcome change from the concrete expanses and from the feverish splashing activities. You are again welcome to bring your own picnic (although no glass bottles or mugs).

Eight different slides, including a patented non-stop surfing challenge called **Wipe-Out**, the usual **Cruisin' Creek**, a 720,000-gallon **Wave Pool** (waves every 15 minutes, up to 4ft high) and three separate kids' areas provide the main attractions, and there is again enough here to keep you occupied for at least half a day. Top of the list for those daring enough to throw themselves down things like Der Stuka is the **Screamer**, an aptly named 72ft-high free-fall speed slide, and the **Abyss**, 380ft of enclosed-tube darkness. The

> BRIT TIP: Kids are again extremely well catered for, and Water Mania can even host birthday parties in Mr Kool's Party Land. Call 407 396 2626 for details.

Anaconda and **Banana Peel** both feature family-sized innertubes down long, twisting, turning slides, while the **Double Berzerker** offers two different ways to be whooshed along and spat out into a foaming pool.

However, the outstanding feature, for both trying and watching, is the **Wipe-Out**, one of only two such attractions in the world. The challenge is to grab a body surfboard and try to ride the continuous wave, risking going over the edge into another pool if you stray too wide, or being sent flying backwards if you lose your balance. A real blast!

Then, when it comes to pint-sized fun for the children, Water Mania is one of the best. The **Rain Forest** is designed for the 2–10s, with a 5,000-sq-ft pool ranging from 3in to 2ft deep and featuring a range of mini-slides, fountains and water guns, all arranged around a wonderful large-scale pirate ship, with more opportunities to climb, jump and generally swashbuckle. Other innovative recent additions are the **Rain Train**, a near life-size locomotive that sprays water out of its stack in the centre of a shallow pool, with other interactive play features and more slides; and **Tot's Town** for the toddlers (and their parents who want to relax a little from supervising their youngsters), which is a partly fenced playground with sand beach and paddling area, with added shade and refreshment hut. Then there is the inevitable **Electric Arcade** of video games for the older children.

In addition to the cooling picnic areas, there are also several snack bars, a mini-golf course, volleyball and basketball courts and a large shop. Much of the park was refurbished and brightened up in 1999, making it even better value for money.

Water Mania is located on Highway 192, just a mile east of the I4 intersection and is open March–October, variously from 9.30 or 10am to 5pm (weekends only in October) Call 407 396 2626 for more details or check out www.watermania-florida.com. Admission is $25.95 for adults and $18.95 for kids 3–12. Parking is $5. **Attraction rating: TTTT**.

STOP PRESS: The big new shopping development of Festival Bay at the top of International Drive (immediately south of Belz Factory Outlets) looks set to have an accompanying mini-theme park, possibly in time to open for the Bay's completion in late 2001.

The **Factory Funhouse and Festival Boardwalk** is planned to be a $60m amusement complex featuring high-tech rides, roller-coasters and fairground attractions. The indoor–outdoor park will have a 200ft Big Wheel, go-karts and a haunted house, plus live international entertainment, with a 15-acre Boardwalk to showcase the main rides, including at least two coasters. It is an extremely ambitious project, and the finance was only just coming together when the *Orlando Sentinel* broke the news in late summer 2000. This means the opening target date could easily be out by as much as a year, but you should expect to see even more major construction in this area throughout 2001.

A new **Trainland** attraction had also just opened on I-Drive, almost opposite the Mercado Center. This features a huge indoor model railway exhibit and an outdoor mini-railroad, which is sure to appeal to enthusiasts and children alike. It is scheduled to open 10am–9pm Mon–Sat, and 10am–6pm on Sun. Call 407 363 9002 for the latest details.

Okay, that sums up the main big-scale attractions on offer, but many people are now looking for the 'something different' factor, so let's explore some alternatives to the mass-market experience …

7

8 Off the Beaten Track
(or, When you're All Theme Parked Out)

After several days in the midst of the hectic tourist whirl of mainstream Orlando, you may find yourself in need of a day or two's rest from the non-stop theme park activities; a holiday from your holiday. Alternatively, you may be a repeat visitor looking for a different Central Florida experience. If either is the case, this chapter is for you.

Hopefully, you will already have noted the relatively tranquil offerings of Cypress Gardens and Silver Springs, but, to get away from it all more completely and to enhance your view of the area still further, the following are guaranteed to take you well off the beaten tourist track. The chapter should really be subtitled **A Taste of the Real Florida**, as it introduces the areas of Winter Park, Seminole County, nature boat rides and eco-tours, and journeys by airboat, balloon, ship, train and plane.

Winter Park

This elegant northern suburb of Orlando is one of its best-kept tourist secrets as it is little more than 20 minutes' drive from the hurly-burly of areas like International Drive and yet a million miles from the relentless commercialism. It offers several renowned museums and art galleries, some top-quality shopping, 20 restaurants (including the top-of-the-range **Park Plaza Gardens**), several pleasant walking tours, a delightful 50-minute boat ride around several of the area's lakes and, above all, a chance to *slow down*.

The central area is **Park Avenue**, a classy street of fine shops, boutiques, two museums and a wonderfully shaded park. At one end of the avenue is **Rollins College**, a small but highly respected arts education centre which also houses the **Cornell Fine Arts Museum** (the oldest collection in Florida, open 10am–5pm Tue–Fri, 1pm–5pm Sat–Sun, admission free) and the **Annie Russell Theater**. The museum features regular art exhibitions and lectures, as well as having its own collection. The **Morse Museum of American Art** is a must for admirers of American art pottery, American and European glass, furniture and other decorative arts of the late nineteenth and early twentieth centuries, including one of the world's foremost collections of works by Louis Comfort Tiffany. The dazzling Chapel restoration from the 1893 Chicago World Expo is now on display in its original form for the first time since the late nineteenth century and is worth the entrance fee on its own. The museum is open 9.30am– 4pm Tues–Sat, and 1–4pm Sun, admission $3 for adults, children under 12 free. The **Albin Polasek Museum and Sculpture Gardens** are also worth a look for culture buffs and the serene, tranquil setting devoted to this Czech/American artist. Open 10am–4pm Wednesday to Sunday, there is no admission charge and it is also a superb setting for weddings. The **Scenic Boat Tour** is located at the east end of Morse Avenue, and offers a charming, narrated tour of the

'Venice of America', travelling 12 miles around the lakes and canals for a fascinating glimpse of some of the most beautiful private houses, boat houses and lakeside gardens (properties in the area start at $750,000 and top $3 million in several instances!). The tours run every day from 10am to 4pm and cost $7 for adults and $3 for children 2–11, and it is one of the most relaxing hours you will spend in Orlando.

An alternative tour is with **Winter Park Bicycle Tours** for a gentle 2-hour overview of the area, covering about 5 square miles of this picturesque neighbourhood on classic 1950s-style bikes, with full guide narration (starting at the Langford Hotel and costing $20; call 407 875 2200 for details). You can also take the **Park Avenue Walking Tour**, with free maps provided by the Chamber of Commerce on New York Avenue.

The shops are also a cut or two above anything you will encounter elsewhere, and while you may find the prices equally distinctive, just browsing is an enjoyable experience with the charm of the area highlighted by the friendliness of everyone hereabouts. Regular pavement craft fairs and art festivals (especially the Spring Art Festival in March/April, which is a big part of the local social scene) also add splashes of colour to an already inviting scenario. In addition to the Park Plaza Gardens, which specialises in continental cuisine (see Chapter 10, Eating Out), you can dine on French, Italian, Thai and Vietnamese offerings.

An additional high point of a visit to Winter Park is the **Kraft Azalea Garden** on Alabama Drive (off Palmer Avenue at the north end of Park Avenue), 11 acres of shaded lakeside walkways, gardens and hundreds of magnificent azaleas.

The main focal point, the mock Grecian temple, is a particularly beautiful setting for the many weddings that are held here. **Mead Botanical Gardens**, on Garden Drive (just off Highway 17/92) offers more beautiful trails through a sub-tropical forest with native birds and plants from around the world. There is no admission charge for either.

Midway between Winter Park and downtown Orlando is another botanical gem, **Leu Gardens**, a 50-acre retreat featuring formal gardens, peaceful walks and a boardwalk overlooking Lake Rowena. The Gardens are open daily from 9am–5pm (9am–8pm in the summer) and cost $4 for adults and $1 for under 13s. They are on the corner of Forest and Nebraska Avenues, via Mills Avenue and Princeton St from Exit 43 of I4.

Winter Park is located off exit 45 of I4, Fairbanks Avenue. Turn right on to Fairbanks and head east for two miles until it intersects with Park Avenue and turn left; public parking is well indicated.

Aquatic Wonders boat tours

To go further into the real world of Florida nature and its wildlife, **Aquatic Wonders** operates a delightful break from the theme park business on Lake Tohopekaliga in Kissimmee. Operated by Captain Ray Robida and limited to a

Airboat rides

8

maximum of six people per trip, the choice of seven 2–5-hour cruises offers a series of gentle adventures that are both entertaining and educational as well as relaxing. Every cruise is a little different depending on the local conditions and Captain Ray's truly individual style, which is wonderfully laid back yet still informative. His local knowledge of the waterways and wildlife is outstanding and children will get a lot out of it if they have enquiring

BRIT TIP: Amazingly, the waterways feeding Lake Toho stretch all the way to Miami in the south. Captain Ray is a mine of fascinating geographical and historical information.

minds.

The 3–4-hour **Aquatic Wonders** cruise studies the complex of local lakes and rivers, water ecology and the fish, insects and other animals of the area ($35 for adults, $26.95 for children 12 and under). The **Eagle Watch Tour** is an ornithologist's delight as it goes out for 2 hours to look at the nesting bald eagles on the lake, rare ospreys and many other species of birds ($18.95 and $12.95). The rather romantic **Sunset Sounds** is another 2-hour trip aboard the 'Eagle Ray' to enjoy the sights and sounds of dusk over the lake as the birds come home to roost ($18.95 and $12.95). **Starlight Wonders** is a 2-hour tour for a spot of star-gazing, gentle music and Native American stories surrounding the origins of the constellations ($24.95 and $14.95, or combine it with Sunset Sounds for $36.95 and $27.95). **Rivers in Time** is a 2-hour journey back in time to the days of the river boat and the Seminole Indian War, a fascinating live history lesson with all the sights and sounds of the lake

for good measure. The **Gator Watch Tour** is a 2-hour night-time journey to view some of the locals hunting, nesting and just hanging out (and there are plenty of them out there!) as well as sounds of the lake at night (again, both are $24.95 and $14.95). **Family Fishing Adventures** offers 4–5 hours of fishing fun with all bait and tackle (but not fishing licence) provided, especially for beginners ($135–$175 for one to six people). There are also games and videos for the kids in case their attention wanders! All tours have non-alcoholic drinks and snacks provided, and Captain Ray is fully licensed by the US Coast Guard, unlike some boat operators in the area, so you are guaranteed a high level of safety as well as entertainment. The Eagle Ray departs daily from Big Toho Marina at the west end of Lakeshore Boulevard off Ruby Avenue in downtown Kissimmee. Call 407 846 2814 for more details and to make reservations for these tours, which are proving increasingly popular, especially the Rivers in Time and Eagle Watch excursions.

Airboat rides

Florida also offers the thrill of airboat rides on many of its lakes, rivers and marshes. An airboat is a totally different experience to any boat ride you will have taken as it is more like flying at ground level. It is as much a thrill as a scenic adventure, but it also has the advantage of exploring areas otherwise inaccessible to boats. Airboats simply skim over and through the marshes, to give you an alternative, close-up and very personal view. Travelling at up to 50mph means it can be loud (hence you will be provided with headphones) and sunglasses are also a good idea to keep stray flies out of your eyes. It is NOT the trip for you if you are spooked by crickets, dragonflies and similar insects that occasionally land inside the boat!

BRIT TIP: Best time to ride is first thing on a weekday morning when the local wildlife is not hiding from the weekend boaters.

There are several operations offering airboat rides in the area, from you-drive boats that do barely 5mph to much bigger rides, but for safety and quality my tip goes to **Boggy Creek Airboat Rides**, especially as they now offer a discounted ticket with Gatorland so anyone purchasing the ride at Boggy Creek saves $4.50 on adult admission to Gatorland and takes a child in free. Boggy Creek's airboats can be found on Lake Toho at Southport Park (all the way down Poinciana Boulevard, off Highway 192 between Markers 10 and 11, and across into Southport Drive) or on East Lake Toho (their main site). For the latter, you can either take Exit 17 of the Central Florida Greeneway (417) and go south on Boggy Creek Road, then right into East Lake Fish Camp; or, from Highway 192, go north on Simpson Road, which becomes Boggy Creek Road, turn right at the Boggy Creek T-junction, then right into East Lake Fish Camp.

BRIT TIP: Watch out for discount coupons in tourist literature offering up to $3 off airboat rides.

The **Fish Camp** is itself a little gem, offering a variety of boating and angling opportunities (call 407 348 2040 for details) as well as the

wonderfully authentic rural Florida charm of the **restaurant and gift shop** (open 8am–9pm every day). If you are heading for a morning airboat ride, consider arriving early for one of their magnificent (huge!) all-day breakfasts, while the more adventurous will want to try the local delicacies – catfish, frogs' legs and gator tail. For another great slice of local eatin', try their Friday and Saturday night buffets. They are fabulous value at $8.95 and $11.95 per person on an all-you-can-eat basis.

Boggy Creek's half-hour ride features two of the most modern airboats in Florida, skimming over the local wetlands for a close-up view of the majestic cypress trees and wildlife that can include eagles, ospreys, snakes and turtles as well as the inevitable alligators.

You do not need to book in advance, just turn up and go (9am–5.30pm 7 days a week), and rides cost $16 for adults and $10 for children 3–12. They also do a

8

BRIT TIP: Want to sample the Florida Everglades but don't fancy the 3-hour trip south? Boggy Creek Airboats are the perfect substitute, and at a fraction of the cost.

1-hour Night Tour ($25) for a completely different, and quite exhilarating, experience, but you do need to book on 407 344 9550.

Balloon trips

Florida is one of the most popular areas for ballooning and, if you are up early enough in the morning, you will quite often see three or four floating over the countryside. The experience is a majestic one. If

> BRIT TIP: Dresses are not advisable for balloon trips and sensible shoes are essential.

Orlando represents the holiday of a lifetime, then a balloon flight is the ride of a lifetime. Believe me, Disney has nothing to touch this one! The utterly smooth way in which you lift off into the early morning sky is breathtaking in itself, but the peace and quiet of the ride, not to mention the stunning views from 2,000ft above ground, are quite awesome. It is not a cheap experience, but it is equally appealing to all but the youngest children or those who suffer vertigo or a fear of heights. It is a highly personalised ride, as four people make for a full trip. Some baskets can take up to nine, but you need to be on good terms!

Orange Blossom Balloons are the premier company in central Florida, with more than 16 years' experience and a wonderfully laid-back style that stems from their British-owned operation. You meet at the Days Inn Hotel Maingate West on Highway 192, half a mile past Splendid China at 6am (the best winds for flying are always first thing in the morning) and then transfer to the take-off site, where you help the crew set up and inflate one of their three balloons. Owner-operator Richard Ornstein and his team are a real hoot, and you are soon up, up and away in awe-inspiring style, floating serenely up to 2,000ft or sinking down to skim the surface of one of the many lakes (disturbing the occasional gator or deer). After about an hour you come back to earth for a traditional champagne landing ceremony and return to Days Inn for a full breakfast and your special balloonist's certificate. The full experience lasts 3–4 hours and the cost is $169 per adult (inclusive of tax; $175 from January 2001) and $85 for 10–16s (under 10s go free with their parents). Hotel pick-up is also available at $10 per person round-trip. Call 407 239 7677 for reservations as they are usually popular (especially for Brits).

Everglades and the Bahamas

Day trips are increasingly being offered from Orlando south to the Everglades, Miami and the Florida Keys, and, if you are prepared to put up with a long day out (up to 16 hours) you can see a lot of the state this way. However, they are not well-suited to children, with long periods on a coach, while the half-hour airboat ride once you get to the Everglades is a pretty brief highlight in all that time.

The only company I would really recommend in this instance is **Real Florida Excursions**, who work with many of the main tour operators and offer nine tours, from an Orlando Shop Til You Drop excursion to a Miami–Bahamas 2-day getaway, which is currently one of the most popular trips for the something-different factor (especially if your tour is led by Bill Vitanyi, one of the most personable and knowledgeable

Up, up and away ...

guides). You travel down to **Miami** (4 hours) by luxury coach, get to shop at the smart **Bayside Marketplace** complex, or take the 1-hour optional Miami waterways cruise, and then take the 22-minute **flight** to the Bahamas for an overnight stay. The following day can be spent on the beautiful beaches or at your hotel in Freeport, the Bahamia Resort & Casino, before you **cruise** back to Fort Lauderdale in some style (great food in particular) and then catch the coach back to Orlando. This excellent package costs just $139 for adults and $99 for children 2–12 (although local taxes can add another $50). An overnight trip to **Miami** and the sizzling **South Beach** art deco district, with its hot night-life, is another attractive proposition. You get deluxe coach transport, a guided tour, good quality accommodation and the best part of a day on the beach for $99 and $39 (3–12s). Alternatively, you could try their **Naples–Everglades Adventure**, with a 30-minute airboat ride through the Everglades, lunch in the beautiful city of Naples and a late afternoon cruise along the Gulf Coast waterways. This is $89 for adults and $49 for 3–12s. Check with your tour operator for details or call Real Florida Excursions on 407 345 4996, ext. 3012.

Flying Tigers Warbird Restoration Museum

Vintage aeroplane and nostalgia buffs will want to make a note of this offbeat museum adjacent to Kissimmee Airport, which builds and restores old World War Two fighters and bombers. Kids who enjoyed building Airfix kits will especially enjoy the 1-hour tour of the facilities, which basically represent a couple of large hangars with aircraft in various stages of restoration and repair. It is

The author takes the front seat with Warbird Adventures

one of the most amazing programmes of its kind you will find, with the exhibits ranging from a fully restored B-25 Mitchell bomber and a P-51 Mustang to scraps of fuselages and engines that will gradually be incorporated into the latest rebuilding project. It's a place where you see, smell and touch the history of the old 1940s newsreels. The tour guides have a detailed working knowledge of everything they show you. You could be forgiven for thinking you have walked into a scrapyard on your way in, but the main hangars reveal the full scale of the operation, with the wholesale restoration of a B-17 Flying Fortress being their pride and joy. In fact, owner Tom Reilly insists: 'All those clean, tidy sterile museums you have seen in the past, well, this isn't one of them. We have oil on the floor we refer to as *bomber blood* and if you are lucky, you might get some on you to take home as a souvenir.' In progress in 2000 was a unique project to restore a WWII Focke-Wulf FW190 fighter-bomber back to flying condition. The site detail includes a charming little gift shop that houses

8

some more museum pieces, uniforms and memorabilia from World War Two. It is open 7 days a week 9am–6pm (9am–5pm on Sun), and there is always some reconstruction work under way. Charges are $8 for adults, $7 for over 60s and $6 for under 12s (under 6s free). The museum can be found just off Highway 192, half a mile down Hoagland Boulevard on the left.

Anyone captivated by the sights, sounds and stories of this magnificent exhibit (also known as Bombertown) can also join in. **Warbird Restoration School** is an intensive 5-day course covering the whole rebuild process, from sheet-metal fabrication to welding and fuel systems. It culminates with a flight in a restored B-25J Mitchell bomber, but is definitely for enthusiasts only – it costs $995. Call 407 933 1942 for details or see their website www.warbirdmuseum.com.

Warbird Adventures

Once you have seen the displays, you should consider neighbouring **Warbird Adventures**. *This is the best ride in town, bar none, guaranteed.* Not only do you get to fly in a 1945 T-6 Harvard fighter-trainer, but also, after a while getting used to the front seat of this vintage two-seater … *you get to fly it!* And you don't just handle the controls, your instructor will get you doing loops, barrel rolls and all manner of aerobatics. This is simply the most memorable and exhilarating ride I have done anywhere in the world, enhanced by in-flight video and wingtip camera to record every moment. It is the only place where you can walk in off the street and, 20 minutes later, be flying a plane *with no previous flight experience.* My instructor was the excellent Thom Richard and, despite my initial reluctance and disbelief, he had me doing the full aerobatic business before long. Roller-

coasters? They're for wimps! Mind you, this is not a cheap experience – a 15-minute flight costs $140, while a 30-minute trip is $240 and an hour $440. Aerobatics (on 30- or 60-minute flights only) cost $30, while the PAL video is $40 and the stills $15 (or all three 'extras' for $60), but this is truly a memory to last a lifetime. Call 1-800 386 1593 for details or check out www.warbirdadventures.com.

Green Meadows Petting Farm

From one extreme to another, here is guaranteed fun for kids of 2 up to about 11, and their parents (and don't forget your cameras). It's the ultimate hands-on experience as, on your 2-hour guided tour, you get the chance to milk a cow, pet a pig, cuddle a chick (or duckling), feed goats and sheep, meet buffalo, chickens, peacocks and donkeys and learn what makes an animal farm tick. There are pony rides for the young 'uns and tractor-drawn hay rides for all, plus the Green Meadows Express steam train for a scenic ride through the farm and a new play area of slides and swings. The shaded acres, free-roaming animals and peaceful aspect all make for another pleasant change of pace, especially as Green Meadows is barely 10 minutes from the tourist hurly-burly of Highway 192 (south on Poinciana Boulevard). It is open from 9.30am to 5.30pm daily (last admission at 4pm) and costs $15 per person (under 2s free), and you should allow 3–4 hours for your visit. Drinks, snacks and gifts are available, but it is also the ideal place to bring a picnic. Call 407 846 0770.

Disney and cruising

Taking a cruise is fast becoming a regular option with your Orlando stay and, with the advent of Disney Cruise Line in 1998, you will now see a lot of publicity for these competitively priced 2-, 3-, 4- and 7-day sailings out of fast-developing Port Canaveral.

Although they are cruise newcomers, **Disney** have set their stall out with some of the most breathtaking hardware in the form of their first two ships, the 83,000-ton *Disney Magic* (1998) and *Disney Wonder* (1999). Classic design plus the usual Disney imagineering have produced these two vessels, which are big even by modern standards and incorporate special features for kids, teenagers AND couples without children. Both ships boast an amazing destination experience in their own right, each with four restaurants, a 1,040-seat theatre, cinema, night-club complex, sports club and a full health spa, while they also visit the Bahamas and Disney 's truly stunning private island. It is not a cheap option and a 3- or 4-day cruise can usually be purchased only as a week's package with a *Walt Disney World* Resort stay, but the advent of 7-day cruising in 2000, taking in St Maarten and St Thomas in the Caribbean as well as their private island, promised to provide much better cruise value.

The ships are identical in practical terms, and the week's cruise gives you more chance to enjoy the wide range of facilities. The impact of the four-restaurant set-up (where you dine in a different one each night, including the amazing Animator's Palate which comes to life all around you), the fabulous entertainment 'district', the vast array of kids' facilities (including Buzz Lightyear's Cyberspace Command Post), the wonderfully picturesque beaches of their Castaway Cay island and the sheer ocean-going quality throughout fair knocks your socks off.

Most tour operators now feature Disney Cruise Line, while the Walt Disney Travel Company (call 0870 2424 900) have the most comprehensive programme on offer.

Other cruises out of Port Canaveral include 2- and 4-day trips to the Bahamas and Key West with **Cape Canaveral Cruise Lines** (an older ship, but good value for money; tel 1-800 910 7447), the glitzy **Carnival Cruise Lines** (all-modern hardware, party atmosphere; tel 1-800 327 9501) with 3- and 4-day Bahamas voyages, **Premier Cruise Lines** (again, older budget-style ships; tel 1-800 990 7770) offering the Bahamas and 7-day Caribbean sailings, and **Royal Caribbean International** (modern glamorous vessel, tel 1-800 327 6700) to Nassau and their private island of CocoCay. For more advice on cruising, may I also recommend my book *Choosing A Cruise*, and the specialist UK travel agent The Cruise Line Ltd on 01273 835252.

For a smaller and more low-key approach, the **Rivership Romance**, daily out of downtown Sanford, is highly recommended, especially for their lunch cruises on the wildlife-rich St John's River. Their old-fashioned steamer can take up to 200 in comfort and adds a fine meal, live entertainment and a river commentary, as well as providing a relaxing alternative to the usual tourist scenario. You choose between the 3-hour lunch cruise (Wed, Sat and Sun, 11am–2pm) at $35 a head, the 4-hour cruise (Mon, Tue, Thur and Fri, 11am–3pm) at $45 or an evening dinner-dance voyage (Fri and Sat, 7.30–11pm) at $50. For reservations and information call 1-800 423 7401. Find Rivership Romance off exit 51 of I4, east into Sanford, then left on to Palmetto Avenue.

8

Seminole County

Having arrived in the historic town of Sanford, the heart of Seminole County, it is worth pointing out the possible diversions of a day or two in this area that will get you well off the beaten track. The **Central Florida Zoological Park** is a private, non-profit-making organisation that puts a pleasant, natural accent on the zoo theme, set in 109 wooded acres of unspoilt Florida countryside and with boardwalks and trails around all the attractions. These include more than 100 species of animals, weekend feeding demonstrations, educational programmes, a picnic area, pony rides and a butterfly garden, plus the Zoofari Outpost gift shop. It's good value, too, at $7 for adults and $3 for kids 3–12, and the park (off exit 52 of I4) is open every day (except Thanksgiving Day and Christmas Day) 9am–5pm.

Bill's **Airboat Adventures,** on the St John's River east of Sanford, offer 90-minute tours in the company of conservationist and river historian Captain Bill Daniel for $30 ($15 for under 14s). Call 407 977 3214 to book. **Possum Bay Fish Camp**, out on East SR 46, has a full range of

Wekiva Marina, Seminole County

airboat rides, fishing boat rentals, wave-runner rides, camping, picnics and country store (tel 407 349 0090), while **Black Hammock Fish Camp and Restaurant** (off Exit 44 of the Central Florida Greeneway, take SR 434 east, turn left on Deleon St and left on to Black Hammock Road) is another peaceful backwater on Lake Jesup where you can try fishing or airboating – and don't miss their great restaurant for local specialities (tel 407 365 2201).

Sanford itself is a designated historic centre, full of brick-paved streets and antique shops. It is very much small-town America, having lost the growth battle with Orlando many years ago, but it makes a peaceful diversion. It also offers the **Rose Cottage Tea Room**, one of

Rivership Romance in Seminole County

Daytona Beach

the prettiest restaurants you will find in Florida, which serves a mouth-watering array of soups, sandwiches, salads and quiches, as well as fabulous fruit teas. This little treasure of the culinary world (open 11am–3pm Tue-Sat) can be found on Park Avenue, 13 blocks out of Sanford town centre, call 407 323 9448 for reservations (which are usually required). For more details on all of the above, look up www.visitseminole.com.

Eco-tourism

Genuine eco-tourism is still in its infancy, in general terms, in central Florida, but there are two major exceptions worth knowing about.

Forever Florida is, for my money, one of the most outstanding, non-theme park attractions of all. It is both a 3,000-acre wilderness preserve and a working ranch. As well as a close-up of Florida's flora and fauna and its conservation issues, you get a taste of the original

Forever Florida

cowboy life, Cracker style (Crackers were the 'real' cowboys, pre-dating their Western counterparts by 50 years), which is a fascinating slice of history. Eco-safaris, covered wagon tours, horse rides, bike trails, nature walks and, for the kids, pony rides and a free petting zoo, are the highlights, as well as the magnificent Restaurant and Visitor Center, which offers an essential 30-minute orientation programme into the Conservancy's creation. Forever Florida began as a dream of gifted young biologist and ecologist Allen Broussard and has been carried to fruition after his death from complications of Hodgkin's disease by his parents, Dr William and Margaret Broussard, who own the neighbouring Crescent J Ranch and continue to give their time and energy to building the wilderness as a non-profitmaking memorial to

Airboat ride

their son. The education element alone is awesome, and tours feature a strong conservation message in this tranquil, untouched corner of Florida. The **Cracker Coach Tour** ($28 for adults, $18 for under 13s) – a kind of open-sided, large wheeled buggy – is their stock-in-trade, a 2-hour-plus trundle around much of the woods, swamp and prairie that make up the ranch and Conservancy, in the company of an education coordinator who provides the low-down on the history and

8

environmental issues of the ecosystems. You are likely to encounter alligators (at a safe distance), whitetail deer, armadillos and a host of bird-life – including bald eagles – and leave with a good understanding of the real Florida. Guided **horse rides** vary from $35–$52 (1–3 hours; $24–$31 for children), and **covered wagon tours** of the Ranch are $14 and $11. **Trail bike** rentals are $8 an hour and **pony rides** $5 for the first ride, $3 for a second. There is even an overnight horse ride or ranch experience for the ultimate Cracker appeal, but it is distinctly expensive at $275 and $255. Regular tours run Fri–Sun at 9am, 12.30pm and 3.30pm but should be booked on 1-800 957 9794. For more details, look up www.foreverflorida.com. The Conservancy is a good 80-minute drive out of Orlando, some 40 miles east on Highway 192, through St Cloud as far as Holopaw, then 7.6 miles south on US Highway 441. **Rating: AAAAA.**

On an equally authentic scale is **Disney's Wilderness Preserve,** run by the Nature Conservancy in Poinciana, south of Kissimmee. This restoration of an 11,500-acre preserve is a work in progress and allows visitors in for various hiking trails, a 1-hour guided tour on Saturdays (at 9.30am) and 2-hour buggy tours on Sundays (1.30pm). Entry fee is $2 for adults and $1 for children, while the buggy tours are an additional $7 and $5. The Preserve is located at the end of Pleasant Hill Road (follow Hoagland Boulevard south off Highway 192). Call 407 935 0002 for more information. **Rating: AAA.** The Kissimmee Convention and Visitors' Bureau also publishes an excellent **eco-guide**, if you drop by their Visitor Center on Highway 192.

Beach escapes

When the temperatures start to soar, the lure of Florida's many white-sand beaches becomes strong, and there are some excellent choices little more than an hour's drive away. Be warned first, though, that Orlando natives all get the same idea at the weekend, so unless you head out EARLY (i.e. before 9am) and come back late (i.e. after 8pm) you are likely to encounter some serious traffic. The choice is actually quite simple for a change. If you head EAST, you have **Cocoa Beach**, at about 40 miles the closest to Orlando (straight along the Beeline Expressway, then south on Highway A1A) and a great mix of wide sands, gently sloping beaches and moderate but fun surfing waves. As it's the Atlantic, the sea can be pretty chilly from November to March, but Cocoa Beach is rapidly developing into a major coastal resort, so the facilities are excellent. While in Cocoa Beach, be sure to visit **Ron Jon's Surf Shop**, a mind-boggling pink and purple emporium of warehouse proportions open 24 hours a day, stocking every kind of beach paraphernalia imaginable. From here north to **Daytona Beach** you have almost 100 miles of beautiful beaches that have been developed to a lesser extent, while Daytona itself (home to some great annual motor sport) is one of the most famous beaches in the world. To reach Daytona Beach direct from Orlando, it is about 90 minutes' drive along I4 east, pick up I95 north then Highway 92 east, which turns into International Speedway Boulevard and leads to the beaches.

To the WEST you have the **Gulf Coast**, which is a good 90 minutes' drive down I4 and through Tampa on I275 south to **St Petersburg Beach** (105 miles) or **Clearwater Beach** (110 miles) or two hours-plus down I4 and then I75 to **Bradenton**

(130 miles), **Sarasota** (140 miles) and **Venice** (160 miles). The beaches are less 'hip', that is, more relaxed and refined, and the sea a touch warmer and much calmer, so it is better for families with small children. You will find it easier to get away from the crowds here, too. **Naples** is another hour further south on I75 but is currently rated one of the most welcoming beach destinations in Florida.

Sport

In addition to virtually every form of entertainment known to man, central Florida is also one of the world's biggest sporting play-grounds, with a huge range of opportunities either to watch or to play your favourite sport.

Golf

Without doubt, the number one activity is **golf**, with almost 150 courses within an hour's drive of Orlando. The weather, of course, makes it such a popular pastime, but some spectacular courses add to the attraction, and there are numerous holiday packages geared entirely towards keen golfers of all abilities. With an 18-hole round, including green fees, cart hire and taxes, from as little as $40 on some courses (and they average around $75), it is an attractive proposition and a very different one from those used to British courses. If you go in for 36-hole days, it is possible in most cases to save up to $30 by replaying the same course. Sculptured landscapes, manicured fairways and abundant use of spectacular water features and white-sand traps make for some memorable golfing. January to May is the busiest golf 'season', but many courses are busy year-round. Check also when you book about each club's dress code, as there are differences from course to course.

Disney have been quick to attract the golf fanatic, with five championship-quality courses, including the 7,000yd Palm, rated one of Golf Digest's top 25. Fees vary from $90–$120 for Disney Resort guests and $100–$130 for visitors, with half-price reductions after 3pm. Call 407 939 4653 for tee-times.

Other quality courses open to the public include the **Grand Cypress**, next door to *Walt Disney World* Resort (tel 407 239 1904, rates from $100–$140), **Metro West Country Club**, on South Hiawassee Road off Conroy-Windermere to the north of Universal Studios (tel 407 299 1099, $75) and **Marriott's Orlando World Center** (tel 407 238 8660, $60–$110). Alternatively, **Tee-Times USA** (tel 1-800 374 8633) offer a unique advice and reservation service, while **Stand-by Golf** will get you discounted prices and guaranteed times at many of the major courses (tel 813 899 2665).

For the personal touch, the all-in-one service of **Professional Golf Guides of Orlando** is designed for Florida visitors, taking one to three people out in the company of a PGA professional to get the best possible tuition and low-down on one of the local courses. Call 407 894 0907 or look up www.progolfguides.com.

Seminole County is another golf haven, with 18 public or semi-private courses, and offers golf-and-hotel packages from $65. Call 1-800 555 9589 for details or look up their entry on www.visitseminole.com.

Fishing

Fishing also attracts a lot of specialist holiday-makers, and it is fast catching on as a highly enjoyable day out with us foreigners as well. The abundance of lakes and rivers makes for plentiful sport of the angling variety, with bass the prime catch. A 7-day licence will cost you

8

Golfing is popular in Orlando

$17.50 (available from all tackle shops, fishing camps, sports stores and Wal-Mart and K-Mart supermarkets), and there are dozens of boats for hire on the St John's River, Lake Toho in Kissimmee, Lake Kissimmee and both coasts for some serious sea fishing. Expect to pay $160–$195 for half a day and $200–$295 for a full day bass fishing. For the most complete angling service try **Cutting Loose Expeditions**, a highly experienced, personalised operator who can organise fresh- or sea-water expeditions and arrange hotel pick-up if necessary. All your bait and licence requirements are included. The service is run by A Neville Cutting, one of America's greatest fishing adventurers, and he maintains high standards with his guides and other staff. Rates start at $200 for a half day's bass fishing (two fishermen per boat with a licensed guide), but other trips, including offshore for marlin, can be arranged. Phone 407 629 4700, visit www.ucutloose.com on the Net or write to Cutting Loose Expeditions, PO Box 447, Winter Park, Florida 32790–0447. Alternatively, **AJ's Freelance Bass Guide Services** specialise in trophy bass fishing on West Lake Toho in Kissimmee with professional guides (all US Coastguard-licensed captains). Full-day trips (9 hours

from first light) are $225 for one to two people, a half day (4½ hrs) is $175 and it is $60 or $30 extra per person, plus your licence and bait. Hotel pick-ups ($20) can also be arranged, call 407 348 8764 or check out www.orlandobass.com.

Water sports

Florida is also, of course, mad keen on **water sports** of all persuasions. Consequently, on any area of water bigger than your average pond don't be surprised to find the locals water-skiing, jetskiing, knee-boarding, canoeing, paddling, wind-surfing, boating or otherwise indulging in watery pursuits. *Walt Disney World* Resort offers all manner of boats, from catamarans to pedaloes, on the main **Bay Lake**, as well as the smaller lakes of **Seven Seas Lagoon**, **Crescent Lake** and **Lake Buena Vista**. There are several operators on the lakes around Orlando and Kissimmee, too, but some of them leave much to be desired, safety-wise. **Dave's Ski School** on Lake Bryan at Lake Buena Vista (right next to the Holiday Inn Sunspree Resort) get our official recommendation for their safety-conscious approach and their virtual guarantee to get beginners up and water-skiing. Their Watersports Adventure includes an hour's water-ski lessons and rides, a tube ride and a wave-runner ride ($55 adult, $48 child), and lasts up to 3 hours, while you can also rent wave-runners at $35 for half an hour. Many of the main tour operators also endorse this ski school and for more details, call 407 239 6939 (or look up www.bvwatersports.com).

For a more gentle experience and a close-up of the local wildlife try **Katie's Wekiva River Landing**. Here you can try up to a full day's canoeing on some of the most scenic waters of central Florida (take I4

Waterskiing at Dave's

[north] east to exit 51 and Highway 46 west for almost 5 miles, and Wekiva Park Drive is on your right). It's fairly leisurely, but does have its faster-flowing sections, and you can take time-outs for a picnic or to go fishing. The entire portion of the Wekiva River here has been designated a protected 'Scenic and Wild' area, while the neighbouring forest with its hiking trails is an official aquatic preserve. Thick cypress forest, clear, spring-fed waters, abundant water and wildlife, it's all here for nature-lovers. Katie's offers five different canoe trips, from a leisurely 2-hour, 6-mile paddle to a 19-mile overnight camping trip, all with a pick-up service at the end or transport up-river to start with. Prices range from $14.50 for a 2-hour paddle to $25 for all day (children 3–11 half-price), and the trips are suitable for beginners and more experienced canoeists alike. Katie's also offers trail bikes, camping, boating and fishing. For more details call 407 322 4470, or log on to www.ktland.com.

Mini-golf

Not exactly a sport, but definitely for tourist consumption are the many and quite extravagant opportunities for **mini-golf** around Orlando. Not only are they quite picturesque, some of them offer prizes for particularly tricky shots. They are a big hit with kids and good fun for all the family (if you have the legs left for 18 holes after a day at the theme park!). Several other attractions and parks offer mini-golf as an extra, but for the best, try out the self-contained centres, of which there are six main ones.

Predictably, Disney have seen the growth in the popularity of this type of attraction and come up with some terrific varieties of their own. **Disney's Fantasia Gardens Miniature Golf**, next to the Swan Hotel just off Buena Vista Drive, is a two-course challenge over 36 of the most varied holes of mini-golf you will find. Hippos dance, fountains leap and broomsticks march on the 18-hole crazy golf-themed **Fantasia Gardens** – yes, its style is taken from the Disney animated classic *Fantasia*, and that means lots of cartoon fun along the way as the park's imagineers challenge you with a riot of visual gags as well as some diabolically difficult mini-golf. Watch out for *Toccata and Fugue in D Minor* where good shots are rewarded with musical tones, and *The Nutcracker Suite*, where obstacles include dancing mushrooms! **Fantasia Fairways** is a cunning putting course on undulating astroturf, complete with fairways, rough, water hazards and bunkers which will test even the best golfers. The 18 holes range in length from 40 to 75 feet, and it can take well in excess of an hour to play a full round. It costs $9 (adult) and $7.50 (child) for Fantasia Gardens, and $9 and $8 for Fantasia Fairways, and they are open from 10am to

8

midnight every day. Their newest offering is the 36-hole **Winter-Summerland** course at the entrance to *Disney's Blizzard Beach* Water Park. Divided into two 18-hole courses, these mini works of art feature a 'Summer' setting of surf and beach tests (watch out for squirting fish), and a 'Winter' variety of snow and ice-crafted holes, all with a welter of visual puns as befitting the vacation resort of Santa's elves (yes, that's the theme, and kids will love it – there are even skid marks where Santa landed his sleigh). An adult round is $9.25 (3–9s $7.50), a double round is 50 per cent off and it is open 10am–11pm. **Pirate's Cove** has a twin-course set-up at Lake Buena Vista (by the Crossroads shopping plaza) and International Drive (just south of the Mercado Center), with mountain caves, waterfalls and rope bridges to test your skill and please the eye. **River Adventure Golf** (on Highway 192, almost opposite Medieval Times) offers a Mississippi River adventure with rolling rapids, waterfalls and an authentic water wheel. **Bonanza Miniature Golf and Gifts** (next door to the Magic Mining Co. restaurant on the western side of Highway 192) has another imaginative – and tricky – 36 holes set in a gold-mine theme with the backdrop of huge waterfalls. **Pirate's Island** (further along Highway 192 to the east) is another spectacular 36-hole spread, while arguably the most impressive of the lot is the **Congo River Golf and Exploration Co.**, which has courses on Highway 192, International Drive and Highway 436 in Altamonte Springs. They could almost be Disney-inspired, they are so artificially scenic. The Kissimmee location also has paddle boats to try, while International Drive has the option of go-karts, and all three have games and video arcades. Charges are $6–$8 per round, but look out

for coupons which all have a couple of dollars off each one. They open from 9am to 10pm or 11pm daily. **Million Dollar Mulligan** is also worthy of mention here, although it is neither mini-golf nor the real McCoy. Instead, Million Dollar Mulligan, just off Highway 192 on Florida Plaza Boulevard (next to Old Town – look for the giant golf ball), is a nine-hole, floodlit pitch-and-putt course, plus driving and target range, that looks spectacular at night with its lake and fountains lit up. The pitch-and-putt is $12 ($8 for kids), a practice bucket for the range $5, while there is also a natural grass putting course ($6 and $4), all open from 9am to midnight.

Horse riding

If **horse riding** takes your fancy (or your children's), you will certainly want to know that Orlando is home to one of the foremost equestrian centres in America, if not the world. It is the **Grand Cypress Equestrian Center**, part of the 1,500-acre Grand Cypress Resort, and all its rides and facilities are open to non-residents. This stunningly well-equipped equine haven offers a dazzling array of opportunities for the horse enthusiast of all abilities. A full range of clinics, lessons and other instructional programmes are available, from half-hour kids' sessions to all-summer academies, plus a variety of trail rides. Serious horse riders will note that this was the first American equestrian centre to be approved by the British Horse Society, and it operates the BHS test programme. Inevitably, this five-star facility does not come cheap, but, especially for children, it is a worthwhile experience. Private lessons are $45 per half hour or $75 per hour, while a week's package of eight half-hour lessons is $270. Young Junior Lessons (15-minute supervised rides for under 12s) are $25, while the Western Trail Ride (an hour's excursion for novice riders) is $30 per person and the Advanced Trail Ride $45. The centre is open from 8am to 5pm daily and can be found by taking exit 27 on I4 on to Route 535 north, turning left after half a mile at the traffic lights and then following the road north for a mile (past the entrance to the Hyatt Regency Grand Cypress Hotel) until the equestrian centre is on your right. For more details call 407 239 1938. On a smaller scale and none the less charming is the **Horse World Riding Stables** on Poinciana Boulevard, just 20 minutes south of Highway 192. This gets you more out into the wilds as it is further away from the main tourist areas, and you can spend anything from an hour to a full day enjoying the different rides and lessons on offer. Their three main trail rides are the Nature Trail ($29.95), a 45-minute to one-hour ride for beginners aged 6 and up through 750 acres of untouched Florida countryside, the Intermediate Trail Ride (ages 10 and up) for nearly one hour ($34.95), and the Advanced Private Trail Ride, a 90-minute trip for advanced riders with a private guide ($44.95). There is also a picnic area with fishing pond, playing fields, pony rides for under 8s and farm animals to pet. There is no charge for just looking around, and the stables are open 9am–5pm daily. Call 407 847 4343 or check out their website at www.horseworldstables.com for details and reservations.

Similarly out in the wilds (in the Rock Springs Run Wildlife Preserve in Seminole County, to be precise) are **Rock Springs Riding Stables**, another slice of native Florida, with rides varying from a 1-hour Turkey Trail to a full day's Wildlife Wander, all led by trained guides. The park's 6,000 acres guarantee plenty of wildlife, from otters and coyotes to the occasional wild boar and even bears, and the rides go out every day 9am–6pm, costing $25–$100, with $10 pony rides for under 8s. To find Rock Springs, take I4 to exit 51 (Sanford-SR46) and go west 8 miles before turning left into the Preserve. Take the dirt road first left and follow all the way to the horse barn, or call 407 314 1000 for more info or reservations.

Spectator events

When it comes to **spectator events**, Orlando is not quite so well furnished as other big American cities, but there is always something on offer for the discerning sports fan who would like to sample the local version of the big football or cricket match. There are no top-flight American Football or baseball teams in Orlando, but there is an indoor version of gridiron, called Arena Football, plus two Minor League baseball teams. The big sport in town, though, is **basketball** and the Orlando Magic of the NBA. The basketball season runs from November to May (with exhibition games in October), and the only drawback is that the state-of-the-art, 16,000-seat Orlando Arena where they play (on Amelia Street, exit 41 off I4, turn left, then left again) is occasionally fully booked for home games. The Arena box office (407 649 3245) can always tell you if there are any tickets left, although you need to call in person to buy them (from $16 up in the gods to $58 courtside), or you can try calling Ticketmaster on 407 839 3900 for credit card bookings. The Orlando Predators, one of America's top **Arena Football** teams, are also popular at the same venue (from May to August, ticket prices $10–$30) and you would need to call several days in advance to avoid

The Florida Citrus Bowl

missing one of their lively home games that feature some great entertainment as well as their fast, hard-hitting version of indoor American Football in the magnificent Arena. For the Real Thing in gridiron terms, the nearest teams in the **National Football League** are the Tampa Bay Buccaneers, 75 miles to the west, the Miami Dolphins, some 3½ hours' drive to the south down the Florida Turnpike or the Jacksonville Jaguars way up the east coast past Daytona, a 3-hour drive up I4 and I95. Again, Ticketmaster can give you ticket prices (they vary from $20 to $40) and availability. College American Football is also a big draw in America and Orlando's **Citrus Bowl Stadium**, which staged four World Cup games in 1994, is home to one of the biggest annual games, the New Year's Day Citrus Bowl, which pits two of the season's top college teams in an end-of-season play-off. However, tickets are again hard to come by as it is nearly always a sell-out, so call the Stadium (which is in the downtown area, just off the North Orange Blossom trail, take exit 36 off I4, turn left then right) on 407 423 2476 at least a month in advance if you are interested.

Disney's Wide World of Sports Complex

The newest sports facility in the area is inevitably a Disney project to bring in some world-class events and competitors. **Disney's Wide World of Sports Complex** is a 200-acre, state-of-the-art complex, featuring more than 32 sports and is quite awesome to wander round even when no one is playing! A recent addition is a permanent version of the **NFL (American Football) Experience**, which gives you the chance to test your skills as a gridiron star in an interactive playground for adults and kids alike. The complex's main features are a 7,500-seater baseball stadium, a softball quadraplex, an 11-court tennis complex, beach volleyball and the **All Star Café** with a massive array of sports memorabilia and even themed food. The baseball stadium is home for spring training of the mighty **Atlanta Braves**, and the crowds positively flock in for their pre-season games. Once the season gets under way in April, the WWoS is home to the minor league **Orlando Rays**, and there are often

Orlando Predator in action

games five or six evenings in succession, with Disney putting on an excellent stage, with plenty of hoopla, for every one. Other prime events include the US Men's Clay Court Tennis Championship (in April), Harlem Globetrotters basketball and international beach volleyball. The facilities alone should inspire world-class performances in any athlete. Standard admission is $8, increased for the big events like the baseball, but it is one of your optional extras

The Orlando Rays

> BRIT TIP: Spring training is a big deal in baseball. Games can be extremely competitive as players are battling to make their team's squad for the season.

with a Park Hopper Plus Pass (although that does not cover special events), and *Disney's Wide World of Sports* Complex can be found off Osceola Parkway, on Victory Way. Call 407 363 6100 for current events and ticket prices.

Baseball and hockey

Baseball is, of course, America's traditional sporting pastime, and, if the Braves' and Rays' games are sold out, you can still get a taste of the action with two other spring training

outfits and another minor league team. **Baseball City** (just off exit 23 of I4 going [south] west) is home to the Kansas City Royals for spring training (March and April) while the Houston Astros set up their pre-season HQ at impressive **Osceola County Stadium** on Bill Beck Boulevard on east Highway 192. The Astros' Minor League team, the **Kissimmee Cobras,** then play here from April to August. The Cobras usually have several games a week, priced $3.50, $4, $5 and $7 (tickets always available at the gate) and are well worth checking out. Call 407 933 5400.

Ice hockey is also in town with the Orlando Arena, home to the International Hockey League's Orlando Solar Bears. It is a real family atmosphere and the season runs from September to April, with tickets from $6 to $30 available from Ticketmaster on 407 839 3900 or the Bears office 407 872 7825, with special offers often available.

8

© Disney Enterprises, Inc.

The Richard Petty Driving Experience at Walt Disney World® Resort

Rodeo

For another all-American pursuit straight out of the Old West, go and see the twice-yearly **Silver Spurs Rodeo** at Osceola County Stadium. This is the biggest event of its kind in the south-east United States and is held the first week in October and the last week in February every year, but it sells out fast so you need to call at least a month in advance for tickets on 407 677 6336. The event features classic bronco and bull riding and attracts top rodeo competitors from as far away as Canada.

On a slightly smaller scale but still worth a visit, the **Kissimmee Rodeo** is held every Friday at 8pm (except when the Silver Spurs is on) at the Kissimmee Sports Arena, on Hoagland Boulevard 2 miles south of Highway 192. Events include calf roping, steer wrestling and bull riding, and admission is $10 for adults and $5 for children 12 and under. Children especially seem to enjoy the live action, which can be surprisingly rugged (not to mention dangerous), and there is even a kids' contest – grab the ribbon from the calf's tail. It goes down a storm! Their new Catch Pen Lounge is open Friday and Saturday 8pm–2am, and Sunday 6pm–2am, with line dancing 6–8pm and $1 drinks. Call 407 933 0020 for more details.

Motor sport

For the guaranteed ultimate in high-speed thrills, *Walt Disney World* Resort has its own speedway oval which is home to the **Richard Petty Driving Experience**, taking you out in one of their 650bhp stock cars as either driver or passenger at up to 145mph. The programmes have been devised by top NASCAR driver Richard Petty and offer the three-lap **Riding Experience**; a 3-hour **Rookie Experience** (with tuition and eight laps of the speedway); the **Winston Experience** (tuition plus 16 laps in two sessions); and the **Experience of a Lifetime** (an intense 30-lap programme in three sessions). The Riding Experience will probably appeal to most, three laps of the 1.1-mile circuit with an experienced, race-proven driver lasting just 37 seconds a lap but an unbelievable blast all the way. Your initial take-off from the pit-lane takes you 0–60mph in a couple of seconds and you are straight into Turn One with your brain some distance behind. It is a bit like flying at ground level, it is hot and noisy and you must wear sensible clothes (you have to climb in through the window), but it is definitely the Real Thing in ride terms and a bigger thrill than anything else in *Walt Disney World* Resort. You don't need to book for the Riding Experience from mid-February to the end of September. There is also no admission fee, so you can come along just to watch. The three driving programmes all require reservations, while the track is occasionally closed for race testing from October to February. However, before you get carried away, wait for the prices: $89.99 for the Riding Experience, $329.99 for the Rookie Experience, $699.99 for the Winston and $1,099.99 for the Lifetime Experience. For more details, or to book, call 407 939 0130.

Race fans will also want to check out the **Daytona Speedway** (take I4 east, then I95 and Highway 92) for more big-league car and motorcycle thrills, notably the Daytona 500 on the first Sunday in July, while the **World Center of Racing** is a fascinating interactive museum. Call 904 253 7223 for details. Race fan Alan Rogers of Chester rates the museum highly. 'Try the hands-on Pit Stop Live, the excellent Daytona 500 movie and the 30-minute tour of the track. It's a real thrill.'

Orlando by Night
(or, Burning the Candle at Both Ends)

Hands up those who still have plenty of energy left! Right, this chapter is especially for you. If we can't wear you out at the theme parks and other attractions, we'll have to resort to a full-frontal assault on your sleep time – and take most of it away.

For, when it comes to night-time fun and frolics, Orlando again has a dazzling collection of possibilities, from its four purpose-built entertainment complexes, through its range of evening dinner shows and on to a full array of bars and night-clubs. The choice is suitably widespread and almost always high in quality.

The original development that started the evening entertainment ball rolling was Church Street Station in the heart of the downtown area, which opened in 1974 with **Rosie O'Grady's Goodtime Emporium** and added six more clubs and restaurants in the next 12 years to become the essential focal point of the city district. The Station recently changed ownership to a British company and a new wave of updating and refurbishing is planned for this complex. Disney opened **Pleasure Island** in 1987 to provide its own source of entertainment, with an imaginative range of clubs, discos and restaurants, and is still adding new or revamped venues as part of the area's conversion to Downtown Disney. **Disney's BoardWalk**, which opened in 1996, added still further to the night-time amusement options.

International Drive joined this process in 1997 with the **Pointe*Orlando** which, while not strictly an entertainment complex as it is mainly shops and restaurants, offers an array of lively bars, plus the big Muvico 21-screen cinema centre. It also has space for a night-club after an abortive attempt to introduce one soon after it opened.

Finally, Universal Orlando got with the beat in late 1998 and early 1999 with the opening of **CityWalk**, arguably the most elaborate and sophisticated entertainment centre of the lot.

Altogether, they represent yet another slick opportunity to be dazzled and relieved of your cash in the name of holiday fun, but you should count on visiting at least one of them if your wallet can take the strain.

Church Street Station

This converted old railway depot remains the focal point of Orlando night-life, with a number of bars, night-clubs, restaurants and other minor attractions springing up all around it. Its combination of shops, restaurants and bars has highly sophisticated touches, but this is largely a lively, occasionally raucous, centre that caters for contrasting musical tastes from Dixieland jazz, country and western to disco and rock and roll. New in late 1999 was the revamped haunted house attraction, **Terror on Church Street** (not for the faint-hearted!). It is open all day, but from 5pm there is an admission charge of $17.95 for

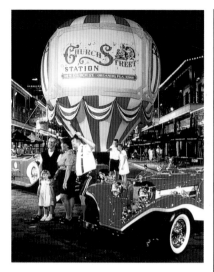

Church Street Station

adults and $11.95 for children (4–12) to the Station (children must be accompanied by their parents). If the attractions of New Orleans-style trad jazz and Can-Can girls, live country and western music with line dancing, or 50s to 90s rock classics played by the resident band do not appeal, visit Church Street during the day just to browse in the shops, look inside each of the venues and marvel at the magnificent interior architecture and furnishings. The Cheyenne Saloon, in particular, is visually stunning with its intricate oak railings and panelling. They also serve a couple of howitzer house cocktails, but, at $9.98 a time (including souvenir glass), it's a one-off rather than an oft-repeated experience! Here's a full rundown of the entertainment: **Rosie O'Grady's Good Time Emporium** (formerly the dilapidated Orlando Hotel) is the centrepiece of Church Street and a must-see venue for its Dixieland saloon setting, lively jazz music and trademark Can-Can girls who dance on the bar. Rosie's also serves deli sandwiches and hot-dogs. The **Cheyenne Saloon** hosts the country and western scene, but if you're not a fan of the music don't let it put you

Church Street Exchange shopping centre at night

Downtown Disney looks superb at night

off as the magnificent setting and atmosphere are definitely worth sampling, while the sight of the locals doing their line dancing is equally fascinating. The **Orchid Garden** belies its peaceful-sounding name by hosting the rock 'n' roll scene in another superb setting of ironwork and glass in a mock-Victorian style. Finally, Phineas Phogg's is the lively, late-night disco (see page 211). For all four of these night-clubs, you need to pay the one-off admission charge, but not if you just want to go shopping in the Church Street Exchange (11am–11pm), sit for a drink in **Apple Annie's Courtyard** (11am–1am) or visit one of the restaurants: **Lili Marlene's** (11.30am–4.30pm for lunch, 5.30–11.30pm for dinner) for excellent prime rib and seafood (and a kids' menu at $6.95); **Cracker's Seafood Restaurant** (4–11.30pm) for Cajun specialities and some of the best seafood in town (and a kids' menu $6.95); or the **Cheyenne Barbeque Restaurant** for succulent pork, chicken, ribs and beef.

The area gets seriously busy at the weekends when the locals come out to play. For a romantic half-hour (or to keep all the family amused), take one of the horse-drawn carriage rides from outside Church Street Station around the whole of the downtown area and its lakes, which are all magnificently lit at night. There is also the lure of Big Mouth Beer Night every Thursday 5–8.30pm in the Cheyenne Saloon, when wide-mouth beer bottles are $2 and barbecue sandwiches $2.50. Stay on to enjoy country music and line dancing with resident band Cheyenne Stampede. Sundays at Lili Marlene's is their special brunch buffet (10.30am–3pm) at $15.95 for adults and $7.95 for kids. Daytime historical tours of the Station are also available, call for reservations on 407 422 2434.

If you are planning more than one visit to Church Street Station it is worth knowing their annual pass ($24.95) is less than the price of two single night admissions, while the Dixie Double Pass ($44.95 for you and a guest) and VIP Pass ($74.95 for four of you) work out cheaper still (and offer discounted drink prices plus discounts at many of the shops). To get to the Station, take

9

Exit 38 (Anderson Street) off I4, turn left on to Boone Street, left again on South Street and right on to Garland Avenue. There are no less than five parking locations in the vicinity.

The surrounding areas of Church Street can be equally lively, with a terrific range of restaurants and bars. Look out in particular for **Pebbles** and **Mulvaney's** (for a touch of the Emerald Isle, especially on St Patrick's Day) and **Chillers** (for an amazing range of daiquiris and frozen specialities). Upstairs is **Ybor's Martini Bar**, an up-scale cigar and cocktail emporium. Above Chillers is the highly recommended bar **Big Bellies**, which features its own micro-brewery and an impressive range of other beers (as well as an outrageous collection of wall art), and above that is the roof-top bar **Latitudes**.

Downtown Disney

The large-scale development of what is now **Downtown Disney** (the old Village Marketplace and Pleasure Island) has evolved into a three-part complex (*Downtown Disney Marketplace, Pleasure Island* and *West Side*) doubling the size of the old site and providing two key evening entertainment sources.

Downtown Disney Pleasure Island: this is the traditional night-club zone which packs in the locals as well as the tourists and where every night is New Year's Eve. The Island (which forms the centrepiece, or linking part, of Downtown Disney) comprises the **Rock 'n' Roll**

BRIT TIP: For the full run-down of Downtown Disney's Marketplace, see page 239 in the shopping chapter. Wallets beware!

Beach Club, a live music venue featuring 40 years of classic rock (and some outrageous DJs); the **Pleasure Island Jazz Company**, for excellent modern jazz and blues in a 30s-style nightspot; **Mannequins Dance Palace** (21s and over), a huge, popular disco featuring a revolving dance floor and live entertainment from the Explosion Dancers; **Comedy Warehouse**, improvised acts from up-and-coming comics and occasional big-name acts; **8Trax**, a homage to 70s music, dance and styles (again over 21s); the **West End Stage**, which hosts the Island's resident band and occasional big-name acts and is the focus for the street party and midnight fireworks; the unmissable **Adventurers' Club**, a multi-level live entertainment lounge where the place comes to life all round you (watch the animal heads and masks!) and the stars of the show are as likely to be next to you as on stage; **BET Soundstage Club**™, with an interactive VJ/DJ and featuring the best of R&B, soul and hip-hop sounds; and the **Wildhorse Saloon**®, which showcases live country and western acts and dancing, as well as an American barbecue restaurant. As well as the clubs, the Island also has a range of shops, including **Music Legends** for rock memorabilia, **DTV**, an up-scale Disney fashion store and **Avigators Supply**, offering some stylish men's and women's clothing. There is also a fine choice of eating outlets either on or next to the Island. **Planet Hollywood**® (the largest of this world-wide movie-themed chain) is the busiest restaurant in all *Walt Disney World* Resort and therefore draws big queues in the evening, while the **Portobello Yacht Club** offers excellent northern Italian cuisine in smart, lively surroundings and **Fulton's Crab House** serves up some of the best seafood in Orlando (although at a price – average $35 for a three-course meal – and with serious queues from 6pm). You can also enjoy **Captain Mickey's Character Breakfast** here at 8am and 10am daily for $13.95 adults and $8.95 kids 11 and under. *Downtown Disney Pleasure Island* is free before 7pm when the entertainment kicks off, then there is an $18.95 charge with strict age restrictions (under 30s should take passports as ID). The eight shops here, plus the outstanding ice cream and coffee bar **D-Zertz**, are all open from 11am, and the 7pm admission is, of course, an option on your Park Hopper Plus Pass.

Downtown Disney West Side is the newest element of the Downtown expansion and incorporates the **AMC® Theater Complex**, which has been increased to 24 screens, with 5,400 seats in state-of-the-art cinema surroundings.

The most eye-catching part of West Side is home to the greatest show on earth (or at least, the greatest I've seen anywhere in the world), the **Cirque du Soleil** production *La Nouba*. Twice a day, five times a week, this purpose-built, eye-catching 1,671-seater theatre stages the most stupendous combination of dance, circus, acrobatics, comedy and live music that makes up this 90-minute show with more than 60 performers. Anyone familiar with the unique styling and outrageous costumes of the Cirque company will have an idea of what to expect, but even they will be left in awe by this multi-dimensional assault on the senses which includes trampolines, trapezes, balancing acts and even mountain bikes, interspersed with innovative dance routines and spell-binding music all with the most awesome staging. Words alone do not do it justice – go and see it. Even at $62 a ticket ($38 for children 3–9), it is worth every cent, but you

often have to book in advance, and reservations can be made up to 6 months before your visit on 407 939 7600. Performances are at 6pm and 9pm Thursday to Monday.

The other *Downtown Disney* elements are a fantastic mix of live music, fine dining, unique shopping and the ultimate in interactive game arcades, *DisneyQuest*. The cavernous **House of Blues®**, in backwoods Mississippi style, is a must for anyone even vaguely interested in blues, rock 'n' roll, R&B, gospel, jazz and Brazilian rock. Check out their magnificent Gospel Brunch on Sundays (8.30am, 1pm and 3.30pm), Wednesdays and Fridays (8.30am and 10.45am) or the 500-seat restaurant next door to the stunning main hall for some fine food, including catfish, jambalaya and a host of delicious Cajun dishes. The inevitable gift shop stocks some quality merchandise.

Similarly, **Bongos Cuban Café™** (co-owned by Gloria and Emilio Estefan) brings the sights, sounds and tastes of Old Havana to another imaginative setting (check out the bongo-drum bar stools!), with red-hot Latin music and some of the best Cuban food in America. The **Wolfgang Puck® Café** also offers a rich experience from the renowned Californian chef, with no less than four dining options: Wolfgang Puck Café, gourmet food in a casual setting; Wolfgang Puck Express, the fast-food version; B's Bar for sushi, seafood, pizzas and micro-brew beers; and the Dining Room, the up-scale restaurant.

The shopping is also original and engaging, from the basic sweet shop **Candy Cauldron** that still resembles a fairytale dungeon, through the one-off outlets like **Sosa Family Cigars, Celebrity Eyeworks' Studio** and the stylish art in glass and ceramics of **Hoypoloi**, to the more predictable souvenir stores of **All Star Gear** and

9

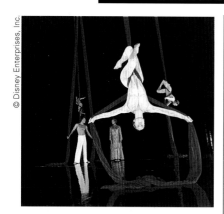

La Nouba **show from Cirque du Soleil**

Wildhorse Saloon® and finally the truly mega **Virgin™ Megastore**, the largest music store in Florida, with 300 listening stations, a full-service café, hydraulic outdoor stage and a mean sound system!

The most unusual element opened in June 1998 and brought yet another novel idea to life. **DisneyQuest** is described variously as 'an immersive, interactive entertainment environment', the latest in arcade games, a series of state-of-the-art adventure rides or, as one employee told me, 'a theme park in a box'. It houses 11 major adventures, like CyberSpace Mountain (design and ride your own roller-coaster!), Virtual Jungle Cruise (shooting the rapids, prehistoric style) and Aladdin's Magic Carpet (more virtual reality, riding in best cartoon fashion), a host of old-fashioned video games in the Replay Zone (do you remember Asteroids and Galaxian?), the latest sports games, a test of your imagination in Animation Academy and two futuristic cafés, one with computers and Internet tables, the other, Food Quest, straight out of a space-age comic book. Two new elements in 2000 were SongMaker (a computer-generated professional audio system that creates a CD with you as the star!) and Pirates of the Caribbean (an amazing 3-D immersion into a swashbuckling adventure as teams of four stage a Battle for Buccaneer Gold). *DisneyQuest* is open 10am–2am daily, but, if you want to avoid the queues (the building admits only 1,500), go during the day. A 1-day ticket costs $27 ($21 for 3–9s, although it is a bit too elaborate for the youngsters) and is an excellent way to keep teenagers in particular amused for 5 hours or more.

Finally, the whole of *Downtown Disney West Side* is characterised at night by outstanding lighting and special effects and a vibrant, thrilling atmosphere that is almost intoxicating. Words alone do not do it justice – go see it!

Disney's other big evening entertainment offering is **Disney's BoardWalk** resort, where the waterfront entertainment district contains two notable venues for non-residents (three if you count the excellent micro-brewery of the Big River Grille and Brewing Works). **Jellyrolls** is another variation on the duelling piano bar, with the lively pianists conjuring up a raucous evening of audience participation songs, while the **Atlantic Dance Club** offers more mainstream dance sounds, plus a Martini bar. Both have a $3 admission charge ($5 at weekends) and you MUST be 21 or older to enter, so remember your passports for ID as they are strict.

Downtown Disney Cirque du Soleil

Hard Rock Café on CityWalk

The Pointe*Orlando

This eye-catching new development on International Drive, almost opposite the Convention Center, is a mix of unique shops, cinemas, restaurants and the WonderWorks science centre. It is open all day but has plenty of evening appeal, too (and recently opened a novel magic-themed dinner show; see later in the chapter).

The big-name stores are all up-scale and include some hugely imaginative touches that make them stand out from mere shops. The collection of bars and restaurants strive to be different too, with **Lulu's Bait Shack** leading the way for New Orleans-style cuisine and entertainment (it looks like an old shack blown in from Bourbon Street), **Johnny Rockets** 50s-style diner, **Adobe Gila's**, a fine Mexican cantina stocking more than 100 different tequillas (ouch!), **Monty's Conch Harbor**, for fine seafood, and **Dan Marino's Town Tavern**, sports-themed dining with the great Miami Dolphins quarterback. Lulu's and Adobe Gila's see most of the evening action, with their bars often packed at weekends.

Additionally, the 21-screen **Muvico cinema,** with its wonderfully vast and themed (inevitably) entrance foyer, boasts state-of-the-art stadium seating and sound systems, and the only IMAX cinema in Orlando, complete with 3-D capability. You can take in a new-release film here several months before it is released back home! The Pointe was also developing a new interactive entertainment venue at the time of writing, to open in Spring 2001. Called **XS Entertainment,** it is being designed by video game giants Namco and promises a high-energy mix of restaurant, bar and arcade.

Universal's CityWalk

As part of the big Universal Orlando development – and in direct competition with Downtown Disney – comes this 30-acre spread of just about everything in the entertainment world. The resort's hub is a busy, bustling expanse of shops, restaurants, snack bars, open-air events and night-clubs. It offers a huge variety of cuisine, from fast

9

Universal's CityWalk

food to fine dining, an unusual mix of speciality shops and a truly eclectic nightclub mix, from reggae to Motown to salsa and high-energy disco. Unlike Pleasure Island, there is no entry fee, but you do pay a cover charge ($3.25–$9) at the eight clubs. You can also buy a **CityWalk Party Pass** ($8.43) or Party Pass with Movie (one free film at the 20-screen Universal Cineplex; $12.67) for entry to all eight (except one-off concerts at Hard Rock Live) or get the 2- or 3-Day Universal Studios Escape Pass with a Party Pass as well.

The area splits into three, with the main **Plaza** featuring shopping and restaurants. Among the most original (and entertaining) of the 13 main shops are **Endangered Species**, with merchandise designed to raise eco-awareness; **Quiet Flight**, a radical surf and beachwear emporium; the retro-American decor of **Fossil** for leather goods, watches and sunglasses; the wacky world of **Captain Crackers** for toys, moving animals and outrageous T-shirts; the inevitable **Universal Studios Store** for character merchandise; and **All Star Collectibles** for (American) sports fans.

When it comes to eating, you have the **NASCAR Café** (a must for motor racing fans, 10am–10pm) with full-size stock cars and racing memorabilia, videos and interactive games while you dine on burgers, ribs, roasted sirloin and popcorn shrimp. **Pastamore** is a delightful al fresco Italian diner, with the choice of full-service dining (5pm to midnight) for pizza, pasta, grilled chicken and steaks or the Pastamore Café (8am to midnight) for sandwiches, pastries and ice cream. **Emeril's** restaurant is the five-star end of the range here, a sophisticated and vibrant journey into the cuisine of New Orleans master chef Emeril Lagasse. Fine

wines and a cigar bar both add to Emeril's Creole-based gourmet creations, and if you don't try the Louisiana oyster stew here, you have missed a real treat (lunch 11.30am–2pm, dinner 5.30–10pm, 11pm Fri and Sat). **Jimmy Buffet's Margaritaville** (11am–2am) is an island homage to Florida's laid-back musical hero, with 'Floribbean' cuisine (a mixture of Key West and Caribbean), live music and three bars, including the Volcano Bar which 'erupts' margarita mix when the blender needs filling (I'm not kidding!). There is a cover charge ($3.25) after 10pm when the band hits the stage.

Across the CityWalk waterway is the **Lagoon Front** location of another huge dining experience, the two-storey **NBA City** which is sure to thrill basketball fans with its Cage dining area, interactive Playground area and Club lounge where you can watch live and classic games (all 11am–2am). Right next door is the massive mock-Coliseum architecture of **Hard Rock Live**, a 2,500-seat concert venue with state-of-the-art staging and sound. Big-name bands and performers are on stage several times a week in this slightly retro rock 'n' roll theatre; call 407 839 3900 for up-to-date details or check out the Universal Orlando website. Of course, you can't miss dining at the **Hard Rock Café** here, the world's largest example of this international chain, with its collection of rock 'n' roll memorabilia (including a 1959 pink Cadillac). It remains incredibly popular, so try to get in early for lunch or dinner (11am–2am) to sample their classic diner fare (notably the Pig Sandwich). Collectors of Hard Rock souvenirs will also find prices a little more to their liking here than the UK.

Finally, you come to the **Promenade** area, which offers the choice of night-clubs and some more fine dining (notably in the case of Latin Quarter). **Motown Café** (also with an entrance on Plaza level) is a homage to all the performers of the Motown record label, from the Four Tops and Jackson Five to modern artists, with a full-service restaurant, retro-style lounge and two revue stages featuring the Motown Moments, who emulate the likes of the Temptations and Supremes (cover charge $3.25, 5pm to midnight Sun–Thur, 5pm–2am Fri and Sat). **Bob Marley – A Tribute to Freedom** is a clever recreation of Marley's Jamaica home, turned into a courtyard live music venue, restaurant and bars. The bands are excellent, the atmosphere authentic and the place really swings at night (4pm–2am, 21 and over on Fri and Sat; cover charge $4.25 after 7pm).

Next up is **Pat O'Brien's**, a faithful reproduction of the famous New Orleans bar and restaurant, with its flaming fountains courtyard, duelling piano bar and main bar (6pm–2am, cover charge $3.25 for the piano bar – you also need to be 21 or over here, so remember to take your passport as ID). Excellent Cajun food and world-famous Hurricane cocktails are also the order of the day here, but don't drink too many and expect to walk home! **CityJazz** is a real contrast, a hip, up-market centre combining history, education and live music from a series of local and international musicians, with tapas-style food. Visually and in sound quality it is stunning and, if you're keen on the live music (8.30pm–1am, cover charge $5.25), you can easily spend all night here. For the younger club-minded visitors, **the groove** is the next generation in night-club entertainment, a vivid, pounding, high-energy dance venue designed like a Victorian theatre but with the very latest in club music, lighting and special effects (9pm–2am, cover charge $5.25 and 21 and over only).

Finally, completing the Promenade tour is the **Latin Quarter**, a truly sensational venue-cum-restaurant that serves up a genuine slice of Latin American style, in its atmosphere, music, dance, decor and cuisine. Quite simply, the food is outstanding – a combination of beef, fresh fish and poultry with tangy fruit sauces, spicy salsas and mouth-watering marinades (don't miss their version of rack of lamb at all costs) – the ambience is mesmerising and the sounds are so wonderfully vibrant and alive, you can't help dancing even in your seat. From Cuba to Chile, here is a great experience, with the 13-piece orchestra whipping up a samba and salsa storm. You can even take lessons from the Latin Quarter Dance Troupe. Drop in for dinner (5pm–2am) or just check out the music on Fridays and Saturdays (cover charge $3.25 after 10pm).

Breathless yet? Well, there's still the **Universal Cineplex**, a 20-screen cinema complex with a 5,000 capacity and the latest in stadium seating, curved-screen visuals and high-tech sound systems.

Hey, I'm exhausted and I'm only *writing* about it!

Disney shows

Walt Disney World Resort's other night-time extravaganzas are often overlooked by visitors unless they are staying at one of the main hotel resorts within *Walt Disney World*. The most popular with those in the know (and it's free!) is the nightly **Electrical Water Pageant** on Bay Lake and the Seven Seas Lagoon in front of the *Magic Kingdom* Park. It lasts just 10 minutes (from around 9pm) so it is easy to miss, but it is almost a waterborne version of the SpectroMagic parade in the *Magic Kingdom* Park itself, with thousands

The Latin Quarter

of twinkling lights on a floating cavalcade of boats and mock sea creatures. The best points to see it are outside the *Magic Kingdom* Park (in high season only), *Disney's Polynesian Resort* and the shores of *Disney's Fort Wilderness Resort & Campground*, but it can also be seen from Disney's Contemporary Resort, Disney's Grand Floridian Resort and Spa and Disney's Wilderness Lodge. For a night of South Seas adventure and entertainment, try the **Polynesian Luau Dinner Show** (open to non-residents at *Disney's Polynesian Resort*). It's a bit expensive at $44 for adults, and $22 for under 12s, but the entertainment is quite thrilling (fire jugglers, hula-drum dancers and clever musicians) even if the food, in keeping with most of Orlando's dinner shows, is nothing out of the ordinary. For reservations (usually necessary), call 407 939 3463. The **Hoop-Dee-Doo Musical Revue** at *Disney's Fort Wilderness Resort & Campground* is an ever-popular nightly dinner show that carries on where the Diamond Horseshoe Saloon Revue in the *Magic Kingdom* Park leaves off, and has great food. Especially loved by children, it

features the excellent joking, dancing, singing Pioneer Hall Players in a merry American hoedown-style show, with barbecued ribs, chicken and corn on the cob while you're watching. Okay, it's corny and a tad embarrassing to find yourself singing along with the hammy action, but it is performed with great gusto, and you're on holiday, remember! The Revue plays three times a night (5pm, 7.15pm and 9.30pm) at the Pioneer Hall, admission $38 for adults, $19.50 for under 12s, and reservations are ALWAYS necessary (tel 407 939 3463).

For British visitors only, there is also the **Disney Backyard Barbecue** several times a week, with a chance for the kids to chow down in best barbecue style with Mickey, Minnie and Co. An excellent all-you-can-eat buffet, including transportation, beer and wine, line dancing lessons and lots of Disney fun add up to a good evening out – but at a price: $55, and $42 for 3–12s ($39 and $26 without transportation). Many of the tour operators offer this excursion, or you could call Real Florida Excursions on 407 345 4996 ext. 3012.

Dinner shows

Having stumbled into the topic of themed dinner shows, it would be appropriate here just to outline this particularly Orlando-based type of attraction for first-time visitors. As the name suggests, it is live

Arabian Nights

entertainment coupled with dinner in a fantasy-type environment where even the waiters and waitresses dress in costume and act out roles. The staging is always of a large-scale, elaborate nature, the acting on the hammy side and the food hearty, plentiful but distinctly ordinary, usually accompanied by unlimited beer, house wine or soft drinks. There is always a strong family appeal and they nearly all seat you on large tables where you can get to know other folks, too, but, at an average of $35–$40 for adults, they are not cheap (especially when you add on the taxes and tips). Beware, too; the almost constant attempts to shake an extra few dollars out of you with photos, souvenirs, flags, etc.

There are a whole range of different shows vying for your attention, so take your pick from the following:

Terror on Church Street

Arabian Nights

This lovingly maintained, family-owned attraction is the largest-scale production and one of the most popular with locals as well as tourists. It's a real treat for horse lovers, but you don't need to be an equestrian expert to appreciate the spectacular stunts, horsemanship and marvellous costumes as more than 50 highly trained horses perform a 25-act show, loosely based on

the celebration of Princess Scheherezade's engagement to Prince Khalid, in the huge, covered arena at the centre of this 1,200-seater Palace. The magnificent close-quarter drill of the Lipizzaner stallions, the daring riding and the thrilling chariot race all add up to a memorable show that kids, in particular, adore. The recent addition of new characters, costumes and special effects, plus the incorporation of a bumbling genie, have given Arabian Nights a real boost and helped to keep their appeal fresh. The food – green salad, oven-roasted prime rib with new potatoes, and a dessert (vegetarian meals on request) – is above average, and it is decent value at $37.95 for adults and $24.95 for kids 3–11. Arabian Nights, which is located just half a mile east of I4 on Highway 192 (it's on the left, just to the side of the Parkway shopping plaza, or just past Water Mania if you are coming from the eastern end of 192), runs every evening at 7.30 or 8.30pm, with occasional matinees, lasting about 2 hours, and tickets may be purchased at the box office between 10am and 6pm or by credit card if you phone 407 239 9223.

9

Pirates Dinner Adventure

Pirates Dinner Adventure

This show features one of the most spectacular settings, with the centrepiece Spanish galleon pirate ship being 150ft long, 60ft wide, 70ft tall and 'anchored' in a 300,000-gallon lagoon, and also delivers good value for money with its pre-show elements, plentiful (if ordinary) food and drink, after-show Buccaneer Bash disco (until 10.30pm) and the Pirate's Maritime Museum which guests are free to wander around. The basic premise of the audience being 'hi-jacked' by the wicked eighteenth-century pirates is a clever one, even if the actual storyline is hard to follow. Chaos and mayhem ensue, some of it inaudible thanks to the poor acoustics of the arena, but there is swashbuckling galore, sword-fights, acrobatics and boat races, and the goodies (inevitably) triumph over evil Captain Sebastian and his crew. There are plenty of stunts and special effects and ticket prices are $38.95 for adults and $23.95 for 3–11s (but watch out for discounts especially here). The Pirates can be found on Carrier Drive between International Drive and Universal Boulevard daily from 6.30pm, with appetisers served until 7.45pm, when show seating begins. Call 407 248 0590 for reservations.

> BRIT TIP: NEVER pay full price for the dinner shows as there are always discounts to be had. Watch out for coupons among the tourist brochures and magazines or ask your holiday company.

Mark II Dinner Theater

This variation on the dinner show theme offers a full-scale Broadway musical or comedy after you have been able to dine well on another well-stocked buffet and salad bar, with home-made desserts and an

(extra) full cocktail service and wine list. The quality productions change every 6 weeks or so, but include works like *Fiddler on the Roof, La Cage Aux Folles* and *Cabaret*. The interior is tastefully designed with tables of two or four in tiered ramps surrounding the stage. An additional feature after Friday and Saturday evening performances is the Afterglow, a chance to meet the performers in the lobby, enjoy a few drinks and join in with a few well-known songs or even have a go in the spotlight yourself! There are eight performances a week, with prices ranging from $28.50–$37 for matinees (11.30am Wed, Thur and Sat), and $33–$42 for evening shows (6pm Wed–Sat, 4.30pm Sun). Call 407 843 6275 for details of the current show and reservations. The Theater can be found off exit 44 travelling (north) east on I4, turn left on to Par Avenue and one mile on the left in the Edgewater Plaza.

Medieval Times

Eleventh-century Spain is the entertaining setting for this 2-hour extravaganza of medieval pageantry, sorcery and robust horseback jousts that culminate in furious hand-to-hand combat by the six knights. It is worth arriving early to appreciate the clever mock-castle design and costumes of all the staff as you are ushered into the pre-show hall and then taken into the arena itself with banks of bench-type seats flanking the huge indoor battleground. The weapons used are all quite real and there is a lot of skill, not to mention hard work, involved, plus some neat touches with indoor pyrotechnics and other special effects. You need to be in full audience participation mode as you cheer on your own knight and boo the others, but kids (not to mention a few adults) get a huge kick out of it and they also love the fact that eating is all done without cutlery – don't worry, there are handles on the soup bowls! The elaborate staging takes your mind off the fact that the chicken dinner is only average, but there is positively heaps of it and the serfs and wenches who serve you make it a fun experience. Admission (also includes Medieval Life) is $38.95 for adults and $23.95 for kids 3–12 and the doors open 90 minutes prior to each performance, the times of which vary according to the season, so call 1-800 229 8300 for details. The castle is located on Highway 192, 5 miles east of the junction with I4. If you have 45 minutes to spare before the show, the adjoining **Medieval Life** exhibition makes an interesting diversion. This mock medieval village re-enacts the life and times of 900 years ago, with artisans demonstrating the crafts of pottery and tool-making, glass-blowing, spinning and weaving. There is also a Chamber of Horrors that might be a touch gruesome for small children.

Sleuth's

Here's another fun variation, a real live version of Cluedo acted out before your eyes in hilarious fashion while you enjoy a substantial meal and unlimited beer, wine and sodas. There are eight different plot settings, including the new *WKZY TV* – a clever skit on trash television – that all add up to some elaborate murder mysteries, with the action taking place all around you and even with some cameo roles for various audience members. The quick-witted cast keep things moving well and keep you guessing during the 40-minute show, then you have the main part of dinner to formulate some questions to interrogate the cast (but be warned, the real murderer is allowed to lie!). If you solve the crime you win a prize, but

that is pretty secondary to the overall enjoyment – and this is a show I do enjoy a lot. Prices are $38.95 for adults and $22.95 for children 3–11 and again showtimes vary, so call 407 363 1985 for details. Sleuth's Mystery Dinner Theater is located in Republic Square, on Universal Boulevard, just off International Drive (turn right past Wet 'n Wild).

Due to make its debut in late summer 2000 was the **Shazam** dinner-show at WonderWorks on The Pointe*Orlando, a 'magical, musical comedy' featuring a variety of illusions, magic tricks, original music, lighting effects and an all-you-can-eat pizza buffet. The 90-minute show was scheduled for twice-nightly performances (Tue–Sun) at 6pm and 8pm. WonderWorks will also offer a 'Night of Wonder' package

---

American radio stations come in a vast number of types and styles that conform to fairly narrow musical tastes. Here is a quick guide to finding the main ones in your car:

9

ADULT CONTEMPORARY	**CLASSICAL**
98.9 FM (WMMO)	90.7 FM (WMFE)
99.3 FM (WLRQ)	91.5 FM (WPRK)
105.1 FM (WOMX)	
107.7 FM (WMGF)	**JAZZ**
	89.9FM (WUCF)
POP	103.1 FM (WLOQ)
99.9 FM (WFKS)	
106.7 FM (WXXL)	**COUNTRY**
	92.3 FM (WWKA)
	97.5 FM (WPCV)
OLDIES	98.1 FM (WGNE)
100.3 FM (WSHE)	102.7 FM (WHKR)
105.9 FM (WOCL)	
790 AM (WLBE)	**ROCK**
	91.5 FM (WPRK)
NEWS/TALK	93.1 FM (WKRO)
90.7 FM (WMFE)	96.5 FM (WHTQ)
104.1 FM (WTKS)	101.1 FM (WJRR)
SPORT	
540 AM (WQTM)	

Sleuth's dinner show

including Shazam and unlimited use of the upside-down attraction at $29.95 for adults and $24.95 for under 13s and seniors. For ticket information, call 407 351 8800.

Night-clubs

Orlando is also blessed with a huge variety of other night-life, from common or garden discos to elaborate live music clubs and no less then three 'duelling piano' bars. The majority are situated in the downtown area, i.e. away from the main tourist centres. The local paper, the *Orlando Sentinel*, has a regular Friday listing section called 'Calendar' which details every local nightspot worth knowing about as well as individual events and one-off concerts, and it is worth checking out as there is an amazing turnover in the success/failure rate of bars and discos. Don't be surprised if a night-club suddenly undergoes a complete change of name and personality, as this is fairly common too. The basic distinctions tend to be **Live Music Clubs, Mainstream Night-clubs**, which also have the occasional live band, and then **Bars** which specialise in evening entertainment.

Live Music

The following should give you a representative taste of the most popular venues (for those 21 and over only in most cases), starting with the Live Music clubs.

The rock 'n' roll piano idea was pioneered here in Orlando, by the wonderfully named **Howl at the Moon Saloon** on west Church Street and is equally popular there (6pm–2am Sun–Thur, and 5pm–2am Fri and Sat). Classic rock 'n' roll, show tunes, current hits, the Saloon's duelling pianists play them all, with full audience involvement and non-stop banter. There is no cover charge Sun–Tues, while Wed–Thur it is $3 after 7.30pm, on Fri it's $5 after 6pm and Sat is $5 after 5.30pm, and the live piano action begins at 8pm every night (it also gets distinctly rowdy and even bawdy later on, so remember your sense of humour).

Then, of course, you will have already noted **Jellyrolls** at *Disney's BoardWalk Resort* and **Pat O'Brien's** (the original New Orleans version) at Universal's CityWalk, which are both hugely popular with locals and tourists alike.

Lord Mansfield's Fox Hunt

DisneyQuest

Country music fans – and others in search of the 'in' crowd – will definitely need to check out **:08 Seconds**, a huge, multi-level entertainment centre. It earns its 'unique' tag by hosting live bull riding(!) and monster truck wars as well as having a huge dance hall with live bands, line dancing lessons, 12 bars (and bottled beer at $2, a real bargain), a pool hall, game room and classic country barbecue. The atmosphere is both authentic and infectious, right down to their well-stocked and excellently priced gift

BRIT TIP: Downtown Orlando is really the heart of the night-club scene, with a host of clubs within walking distance along Orange Avenue between Church Street and Jefferson Street.

shop. This is one of my favourite clubs in town. On West Livingston Street in the heart of downtown, it has bags of style, but call 407 839 4800 for the latest details (usually, ladies' night Wed, monster trucks Fri, and bull riding Sat).

Blues and Jazz are the staples of **Sapphire**, at 54 North Orange Avenue, where resident DJs, bands and special guest acts vary from week to week. Call for details on 407 246 1419. This has the reputation as the 'hippest' place to be seen, with its San Francisco-inspired decor.

As a complete alternative from the music scene, **Sak Comedy Club** (on West Amelia Avenue, in the Orlando Centroplex) is like a live version of the TV show *Whose Line Is It Anyway?* Fast-paced and funny, the Sak performers do a mix of competitive improv comedy, with every show offering something different and the young performers living on their wits. On stage Tue–Sun, with three shows on Fri and Sat (the 9.30pm one is usually packed), admission is $12. Call 407 648 0001 for reservations and find out why Sak's has been consistently voted the best live comedy in Florida.

Discos

In addition to the mainstream DJ dance centres at Downtown Disney's Pleasure Island and Universal's CityWalk, the **Zuma Beach Club** (on North Orange Avenue, just up from Church Street) appeals widely to the disco crowd with its beach-party atmosphere (including staff in bikinis or cut-off shorts, and 'lifeguards') and Top 40 sounds 9pm–3am Wed–Sat (and some live concerts on Sun). The atmosphere

Rosie O'Grady's

9

can be pretty basic and raucous, but it definitely appeals to the younger crowd. Call 407 648 8363 for the latest details. For more mainstream disco style, **Phineas Phogg's**, in Church Street Station, is open until 2am every night. Admission (21 and over only) is part of the Station's $17.95 entry fee.

Progressive

The alternative scene can boast several lively clubs that offer what the Americans term 'progressive' music but in real terms is more likely to be a techno-dance or even rave style. **Barbarella**, on Orange Avenue on the corner of Washington Street, offers alternative and new wave music 9pm–3am most nights. Again, it is more of a techno-dance sound, but with various retro-progressive, old wave and 'Bad Disco' nights. Cover charge varies from $3 to $6, call 407 839 0457 for details. **The Club at Firestone** is almost impossible to categorise as it ranges from mainstream disco to acid jazz lounge, with something different each night from Wed–Sat (including gay nights on Wed and Sat). About half a mile north of Church Street on the corner of Orange Avenue and Concord Street, it is open 9pm–3am with the cover charge ranging from $5 to $9. Call 407 426 0005 for night-by-night information (or look up www.clubatfirestone.com). Other current hot-spots at the time of writing include the high-energy dance of **Club Volcano** on Orange Avenue (9pm–3am, with live rock bands occasionally, call 407 999 0033) and the eclectic sound of the **Blue Room** on West Pine Street (10pm–2.30am Wed, 8pm–2.30am Thur–Sat, ladies drink free on Thur).

Bars

Bars of all types simply abound in Orlando, but there are again several which offer a particular tourist appeal, especially to newcomers to the scene. Live entertainment, extrovert barmen, sports-themed bars and raw bars (offering seafood, often by the bucket!), the choice is, as ever, wide-ranging, but here are a few of the best.

Travel out past Church Street (and the bars mentioned in conjunction with Church Street Station), and into Orange Avenue and you are into real locals' territory with the likes of **One-Eyed Jack's**, with its party pop atmosphere and live music sing-alongs, and its neighbouring connected bars of the **Loaded Hog** and **Wall Street Cantina**, which get packed at weekends. Turn left on to West Central Boulevard and you find **Kate O'Brien's Irish Pub** for more lively bar entertainment (and a neat beer garden), while the similarly Irish-themed **Scruffy Murphy's** is another block further north on Washington Street. Again, there is no cover charge and it boasts a real good-time atmosphere when it is busy (which is most nights). Back on Orange Avenue, the **Have a Nice Day Café** is part bar, part 70s disco (4.30pm–2am Mon–Sat), while heading south on Orange takes you to **Tanquerary's Bar and Grille** with live music on Fri and Sat.

The eclectic trio of the **Kit-Kat Club, Harold and Maud's** and **The Globe** (the latter an off-the-wall 24-hour diner) are also worth seeking out for a lively drink or three on Wall Street, just off Orange. The three are interconnected, which is mildly disconcerting, but boast a range of bars, a pool hall and live music, as well as the fun eating style of The Globe.

Sports bars

Finally, with the multitude of sports bars that are another particularly American pastime, **Friday's Front Row Sports Grill** on International Drive (just south of the Sand Lake Road junction) really sticks out as a major tourist trap which even the locals enjoy. Here you can catch ALL the action (and, yes, they do show soccer as well) on 84 TV screens, plus enjoy some 100 beers from around the world (and bar features like $1 domestic 12oz drafts!), as well as try out their basketball nets, pool tables and shuffleboard, and rub shoulders with the local sports stars from time to time. The food is good, standard American diner fare and there is plenty to keep the kids amused, too (like crayons to colour in the paper tablecloths and a huge range of video games). The atmosphere varies according to the time of day and the sports event (VERY rowdy for Orlando Magic basketball games!), so call 407 363 1414 for up-to-the-minute info. There is never a cover charge, reservations are not accepted and it is open from 11am–2am Mon–Sat, 11am–midnight on Sun.

Other choices for the sports bar experience include the massive **Sports Dimension** on Curry Ford Road – 87 TV screens, with 12 big-screens – open 11am–2am every day (407 895 0807) and **Headlightz Sports Bar** on East Colonial Drive, which also offers live music (tel 407 273 9600). Another personal favourite is the **Orlando Ale House** on Kirkman Road, just opposite Universal Studios (tel 407 248 0000). Boasting more than 30 TVs, a raw bar and some great seafood, it also carries an above-average range of beers. *Walt Disney World* Resort can boast the excellent **ESPN Club** at *Disney's BoardWalk Resort*, a full-service restaurant with sports broadcast facilities, video games, more than 70 TV monitors, giant scoreboards and even a Little League menu for kids. No sports fan should miss it. Equally, **NBA City** at Universal's CityWalk, and the **Cricketers' Arms** in the Mercado Center should not be overlooked as great sports venues, especially for TV/video addicts.

Now, you will also want to know a lot more about where, when and how to tackle that other holiday essential – FOOD. So, read on …

9

Eating Out
(or, Watching the Americans at Their National Sport)

If eating was an Olympic event, the Americans would take gold, silver and bronze every time. Forget baseball, basketball or American football: eating is their national sport! To say they take meal times seriously would be the understatement of the year.

I know I am doing a vast disservice to the majority of the inhabitants of their huge country, but it is hard to dispel the notion of the average American as a walking food intake, especially when so many of the local tourists you will encounter are so, well, not to put too fine a point on it, fat.

Variety

As a consequence, the variety, quantity and quality of restaurants, cafés, fast-food chains and hot-dog stalls is in keeping with this great tradition of eating as much as

Emeril's of CityWalk

possible, as often as possible. It is not out of the question to be able to eat around the clock, i.e. 24 hours a day, and at first glance the full selection of food is rather overwhelming (hence this chapter). Cruising along either of the main drags of International Drive or Highway 192 will quickly reveal a dazzling array of different eating houses, the choice of which can be quite bewildering.

As a general rule, food is plentiful, relatively cheap, readily available and nearly always appetising and filling. You may not encounter many gourmet establishments (although Orlando DOES possess some outstanding high-quality restaurants, like Emeril's on CityWalk), but you will get good value for money and you probably won't need to eat more than two proper meals a day, unless your appetite is of a similar transatlantic nature. Put simply, portions tend to be large, food of a heavily steak-, chicken- or pizza-based variety, service of an efficient, friendly character, and it is ultimately hard to come by a really BAD meal. The one possible exception (as pointed out by several readers) is if you like a good supply of fresh veg with your meals. The US diet often seems to overlook this staple, but if you look up the vegetarian options lower down or check out one of the outlets of **Chamberlain's**, notably at the Market Place on Dr Phillips Boulevard and in the new Winter Park Village shops, you will find a healthy, balanced choice.

Exceptional deals

In keeping with the climate, most restaurants tend towards the informal (T-shirts and shorts are usually acceptable) and cater readily for families. This also leads to two

> BRIT TIP: A buffet breakfast at Ponderosa, Sizzler or any other similar establishments will probably keep you going until tea-time and is a good way to start the day if you are tackling one of the Big Eight theme parks.

exceptional deals for budget-conscious tourists, especially those with a large tribe to keep happy. Many of the main hotels now offer 'kids eat free' deals, provided they eat with their parents. The age restrictions can vary from under 10s to under 14s, but it obviously represents good value for money if you are staying there. The second item of interest is the 'all-you-can-eat' buffet, another common feature of many of the large chain restaurants in particular, and, when you consider they are catering for the American appetite, it means you can have a pretty hearty meal for not too much and probably eat enough at, say, breakfast, to keep you going until dinner! A few establishments also offer 'early bird' specials, a dinner discount if you dine before 6pm.

Don't be afraid to ask for a doggy-bag if you have a fair amount left over (and even if you haven't brought the dog!). It is common practice to take away the half of that pizza you couldn't finish, or those chicken legs or your leftover salad. The locals do it all the time and, again, it is wallet-friendly. Just ask

for the leftovers 'to go'. (PS: it's not usually a bag, either!)

Don't hesitate to tell your waiter/waitress if something isn't quite right with your meal. Americans will readily complain if they feel aggrieved, so restaurants are keen to make sure everything is to your satisfaction.

And, please, don't forget to tip. The basic wage rate for waiters and waitresses is low, so they rely heavily on tips to supplement their wages. Unless service really is shoddy, in which case you should mention it, the usual rate for tips is 10 per cent of your bill at buffet-style restaurants and 15 per cent at full-service restaurants. However, it is usually worth checking to see if service has already been added to your bill. It is a common practice in many British restaurants nowadays, but not so common in America.

> BRIT TIP: Another way to save money given the large portions usually on offer is to share an entrée, or main course, between two. Your waiter/waitress will be happy to oblige (provided you keep their tip up to the full rate).

10

Having implied that the majority of eating outlets tend to be of a hearty rather than quality- and variety-conscious kind, it is still quite easy to encounter a monumental array of food types. Florida is renowned for its seafood, which also comes at a much more reasonable price than in the Mediterranean. Crab, lobster, shrimp (of a size which we would call king prawns), clams and oysters can all be sampled without fear of breaking the bank, as well as several dozen varieties of fish, many of which you won't have come across before.

Cuban, Cajun/creole and Mexican are other more local types of cooking which are well represented here (if you haven't eaten Mexican food, try fajitas – pronounced faheetas – they're delicious!), and you'll also be spoiled for choice of Oriental fare, from the more common Chinese and Indian to Japanese, Thai and even Vietnamese.

The big shopping complexes and malls also offer a good choice of eateries in their food courts, and again they often represent particularly good value for money. Cracker cooking is original Floridian fare, and the more adventurous will want to try the local speciality – alligator meat. This can be stewed, barbecued, smoked, sautéed or braised. Fried gator tail 'nuggets' are an Orlando favourite, while barbecued gator ribs are the 'unofficial' food of Central Florida, according to the local press.

Ordering

Ordering your food can also be an adventure in itself. The choice for each item is often the cue for an inquisition of exam-type proportions from your waiter/waitress. You can never order just 'toast' – it has to be white, brown, wholegrain, rye, muffin or bagel; eggs and bacon come in a baffling variety of types; an order for tea or coffee usually provokes the response 'Regular or decaf? Iced, lemon or English?'; and salads have more dressings than the National Health Service. Whenever I've finished ordering I'm tempted to ask 'Have I passed?' after the barrage of questions. (NB: American bacon is always streaky and crisp-fried and sausages are chipolata-like and on the spicy side.) Don't be worried about going in to a restaurant and asking to see their menu if it isn't prominently displayed. It is

no big deal to Americans and the restaurant won't feel insulted if you decide to look elsewhere.

Vegetarian options

In a culinary country where beef is king, vegetarians often find themselves hard done by, and Orlando is little different to the general American rule. However, there are a couple of bright spots, plus a handy hint when all seems lost. Firstly, there are two speciality vegetarian restaurants in Orlando, The **Lower East Side** at 3401 LB McLeod Road (tel 407 648 4830) and the Chinese cuisine **Garden Café** on West Colonial Drive downtown (tel 407 999 9799), while the tapas-style **Café Tu-Tu Tango** on International Drive serves a number of veggie dishes. Most of the up-scale restaurants should be able to offer a vegetarian option and will be happy for you to ask in advance. *Walt Disney World* Resort is slightly more enlightened in that the California Grill (in Disney's Contemporary Resort), Seasons (Disney Institute), Citricos (Disney's Grand Floridian Resort and Spa) and Spoodles (Disney's BoardWalk) feature vegetarian dishes, while all the full-service restaurants (notably Bongos Cuban Café™ and Wolfgang Puck's® Café in Downtown Disney), plus some of the counter-service ones are usually keen to try to cater for non-menu requests. It is always worth asking. An excellent section of the Unofficial WDW Information Guide also lists a lot of special dietary requests, including vegetarian and vegan, on www.wdwig.com/special.htm.

Drinking

Drinking is another matter altogether. Most British towns now have their share of American bars and diners and they give you a pretty

BRIT TIP: If there are several of you, ordering a pitcher of beer will work out cheaper than by the bottle or glass.

good idea of what to expect, only there is a lot more of it here. The biggest complaint of Brits on holiday in the USA is of the beer. With the exception of a handful of English-style pubs (see page 222), American beer is always lager, either bottled or on draught, and ice-cold. It goes down great when it's really hot, but, as a general rule, it is weaker and fizzier than we're used to. Of course, there are exceptions and they are worth seeking out (try Killian's Red, Michelob Amber Bock or Dos Equis for a fuller flavour), but if you are expecting a good, old-fashioned British pint, forget it. But I would suggest if you can't do without your pint of Tetley's, or whatever, for a couple of weeks, then you're probably going on the wrong kind of holiday here! Spirits (always called 'liquor' by Americans) come in a typically huge variety, but beware ordering just 'whisky' as you'll get bourbon instead. Specify if you want Scotch whisky or Irish whiskey and demand it 'straight up' if you don't want it deluged under a mountain of ice! If you fancy a cocktail, there is a massive choice and most bars and restaurants have lengthy happy hours where prices are very consumer-friendly (hic!). Californian wines also work out much better value than imported European ones (and are usually of equally good quality). If you are sticking to soft drinks ('sodas') or coffee, most bars and restaurants will give you free refills. You can also run a tab in most bars and pay when you leave to avoid having to shell out for each round.

Another few words of warning.

Florida licensing laws are stricter than ours and you need to be **21 or over** to enjoy an alcoholic beverage in a bar or lounge. Even if you are over 21 you will often be asked for proof of your age before you are served (or allowed in entertainment complexes like Downtown Disney Pleasure Island), and this means your *passport*, as it contains a picture of you (Americans use their driving licences as proof of ID because it also has to carry a photo of the owner). It's no good arguing or trying to reason with a reluctant barman. Local licensing laws are strict and they cannot afford to take any chances. No photo ID, no beer! Anyone under 21 may NOT sit or stand near a bar either.

Right, that gives you the inside track on HOW to eat and drink like the locals, now you want to know WHERE to do it, so here's a handy guide to that veritable profusion of culinary variety. At the last count there were 3,800 restaurants in the metro Orlando area, with new ones being added and some biting the dust all the time, and, while it would be a tall order to try to list every one, the following section will cover the main tourist areas and all the chain groups, as well as provide an insight into the more specialist, one-off establishments.

Fast food

If you are a **McDonald's** fan you are coming to the right place as there are no less than 70 outlets in the greater Orlando area, varying from small drive-in types to the mega, 24-hour-a-day establishment on Sand Lake Road (near the junction with International Drive) that also has the biggest play area for kids of any McDonald's in the world and a number of differently themed eating areas. **Burger King** is also well represented, with 50 outlets, as is another familiar American franchise

End Zone Food Court at Disney's All-Star Sports Resort

in Britain, **Wendy's**, which has 27 restaurants. If you're a burger freak and want to sample a variation on the theme, give **Checkers** (25 outlets) or **Hardees** (11) a try.

Kentucky Fried Chicken (or KFC as it now likes to be known) has no less than 28 restaurants around the area, but you might like to try the local variations on the chicken theme at **Popeye's Famous Fried Chicken** (12).

If it's pizza you're after there is also a wide choice, from the well-known **Pizza Hut** (with 54 restaurants) to the local varieties of **Flipper's Pizza** and **Domino's**, who all offer a local delivery service, even to your hotel room.

A particularly American form of take-away is the Sub, or torpedo-roll sandwich. This is what you will find at any one of the 31 local branches of **Subway**, or the 29 of **Sobik's** or nine of **Miami Subs**. They're a rather more healthy option than yet another burger, and offer some mouthwatering varieties. Two other minor variations on the fast-food theme are **Arby's** (with 11 outlets), which offers a particularly appetising roast beef sandwich and other beefy delicacies, and **Taco Bell** (44 outlets), which does for Mexican food what McDonald's does for the hamburger. If you've never had Mexican food before, this is not the place to start, but for anyone familiar with their tacos, nachos and tortillas, it's a quick and cheap spicy meal.

Practically all of these establishments will also have drive-through windows which are fun to try at least once on your Orlando visit. Simply drive around the side of the building where indicated and you will find their take-away menu with a voice box that will take your order. Please, don't wait for the food to be miraculously produced from the voice box! Carry on around the building and your food will be served from a side window where the cashier will also take your money. You will probably find your car has a slide-out tray from the central dashboard area that will take your coffee or soda cup and you can drive along with your meal and pretend to be really American!

Family restaurants

This is a section that may, at first appearance, seem similar to the American Diner type, but there are two quite major differences. First, they are only restaurants. You usually won't find a bar here and some don't serve alcoholic drinks at

> **BRIT TIP:** Tourist brochures often include money-off coupons for many restaurants so you can find some useful savings.

all. And second, they make a big effort for family groups in terms of kids' menus and activities (in many cases the kids' menu doubles up as a colouring and puzzle book) and budget-conscious prices. They also all serve breakfasts, and you will find the best of the all-you-can-eat buffet deals here. Nearly all are chain groups in the same way as you find Little Chef and Happy Eaters all over Britain, but there are one or two individuals worth knowing about.

Leading the way in terms of popularity with British tourists are the **Ponderosa Steakhouse** group and **Sizzler**. Whether it's breakfast, lunch or dinner, you will find great value and good, reliable food. In terms of style they are almost indistinguishable: you order and pay for your meal as you enter and are then seated, before being unleashed on some of the biggest buffet and salad bars you will have seen. Ponderosa have the rather flashier style, but you'd be hard pushed to tell whose food was whose. Expect to pay about $4–$5 for their breakfast buffets and $6–$9 for lunch and dinner (there IS a difference in price depending on location, with the International Drive area tending to be a dollar or two dearer than elsewhere). Standard fare includes chicken wings, meatballs, chilli, ribs, steaks and fresh seafood, while their immense salad bars in particular represent major value for money. Both are open from 7am until late evening and are handily located in all the main tourist spots.

A more homely touch can be found at the following selection of restaurant chains, with equally good if not better value for money. **Bob Evans** restaurants (open 6am–10pm, or 6am–11.30pm Friday and Saturday) traditionally specialise in American down-home breakfasts, with all manner of pancakes, omelettes and egg platters guaranteed to fill you up without breaking the bank. They also do the inevitable burgers and hot sandwiches and a special dish of the day that might be shepherd's pie, roast turkey or hickory-smoked ribs. Their restaurant on Canadian Court, just off International Drive, is entered through a delightful General Store where you can buy country crafts and some of the homestyle foods on their menu. If it's a hearty breakfast you want at any time of day, then the **International House of Pancakes** (otherwise known as IHOP) or the **Waffle House** will both appeal to you. You will struggle to spend more than $5 or $6 on a full meal, whether it be one of their huge breakfast platters or a hot sandwich with fries. Waffle Houses are also open 24 hours a day, while IHOPs open from 6.30am right through to 1.30am. Another traditional American 24-hour family diner is **Denny's Diner**, the nearest thing to our Little Chefs. Again, they make a traditional bacon 'n' egg breakfast seem ordinary with their wide selection, and they do an excellent range of hot, toasted sandwiches and some imaginative dinner meals, like grilled catfish, as well as a Senior Selections menu, featuring smaller portions at reduced prices for the over 55s. Similarly, **Perkins Family Restaurant** is also open around the clock with a lookalike menu. For a really hearty breakfast try Perkins Eggs Benedict (two eggs and bacon on a toasted muffin with hash browns and fresh fruit), while their bread-bowl salads are an equally satisfying meal. A new chain who impress for their clean, fresh style are **Golden Corral**, who have already chalked up a number of reader recommendations, and offer a delicious Carver's Choice of hand-carved meats in addition to the usual buffet deals and a terrific dessert bar.

If you are travelling on the major highways of Florida one of the 34 branches of **Cracker Barrel** may catch your attention, in which case you should definitely check out their delightful Old Country Store style, with mountainous breakfasts, well-balanced lunch and dinner menus, Kid's Stuff choices and a real old-fashioned charm that is a nice change from the usual tourist frenzy.

10

One of the most popular one-off restaurants for wide family appeal is **Captain Nemo's**, on Highway 192 opposite Fort Liberty. It serves breakfast from 8am to noon, lunch until 3pm and dinner until 11pm, and its seafood and steak menu means mum and dad can try oysters, lobster, salmon, swordfish or grouper while the kids still get their burger fix. Prices are also budget-orientated, with daily specials and a Happy Hour 3–7pm.

For a real fun family treat (and the biggest crossover into the diner-type restaurant), take the clan to one of the two **Jungle Jim's** in the Orlando area (at Crossroads of Lake Buena Vista, and West Church Street). From the parrots that welcome you to the restaurant, you know you are in for an unusual dining experience, and sure enough you will eat in an entertaining jungle setting, with the menu promising 'An epic dining adventure of lost legends, forbidden pleasures and ancient rituals'. There are 63 (count them, 63!) choices of burger, including the World Famous Headhunter, a one-pound burger, with ham, bacon and cheese and a full pound of fries – polish off the lot and your next one is free! The alternatives are ribs, steak or chicken, but it would be a shame not to try at least one of the 63 varieties. The kids' menu is suitably varied, and there is a huge range of cocktails served by Dr S'Tiph Shotta Likker (ouch!). They are open 11am–1.30am Sun–Thur, 11am–2am Fri–Sat.

British

To complete this section, it would probably be appropriate to mention the handful of British pubs and diners which seek to attract the UK visitor. All offer a fairly predictable array of pub grub along the lines of pies, pasties and fish and chips and a few imported British beers (Guinness has become very popular since the Irish were here for the World Cup in 1994!). You'll find the odd Brit or two working behind the bars, and you can happily take the kids into all of them, providing they don't sit at the bar. First and foremost among them is the **Cricketers' Arms** in the Mercado Mediterranean Village on International Drive. This has become a favourite haunt for many British visitors due to the large selection of beers, appetising food, live evening entertainment and (soccer fans take note) live Premiership matches on their giant TV screen on a Saturday morning (from 10am – remember the time difference). It gets busy in the evenings, their live music is usually pretty good, and many of the staff are Chelsea fans, but we won't hold that against them! There is usually a cover charge for soccer matches.

Highway 192 in Kissimmee sports a number of fairly derivative pubs all keen to appeal to the home market. The best of them are **Harry Ramsbottom's** at Fort Liberty (between Markers 10 and 11), which also has its own fish 'n' chippie, and the wonderfully kept **Stage Door**, six miles west of the junction with I4 (and west of Marker 4, just past Lindfields Boulevard). This bar/restaurant gets full marks from the locals too.

American diners

This section is the one where it would be easiest to go OTT. Not surprisingly, there are so many American-style restaurants of one kind or another it would be a full-time job just to keep track of them all. Therefore, I will limit this particular survey to the main tourist areas of International Drive and Highway 192, plus a couple off the beaten track that are well worth finding. The **$ price listings** are intended only as a rough guide for a three-course meal in each case.

$	=	$10–$15
$$	=	$15–$20
$$$	=	$20–$25
$$$$	=	$25–$30
$$$$$	=	$30 plus.

Steak and Ale is a popular choice and can be found at seven locations around Orlando (11.30am–10pm Mon–Thur, 11.30am–11pm Fri, noon to 11.30pm Sat, noon to 10pm Sun; **$$**). They do some great steaks and ribs, plus tempting seafood and chicken dishes, with early bird specials of a three-course set meal 4–7pm (4–6pm November–March), and two-for-one drink specials at the same time. **TGI Friday's** will already be well-known from their outlets springing up all over Britain and their fun style of lively meal-times is served up in exactly the same way in their eight Orlando restaurants. (11am–1am; **$$**.) They do a great range of burgers, plus Mexican dishes, pizza, pasta, steak, ribs and seafood. The nationwide chain **Bennigan's** has ten outlets in Orlando and is a particular personal favourite for their friendly, efficient service, smart decor and tempting menu, especially at lunchtime (11am–2am; **$$**). They make the ordinary seem appetising and have a bar atmosphere straight out of the TV programme *Cheers!* Their Irish flavour really comes into its own on St Patrick's Day (17 March), and they have happy hours (!) every day 2–7pm and 11pm to midnight. Another enjoyable dining experience can be found at the two branches of **Darryl's** (one on International Drive, the other at Fort Liberty on Highway 192). Their weird and wonderful decor is totally original; they also have a great bar area and a nicely varied menu with some interesting choices, like Cajun-fried shrimp (11am–1am; **$$**). Thick, wood-fired steaks, delicious burgers and Southern-style dishes are their

main fare, but they also offer some tasty soups and quiches.

Hooters makes no bones about its style. 'Delightfully tacky yet unrefined' declares the menu proudly, and sure enough here is a relatively simple, lively establishment, especially popular with the younger crowd for its beach-party atmosphere (11am–midnight Mon–Thur, 11am–1am Fri–Sat, noon–11pm Sun; **$**). Their seven restaurants have a truly entertaining menu featuring great value seafood, salads, burgers and Hooters Nearly World Famous Chicken Wings that come in five strengths: mild, medium, hot, 3 Mile Island or Wild Wing. You have been warned!

By contrast, **Pebbles** (five restaurants) goes for the casual but sophisticated style, with a genuinely imaginative menu that will appeal to the amateur gourmet and won't cost you a fortune (11am–midnight; **$$$**). You can eat burgers or roast duck, salad or steak and be sure of an individual touch with every meal. Their pastas are particularly appetising and they also do a kids' menu. **Uno Chicago Pizzeria** is the place to go if Pizza Hut has become *passé*. Their six outlets offer great deep-dish pizzas with the addition of pastas, chicken dishes, steaks and salads (11am–midnight; **$$**). The **Olive Garden** restaurants (12 of them) are one of America's big success stories in recent years as they have brought Italian food into the budget, mass-market range (11am–10pm Sun–Thur, 11am–11pm Fri–Sat; **$$**). Their light, airy restaurants make for a relaxed meal and, while they don't offer a huge choice, what they do they tend to do pretty well and in generous portions. Pastas are their speciality, but they also offer chicken, veal, steak and seafood and some great salads, and there are unlimited refills of garden salad,

10

Planet Hollywood® at Downtown Disney

garlic breadsticks and non-alcoholic drinks that add to their good value.

Jack's Place (in the Clarion Plaza Hotel on International Drive) refuses to be easily categorised. Here in this lively eatery you dine surrounded by 'the stars' – dozens of signed celebrity caricatures by the famous New York artist Jack Rosen. The menu is pretty good, too – grilled yellow fin tuna, rosemary roasted pork and slow-roasted prime rib, as well as some more delicious pasta and steak dishes (5.30–11pm; **$$$**).

The **Bahama Breeze** on International Drive is a must for its striking Caribbean styling – and its packed car park and queues (up to an hour's wait at peak periods!). As the Bahamas are not strictly in the Caribbean, their theming is a little suspect, but we'll forgive them as it makes for a memorable experience with well above average food for a typical diner. Try West Indies Patties or Creole Baked Goat Cheese as a starter, while the main courses (primarily pastas, seafood, chicken, beef or pizza) feature outstanding items like Black Pepper Seared Tuna or the Cuban beef stew Ropa Vieja, with every dish coming up immaculately fresh. The plantation-room styling, delightful outside wooden deck for enjoying a pre- or post-dinner drink and live music most nights fully endorse their own slogan of: 'At Bahama Breeze there are no worries, just happy, friendly people and island hospitality!' (4pm–2am Mon–Sat, 4pm–midnight Sun; **$$$**.)

Ribs

When it comes to steaks, ribs and barbecue food, Orlando has a magni-ficent array of one-off restaurants that all proudly proclaim some kind of 'world famous' variety. In many instances they are right, and here's a good selection of the best on offer.

Lazy Bones Ribs (on Highway 192, just past the junction with State Road 535 going east), is an authentic barbecue diner that also has a kids' playroom. Baby back pork ribs, prime beef ribs, steaks, chicken and seafood are all succulent choices, plus there are gator ribs for the really brave (4pm–11.30pm, with the Riverboat Bar and Lounge open until 2am; **$$**).

While in the Mercado Center, you may decide to try **Damon's**, which pronounces itself The Place for Ribs. While they also do salads, chicken, seafood and burgers, their rib platters are simply humongous. (11am–10pm; **$$$**.) Try their onion loaf as a starter as it is rightly 'famous', while their lunch selections are particularly good value and, they promise, served within 15 minutes with their 'express' label. Damon's new restaurant in Old Town is one of their sports-themed Clubhouse variety, with interactive sports and trivia games to add to their appeal (and is owned by former American Football star Fred Marion of the New England Patriots).

Cattleman's Steak House (on Vineland Road, Kissimmee, near the junction with Highway 192 and International Drive) goes for the cowboy approach once again, with a neat saloon bar (happy hour 4–7pm), early bird specials 4–6pm and the Little Rustlers' Round-up menu for the kids. Steaks are again the order of the day, but you can also order chicken and seafood, while their Heavenly Duck is worth trying for something different (4–11pm, saloon open until 2am; **$$$**). The up-market version of this type of establishment is **Wild Jack's** (on International Drive, just north of Sand Lake Road) where you are greeted by the most magnificent wood-smoked barbecue aroma as you walk in the door. The huge, western-themed interior features a big, open pit-barbecue where you

can watch your food being cooked (11.30am–11pm; **$$$**). Steaks, ribs, chicken and turkey represent your main choices and they are all served up with bags of panache and a big helping of Wild West style. There is happy hour 4–7pm, kids eat free with a full-paying adult and you can even buy yourself a Wild Jack's souvenir boot-shaped beer mug.

BRIT TIP: Don't miss Wild Jack's jalapeño mashed potatoes, their dynamite chicken wings, cowboy baked beans and the Jack Daniels chocolate cake for dessert!

Another restaurant to pull in a lot of complimentary reader feedback is **Key W Kool's Open-Pit Grill** on Highway 192 (just opposite Splendid China). Choice cuts of meat, mouth-watering steaks and prime rib and a wonderfully succulent, inviting aroma add up to an outstanding dining choice, and at good prices, too (4–11pm; **$$$**). Highly recommended.

BRIT TIP: reader Mrs Gillian Austin from Horsham in West Sussex, recommends **JT's Prime Time** (at the western end of Highway 192 out towards Highway 27), a down-to-earth, good-value locals' eatery, with a good kids' menu, early bird dinner specials (before 6.30pm for $6), offering barbecue chicken, steaks and 'wonderful burgers. It knocked the spots off TGI Friday's.' Ouch!

10

I can also heartily recommend any of the seven restaurants of **Tony Roma's,** which pronounce themselves Famous for Ribs, and rightly so. The airy but relaxing decor and ambience, clever kids' menu (the Roma Rangers Round-up, full of puzzles and games), junior meals, and their melt-in-the-mouth ribs (try their Original Baby Backs if you don't believe me!) all add up to a winning combination. You can still get chicken, burgers and steaks, but why ignore a dish when it's done this well? The Rib Sampler is a great platter, and there are also chicken- and shrimp-rib combos (11am–midnight Sun–Thur, 11am–1am Fri and Sat; **$$**).

Tex-Mex

What the Olive Garden does for Italian cuisine, **Chili's** does for Mexican. Actually, it's an Americanised version of Mexican cooking originating in Texas (hence Tex-Mex), with the emphasis more on steak and ribs and less on tortillas and hot spices (11am–1am Mon–Sat, 11am–11pm Sun; **$$**). Service is frighteningly efficient, and, if you are looking for a quick lunch or dinner, you'll be hard-pushed to find a quicker turnaround. Atmosphere is lively and bustly and they do a good kids' menu that is also a colouring/puzzle book.

The newest and most elaborate Mexican offering is the cavernous **Don Pablo's**, next to the Visitor Center on I-Drive. Clever theming, lively atmosphere (especially around the Cantina bar!) and a classic, well-explained menu add up to a real fun experience (11.30am–10pm Sun–Thur, 11.30am–11pm Fri–Sat; **$$**). Another one-off restaurant that has a lot of Brit appeal is **Café Tu Tu Tango** on International Drive, next to Austin's. The accent is artist-colony Spanish (whatever that means), with a really original menu, live entertainment and art-work all over the walls that changes daily. Vegetarians will find themselves well catered for here, while you can also try some particularly succulent pizzas, seafood, salads and paella. Mexican and Chinese dishes also make an appearance, and there is a thoughtful kids' menu (11.30am–midnight; **$$**). The overall style is based more on a tapas bar, so you order a number of different dishes rather than a starter and main course. Ultimately, it is as much an artistic experience as a meal, and the fun atmosphere perfectly complements the rich array of dishes.

Steakhouses

Serious steak-lovers will have to pay a visit to **Ruth's Chris Steak House** (with a new restaurant location in the Winter Park Village) where prime beef in a mouthwatering variety of choices is the order of the day. It isn't cheap, but you'll be hard-pushed to get a better steak anywhere (5–11pm Mon–Sat, 5–10pm Sun; **$$$$$**). 'Only the best', proclaims the restaurant's slogan. 'Come judge for yourself, but come hungry.' Nuff said. Similarly, the **Butcher Shop** (in the Mercado Center on International Drive) offers steaks, steaks and more steaks. Hugely impressive is the cold counter where you can select your own piece of meat, and the hickory charcoal open grill where you can actually cook your steak to the desired degree (of course, there is also a chef to do it for you or offer advice) (5–10pm Sun–Thur, 5–11pm Fri–Sat; **$$$$**).

> BRIT TIP: Don't miss the Butcher Shop's skillet-fried mushrooms in garlic and butter sauce!

Charley's Steak Houses (of which there are three, the biggest on International Drive just north of the Mercado Center) continue the theme of excellent steaks, cooked over a specially built pit woodfire. It's not cheap (although their Orange Blossom Trail location, 2 miles north of the Florida Mall, is noticeably cheaper than the other two), but the decor and bar area are splendidly furnished, and if you don't fancy steak, which you can watch being grilled on their large, hardwood grill, there are seafood choices as well (5–11pm; **$$$$$**). Another new and imaginative choice is **Vito's Chop House** in front of the Castle Hotel on I-Drive. Their choice beef cuts are aged 4–6 weeks and cooked over wood fires, while they also offer trademark pork chops, seafood and pasta, as well as an extensive wine list (5–10.30pm Sun–Thur, 5–11pm Fri–Sat; **$$$$**). PS: check out the Tuscan T-Bone.

For more steak-induced hedonism, **Morton's** of Chicago (on the Market Place at Dr Phillips Boulevard) is hard to beat. Its rather more up-market (and sometimes pretty smoky) style is offset by a lively ambience that fully adds to the enjoyment of its trademark steaks, which you can watch being cooked on an open range. You are provided with a fully exhibited menu (they bring examples to the table!) and invited to enjoy some of the biggest, most succulent steaks it has been my pleasure to sample. The Porterhouse is an inspired choice, as is one of the principal alternatives, Shrimp Alexander. Needless to say, this homage to bovine cuisine does not come cheap, especially as your vegetables are extra, but it is a thoroughly memorable experience (5pm–midnight Mon–Sat, 5pm–11pm Sun; **$$$$$**). Similarly, the new **Shula's Steak House** in the Walt Disney World Dolphin Hotel is both expansive (on your waistline)

and expensive. The porterhouse and prime rib are truly outstanding, and this restaurant (the latest in a chain owned by famous former American Football coach Don Shula) is extremely popular with locals (5–11pm; **$$$$$**). **Black Angus** and **Western Steer** complete the line-up of steakhouses along more budget lines as they also serve breakfasts and aim for the family market. Black Angus (down at the east end of Highway 192) offers an all-you-can-eat breakfast buffet as well as a typical range of steaks, and also has a nightly karaoke session (7am–11.30pm; **$$**). Western Steer (on International Drive, opposite Wet 'n Wild) offers a breakfast buffet as well as a dinner buffet. Steaks are still the main fare, and with a large tribe to feed it's great value (7am–11.30pm; **$$**).

Seafood

After that exhausting trek through the steakhouses of Orlando, you won't be surprised to learn that the choice of seafood restaurants is equally large. The **Crab House** (locations on Goodings Plaza on International Drive and Palm Parkway) should be self-explanatory. Garlic crabs, steamed crabs, snow crabs, Alaskan king crabs, etc. Yes, this is THE place for crab. You can always try their prime rib, pasta or other seafood, but it would be a shame to ignore the house speciality when it's done this well (11.30am–11pm Mon–Sat, noon–11pm Sun; **$$$**). **Red Lobster** (nine restaurants) is from the same company that has made a success of the Olive Garden chain. This is seafood for the family market, with a varied menu, lively atmosphere and one of the best kids' menus/activity books you'll find. And, while lobster is their speciality, their steaks, chicken, salads and other seafood are equally appetising, and they do a

10

Morton's Steakhouse

great variety of combination platters
(11am–10pm Sun–Thur,
11am–11pm Fri–Sat; **$$$**). **Charlie's
Lobster House** (on International
Drive at the Mercado Center) has a
similar menu, with nightly fresh fish
specials and reservations
recommended. The bar areas are
immaculately finished and service
has that extra bit of charm (4–10pm
Sun–Thur, 4–11pm Fri–Sat; **$$$$**).
Completing the chain restaurants
here are the three outlets of the
Boston Lobster Feast, with
elaborate nautical decor and an
unlimited lobster and seafood buffet
(hence the 'Feast', you see). They
have early bird specials from
4.30–6pm Mon–Fri, 2–4.30pm
Sat–Sun (and that represents
excellent value), while their 40-item
Lobster Feasts are guaranteed to
stretch the stomach more than a
little (4.30–10pm Mon–Fri, 2–10pm
Sat–Sun; **$$$$**).

Of the one-off restaurants, **Ocean
Grill** (on International Drive, just
north of the Sand Lake Road
junction) offers great seafood at
moderate prices. Daily specials,
including the early bird variety from
4–6pm, jostle with the likes of fried
clams, South-western swordfish,
fried catfish, shrimp creole and
seafood lasagne. Their plain old fish
and chips would put most British
chippies to shame, and for the
really hearty appetite they do a
magnificent surf 'n' turf (lobster or

shrimp and steak), although
admittedly at a hearty price
(4–11pm; **$$$**).

The **Atlantic Bay Seafood Grill**
(on Highway 192, just east of I4)
surprisingly offers a breakfast buffet
on top of its full range of well-priced
seafood dishes, early bird specials
4.30–6.30pm, and steaks, ribs and
pasta. It's not gourmet fare but it is
hearty and good value, especially
their all-you-can-eat seafood bar
(4–11pm; **$$**).

Inside the new Omni Rosen hotel
on International Drive is the
Everglades Restaurant, an up-
market seafood and steak choice
which again combines unusual decor
(an environmental look at the
Everglades, complete with manatee,
swamp scenery, tropical music and a
12ft aquarium) with fine cuisine.
The daily seafood specials jostle with
the likes of wild boar, venison and
buffalo steak, while the gator
chowder is a must-try starter. There
is a relaxing adjacent bar area in
this cavernous hotel, and diners at
the Everglades also enjoy
complimentary valet parking
(5.30–11pm 7 days a week; **$$$$**).

New at Pointe*Orlando is
Monty's Conch Harbor, where
Key West is the relaxed, casual
theme and the specialities include
conch chowder, clams, oysters, stone
crabs and Cajun-spiced tuna. Their
fresh fried seafood baskets are also a
real treat and key lime pie is a must
for dessert (11.30am–11pm; **$$$$**).

However, my vote for the most
memorable seafood dining
experience in town is **Fulton's Crab
House** in Downtown Disney's
Marketplace. This mock riverboat
has six differently themed dining
rooms (albeit with the same menu),
plus the Stone Crab Lounge which
features a complete raw bar (and
always seems to be busy). Nautical
props, photos and lithographs fill the
interior, giving it a wonderfully
eclectic, period atmosphere, but the

Fulton's Crab House

real attraction is the food – some of the freshest and most tempting fish, crab and lobster dishes in all of Florida. The Alaskan king crab is a rare treat, as is their tuna *filet mignon*, but there are fresh specials every day (the air shipping bills for which are posted in the main hall), as well as a children's menu. Fulton's also features an extensive wine list, micro-brewed beers and its own specialities, but the restaurants often have a queue as early as 6pm, so it is advisable to book (407 394 2628). The Stone Crab Lounge serves lunch and dinner 11.30am to midnight, while the Crab House is open for dinner 5–11pm. **$$$$**.

The Fab Four

There are four other restaurants that sort of fit into the American Diners category but are really delightful, one-off restaurants in their own right. All four will provide a genuinely exciting dining experience in novel settings that will linger long in the memory, and without costing you a fortune.

Planet Hollywood®: The largest restaurant in the recently troubled world-wide chain of this glitzy, showbiz-style venture is next door to Downtown Disney Pleasure Island and is a pure fun entertainment venue. The food is fairly predictable diner fare, although everything is served up with pizazz, but the

cavernous interior lends itself to a party atmosphere, complete with numerous film clips and a stunning array of movie memorabilia. Some memorable house cocktails, too, but visit either mid-morning or mid-afternoon to avoid the serious queues! (11am–2am; **$$$**).

B-line Diner: Inside the Peabody Hotel on International Drive lurks an amazing art deco homage to the traditional 50s-style diner, faithful to every detail, including the outfits of the staff. You sit at a magnificent long counter or in one of several booths, with a good view of the chefs at work, and with a rolling menu that changes four times a day (which isn't bad when it is open around the clock!). The food is way above usual diner standard, but the prices aren't, so you can munch away on catfish in a papaya-tartare sauce or pork chops with apple-sage chutney, as well as the traditional favourites of burgers, steaks and ribs, happy in the knowledge you won't break the bank. Their desserts are displayed in a huge glass counter and I defy you to ignore them! (Open 24 hours; **$$**.)

Rainforest Café: The two versions of this eco-aware jungle-themed restaurant chain are adjacent to *Disney's Animal Kingdom* Theme Park and in the heart of *Downtown Disney Marketplace*, one with a huge waterfall exterior and the other topped by an active, smoking volcano, and they have to be seen

The fabulous Planet Hollywood

to be believed. You don't dine, you go on a 'safari adventure' in a rainforest setting amid audio-animatronic animals (including elephants and gorillas), thunderstorms, tropical birds, waterfalls, aquariums and some of the cleverest lighting effects I have seen. It is an amazing experience, especially for children, and the food is well above average. Try the Rasta Pasta or Mo' Bones ribs, but the menu alone will take a while to negotiate. Unless you arrive before midday, you will have to wait for a table, but that is no hardship given their locations. Beware the café's huge gift shop, too! (11am–11pm; **$$$**.)

Another unmistakable landmark on International Drive is the super-charged, super-large restaurant of **Race Rock**, packed with rare motor-racing memorabilia and eye-catching machines of all kinds. This does for motor sport what the Hard Rock does for music, and how! Two giant car transporters line the entrance, which also boasts a giant-wheeled buggy, two dragsters and a hydroplane speedboat, welcoming you in to the circular, 20,000-sq-ft restaurant itself. Giant TV screens and a host of regular TVs, video games, virtual-reality racing machines and loud, loud music and chequered flag tables complete the atmosphere, while the central bar sports an upside-down racing car circulating as the world's biggest ceiling fan! The food is traditional diner fare given a few tweaks like Start Your Engines (the starter selections), Circle Tracks (pizza), Stock and Modified (burgers and sandwiches), Pole Position Pastas and The Main Event (ribs, chops, chicken and salmon – I rate the Road Runner chicken, marinated in lime juice, olive oil and garlic and char-grilled). There is a Quarter Midget menu at $4.99 for children 12 and under (11.30am–midnight;

$$). Race Rock is also included in the Day on the Drive package.

Speciality restaurants

This final section requires least preamble as the type of fare is fairly obvious. As I have already mentioned, the food on offer varies enormously from American to Japanese, through all kinds of Asian, to the Middle East, through Europe and back again. Here are the main varieties.

Chinese

Chinese food is well established in America and well represented in Orlando. **Ming Court** on International Drive, just south of King Henry's Feast, is the Rolls Royce of local Chinese restaurants. With the magnificent setting and live entertainment you could easily convince yourself you had been transported to China itself. The menu is extensive and many dishes can be had as a side order rather than a full main course to give you the chance to try more (11am–2.30pm and 4.30pm–midnight; **$$$**). **Bill Wong's Famous Super Buffet** (yes, they really do call it that) on International Drive offers a cross between Chinese and diner-type fare. Their all-you-can-eat buffet features jumbo shrimp (and they mean Jumbo!), as well as crabs, prime rib, fresh fruit and salad (11am–10pm; **$$**). A rather classier version of this style is the new **China Garden Buffet** at the Mercado Center. The elegrant surroundings are the perfect complement to the extraordinary buffet choice, with more than 50 items – from spring rolls to chilled crab claws – on offer at any one time. There is also a full à la carte selection, but the buffet price of $14.95 for adults and $6.95 for 3–10s ($7.59 and $3.95 at lunch) make this one of the best meal deals in town (10am–11pm; **$$**). Similarly, the **Sizzling Wok**, on Sand Lake Road, just across from the Florida Mall, offers an opportunity to get stuck into a massive Chinese buffet at a very reasonable price (11am–10pm Sun–Thur, 11am–10.30pm Fri–Sat; **$$**). Out on Highway 192 you'll find a number of fairly predictable, budget-priced outfits, the best of which is **Peking Gardens**, which goes slightly more up-market with a tempting range of Szechuan, Hunan and Cantonese cuisine (noon–11pm Sun–Thur, noon–midnight Fri–Sat; **$**). **Trey Yuen** and **China Jade Buffet** complete the tourist area Chinese offerings, and are fairly typical of Chinese restaurants in Britain. Both are located on the northern stretch of International Drive, with Trey Yuen specialising in the appetising small bite *dim sum* selections and offering a local delivery service (11am–midnight; **$**) and China Jade sticking to a more limited range of specialities but again at a sound all-you-can-eat price (11am–11.30pm; **$**).

Japanese

The more adventurous among you (and those already familiar with their cuisine) will want to try one of the fine Japanese restaurants with which Orlando is blessed. **Shogun Steakhouse**, on International Drive under the Rodeway Inn, is ideal for those who can't quite go the whole hog and get stuck into sushi (raw fish). If you decide to 'chicken' out, you can still order a no-nonsense steak or chicken, but their full Japanese menu is well explained and vividly demonstrated by their chefs in front of you at long, bench-like tables (6–10pm Mon–Thur, 6–10.30pm Fri–Sun; **$$**). **Kobe** also brings a touch of Americana to its dining content. With six locations around the area, Kobe go for the mass-market appeal but still achieve individual style with the chef preparing your food at your table in a style that is as much showmanship as culinary expertise (11.30am–11pm; **$$**). **Ran-Getsu**, on International Drive opposite the Mercado Center, does for Japanese cuisine what the Ming Court does for Chinese, i.e. it's stylish, authentic and as much an experience as a meal, and it is still reasonably priced. The setting is simple and efficient, and you can choose to sit at conventional tables or their long, S-shaped sushi bar (5pm–midnight; **$$$**). **Benihana** completes a formidable quartet of outlets, situated in the Hilton Hotel at Walt Disney World Village, Lake Buena Vista. Again, it's a memorable experience, with everything cooked right in front of you by their expert chefs, and their steaks are among the most tender you will ever taste (5–10.30pm; **$$$**).

Indian

If you have come all this way and still fancy a curry, believe it or not you will be able to get one as good as any you have tried back home. There are already more than a dozen Indian restaurants around the Orlando area and they all maintain a pretty fair standard, from the up-market **Far Pavilion**, at the intersection of International Drive and Kirkman Road, to the budget-price **New Punjab** at the upper end of International Drive and on West Vine Street, Kissimmee, with its excellent lunch and dinner specials. For a medium-range restaurant, **Passage to India** (also on International Drive) gets the locals' vote as best Indian restaurant and is a cut above the average, too, with unusual and exotic chicken dishes and vegetarian Sabzi Dal Bahar (11.30am–midnight; **$$$**). It is a particular personal favourite for

10

Inside Race Rock

its attentive service and relaxed atmosphere, and you will probably find yourself dining with a few fellow Brits, too. Rock band The Cure and cricketer Imran Khan have also eaten here and left the photos to prove it!

Thai and more

For other types of Oriental cooking, the **Siam Orchid** (on Universal Boulevard, just around the corner from Wet 'n Wild) offers exceptional Thai food in a picturesque setting overlooking Sandy Lake (5–11pm; **$$**). If you'd like to try another variation, **Little Saigon** (on East Colonial Drive) will introduce you to Vietnamese cuisine and a whole new array of soups, barbecue dishes, fried rice variations and other interesting treats that take up where Chinese food leaves off (10am–9pm; **$**). Cuban food is a Floridian speciality and you will find some of

the best examples at **Rolando's** (on Semoran Boulevard, in the suburb of Casselberry, head east from I4 exit 48). Try the red snapper or pork chunks and find out why the *Orlando Sentinel* rates this the best Cuban food north of Havana (11am–9pm Tue–Thur, 11am–10pm Fri–Sat, 1–8pm Sun; **$**).

Italian

No survey of Orlando's restaurants would be complete without mention of its fine tradition of Italian cooking. **Pacino's** on Highway 192, opposite Old Town, goes for the family market and scores a big hit with value for money, friendly atmosphere and Sicilian style, with clever animated puppet operettas, a fountain that occasionally spouts flame and a relaxing open-air feel that is enhanced by the clever use of the differently arranged seating areas (4pm–midnight; **$$$**). **Bergamo's**, in the Mercado Center, is actually German-owned but nonetheless authentic for all that. Don't be surprised if your waiter suddenly bursts into song – it's all part of the unique charm of this extremely tempting and ultimately highly entertaining restaurant (5–10pm Sun–Thur, 5–11pm Fri–Sat; **$$$$**).

Race Rock

Hard Rock Café

Italianni's (on International Drive just south of its Sand Lake Road junction) won't hurt your wallet quite so much and does a great pizza among a typical selection of Italian fare. Don't miss their home-made cheesecake for dessert (11am–11pm; **$$$**). The five-star version of Italian cuisine here belongs to two contrasting restaurants, **Christini's** on Dr Phillips Boulevard, and **Michaelangelo** on Kirkman Road. Strolling musicians, elegant surroundings and a 40-year history of award-winning cuisine characterise Christini's, where their home-made pasta and *filet mignon* are as good as anything you will find in Italy (5–11pm; **$$$$$**). Michaelangelo, just north of Universal Studios in Turkey Lake Village, promotes a candlelit atmosphere with live music in the cocktail lounge, formal, dinner-jacketed staff and a northern Italian cuisine that features delicious veal, snapper and pasta delicacies. Their pasta, bread and desserts are all home-made and it is all presented in an old-world style that is a million miles away from the tourist hurly-burly of the theme parks (6–11pm, 6pm–2am in the bar; **$$$$$**).

German

A recent and highly worthwhile discovery of mine is **Gain's German Restaurant** on the South Orange Blossom Trail (just past Oakridge Road going north), both for their food and their excellent selection of bottled and draught beers. The friendly welcome, authentic Bavarian decor and tempting menu come as a real surprise in the heart of tourist Orlando, but owners Hans and Kessy Gain have lavished much care and attention on building up their trade here. A tasty ragout is an ideal appetiser, while there are sausage specialities (naturally), wiener schnitzel (of course), and rotisserie chicken and pan-fried rainbow trout (for something different). Apple strudel and Black Forest cake are the ideal desserts, while the Diebels amber ale is a fine choice for beer connoisseurs. Call 407 438 8997 for reservations (11.30am–2.30pm and 4.30–10pm Tue–Thur, 4.30–11pm Fri and Sat, 4.30–10pm Sun; **$$–$$$**).

Splashing out

Finally, if you fancy really splashing out, there are three notable restaurants I would always recommend for a memorable occasion. The **Park Plaza Gardens** is part of the Park Plaza Hotel on Park Avenue, Winter Park and this

Sunday brunch at the Renaissance Hotel

10

beautiful courtyard restaurant gives you the feel of outdoor dining with the air-conditioned comfort of being indoors. Attentive service is coupled with an elegant, versatile menu that offers the choice of a relatively inexpensive lunch or a three-course adventure featuring escargot, pasta with salmon, medallions of beef or one of several tempting fish dishes. Cuisine is distinctly *nouvelle* rather than American, but nonetheless satisfying for all that. Its setting becomes even more intimate and charming in the evening with lights scattered among the foliage.

Enjoy a very pleasant happy hour in the lounge 5–7pm (with complimentary buffet Thursday and Friday), while their popular three-course Sunday brunch features unlimited champagne and live jazz (11.30am–3pm Mon–Sat and 11am–3pm for Sunday brunch, 6–10pm Mon–Thur, 6–11pm Fri–Sat, 6–9pm Sun; **$$$$$**).

Not strictly on the main tourist track but definitely worth seeking out for that superior dining experience is the **Atlantis** restaurant inside the Renaissance Orlando Resort Hotel on Sea Harbor Drive next to SeaWorld. This wonderfully elegant and quite intimate corner of an equally smart hotel offers fine dining in the normal course of events, but their signature new meal is the seven-course *Titanic* **dinner**, in keeping with the new *Titanic* attraction at the Mercado Center. In true maritime first-class style, the Atlantis has researched and recreated a series of fine dishes that bear the hallmark of the ship's immaculate cuisine. The likes of Consommé Olga, Lobster Thermidor with Mousseline Sauce, Roast Sirloin of Beef Forestière (or Calvados-glazed Duck Breast with apple sauce) and

Waldorf Flan all hint at a bygone age of high-society restaurant style, but it is served up in modern-day splendour. Truly, a meal not to be missed – but at a price: $55 a head or $80 with pre-selected wines and champagne. Otherwise, Atlantis features a full seafood-orientated à la carte dinner menu (5–10.30pm; **$$$$$**). PS: for another meal with a difference check out the Renaissance's Sunday Brunch, which is something of an Orlando tradition. Not so much a buffet as a 100-item banquet, it costs $29.95 for adults and $14.95 for children 4–12. Try this and brunch will never be the same again.

Finally, new in the Mercado Center on I-Drive and a really pleasant surprise for their up-scale style in this largely mass-market location is **DiVino's**, a slightly rural Italian restaurant with the full essence of Tuscany. Relatively simple pastas jostle with wood-grilled swordfish, braised chicken and the trademark Osso Buco (roast veal shank), plus some excellent daily specials (seafood especially) to offer a genuine slice of Italiana. It is not a cheap exercise by any means (most main courses are $20, some are $28 or $30) but the deep flavours, allied with excellent service, make for a thoroughly memorable meal. Reservations are advisable as it gets pretty busy most evenings around 8pm, on 407 345 0883 (5–11pm daily; **$$$$$**).

Now on to another of my favourite topics. As already mentioned, and in keeping with the area's great diversity of attractions, the other main way in which Orlando will seek to separate you from your hard-earned money is in shopping. The choice is suitably wide-ranging …

11 Shopping

(or, How to Send Your Credit Card into Meltdown)

The vast area that constitutes metropolitan Orlando is a positive shopper's paradise, with a dazzling array of specialist outlets, malls and complexes, flea markets and discount retailers. It is also one of the most vigorous growth markets, with new centres springing up seemingly all the time, from the smartest of malls to the cheapest and tackiest of tourist gift shop plazas (and you can hardly go a few yards in the main tourist areas without a shop insisting it has the best tourist bargains of one sort or another).

You will be bombarded by shopping opportunities every way you turn, and the only hard part is avoiding the temptation to fill an extra suitcase or two with the sort of goods that would cost twice as much back home. As a general rule you can expect to pay in dollars what you would pay in pounds for items like clothes, books, records and CDs, while there are real bargains to be had in jeans, trainers, shoes, sports gear and T-shirts.

But beware! Your duty-free allowance in the catch-all duty category of 'gifts' is still only £145 per person, and it is perfectly possible to exceed that sum by some distance. Paying the duty and VAT is still often cheaper than buying the same items at home, however, so it is worth splashing out, but remember to keep all your receipts and go back through the red 'goods to declare' channel on your return. You will pay duty of up to 19 per cent on the total purchase price (i.e. inclusive of Florida sales tax, see below) once you have exceeded your £145 allowance, and then VAT at 17.5 per cent. Unfortunately, you can no longer pool your allowances to cover one item that exceeds a single allowance. Hence, if you buy a camera, say, that costs £200, you have to pay the duty on the full £200, taking the total to £213.20, and then the VAT on that figure. However, if you have a number of items that add up to £145, and then another which exceeds that, you pay the duty and VAT only on the excess (and the customs officers will usually give you the benefit of the lowest rate on what you pay for). To give you some examples of duty rates (which fill three volumes and are up-dated regularly), golf clubs are charged at 2.7 per cent, cameras at 4.2 per cent and mountain bikes at a whopping 15 per cent, all plus VAT. If you have any queries, consult the Customs and Excise office located in the departure lounge before you leave your home airport.

Your ordinary duty-free allowances from America include 200 cigarettes and a litre of spirits or two litres of sparkling wine and two litres of still wine. Alligator products, which constitute an endangered species, require a special import licence, and you should consult the Department of the Environment first.

Be aware, also, of the hidden 'extras' of shopping costs. Unlike our VAT, the local version in Orlando, the Florida State sales tax, is NOT added to the displayed

KEY TO ORLANDO – SHOPPING CENTRES

A = CHURCH STREET EXCHANGE
      AND CHURCH STREET MARKET
B = OLD TOWN
C = KISSIMMEE HISTORIC DISTRICT
D = SEMINOLE TOWNE CENTER
E = ORLANDO PREMIUM OUTLETS
F = OVIEDO MARKETPLACE
G = DOWNTOWN DISNEY MARKETPLACE
H = MERCADO CENTER
I = GOODINGS INTERNATIONAL PLAZA
J = CROSSROADS OF LAKE BUENA VISTA
K = BELZ FACTORY OUTLET WORLD
L = QUALITY OUTLET CENTER
M = KISSIMMEE MANUFACTURERS' OUTLET MALL

N = FLEA WORLD
O = OSCEOLA FLEA AND FARMERS' MARKET
P = FLORIDA MALL
Q = ALTAMONTE MALL
R = OSCEOLA SQUARE MALL
S = COLONIAL PLAZA MALL
T = ORLANDO FASHION SQUARE MALL
U = WINTER PARK VILLAGE
V = LAKE BUENA VISTA FACTORY SHOPS
W = THE MARKETPLACE
X = THE POINTE*ORLANDO
Y = PARK AVENUE
Z = BELZ INTERNATIONAL OUTLET CENTER

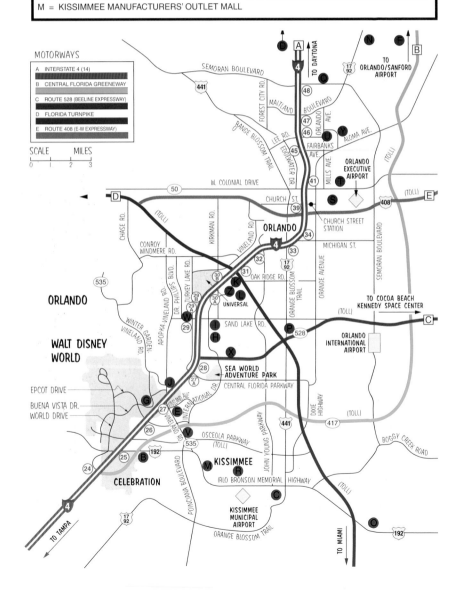

MOTORWAYS

A	INTERSTATE 4 (14)
B	CENTRAL FLORIDA GREENEWAY
C	ROUTE 528 (BEELINE EXPRESSWAY)
D	FLORIDA TURNPIKE
E	ROUTE 408 (E-W EXPRESSWAY)

SCALE   MILES
0   1   2   3

purchase price, so you should add 6 or 7 per cent (depending on which county you are in) to arrive at the 'real' price. This frequently catches visitors out. The sales tax is added to everything you buy in Orlando, from your theme park tickets to a beer at the hotel and all meals (but not supermarket groceries, which are classed as 'essentials').

Here is a rundown of the main shopping attractions and the sort of fun and bargains that can be had, divided into four categories. First, the purpose-built speciality shopping complexes, specifically out to catch the tourist; second, Orlando's speciality flea markets and discount outlets; third, the large shopping malls; and finally a few shops for the bargain-hunter.

Shopping complexes

The originators of the first category must be **Church Street Exchange** and **Church Street Market**, two separate but similarly intentioned restorations full of one-off gift shops in downtown Orlando. The Exchange is part of the Church Street Station entertainment complex, but there is no admission charge to go shopping here. It is a grand, eye-catching old railroad station conversion now housing three levels of gift shops, cafés and restaurants, split into two sides, with live entertainment and sideshows in the evenings and at weekends. Open from 11am to 11pm every day, it also features Commander Ragtime's Midway of Fun, Food and Games, a

Shopping in the Old Town

BRIT TIP: If you are tempted to use 'doctored' receipts to show a lesser value – don't, it is illegal. Your goods will be confiscated and there are heavy fines. Also, you can't escape the duty by saying the items have been used (in the case of golf clubs, for example) or that they are gifts for someone else.

floor of antique, carnival-style games and a usually uncrowded food court. Stores vary from the exclusive and expensive to typical tourist fare, but all with a distinctly stylish, Victorian flavour. Look out for the Bumby Emporium, Church Street Station's elaborate gift shop, and the Buffalo Trading Company, for all things Western. Although the two tend to merge into each other, the two-storey Market is separately owned and run, built around a large brick courtyard, and consists of another two dozen specialist stores (check out Laser Magic for some clever holograms and Brookstone for all manner of useful and useless gadgets), craft stalls and street performers, plus restaurants like the young and trendy Hooters and the excellent budget Italian eatery, the Olive Garden. The Market is open until 10pm (6pm on Sun) and for both take exit 38 off I4. Parking is available and well signposted in either multi-storey or ground-level facilities.

Kissimmee's version of the purpose-built tourist shopping centre is **Old Town**, an antique-style offering in the heart of Highway 192. Some 75 shops – from standard souvenirs, novel T-shirt outlets, Disney merchandise and sportswear to motorbike fashions – line the brick-built streets, along with eight restaurants, a **haunted house** attraction, the Yellow Submarine play area (great for letting the youngsters loose for a while!) and a host of fairground rides, including the 60ft-tall Century Wheel, the Windstorm roller-coaster, go-karts, a Kids' Town area of junior rides and the Skycoaster mega-ride. Allow for up to four hours here and try at all costs to take in the weekly **Saturday Nite Cruise** at 8.30pm, a drive-past of 300-plus vintage and collector cars from all over America (and a new **Friday Nite Cruise** featuring cars built from 1973–85, live music and prizes). Parking is free and Old Town is open 10am–11pm seven days a week. The new Damon's Clubhouse restaurant is the stand-out dining choice, but the Cadillac Diner is a fun alternative. The whole place really comes alive in the evening, too.

Other Kissimmee tourist-orientated shopping centres include the recently revamped **Historical District of Kissimmee** on Broadway, which can be found two blocks south of Highway 192 on Route 17–92. These are a number of restored turn-of-the-century homes featuring gift shops, a children's boutique, country store and Chef's Pantry restaurant. The Historical District shops are open 10am–5pm (10am–3pm on Saturdays).

BRIT TIP: As with parks and restaurants, there are special coupons and discounts in the various tourist hand-outs for some of the shops. A few are worth keeping but the majority are pretty tacky.

Computer addicts may want to check out the **netkaffee** here for the chance to send and receive e-mail (9am–9pm). PS: you can also take advantage of free e-mail services at main public libraries (says reader Ann Tootell of Leicester).

Downtown Disney

Not to be outdone, Disney have a major shopping experience in their *Downtown Disney* development. **Downtown Disney Marketplace** is typical Disney, a beautiful location, imaginative building and landscaping and a host of one-off elements that make shopping here a pleasure. Don't miss the awesome **World of Disney** store, the largest of its kind in the world, the new **Lego Imagination Center** (an interactive playground and shop), **Summer Sands** for swimwear and accessories and **Team Mickey's Athletic Club**. Dancing fountains and squirt pools (where kids tend to get VERY wet), the lakeside setting and boating opportunities all add to the appeal. Restaurants include the superbly themed **Rainforest Café** and the first **McDonald's** in *Walt Disney World* Resort. Once you have taken in *Downtown Disney Marketplace*, stroll over to **Downtown Disney West Side** and see a film or visit the world's largest **Virgin Megastore**. The whole complex is open 9.30am–11pm every day. It is found off exit 26A of I4 and is well signposted (avoid exit 27 for the increasing traffic congestion).

Similarly cleverly built to attract the eye of passing tourists is the **Mercado Center** in the heart of the southern International Drive tourist drag, with more than 30 speciality shops, six superb restaurants (including Bergamo's, Charlie's Lobster House, China Garden Buffet, DiVino's and the Butcher Shop), the Blazing Pianos nightclub, live evening entertainment

(Wed–Sun in the courtyard) and an impressive international food court (especially for the budget-conscious). The wonderful Spanish architecture encourages browsing along the 'streets', lined with one-off shops. The Mercado is open 10am–10pm daily (longer at the bars and restaurants), and will amuse you and your wallet for several hours. Speciality shops like Kandestix, Krazy Kites, Conch Republic and American Cola Cola Company are good for unusual gifts, or try the Cricketers Arms for a drink.

A recent addition is the hugely elaborate **Pointe*Orlando** (already discussed in Orlando by Night in Chapter 9), which is as much an evening adventure as mere shopping. The 60-plus stores here are all more up-market than usual tourist fare, and you can indulge your passion for fashion at places like Ocean Drive Fashion, Gap and Gap Kids, Disney Worldport, Samsonite Travel Expo, Abercrombie & Fitch and Armani Exchange. If nothing else, you should let the kids loose in the huge interactive toy shop FAO Schwarz, go to the Muvico cinema complex, and finish up with a meal at lively Johnny Rockets American diner.

Discount outlets

Belz Factory Outlet World is by far the most impressive of the second category of shops, the 'factory' or discount outlet, and is a positive Mecca for all serious shoppers. Actually, it almost defies description as it is too widespread to be a full shopping mall, too elaborate to be a flea market and too down-to-earth to be a straightforward tourist trap (the locals do a lot of shopping here, too). Belz can be found on West Oak Ridge Road at the top of International Drive and consists of more than 160 shops arranged in two indoor malls (both with lively

11

The Mercado Center

food courts and one with a vintage carousel to amuse the kids), plus four separate annexes that all require a separate journey by car (unless you want to wear out a lot of shoe leather!). Avoid Belz at weekends, if you want to beat the crowds. The aim is to sell name brands at factory-direct prices and, while you may have to wade through a fair amount of stuff you wouldn't want if they were giving it away, you will find shoes, clothes, books, jewellery, electronics, sporting goods, crockery and much more at bargain rates. Check out the Calvin Klein outlet (Annex 2), Reebok footwear (Annex 4), the Van Heusen factory store (Malls 1 & 2), OshKosh kidswear, the Umbro store and Guess Jeans (all Mall 2). Serious shoppers will

Belz Factory Outlet

want to spend several hours here, and Belz is conveniently open 10am–9pm Mon–Sat and 10am–6pm Sun. **Quality Outlet Center** (9.30am–9pm Mon–Sat, 11am–6pm Sun) further down International Drive offers much of the same, although not in the same quantity. (Disney Gifts for heavily discounted Disney merchandise is worth a look.) For a classier version, the **Belz Designer Outlet Center**, just south of Belz on I-Drive has a more up-market range of shops, including Donna Karan, Rocky Mountain Chocolate Factory and Westpoint Pepperell for fine linens (10am–9pm Mon–Sat, 11am–6pm Sun).

The Pointe*Orlando

The Belz Enterprises company is also busy building its newest retail centre adjacent to the Factory Outlet World at the top of I-Drive. **Festival Bay** will be 25 acres of 'lifestyle retail complex', which is marketing-speak for shops, restaurants and entertainment. The Bay will feature major outlets of Ron Jon's Surf Shop, Vans, a trendy sports footwear specialist who will open up as a 'skate park', as well as a Cinemark 20-screen movie theatre. Shops will include fashion and designer labels, plus themed restaurants, all due to open in autumn 2001 (although the amazing Bass Outdoor World store – worth a visit on its own – and the cinema complex are already open).

Kissimmee's version of the

BRIT TIP: For the best value genuine Disney merchandise, try the Character Warehouse in Belz Mall 2 and Character Premiere in Mall 1.

discount outlet is the **Kissimmee Manufacturers' Outlet Mall** on Old Vineland Road (just off the central drag of Highway 192, between Markers 13 and 14). Again featuring name brands like Nike, Levis and London Fog, it is open 10am–9pm Mon–Sat, 11am–5pm Sun.

The newly expanded **Lake Buena Vista Factory Stores** offer another range of big-name products at discount prices, from Adidas, Reebok and Starter Athletic Wear to a budget-priced Disney Character Corner, OshKosh B'Gosh and (the better-priced) Carter's Childrenswear, plus a lively food court and a kids' playground. A 1999 expansion added Gap and Liz Claiborne stores, and it all has the added bonus of being the closest outlet shopping centre to Disney's attractions. They can be found on SR 535 (2 miles south off Exit 27 of I4) and are open 10am–9pm Mon–Sat, 10am–6pm Sun, and they have a daily shuttle service that picks up at various hotels and timeshare units in a 10-mile radius (call 407 238 9301 for more info). Another recent development (and worth a look

BRIT TIP: American video tapes are **NOT** compatible with European VCRs, so you will be wasting your money unless the video is marked **PAL**, which signifies European use.

because they are off the beaten tourist path) are the shops and restaurants of Disney's town of **Celebration**, a unique collection of speciality stores, an ice cream and candy shop, cinemas, lakeside dining and Saturday Farmers' Market, plus boat and bike rentals. Follow the signs to downtown Celebration down Celebration Avenue, just off Highway 192 ¼-mile east of its junction with I4. The shops are open 10am–9pm Mon–Sat, noon–6pm Sun.

BRIT TIP: Despite the attractive prices, avoid the temptation to collect a house-load of electrical goods as they are geared to run on American 110–120 volt supplies and not our 220, and you would have to buy special adapters to use them back home.

Brand new in 2000 and quite a fresh alternative on the factory retail front was the **Orlando Premium Outlets** centre between International Drive and I4 (just south of SeaWorld; Exit 27 off I4). Some 110 stores of brand names (like Timberland, Adidas, Banana Republic, Ralph Lauren and Calvin Klein) are spread out through four themed areas, with quite a relaxing aspect, easy parking, a good food court and the convenience (from autumn 2000) of being at the southern end of the I-Ride Trolley. Watch out also for big Disney bargains at the Character Premiere and Nike Factory Store. Opening hours are 10am–10pm (Mon–Sat) and 10am–7pm (Sun). Highly recommended.

Flea markets

Flea World boasts America's largest covered market, with 1,700 stalls

11

spread out over 104 acres, including three massive, themed buildings, plus a 7-acre amusement park, Fun World, that will keep the kids amused for a good hour or two. It is open Friday, Saturday and Sunday only from 9am to 6pm and can be found a 20-minute drive away on Highway 17–92 (best picked up from exit 47 of I4) between Orlando and Sanford (to the north). The stalls include all manner of market goods, from fresh produce to antiques and jewellery and a whole range of arts and crafts (try Rag Shoppe USA for some real bargains in materials and lace), while there is a full-scale food court and a 300-seat pizza and burger eatery, the Carousel Restaurant, plus free entertainment on the Fun World Pavilion stage.

On a smaller scale is the **Osceola Flea and Farmers' Market** at the eastern extremity of the tourist area of Highway 192 in Kissimmee.

Malls

The area's big indoor malls tend to run a touch more expensive than the outlets already mentioned, but they do boast a huge range of pretty stylish shops. The outstanding **Florida Mall** features more than 200 shops, with six large department st___ and an excellent food court _____ a choice of 19 eating _____plus the lively bar-_____t, Ruby Tuesday and the _____new California Café Bar & ____located on the South ____Blossom Trail, on the corner ___Lake Road, and is open ___9.30pm Mon–Sat, 11am–6pm ____ recent addition is the up-____et (but expensive) Saks Fifth Avenue, while OshKosh baby gear can be bought, usually at reduced prices, at JC Penney. Florida's oldest (and biggest) department store, Burdine's, opened a branch here in 1999 as part of an impressive expansion scheme, adding 39 more

shops, another restaurant and an extra 2,500 parking spaces. The whole project included a face-lift for other parts of the Mall, and there is more in the pipeline, with the fashion retailer Nordstrom due to open a major department store here in Spring 2002.

The huge two-storey **Altamonte Mall**, on Altamonte Avenue in the suburb of Altamonte Springs (take exit 48 on I4 and head east for half a mile on Route 436), is also well above average. It is one of the largest in America, featuring 175 speciality shops, four major department stores, a choice of 15 eating outlets in Treats food court, plus another three restaurants, including Ruby Tuesday, and an elegant overall design with marble floors that makes visiting a pleasure. You can also get away from the usual tourist hordes here to do some serious shopping from 10am–9pm Mon–Sat and from 11am–6pm Sun (weekdays are best, though). Out-of-town visitors can benefit from the mall's Visitor Savings shopping programme, which offers discounts in many of the stores. Simply show your hotel room key or your driving licence or passport at the Customer Service Center in the middle of the lower level to pick up your Savings Passport.

One of the most extensive mall developments is the hugely spacious **Seminole Towne Center** just off I4 to the north of Orlando on the outskirts of Sanford. This vast complex offers another two-storey wonderland of designer shops, boutiques and department stores (like Burdine's and JC Penney) as well as craft stalls and a wide-ranging food court. Turn right off exit 51 of I4 and you are there, and it makes a handy place to while away your last few hours if you have an afternoon flight from the nearby Orlando/Sanford Airport.

Another recent Seminole

County addition is the **Oviedo Marketplace**, an impressive development of 100-plus shops just off the Central Florida Greeneway at Red Bug Lake Road (exit 41, head west). With three main department stores, a well-planned food court with children's play area, plus four restaurants and the 22-screen Regal Cinema complex ($4.50 before 6pm, $6.50 after), the Marketplace has yet to be discovered by the masses and is open 10am–9pm Mon-Sat and noon–6pm Sun. In particular, the Oldenberg Brewery & Restaurant (great micro-brewery) and Cha Cha Coconuts (a taste of the Caribbean) are among Orlando's hottest new eateries.

The large and spacious **Osceola Square Mall** (where Highway 192 mysteriously becomes Vine Street along its central stretch) is the only enclosed mall in Kissimmee, with 50 shops and a 12-screen cinema complex (open 10am–9pm Mon–Sat, noon–6pm Sun), including the local outlet of the retail store Ross, which deals in end-of-line items from big-name manufacturers like Calvin Klein, Gap and Tommy Hilfiger. If you are prepared for a good rummage through their packed clothing racks, you can collect some real bargains. 'Ross should be on every Brit's shopping list,' advises reader Mrs B Mair of Stockport.

If you are in Winter Park, look out for the new **Winter Park Village**, which opened in 2000. It is a small, up-scale, open-plan development of boutique shops, larger speciality stores like Borders Books, and some fine restaurants, of which PF Chang's Chinese Bistro (their spicy Szechuan chicken is to die for) is the highlight. The Village replaced the old Winter Park Mall and is on North Orlando Avenue, exit 46 off I4, east on Lee Road then right.

The big Mall news, though, is the building of the most up-scale development to date, the Mall at Millenia, just to the north of Universal Orlando. Scheduled to open in 2002, it will feature New York's most famous department stores, Bloomingdale's and Macy's, among an extravagant list of top-name boutiques. Watch this space, as they say!

Apart from the big chemist chain stores, Eckerd and Walgreens, already mentioned, there are a few more typical large-group stores. The main supermarkets you will find are Publix and Goodings, which are comparable with Asda, Safeway or (in the case of Goodings) Marks and

> BRIT TIP: Need a good book? Make a beeline for **Barnes & Noble** by the Florida Mall or opposite the Colonial Plaza for a magnificent array of titles (especially travel) and a wonderful coffee shop.

Spencer, while for clothes, DIY, home furnishings, souvenirs, toys, electrical goods and other household items the big discount stores are K-Mart, Wal-Mart (open 24 hours for serious shopaholics!) or Target (like a big version of Tesco's, but without the food department makes sense). If there is anything you have forgotten to bring, chances are you can get it at Wal-Mart Supercenters, or Highway 192 just past Medieval Times, the other at the junction of Sand Lake Road and John Young Parkway. For photographic supplies and film processing you should try one of the many branches of Eckerd Express Photo.

Specialist shops

Finally, a few worth making a note of for specific items are the various

Park Avenue, Winter Park

outlets of **World of Denim** (no explanation necessary), **The Sports Authority** and **Sports Dominator**, the former on Sand Lake Road and the latter north of Sand Lake Road, on International Drive, which both offer all manner of sporting goods and apparel, while serious sportsmen and women will also want to visit the magnificent range of the five **Edwin Watts Golf** shops, including their national clearance centre on International Drive, or any of the five **Special Tee Golf & Tennis** shops. On golf clubs in particular you can pick up some great deals and save pounds on the same equipment back home. The **:08 Seconds** store (on Highway 192 opposite Medieval Times) offers the chance to get yourself fully kitted out in the latest cowboy fashions. Once again, check out www.wdwinfo.co.uk for the very latest shopping tips and info.

Now, on to other concerns …

Lake Buena Vista Factory Stores

Safety First

(or, Don't Forget to Pack Your Common Sense!)

From the coverage Florida has received in our media you would be forgiven for thinking any holiday to Orlando could be the equivalent of signing up for a vacation in Crime City, USA. This is simply not the case.

Make no mistake, America is a more violent, crime-worried country than ours, but the newspaper and TV images of Orlando as a mugger's paradise are a long way from the truth. In pure statistical terms, you have more chance of being mugged in your local high street than in Orlando. The only tourist destination in America with a LOWER crime rate than Orlando is Sante Fé in New Mexico, and that handles only a fraction of the numbers that central Florida does. Of course there have been incidents of violent crime in the city, no one could pretend otherwise, but on the whole these have been isolated and unusual, and have drawn so much publicity simply because they are the exception rather than the norm. Again, in terms of the most recent statistics, crimes against visitors to Orlando account for 0.04 per cent of the total crime figures for the area, or something in the region of 4,000 incidents for every 13 million tourists. The area has its own Tourist Oriented Policing Service (or TOPS), centred on International Drive, with more than 70 officers patrolling purely the main tourist areas, arranging crime prevention seminars with local hotels and generally ensuring that Orlando takes good care of its visitors. You will often see the local police in these areas out on mountain bikes, and they are a polite, helpful bunch should you need assistance or directions. Tourism is such a vital part of the local economy that the authorities cannot afford not to be seen to be taking an active role against crime, hence the area has an extremely safety-conscious attitude.

This is most evident in the use of state-of-the-art methods of crime prevention that have gone a long way towards driving tourist crime out of the area. These include the fitting of electronic locks on hotel rooms, designing new hotels with crime prevention criteria, like special landscaping, lighting and the use of particular colours, and putting extra

The security-featured Rosen Centre Hotel

police patrols on duty in motorway areas where tourists encounter difficulties through bad signposting or avoiding the tolls.

Having said all that it would be foolish to behave as if the villainous element did not exist and therefore there are a number of guidelines which all visitors to America in general, and Orlando in particular, should follow. Put simply these are all a question of common sense. For example, just as it would be inadvisable to walk around the darker corners of Soho in London late at night alone, so it would in parts of Florida.

Emergencies

General: In an emergency of any kind, for police, fire department or ambulance, dial 911 (9–911 from your hotel room). It is a good idea to make sure your children are aware of this number, while for smaller-scale crises (mislaid tickets or passports, rescheduled flights, etc.) your holiday company should have an emergency contact number in the hotel reception. If you are travelling independently and run into passport or other problems that require the assistance of the British Consulate in Orlando, their office is located in Sun Bank Towers, 200 South Orange Avenue, with walk-in visitors' hours 9.30am–noon and 2–4pm, or phone 9.30am–4pm on 407 426 7855.

Medical: here's a bulletin from an informed British source who works with American paramedics – if you are taking regular prescription drugs, check with your doctor or pharmacist to see if they have a *different* name in the US. Many do (adrenaline is known as epinephrine) and it is worth finding out and carrying the drug with both names in case of an emergency. (Many thanks to Valerie Mulcare-Tivey for this advice.)

Hotels

While in your hotel, motel or guest house, you should always use door peepholes and security chains whenever someone knocks at the door. DON'T open the doors to strangers without asking for identification, and check with the hotel desk if you are still not sure. It is stating the obvious, but keep your room doors and windows

> BRIT TIP: If your room has already been cleaned before you go out for the day, hang the 'Do Not Disturb' sign on the door.

locked at all times and always use deadlocks and security chains. It is still surprising how many people simply forget basic precautions when they are on holiday (the local police also never cease to be amazed at how many people leave their common sense behind when they leave home!). Always take your cash, credit cards and car keys with you when you go out, and don't leave the door open at any time, even if you are just popping down the corridor to the ice machine. And make a point of asking the hotels about their safety precautions when you make your reservation. Do they have electronic card-locks (which can't be duplicated) and do they have their own security staff?

Don't be afraid to ask reception staff for safety pointers in the surrounding areas or if you are travelling somewhere you are not totally sure about. Safety is a major issue for the Central Florida Hotel/Motel Association, so hotel staff are usually well briefed to be helpful in this area. Using a bumbag (the Americans call them fanny packs!) is a better bet than a shoulder bag or handbag, and if you carry a wallet try to keep it in an inside pocket.

Nothing is guaranteed to get the local police shaking their heads in disbelief and disgust than the tourist who goes round looking like an obvious tourist. The map over the steering wheel is one obvious giveaway, but other no-nos are wearing large amounts of ostentatious jewellery, carrying masses of photographic equipment or flashing wads of cash around. The biggest single giveaway of all is leaving your camera or camcorder on the front seat of the car. If you

> **BRIT TIP:** A handy idea for your journey over is to use a business address rather than your home address on all your luggage. It is less conspicuous and safer should any item be stolen or misplaced.

want to look a bit more like one of the locals, wearing the ubiquitous baseball cap is a good way of blending in, and wearing a hat is a good idea anyway given the local climate.

Finally, and this is VERY strong police advice, in the unlikely event of being confronted by an assailant, DO NOT resist or try to 'have a go', as it more often than not will result in making the situation more serious.

NB: If you want to be extra safety-conscious, you can hire mobile phones, pagers and even two-way radios from as little as $20 a week from **Airwave Communications**, tel 407 843 1166.

Money

Following on from the advice about bumbags and wallets, it is completely inadvisable and totally unnecessary to carry large amounts of cash around with you. US travellers' cheques are accepted almost everywhere as cash and can be readily replaced if lost or stolen, as can credit cards, which are another widespread form of currency. Visa, Mastercard and American Express are almost universally accepted, but don't take unnecessary bank or credit cards with you. The Sun Bank in Disney's Magic Kingdom and Epcot is open seven days a week should you need extra help with any financial transactions. It is also worth separating the larger notes from the smaller ones in your wallet to avoid flashing all your money in public view. Losing £200 worth of travellers' cheques shouldn't ruin your holiday – but losing £200 in cash might.

> **BRIT TIP:** Be forewarned that all American banknotes are EXACTLY the same green colour and size. It is only the picture of the president and the denomination in each corner that change.

In addition, most hotels will offer the use of safes and deposit boxes for your valuables, and many rooms now come equipped with mini-safes in which it is a good idea to leave your passports, return tickets, cameras etc., when you don't need them. Always keep your valuables out of sight, whether in the hotel room or the car. Use the car boot if you're leaving a jacket or camera.

12

Driving

Car crime is one of the biggest forms of criminal activity in America and has led to some of the most lurid headlines, especially in the Miami area a few years back. Once again, it pays to make a number of basic safety checks before you set off anywhere. The first thing is to be SURE of the car's controls before you drive out of the hire company's car park. Which button is the air-conditioning, which side of the steering wheel are the indicators and

BRIT TIP: American freeways, highways and expressways (with the exception of the Florida Turnpike) do not have service stations, so if you need petrol you will have to get off the motorway (although not very far in most cases).

where are the windscreen wipers? Check BEFORE you leave! Also, make sure you know your route in advance, even if it is only a case of memorising the road numbers. Most of the car-hire companies now give good directional instructions on how to get to your hotel from their car park so read them before you set off.

Just about the main item on the list of local police Dos and Don'ts is to use your map BEFORE you set off – trying to drive with the map over the steering wheel is just asking for an accident, let alone marking you out as an obvious tourist. Make sure, too, you put your maps and brochures away in the glove compartment when you leave the car to avoid leaving the obvious sign that says 'Tourist Parked Here'!

Check that the petrol tank is full and never let it get near empty. Running out of 'gas' in an unfamiliar area holds obvious hazards.

If you stray off your pre-determined route, stick to well-lit areas and stop to ask directions only from official businesses like hotels and garages or better still, a police car or station. Always try to park close to your destination where there are plenty of street lights and DO NOT get out if there are any suspicious characters lurking around. Always keep your doors and windows closed (if it's hot, you've got air-conditioning, remember?), and don't hesitate to lock the doors from the inside if you feel threatened by unlikely-looking pedestrians (larger cars have doors that lock automatically as you drive off). And, please, don't forget to lock the doors when you leave the car!

Miami crooks had developed the habit of trying to get cars to stop by trying to look official or deliberately bumping into obvious hire cars from behind. The easily identified hire car plates have now been phased out, but still NEVER stop for a non-official request. Go instead to the nearest garage or police station, and always insist on identification before unlocking your car and getting out of it for an official. It is comforting to know that a unique aspect of driving in Orlando is that none of the main tourist areas have any sort of no-go areas to be avoided. The nearest is the portion of the Orange Blossom Trail south of downtown Orlando. This houses a selection of strip clubs and 'adult bars' that are not particularly attractive and can be downright seedy at night.

Should you require any further information on being safe in Orlando, contact the Community Affairs office of the Orange County Police on 407 836 3720.

Going Home

(or, Where Did the Last Two Weeks Go?)

And so, dog-tired, financially crippled but (hopefully) blissfully happy and with enough memories to last a lifetime, it is time to deal with that bane of all holidays – the journey home.

If you have come through the last week or two relatively unscathed in terms of the calamities that can befall the uninformed or the plain unlucky, there are still one or two more little pitfalls that can catch you out.

The car

First and foremost is the hire car. It has to be returned to Alamo, or

The Airtours children's lounge at Orlando/Sanford airport

Orlando International Airport – Great Hall

whoever, and that can take time if you had to use an off-airport car depot. It is usually a lot easier and quicker to return the car and complete any outstanding paperwork (rare) than to get mobile in the first place, but it is wise to allow half an hour, just in case. The process tends to be even slicker with the firms who operate directly from the two airports.

Orlando International

For reference purposes, the International Airport is 46 miles from Cocoa Beach and 54 from Daytona Beach on the east cost, 84 miles from Tampa and 110 from Clearwater and St Petersburg to the west, 25 from Walt Disney World and 10 from Universal Studios; always allow yourself plenty of time for the journey.

As with all of the major tourist activities in Orlando, car-hire return is a well-organised, highly efficient matter, but the simple numbers involved usually determine that here is one more queue to be negotiated, especially if you leave it until the last minute.

You are now back where you started in terms of your Orlando adventure, and probably with some time to kill, so here is a full guide to the two main airports.

Orlando International is the twenty-fourth largest airport in the world, one of the fastest-growing and one of the most widely acclaimed for its overall passenger satisfaction values (the No. 1 in America and second only to Singapore world-wide in 1999). It was forecast to top 30 million passengers in 2000 for the first time (some 80,000 a day), putting it level with Gatwick and Hong Kong, and with half the traffic of Heathrow (which has four terminals to Orlando's one). It can, therefore, get busy at peak times, but its 854-acre terminal complex usually handles the crowds with ease, and this is one of the most comfortable and relaxing airports from which to depart you will find. It boasts a great range of facilities and services, and its wide airy concourses and halls will make you feel you are in a top-quality hotel rather than an airport (perhaps not too surprising when one end of the terminal is taken up by the airport-run Hyatt Hotel).

Ramps, restrooms, wide lifts and large open areas throughout the airport ensure easy access for wheelchairs, and there are special features like TDD and amplified telephones, wheelchair-height drinking fountains, braille lift controls and companion-care restrooms to assist disabled travellers.

You will also find plenty to do here to while away that final hour or two,

and, should you have more than a couple of hours to spare, it is worth knowing you can leave your hand luggage at the Baggage Checkroom and take the 15-minute taxi ride to the Florida Mall for any last-minute shopping, or take in a film at the big cinema complex just to the north of the airport (a 5-minute journey by taxi). The airport's two information desks (both on Level Three) keep all the cinema timetables, so if you think you have time, consult them and hail a cab!

In keeping with the Orlando area, the International Airport has some wide-ranging plans for staying a step ahead. A recent addition is the **Shipyard Pub and Brewery** in the centre of the terminal, which has bags of Brit appeal. REAL beer (albeit still a little on the cold side), excellent bar meals and the option of a tour of the micro-brewery add up to an above-average airport experience. A fourth satellite arm to the main terminal was added in 2000, and a $1.2billion project to add a complete new terminal, runway, taxiway and control tower is now fully underway, with the first phase due for completion in 2003.

Landside

As with all international airports, you have a division between **LANDSIDE** (for all visitors to the airport) and **AIRSIDE** (beyond which you need to have a ticket). Orlando's **LANDSIDE** is divided into three levels: **One** is the greatly enhanced area for ground transportation, tour operator desks, parking, buses and the car rental agencies; **Two** is the Baggage Claim level (you will probably hardly have noticed it on your way in) and for private vehicles meeting passengers; **Three** is where you should enter the airport on your return journey as it holds all the check-in desks, plus shops, restaurants, lockers, bank and information desks. Level Three is effectively sub-divided into four sections: **Landside 'A'** is the check-in section for Gates 1–29 and 102–126. Here you will find American Airlines, Continental, TWA and AirTran. **Landside 'B'** is home to the check-in desks for Gates 30–99 and the other main airlines, including Northwest, United, USAir, BA, Delta, Britannia, Caledonian and Virgin.

Then, once you have checked in, you can choose to explore the **East** and **West** sections of the main concourse which occupies the centre of Level Three. The **West** end houses the Great Hall, around which are the main shopping and eating areas. Inevitably, Disney & Co. make one last attempt to part you from what's left of your money, so here you will find some more highly impressive, not to mention large, gift shops for Walt Disney World, SeaWorld and Universal (and there is no airport mark-up either), Warner Bros, Bunch-A-Books, Tie Rack, Sunglass International, the Golf Gallery, two newsagents, a highly varied food court (including Burger King, Pizza Hut, Nathan's Famous frankfurters and chilli dogs and Cinnabon) and, up the escalators in the centre of the hall, a restaurant of the lively Chili's chain, a Tex-Mex diner and bar.

The **East** end of Level Three tends to be quieter and more picturesque as it is dominated by the eight-storey Hyatt Hotel atrium, featuring palm trees and a large fountain, and there are fewer shops down here. Universal and SeaWorld both have secondary shops (and they're different, too!), while the Paradies Shop is also worth a look for other gift items. For food and drink there is a Starbuck's coffee shop and the new Shipyard Pub. There is also, up the escalator, the entrance to the Hyatt Airport Hotel if you fancy seeing out your visit in style. McCoy's Bar and Grill (up the escalator, turn right) is one of the smartest bar-restaurants you will find in Orlando, and it has the bonus of a grandstand view of the airport runways to watch all the comings and goings. The surroundings are immensely stylish and a long way removed from the average airport lounge. If you want to go really up-market in your Orlando farewell, go up the escalator, turn left and take the lift to the ninth floor and Hemisphere Restaurant. Not only do you have an even more impressive view of the airport's workings, its northern Italian cuisine

> **BRIT TIP:** Overlooked by many travellers, McCoy's Bar and Grill in the Hyatt Hotel is the perfect little sanctuary to while away that final hour or two before the flight.

provides some of the best fare in the city. It's slightly on the pricey side, but the service and food are five-star.

The central access corridors between the East and West ends, which already housed some service facilities like a bank, travel agent, post office, baggage checkroom and hair salon, now also contain a mini shopping parade with some more impressive stores like Body Shop, Perfumania, Electronics Boutique, Discovery Channel store and a family entertainment games and playroom.

If you still have time to kill after visiting all these establishments and buying those final gift items, wander round the concourse and examine some of the airport's magnificent art collection or view the large aquarium next to the SeaWorld shop at the East end.

13

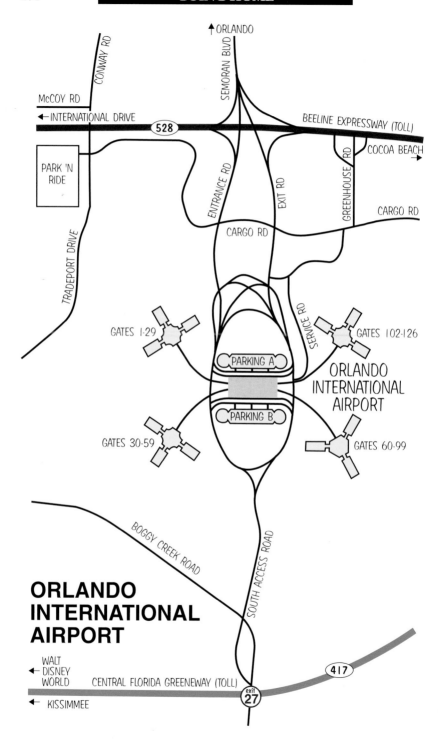

ORLANDO INTERNATIONAL

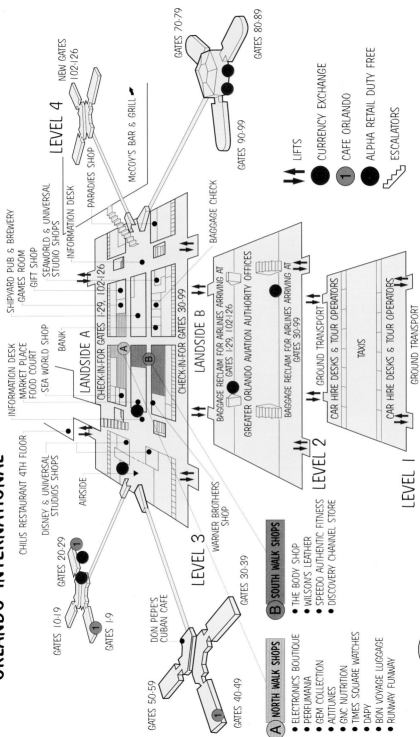

CHILIS RESTAURANT 4TH FLOOR

SHIPYARD PUB & BREWERY
GAMES ROOM
GIFT SHOP
SEAWORLD & UNIVERSAL STUDIO SHOPS
PARADIES SHOP
INFORMATION DESK

McCOY'S BAR & GRILL

LEVEL 4

NEW GATES 102-126
GATES 70-79
GATES 80-89
GATES 90-99

INFORMATION DESK
MARKET PLACE
FOOD COURT
SEA WORLD SHOP
BANK

DISNEY & UNIVERSAL STUDIOS SHOPS
AIRSIDE

LANDSIDE A
CHECK-IN-FOR GATES 1-29, 102-126
CHECK-IN-FOR GATES 30-99
BAGGAGE CHECK

WARNER BROTHERS SHOP

DON PEPE'S CUBAN CAFE

GATES 50-59
GATES 40-49
GATES 30-39
GATES 20-29
GATES 10-19
GATES 1-9

LEVEL 3

LANDSIDE B
BAGGAGE RECLAIM FOR AIRLINES ARRIVING AT GATES 1-29, 102-126
GREATER ORLANDO AVIATION AUTHORITY OFFICES
BAGGAGE RECLAIM FOR AIRLINES ARRIVING AT GATES 30-99
GROUND TRANSPORT
CAR HIRE DESKS & TOUR OPERATORS

LEVEL 2

TAXIS
CAR HIRE DESKS & TOUR OPERATORS
GROUND TRANSPORT

LEVEL 1

↑↓ LIFTS
● CURRENCY EXCHANGE
① CAFE ORLANDO
● ALPHA RETAIL DUTY FREE
⌁ ESCALATORS

Ⓐ **NORTH WALK SHOPS**
- ELECTRONICS BOUTIQUE
- PERFUMANIA
- GEM COLLECTION
- ALTITUNES
- GNC NUTRITION
- TIMES SQUARE WATCHES
- DAPY
- BON VOYAGE LUGGAGE
- RUNWAY FUNWAY

Ⓑ **SOUTH WALK SHOPS**
- THE BODY SHOP
- WILSON'S LEATHER
- SPEEDO AUTHENTIC FITNESS
- DISCOVERY CHANNEL STORE

13

Airside

Once you have decided it is time to move on to your departure gate, you have to be aware of the three satellite arms that make up the airport's **AIRSIDE**.

These are divided into **Gates 1–29, 30–59** (both at the West end of the main terminal) and **60–99** (at the East end). The new satellite arm for **Gates 102–126**, was destined for American domestic traffic only at the time of writing. ALL the departure gates are here, plus the duty-free shops, more restaurants, lockers and nursery services.

The airport's four satellites are each connected to the main building by a mono-rail shuttle service (as exists between the North and South terminals at Gatwick), so you need to keep your wits about you when it comes to finding your departure gate. As is increasingly the case these days, there are no tannoy announcements for flights, so you must remember to ask your departure gate and time when you check in on Level Three. However, there are three monitor boards in the main terminal which display all the necessary departure information. As a general rule, British Airways and Virgin use **Gates 60–99**, as do Delta. NorthWest, United and USAir usually use **Gates 30–59**, while Pan Am departs from **Gates 1–29**, along with American, Continental and TWA.

In most airports, once you have moved Airside it is not possible to return to the Landside area again. However, that is not the case here, and, if you find the crowds milling around your departure gate too much to bear, you can always return to one of the terminal hostelries, for a bit of peace and quiet.

Having said all that, you will find the Airside areas just as clean and efficient as the main terminal, with the added bonus of three duty-free shops just in case your credit card hasn't already gone into meltdown.

As you pass through the ticket and baggage check at the West end of the terminal you will find the Alpha Retail Duty Free immediately on your right. This is the biggest of their three shops and is open only to departing international passengers, so you will need to have your boarding card handy. Unlike the duty-free shops in Britain, you don't carry your purchases out with you. Instead, they are delivered to your departure gate for collection as you get on the plane. This is because the international flights are mixed in with the domestic ones and, of course, duty-free shopping does not apply to internal flights.

Having taken the shuttle to **Gates 1–29**, you will find another duty-free shop, plus a newsagents (the Keys Group News and Gifts), a currency exchange, two bar-lounges of the Café Orlando and another mini-food court, featuring Burger King, Mrs Field's Cookies and TCBY (which really does stand for The Country's Best Yoghurt). **Gates 30–59** is the only satellite arm NOT to have its own duty-free shop, so remember to bag your duty-frees back at their main store just past the Airside ticket check. However, you will still find a Café Orlando lounge bar, Don Pepe's Cuban Café, a food court and a WH Smith's. Travelling from **Gates 60–99** gives you the options of another duty-free shop, a Fenton Hill newsagents, currency exchange and food court containing Burger King (inevitably – it's always the busiest, too), Nathan's Famous frankfurters, etc., TCBY and the Shipyard Brewport for that final beverage. As a bonus for parents with young children, there is a sea-themed children's play area here.

Just like back at your home departure airport, you still have to be near your departure gate a little before time so you can hear the rows being called for embarkation.

For more detail on Orlando International, log on to www.fcn.state.fl.us/goaa

Orlando/Sanford Airport

Returning to what is now the main Orlando gateway for British charter flights should be a relatively simple experience, providing you retrace your route on the Central Florida Greeneway and come off at Exit 49. You go across one set of traffic lights, then turn right at the second set on to Lake Mary Boulevard and follow it all the way back into the Airport. New signs have been posted along all the main routes to make the return journey very straightforward, and the wonderfully efficient ease of the Alamo and Dollar car-rental return adds to this simplicity.

By way of a little more explanation, Orlando/Sanford was created as a full international airport only in the spring of 1996 as an initiative between the airport authorities and several of the main British tour operators. The relatively slow processing of international passenger arrivals at the International Airport, with its double baggage retrieval system, long queues at the Immigration Hall and congested car-hire operations (with many of them having to bus people to off-airport depots) led to the inevitable cries of 'Can't we do it better/quicker/more efficiently?' And so the British charters (Airtours, jmc airlines, Monarch and Air 2000) decided to see if they could speed up their passenger through-put by using the alternative, i.e. Orlando/Sanford. With its small, simple design (straight off the plane into Immigration, one baggage carousel and then a walk across the road into the Dollar or Alamo car-hire offices) it DOES get you mobile appreciably quicker. Of course, you are that much further to the north to

start with, so your journey time is a good 35–40 minutes longer and you have to pay an extra $4–$5 in tolls, BUT, providing you follow the simple directions to the main tourist areas, you can save as much as an hour in overall time taken.

> BRIT TIP: By all means stay in the Sanford area for a day or two to check out their natural attractions, but it is not a great base for visiting the theme parks because of morning congestion along I4.

However, while this new charter gateway is a much simpler operation, it stands to reason that you lose out on the extra facilities of the International Airport, which can be a drawback if there is a delay in the flight home for any reason.

The one departure gate access can also create a bit of a bottleneck, but the airport is in the process of expanding and adapting to ease these growing pains. And, when the airport is not at full capacity or subject to unforeseen delays, its facilities are perfectly adequate for a comfortable stay, with a British-style pub, a restaurant, snack bar, cafeteria and ice cream shop, a video games room, a well-stocked duty-free shop and a fully supervised (free) childcare centre. More facilities are being added all the time, notably a children's shop, a larger outdoor smoking deck (smoking is severely restricted inside) and a VIP travel lounge for customers of Airtours' Premiair service and other up-graded cabin options. The addition of extra departure gates later in 2000 should have gone a long way towards alleviating the pressure of sheer numbers, and ultimately help to

13

ORLANDO/SANFORD
AIRPORT

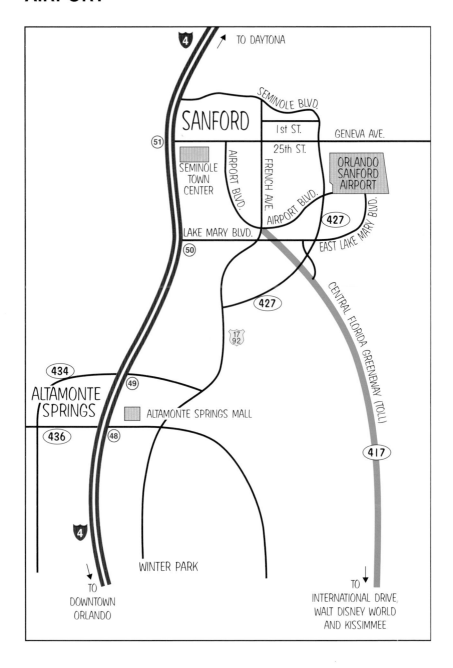

make Orlando/Sanford as smooth a proposition on the way out as it is on your arrival.

After all that, you can expect your return flight to be somewhat shorter than the journey out thanks to the Atlantic jetstreams that provide handy tail-winds to high-level flights. Differences of more than an hour in the two journey times are not uncommon.

Finally, you will land back at Heathrow, Manchester, Glasgow, etc., rather more jet-lagged than on the trip out. This is because the time difference is more noticeable on eastward flights, and it may take a good day or two to get your body's time-clock back on to local time. It is therefore even more important not to indulge in alcoholic beverages on the flight if you are driving home.

And, much as it may seem like a good idea, the best way to beat Florida jet-lag is NOT to go straight out and book another holiday to Orlando!

But, believe me, the lure of this great theme park wonderland is almost impossible to resist once sampled – you *will* want to return.

Now give something back

After hopefully having the holiday of a lifetime, you might like to know about a charity helping children with terminal illnesses to have a memorable time here, too. **Give Kids The World** is a unique, amazing organisation in Kissimmee which provides a week's fantasy holiday for terminally ill children who wish to visit the central Florida attractions. GKTW works with other wish-granting foundations around the world and basically provides all the local facilities for the child – and their family – to find some joy in their lives. It is set up as a village resort and includes all meals, accommodation, transport, attractions, tickets, use of video camera and many other thoughtful touches in a magical setting. It is a truly wonderful charity, one I am happy to support myself, and I hope you will help, too. You can make a donation on their website – www.gktw.org – or send it to: Give Kids The World, 210 South Bass Road, Kissimmee, Florida 34746, USA. Thank you.

13

Your Holiday Planner

You can design your own holiday schedule on pages 262–263 with the aid of the theme park busy day guide on page 264.

Example 1: with 5-day Park Hopper Plus Pass

DAY		ATTRACTION	NOTES
SUN	DAY		
	EVE		
MON	DAY		
	EVE		
TUE	DAY		
	EVE		
WED	DAY		
	EVE		
THUR	DAY	Arrive 2.40pm local time Orlando/Sanford Airport	*NB: 55 mins to drive to hotel*
	EVE	Check out local shops and restaurants	
FRI	DAY	Welcome meeting/UNIVERSAL STUDIOS	
	EVE		
SAT	DAY	DISNEY'S ANIMAL KINGDOM THEME PARK	*(8am start)*
	EVE	Medieval Times Dinner Show	
SUN	DAY	THE MAGIC KINGDOM PARK	*(Open until 10pm today)*
	EVE		
MON	DAY	SEAWORLD	
	EVE		
TUE	DAY	BUSCH GARDENS	
	EVE		
WED	DAY	KENNEDY SPACE CENTER	
	EVE	Skull Kingdom/WonderWorks/Pointe*Orlando	

Disney's 5-Day Park Hopper Plus Pass gives 5 days at the main theme parks, plus TWO of Blizzard Beach, Typhoon Lagoon, River Country, Pleasure Island and Disney's Wide World of Sports; there may be a separate charge for big events at Wide World of Sports.

DAY		ATTRACTION	NOTES
THUR	DAY	DISNEY-MGM STUDIOS	
	EVE		
FRI	DAY	ISLANDS OF ADVENTURE	
	EVE	Universal Studios CityWalk	*(until late!)*
SAT	DAY	Winter Park Lakes/shopping/museums	
	EVE		
SUN	DAY	EPCOT	*(open until 9pm)*
	EVE		
MON	DAY	Fantasy of Flight and Splendid China	
	EVE	Pleasure Island	
TUE	DAY	Aquatic Wonders Tours/Warbird Air Museum	
	EVE	Church Street Station	*Holiday company trip*
WED	DAY	Blizzard Beach/EPCOT	*(Arrive late this time)*
	EVE		
THUR	DAY	Gatorland/Back to airport	
	EVE		*Flight 6pm; return car at 3.30pm*
FRI	DAY	Return Gatwick 7am	
	EVE		
SAT	DAY		
	EVE		
SUN	DAY		
	EVE		

14

Example 2: with 7-day Park Hopper Plus Pass

Disney's 7-Day Park Hopper Plus Pass gives 7 days at the main theme parks, plus FOUR of Blizzard Beach, Typhoon Lagoon, River Country, Pleasure Island and Disney's Wide World of Sports; there may be a separate charge for big events at Disney's Wide World of Sports.

DAY		ATTRACTION	NOTES
SUN	DAY		
	EVE		
MON	DAY		
	EVE		
TUE	DAY		
	EVE		
WED	DAY		
	EVE		
THUR	DAY	Arrive 2.40pm local time Orlando/Sanford Airport	*NB: 55 mins to drive to hotel*
	EVE	Check out local shops and restaurants	
FRI	DAY	Welcome Meeting + UNIVERSAL STUDIOS	*(Open until 8pm)*
	EVE		
SAT	DAY	DISNEY-MGM STUDIOS	
	EVE		
SUN	DAY	THE MAGIC KINGDOM PARK	*(Open until 11pm today)*
	EVE		
MON	DAY	KENNEDY SPACE CENTER	
	EVE	Medieval Times Dinner Show	
TUE	DAY	DISNEY-MGM STUDIOS	
	EVE	Church Street Station	*Holiday company trip*
WED	DAY	Disney's Blizzard Beach/EPCOT	*Late afternoon at Epcot*
	EVE		

DAY		ATTRACTION	NOTES
THUR	DAY	SEAWORLD	
	EVE	Hoop-de-Doo Revue	*(9pm show)*
FRI	DAY	THE MAGIC KINGDOM PARK/River Country	*(Open until 10pm; go to River Country for an afternoon break)*
	EVE		
SAT	DAY	Winter Park Lakes or Silver Springs	
	EVE	Relax!	
SUN	DAY	ANIMAL KINGDOM	*(8am start)*
	EVE	Pleasure Island	*(Open until late!)*
MON	DAY	BUSCH GARDENS	
	EVE		
TUE	DAY	ISLANDS OF ADVENTURE	
	EVE	Wet 'n Wild	*(Open until 11pm)*
WED	DAY	Typhoon Lagoon/EPCOT	
	EVE	Universal Studios CityWalk	*(Final fling!)*
THUR	DAY	Gatorland/Back to Airport	*Check-out by midday*
	EVE		*Flight 6pm; return car at 3.30pm*
FRI	DAY	Return Gatwick 7am	
	EVE		
SAT	DAY		
	EVE		
SUN	DAY		
	EVE		

14

Blank form: your holiday!

DAY	ATTRACTION	NOTES
SUN	DAY EVE	
MON	DAY EVE	
TUE	DAY EVE	
WED	DAY EVE	
THUR	DAY EVE	
FRI	DAY EVE	
SAT	DAY EVE	
SUN	DAY EVE	
MON	DAY EVE	
TUE	DAY EVE	
WED	DAY EVE	

DAY	ATTRACTION	NOTES
THUR	DAY / EVE	
FRI	DAY / EVE	
SAT	DAY / EVE	
SUN	DAY / EVE	
MON	DAY / EVE	
TUE	DAY / EVE	
WED	DAY / EVE	
THUR	DAY / EVE	
FRI	DAY / EVE	
SAT	DAY / EVE	
SUN	DAY / EVE	

14

BUSY DAY GUIDE

	BUSIEST	AVERAGE	LIGHTEST
MON	EPCOT **MAGIC KINGDOM** **DISNEY'S ANIMAL KINGDOM THEME PARK** **ISLANDS OF ADVENTURE**	DISNEY-MGM STUDIOS UNIVERSAL STUDIOS	BUSCH GARDENS SEAWORLD KENNEDY SPACE CENTER WATER PARKS
TUE	EPCOT **UNIVERSAL STUDIOS** **DISNEY'S ANIMAL KINGDOM THEME PARK**	MAGIC KINGDOM DISNEY-MGM STUDIOS	BUSCH GARDENS SEAWORLD KENNEDY SPACE CENTER ISLANDS OF ADVENTURE WATER PARKS
WED	**DISNEY-MGM STUDIOS** **DISNEY'S ANIMAL KINGDOM THEME PARK**	ISLANDS OF ADVENTURE MAGIC KINGDOM WATER PARKS	UNIVERSAL STUDIOS SEAWORLD KENNEDY SPACE CENTER BUSCH GARDENS EPCOT
THUR	**MAGIC KINGDOM** **UNIVERSAL STUDIOS**	EPCOT WATER PARKS DISNEY'S ANIMAL KINGDOM THEME PARK BUSCH GARDENS SEAWORLD	DISNEY-MGM STUDIOS KENNEDY SPACE CENTER ISLANDS OF ADVENTURE
FRI	**WATER PARKS** **EPCOT** **SEAWORLD**	ISLANDS OF ADVENTURE BUSCH GARDENS KENNEDY SPACE CENTER DISNEY-MGM STUDIOS	MAGIC KINGDOM UNIVERSAL STUDIOS DISNEY'S ANIMAL KINGDOM THEME PARK
SAT	**MAGIC KINGDOM** **UNIVERSAL/IOA** **BUSCH GARDENS** **SEAWORLD** **KENNEDY SPACE CENTER** **WATER PARKS**	DISNEY-MGM STUDIOS	DISNEY'S ANIMAL KINGDOM THEME PARK EPCOT
SUN	**DISNEY-MGM STUDIOS** **BUSCH GARDENS** **SEAWORLD** **KENNEDY SPACE CENTER** **WATER PARKS** **UNIVERSAL/IOA**	DISNEY'S ANIMAL KINGDOM THEME PARK	MAGIC KINGDOM EPCOT

15 Index

The author wishes to acknowledge the help of the following in the production of this book:

The Orlando Tourism Bureau in London, The Orlando/Orange County Convention & Visitors' Bureau, Visit Florida, The Kissimmee/St Cloud Convention & Visitors' Bureau in London and Kissimmee, Walt Disney Attractions Inc., Universal Studios Orlando, The Greater Orlando Aviation Authority, Orlando/Sanford International Airport, The Busch Entertainment Corporation, The Orange County Sheriff's Office, Seminole County Convention & Visitors' Bureau, Winter Park Chamber of Commerce, The Orlando Sentinel, Alamo Rent A Car, HM Customs and Excise Office, Canaveral Port Authority.

Plus, Oonagh McCullagh (Orlando Tourism Bureau), Jason Bevan, Margaret Melia (Walt Disney), Danielle Courtenay, Ann Berzansky, (Orlando CVB), Larry White, Loretta Shaffer (Kissimmee CVB), Rhonda Murphy, Linda Buckley, Rick Gregory (Universal), Carolyn Fennell (Orlando Aviation Authority), Kjerstin Dillon, Keith Salwoski, Greg Smith (SeaWorld), Honoria Nadeau, Michael Goldstein (Busch Gardens), Don & Fran Williamson (Unicorn Inn), Brian Wright (Kennedy Space Center), Debra Johnson (Fantasy of Flight), Greg Dull (Orlando/Sanford Airport), Rod Caborn, Suzanne McGovern, Monte Martin (Yesawich, Pepperdine & Brown), Allan Oakley (Alexander & Associates), Warren Wright (Lynx Transport), Todd Hansen (Ripley's), Donna Turner (Medieval Times), Jason Lawrence (Pointe*Orlando), Thom Richard (Warbird Adventures), Joanne Baker (Virgin Holidays) and Kara Phillips (Airtours), and my special research 'assistants' Michele Carpenter, Rich Shallies, Matt Heffernan and Marcia Harris, and travel writer Karen Marchbank. Thank you all.

Special thanks to Pete Werner and all at DIS – you know who you are!

Got a red-hot Brit Tip to pass on? The latest info on Disney's Animal Kingdom™ Theme Park or Islands of Adventure? Found the best new restaurant in town? We want to hear from YOU about how to keep improving the guide each year. Why not drop us a line to:
Brit's Guides (Orlando), W. Foulsham & Co. Ltd, The Publishing House, Bennetts Close, Cippenham, Slough, Berkshire SL1 5AP.
Or e-mail: simonveness.orlando1@virgin.net

Reader tips from: Joan Adebayo, Les Willans, Neil Watts, Alan Salt, Fran Thompson, John Knight, Danielle Lockwood, Sarah Allies-Groom, Dean Knight, Jim Taylor and Malin Dixon (via e-mail); Mrs P Thomasson, Herts; Michelle Russell, Leek, Staffs; Mr and Mrs Snelling, Crewe; Mrs G. Riddle, Newcastle-upon-Tyne; Mr B. Wise, Folkestone, Kent; Mr R. Hyson, Portsmouth, Hants; Mrs E. Marshall, Sevenoaks, Kent.